Parody, Politics and the Populace in Greek Old Comedy

Also available from Bloomsbury

Aristophanes, James Robson
Aristophanes and His Theatre of the Absurd, Paul Cartledge
Athenian Comedy in the Roman Empire, edited by C. W. Marshall
and Tom Hawkins
The Comedian as Critic, Matthew Wright
No Laughing Matter, edited by C. W. Marshall and George Kovacs

Parody, Politics and the Populace in Greek Old Comedy

Donald Sells

BLOOMSBURY ACADEMIC
LONDON · NEW YORK · OXFORD · NEW DELHI · SYDNEY

BLOOMSBURY ACADEMIC
Bloomsbury Publishing Plc
50 Bedford Square, London, WC1B 3DP, UK
1385 Broadway, New York, NY 10018, USA

BLOOMSBURY, BLOOMSBURY ACADEMIC and the Diana
logo are trademarks of Bloomsbury Publishing Plc

First published in Great Britain 2019
Paperback edition first published 2020

Cover design: Terry Woodley
Cover image: Apulian Red-Figure Bell Krater. The J. Paul Getty Museum,
Villa Collection, Malibu, California, Gift of Barbara and Lawrence Fleischman.

A catalogue record for this book is available from the British Library.

Library of Congress Cataloging-in-Publication Data
Names: Sells, Donald, author.
Title: Parody, politics, and the populace in Greek old comedy / Donald Sells.
Description: London: Bloomsbury Academic, 2018. | Includes bibliographical
references and index.
Identifiers: LCCN 2018023339 | ISBN 9781350060517 (hb) | ISBN 9781350060531 (epub)
Subjects: LCSH: Greek drama (Comedy—History and criticism. | Parody in literature.
Classification: LCC PA3161 .S455 2018 | DDC 882/.0109—dc23
LC record available at https://lccn.loc.gov/2018023339

ISBN: HB: 978-1-3500-6051-7
PB: 978-1-3501-6628-8
ePDF: 978-1-3500-6052-4
eBook: 978-1-3500-6053-1

Typeset by RefineCatch Limited, Bungay, Suffolk

To find out more about our authors and books visit
www.bloomsbury.com and sign up for our newsletters.

Contents

Illustrations

Abbreviations

Bernabé	Bernabé, A. (1987), *Poetae Epici Graeci: Testimonia et Fragmenta Pars I*, Leipzig: Teubner.
GMT	Goodwin, W. W. (1889), *Syntax of the Moods and Tenses of the Greek Verb*, London: Macmillan and Co.
KA	Kassel, R. and C. Austin (1983-2001), *Poetae Comici Graeci*, Vols 1–8, Berlin: De Gruyter.
KPS	Krumeich, R., N. Pechstein and B. Seidensticker, eds (1999), *Das griechische Satyrspiel*, Darmstadt: WBG.
LIMC	*Lexicon Jconographicum Mythologiae Classicae*, (1981–1999), 8 vols, Zurich and Munich: Artemis & Winkler.
Perry	Perry, B.E. (1952), *Aesopica*, Vol. 1, Urbana, IL: University of Illinois Press.
PhV	Trendall, A.D. (1967), *Phlyax Vases*, 2nd edn, London: University of London.
PMG	Page, D.L. (1962), *Poetae Melici Graeci*, Oxford: Oxford University Press.
Radt	Radt, S. (1985), *Tragicorum Graecorum Fragmenta*, Vol. 3: Aeschylus, Gottingen: Vandenhoeck & Ruprecht.
	Radt, S. (1977), Tragicorum Graecorum Fragmenta, Vol. 4: Sophocles, Gottingen: Vandenhoeck & Ruprecht.
RFVAp	Trendall, A.D. and A. Cambitoglou (1978), *The Red-Figure Vases of Apulia*, Oxford: Oxford University Press.
RFVAp suppl.	Trendall, A.D. and A. Cambitoglou (1991), *Second Supplement to the Red-Figure Vases of Apulia*, i, London: University of London.

Acknowledgements

The beginning of my comic project was the summer of 2003 when Ralph Rosen recommended the comic fragments as an excellent starting point for research on Old Comedy.

I am extremely grateful to those who have read and commented on individual chapters: Stelios Chronopoulos, Chris Eckerman, Lizzie Nabney, Lisa Nevett, Amy Pistone, Chris Ratté, David Roselli, Piero Totaro, Victoria Wohl. I also thank those who read the whole manuscript at an early stage: Carl Anderson, Sara Forsdyke, Tom Hubbard, Ralph Rosen, and Celia Schultz. Richard Janko, Celia Schultz, Ruth Scodel and Alan Sommerstein gave me feedback on various parts of the book throughout the process.

With funds provided by the Bruce Frier Fund of the Department of Classical Studies at the University of Michigan I was able to examine firsthand many of the vases featured in this study. For help acquiring images and permissions, I would like to thank Alessia Argento (Villa Giulia), the Mustilli Family and Arianna Sacerdoti (Naples).

I thank Bloomsbury's two anonymous readers for many perceptive comments and much encouragement. I am especially grateful to Alice Wright and Emma Payne for patiently shepherding me through the publication process. Christian Axelgard and Nick Geller provided excellent proofreading and comments. Molly Schaub and Scott Morton helped with the indices and bibliography.

Finally, I thank my mentors at Michigan. Scholars in Classics are extremely lucky to be mentored by one eminent scholar. I had two, Richard Janko and Ruth Scodel. I will always be grateful for their support during the process of writing this book.

My greatest debt is to my mom, the strongest person I know.

Introduction

I. Studying parody in Old Comedy

There is currently no study devoted solely to the performance of parody and literary appropriation in Greek Old Comedy. This is odd given parody's pervasiveness in the contemporary world and its role as a mainstay of enduring, perennially successful comedy. Shows such as *Monty Python, Saturday Night Live, The Simpsons* and *South Park*, films like *Airplane!, The Naked Gun* and *Hot Fuzz*, and before them, satirical magazines like *Punch, Mad* and *Private Eye* have earned critical acclaim and devoted fanbases by producing parodies now enshrined in the annals of popular culture. The wide readership of *The Onion* proves that churning out perceptive and clever parody for public consumption is a successful business model in media. Twenty-first-century parody is a powerful means of political, social and cultural criticism in the western world, stoking righteous anger, endangering political careers, occasionally ruining lives, and exposing its creators to threatened and actual violence.[1]

Unfortunately, we know very little about the real-world impact of parody in fifth-century Greek comedy on Athenian society. Nevertheless, scholars continue to study important aspects of this timeless phenomenon of popular culture on its own terms. Since Peter Rau's fundamental 1967 study of Aristophanic paratragedy, *Paratragödia*, several monographs, a few volumes of conference proceedings, and a number of articles have been devoted to parody – mostly paratragedy – in Old Comedy.[2] Given current levels of interest in theatre, the *khorêgia*, music, acting and other interconnected dramatic topics,[3] a comprehensive study of the verbal and visual dimensions of significant literary and visual evidence for parody and appropriation would be a mammoth undertaking. The aim of this book is more modest, a study of Old Comedy's parody and literary appropriation of the prestige genres of fifth-century performance culture – tragedy, satyr play and lyric – as a means of raising the public profile of the individual poet and the genre as a whole.

In the most significant contribution to the subject since Rau's book, Silk's reassessment of Rau's methodology in his 1993 article 'Aristophanic Paratragedy' provided an important way forward in the study of this dynamic part of the comic repertoire. Notwithstanding its exhaustive philological analysis of tropes and scenes, and occasional judgments on the strategy and spirit of parody, *Paratragödia* rarely applies its many categorical distinctions to meaningful analyses of comedy.[4] Silk's more sensitive reading distinguishes the different levels and tones of paratragic language that tended to get lost in Rau's work but, in fact, represent the rewards of reading parody in its own context and with the necessary stylistic nuance. Moreover, since Rau focuses only on lyric poetry of a paratragic kind – this is perhaps only fair given his specific focus – the significant corpus of parodied lyric calls out for study as a comic target in its own right. The strictly textual and linguistic focus of both Rau and Silk – a restriction the latter acknowledges up front – naturally excludes important evidence of parody in performance preserved in contemporary vase painting. Finally, there are still very few analyses of comedy's parody of satyr play, which the comic poets exploited to diversify and defamiliarize their imaginative and political content less explicitly and with more subtlety.[5]

Apart from texts, the iconography of Attic and South Italian vase painting and plastic art preserves a store of extant evidence for late fifth-century and early fourth-century parody. Important studies of such theatre-related material remind us of something easily forgotten in our text-centred discipline: that parody in performance is a visual experience and had a distinctive impact on audiences. Recognizably parodic iconography of this kind preserves valuable testimony for the performative mechanisms of such parody, balancing and occasionally supplementing our textual evidence. Its thematic and narrative evidence reveals the concepts driving such mechanisms, counterfactual experiments, and unparalleled cross-generic scenarios. This study's integration of theatre-related vase paintings with literary evidence thus presents a fuller and more comprehensive picture of fifth-century comic appropriation.

II. Expectations, seriousness and society

The varieties of Aristophanic paratragedy show that the appropriation of other poetic forms cannot easily be reduced to one common, single mechanism or effect. I have already used several terms – 'parody', 'paratragedy', 'appropriation' etc. – to describe the topic. Throughout this investigation, I adhere to, and occasionally expand, Silk's definitions of different forms of paratragedy: 'paratragedy' is an umbrella term that includes parody, which is an essentially negative, subversive appropriation of tragedy as well as other kinds of appropriation.[6] All appropriation of tragedy by comedy is paratragic, though not all instances of paratragedy are parodic. Paratragedy can vary in style and spirit, as do the other 'para-' narratives with which Old Comedy appropriates its two other poetic rivals in fifth-century performance culture, satyr play and lyric. More neutral terms like 'appropriation' and 'adaptation' denote forms of paratragedy, parasatyrism and paralyric that seemingly lack parody's subversive intent.

Silk's categories of paratragedy provide a useful model to which further qualifications are added in my investigation of the verbal and visual evidence of performance in the following chapters. I consider this evidence along two primary conceptual axes. An example of intergeneric engagement is understood along a latitudinal spectrum in 'mechanical' terms, i.e., the linguistic and visual expression of comic engagement. A second, vertical axis measures the broader subtext informing the parody or appropriation, that is, its level of political, social and cultural engagement, e.g., high, medium, low or zero. These measures can only ever be approximate, of course, and readers should understand them generally as guidelines. Paratragedy, parasatyrism and paralyric fall along a continuum that extends from a brief and ephemeral evocation with little or no deeper subtext to, at the other extreme, sustained appropriation of genre that meshes with a larger thematic focus.[7] At one pole, the more straightforward and concrete one, comedy stages awkward and humorous meetings, i.e., 'collisions' between the comic context and the norms or codes (e.g., verbal, visual, ethical) of a second, alien genre that is evoked. At the other pole belong implicit appropriations of genre of a more subtle kind.[8] For example, though collision may be lacking or understated in the purely linguistic terms of a given parody, it might find expression in the juxtaposition of that linguistic register and the physical disposition of the comic speaker, e.g., in his or her ugliness, gesture, conduct and even given dramatic situation. In fact, most of my departures from Silk's thinking are driven by my consideration of these broader performative and political parameters as legitimate evidence of parody.

A general overview of the mechanical and contextual scales in practice should clarify my meaning. Small-scale parody is typically modest in aim: producing a laugh that is quickly forgotten because it is generally inconsequential for scene and plot. Swift designates these 'low-level' allusions in her analysis of lyric in tragedy, i.e., superficial resonances of another genre that range from a reference in which 'genre is almost entirely effaced' to one that is, at most, slightly provocative in effect. In Old Comedy, this might be a generically marked exclamation that momentarily elevates linguistic register, an absurd juxtaposition of rarefied and trivial diction, or a swift repurposing of a memorable line in banal terms. A good low-level example – and one that Silk also adduces – is the Sausage-Seller's abrupt apostrophe in his *agôn* with the Paphlagonian in *Knights* (424 BCE):[9]

Πα. λαβέ νυν πλακοῦντος πίονος παρ' ἐμοῦ τόμον.
Αλ. παρ' ἐμοῦ δ' ὅλον γε τὸν πλακοῦντα τουτονί.
Πα. ἀλλ' οὐ λαγῷ' ἕξεις ὁπόθεν δῷς· ἀλλ' ἐγώ.
Αλ. οἴμοι, πόθεν λαγῷά μοι γενήσεται;
    ὦ θυμέ, νυνὶ βωμολόχον ἔξευρέ τι.

Pa: Now have a slice of cheesecake, from me.
Sa: Have this whole cake, my compliments!
Pa: Well, you don't have a good source of hare to give him. But I do!
Sa: Oh god! Where am I going to get hare's meat!
    Heart! Find some tomfoolery![10]

Eq. 1190–1194

As Silk writes, this moment exhibits the collision of mutually exclusive 'stylistic habitats, tragic and less than tragic'.[11] The Sausage-Seller's distress is not exactly inappropriate to the absurd terms on which the contest proceeds, the competitive bribery for the favour of the senile, boorish master 'Demos'. But the distinctly tragic exclamation (οἴμοι) and apostrophe (ὦ θυμέ) are clearly high style and clash with the everyday comic victual, hare's meat, and the distinctly prosaic νυνί and βωμολόχος.[12] There is an absurd collocation of linguistic registers and (almost certainly) gestures, if we can assume that the verbal was accentuated with some kind of supplementary comic code, gesture or even pitch.[13] *Knights* 1194 simply tries to provoke a momentary laugh and subverts no specific model.

When developed into a longer sequence and contextualized differently, this brief paratragic bit by the Sausage-Seller can have greater significance to the comedy as a whole. Again, Swift's classes of tragic allusion to lyric poetry are useful. Higher-level allusions connect to a play's larger narrative, reinforcing its themes straightforwardly or ironically.[14] One example is Aristophanes' parody (855–919) of Euripides' *Helen* (412 BCE) in *Thesmophoriazusae* (411 BCE). Unmasked as a male intruder of the all-female Thesmophoria and subsequently confined to the stage-altar as a suppliant, the hapless Inlaw imitates the heroine of Euripides' 'new' (850) *Helen* of the previous year, who similarly took refuge on an altar in Egypt under threat of rape. Like Helen, Inlaw hopes to be rescued.

Aristophanes' distortion of the model compresses and combines three distinct episodes, Helen's opening monologue (Eur. *Hel.* 1–67), the unexpected arrival of Teucer from Troy (*Hel.* 68–166), and the ostentatiously delayed recognition between Helen and the shipwrecked Menelaus (*Hel.* 528–596). Inlaw's truncated performance (Ar. *Thesm.* 855–857) quotes (with some comic distortion) merely the first three lines of the heroine's opening speech and thereafter only sporadically (862=*Hel.* 22; 864–865=*Hel.* 52–53; 866=*Hel.* 49). Aristophanes' occlusion of the speech's uniquely Euripidean genealogies and account of the war (859–860; cf. *Hel.* 4–21) infuses a sense of absurdity into the scene. Apart from the occasional bathetic (μελανοσυρμαῖον, 857) and comic vocabulary (προσέρχεται, 867; αἰκάλλει, 869),[15] Inlaw's language maintains a tolerable level of tragic dignity without significant collision, although his pastiche of quotations from multiple tragic characters is amusing. Collision is rather identifiable in Inlaw's interaction with his exasperated female captor, Critylla, whose banal responses show she is both ignorant of and uninterested in the performance. The sophistication of this paratragedy increases with Euripides' eventual entrance dressed as Menelaus, and his participation shows how comic adaptation is designed with audience cognition in mind. After Inlaw prepares the audience for the arrival of 'Menelaus' (οὑμὸς Μενέλεως οὐδέπω προσέρχεται, 867), the character Euripides makes his entry dressed in the mask and ragged costume of the shipwrecked Menelaus while delivering the lines of a different Euripidean character:[16]

Ευ. τίς τῶνδ' ἐρυμνῶν δωμάτων ἔχει κράτος,
ὅστις ξένους δέξαιτο ποντίῳ σάλῳ
καμόντας ἐν χειμῶνι καὶ ναυαγίαις;
Κη. Πρωτέως τάδ' ἐστὶ μέλαθρα.
Κρ.   ποίου Πρωτέως,
ὦ τρισκακόδαιμον; ψεύδεται νὴ τὼ θεώ,
ἐπεὶ τέθνηκε Πρωτέας ἔτη δέκα.

Eur: Who, holding sway in these walled abodes,
would welcome strangers worn down in the storm
and shipwreck of the rolling sea?
In: These are the roofs of Proteus.
Kr: 'Proteus' indeed,
you bastard! He's lying, by the twain, since Proteas
has been dead ten years!

Thesm. 871–876

Euripides' lines are borrowed (in part) from Salaminian Teucer (68), whose arrival in Egypt as an exile actually precedes that of Menelaus in the Euripidean original. Given the recent performance of *Helen*, these lines were probably familiar to at least some in the audience. The next two lines appended to the hero's high-style introductory statement and describing the condition of the castaway Menelaus (cf. *Hel.* 400–401, 408–410) would have made the reference clearer to the audience. The same is true of his immediate encounter with Critylla, here playing the part of the tragedy's abusive Egyptian female porter, whom tragic Menelaus had the misfortune to encounter.

Different kinds of collision occur: in the juxtaposition of speech taken from multiple roles and in the heroes' paratragic responses to the comic Critylla, although not strictly in the linguistic content of statements by individual characters. Critylla's abrupt interjection (ποίου Πρωτέως) in the line's final third rhythmically conveys the collision of the heroes' dignified script and her banal perspective. Such audible discrepancies of register would have been apparent to most (if not all) spectators, but those with greater poetic competence may have recognized the compression of multiple characters into Euripides' one role.

This passage anticipates the primary target of this parody, namely the ostentatiously drawn-out recognition scene of Menelaus and Helen (*Hel.* 541–659), which was initially deferred (*Hel.* 567–596) to great dramatic effect in Euripides' play.[17] In response to *Helen*'s pervasive thematic interest in the differences of appearance and reality,[18] Aristophanes focuses his recognition through his heroes' struggle to effect the recognition of each other while facing Critylla's opposition in his version of the scene. This mid-level parody ultimately meshes with *Thesmophoriazusae*'s larger thematic concern with the unintended consequences of Euripidean tragedy's representation (or misrepresentation) of gender and identity.[19] The parody's cogent expression of the distinctive social and cultural interests of Aristophanes' play thus demonstrates a 'high' level of engagement with its larger comic context.

The different strategies of *Knights* and *Thesmophoriazusae* offer a sense of the range of complexity and diversity that comic parody and appropriation might take. The variety of linguistic, physical and visual codes present in just these two examples justifies the holistic approach adopted in this study. By expanding the terms in which paratragedy, parasatyrism and paralyricism can be understood, I occasionally draw conclusions different from, but not always at odds with, those of Rau and Silk. For example, although he does not analyse this specific passage, I suspect that Silk, who focuses exclusively on linguistic codes, would characterize much of Inlaw and Euripides' performance of *Helen* in

Thesmophoriazusae as paratragic but without collision, and possibly as non-parodic, at least until the unquestionably subversive obscenity of the eventual climactic recognition (*Thesm.* 912–916). I, by contrast, see parodic collision in Aristophanes' combination of statements made by different characters in the original text into the speech of single comic character. Collision occurs not within the language of a single character but in the juxtaposition of various codes in performance: the tragic language clashes with the accompanying visuals of the padded and grotesque comic costume, the characters' lowbrow predicament, and the generically cronish blocking figure of comedy. Critylla's objections repeatedly underscore the incompatibility of tragedy and comedy's ethical worlds.

We might think of comic appropriation at the broadest, macro level as play- rather than scene-specific and shaping the comic plot as a whole. No extant comedy quite fulfills this, although surviving titles certainly attest to such full-scale appropriations. Cratinus's *Eumenides* probably adapted the homonymous Aeschylean tragedy of 458,[20] and lost comic versions of *Phoenissai* by Aristophanes (see fr. 570) and Strattis (frr. 46–53) seemingly parodied Euripides' tragedy (408 BCE) of the same title. The play-based, pseudo-biographical frame of *Thesmophoriazusae* approaches this level with its infiltration and escape subplots that are modelled on successful productions of this plot type in Euripides' *Iphigenia Among the Taurians* (414–412 BCE) and *Helen* (412). The parasatyric but fragmentary *Dionysalexandros* of Cratinus is also a candidate for macro-appropriation if its chorus was composed of satyrs, as is now believed.[21]

One final strategy deserves mention. Comedy sometimes evokes not specific texts, but whole genres through tonal and structural appropriation, i.e., modal representations of distinct, often abbreviated, generic signals. As I discuss in Chapter 3's study of satyr play, Aristophanes evokes tragedy (e.g., in language, action, thought) in his *Clouds* without including the formal structures of a specific model.[22] Modality, admittedly harder to identify with certainty than explicit paratragedy or parasatyrism, is in fact a common appropriative strategy that echoes the styles and tropes of generic models but rarely specific texts.[23] Swift's lucid study of tragedy's appropriation of the verbal and thematic features of lyric poetry documents tragic choruses' use of the form to shape the moral and aesthetic character of plays. Modes in comedy similarly manipulate audience expectation to affect the mood of a scene or episode and temporarily transcend the comic present. Chapter 3 marshals the extant evidence for comedy's use of satyr play along such lines.

Because no single theoretical model can adequately address both the stylistic codes and the topical subtexts of parody and appropriation in Old Comedy, the following chapters draw ideas from several methodologies in order to grapple with the complexities of the evidence as precisely as possible. To convey comedy's visual 'coding' of rival genres, i.e., the conscious appropriation of their visual features (e.g., costume, props, gesture, etc.), and its interpretive demands on theatre audiences, I make use of some tenets of performance studies and theatre semiotics.[24] Mastronarde has aptly compared genre in fifth-century drama to a moving target. To maintain a strong but flexible sense of the comic poets' manoeuvrings in and around these fluid generic frontiers of late fifth-century drama, I apply the relational approach championed by modern genre theory.[25] Alternatively the poetic program implied in the Aristophanic parody of *Telephus* in *Acharnians* – the topic of Chapter 1 – can be best apprehended through marketing theory. However, the most pragmatic methodological approach to Old Comedy's parody, and the one that orients the analyses of each chapter generally, considers the expectations that comic audiences brought to each performance of comedy.

In his brief introduction to comedy, Bevis puts his finger on the importance of expectation in successful comedy (specifically jokes), which invites audiences to reflect upon what they know or think they know: 'The surprise that accompanies getting a joke can prompt us to wonder about the expectations that were toyed with to get us there, and what these expectations may tell us about ourselves.'[26] This is especially true of parody and appropriation, whose success is contingent upon a spectator's ability to recognize, if only in the most rudimentary or intuitive way, that what s/he sees involves at least one 'text' in addition to the present one. For this reason, study of the textual and performative strategies of allusion in comedy must proceed with an awareness of and sensitivity to the audience's abilities and the circumstances of textual production. Since Old Comedy was public, a mass entertainment shaped according to the tastes of Athenian spectators, the general mechanisms of its humour must necessarily appeal to them and what they know. Whatever its intended effect – parodic, serious or a mixture – the success of appropriation lay in its ability to resonate, at some level, with a spectator's experience of festival performance. This experience informed the sense of expectation audiences then brought to subsequent performances.

This regard for comedy's audience drives the theoretical model that regularly, if generally, shapes my analyses of comedy, reader-response theory. Sometimes called 'theory of aesthetic response', reader-response theory was developed most significantly by Hans Robert Jauss and Wolfgang Iser,[27] who argued that the aesthetic experience of a literary work is an active process by which a reader's apprehension of the text interacts with his/her previous reading experience. Jauss redefined literary history according to an abstract hermeneutic process by which a text achieves historicity (or 'eventful character'[28]) through its reception as an aesthetic object by readers. Iser was chiefly occupied with the reading process itself, which he described as a 'dialectic of "protension" and retention, conveying a future horizon, yet to be occupied, along with a past (and continually fading) horizon already filled'.[29] For both thinkers, texts of significant aesthetic value compel readers to do a great deal of focusing and refocusing through the 'horizon of expectations' they bring to texts and develop through successive readings.[30] Initial pre-judgments generate a frame of reference within which what follows is interpreted and subsequently influences the original understanding by challenging or undermining it.

While the present study is neither a reader-response criticism of comedy nor concerned with the psychological particulars of the reading process, the theory's interest in the text's objective status and historicity is relevant to the approach taken here. The 'horizon of expectations' (*der Erwartungshorizont*) provides an important and useful animating principle for the textual analyses of Old Comedy in performance.[31] Of course, as with any methodology, reader-response criticism has certain drawbacks.[32] But the general value of Jauss and Iser's model of expectations to the study of both parody and drama is commonly recognized. One particularly relevant example is Rose's view of parody in the ancient Greek form, which describes Aristophanes and his contemporaries evoking the targeted text in order to prepare the reader (or spectator) for the comic incongruity of a second unexpected version.[33] Scholars of dramatic performance similarly evoke the horizon of expectations as a model for spectator cognition, i.e., the knowledge of texts and conventions acquired by a spectator through 'cultural preparation' from critics and/or acquaintances.[34]

It is a commonplace observation that ancient Greek audiences were reasonably sensitive to distinctions of genre. Parody in spectacle and text elicits this kind of adjudication, first instilling a text or genre's conventions in the mind – conventions acquired through shared experience of dramatic, political, legal and religious institutions – before somehow deviating from them. It is by bearing these expectations in mind, at least approximately and provisionally, that one can understand in at least one sense how comedy engaged spectators 'seriously,' that is, raised questions about politics and other issues relevant to the spectators' lives. The extent of comedy's 'seriousness' is one of the longstanding debates in the study of comedy and satire. For Old Comedy, this discussion emerged through early twentieth-century disagreement about the degree to which Aristophanic comedy expressed its author's political views, if at all. Responding to Gomme's famous scepticism of any coherent political partisanship in the comedies, the Oxford Marxist de Ste Croix attempted to demonstrate what he believed were Aristophanes' clear aristocratic sympathies, pointing out, moreover, the fallacy of assuming that humour precluded serious content.[35] The 'serious' position was boosted significantly by Henderson's influential argument for Old Comedy's unofficial but critical democratic function of vetting politicians and their policies for the Athenian *dêmos* through ridicule.[36] An implicit assumption of many analyses of the serious in Old Comedy is its political nature. Silk helpfully broadened the terms of the serious beyond purely political topics into the 'substantial', i.e., what engages the mind and specifically the imagination.[37] This definition accommodates any topic that could reasonably sustain the interest of an audience.

The wide popularity and vast sums of money used to finance Athenian festivals provide compelling reasons for seeing its performances as inherently relevant to the average Athenian and public life.[38] Comedy's appropriation of various performance types was imbued with the popular interests and concerns of the Athenian public and shaped by their day-to-day experience of the Assembly, the courts, religious ritual and conflict: Telephus's tragic rhetoric is cast as a speech in the Assembly (*Acharnians*); Trygaeus's project stems from the citizen's feeling of powerlessness to stop the war (*Peace*); the disruptions of Euripidean tragedy's controversial politics are measured by their impact on the average Athenian household (*Thesmophoriazusae*). If tragedy inflected myth through a complex of narrative forms that addressed contemporary cultural issues,[39] Old Comedy's (serious or ironic) appropriation and critique of rival poetic forms were undertaken by *infusing* those genres with its own cultural, political and aesthetic concerns. Politics – in the broadest possible sense, i.e., life in the polis – is a primary substrate of fifth-century comic appropriation. While early plays like Cratinus's *Dionysalexandros* and Aristophanes' *Acharnians* use parody to satirize Athenian governance and vice versa, Aristophanes uses social and cultural topics in increasingly intimate and personal settings to parody Euripidean tragedy. Such broad topicality was key to comedy's continued relevance. The next section outlines a more comprehensive explanation of appropriation as a function of the genre's natural drive to innovate in a highly competitive world.

III. Why is parody? Genes and genres

De Ste Croix's observation (1972: 357) that the serious 'message' of Aristophanes and his peers, however one defines it, was more likely to be welcomed by spectators if it was funny seems intuitively correct.[40] A precise explanation of parody's operation on the spectator's mind falls outside my present concerns. However, it is clear enough from the evidence that the comic poets fostered and maintained the relevance of their work by adapting their humour to their audiences' changing tastes (cf. Ar. *Eq.* 515–518). Because Athenian audiences exercised considerable administrative and creative power over the festivals, as both arbiters of the competitions and influencers of the festival judges' verdict,[41] poets strove to accommodate their tastes through a process of 'feedback', as Roselli terms it.[42] Poets' constant calibration of their style of humour and topics in response to spectators' reception of their and their rivals' comedy steered comic innovation. The ability of the individual poet to respond rapidly and creatively to the audience through innovation ultimately determines the life-cycle of the individual poet's career in a given genre in Athens.[43]

Understanding the competitive dynamics of Old Comedy requires an awareness of the particular stakes of victory and defeat in the festival and how they differed from those of other theatrical traditions. The supply-and-demand economic model that governed rival playhouses in the Elizabethan era, for example, is not applicable to this tradition,[44] though Athenian drama was indeed a business in its own way.[45] Although official prizes of the latter half of the fifth century had insignificant monetary value, the prestige that accrued to the participants in a victorious production was valued in its considerable social capital.[46] Although theatrical culture spread beyond Athens and into foreign markets during the later fifth century, limited opportunities and high production costs at the most important occasions for drama in the Athenian Lenaea and Great Dionysia forced playwrights into intense competition for a limited number of slots.[47] Poets lucky enough to make the initial cut and earn the necessary public funding to stage their work then entered a competition pitting poet against poet, *khorêgos* against *khorêgos*, chorus against chorus, and eventually actors against actors and musicians against musicians.[48]

Unlike its dramatic peers, comedy openly acknowledges this competitive dynamic in various ways: on the many occasions fictional comic characters channel the voice of the poet himself in the *parabasis* and almost certainly in institutionalized extra-dramatic moments. The *proagôn* of the Dionysia introduced the cast and chorus to the public in the *ôdeion*; if victorious, the same participants gathered in the post-victory celebration; such victories were sometimes alluded to in subsequent performances by the same poet. To produce the kind of cutting-edge content that helped them stay relevant, poets drew from pools of options in the ever-expanding and always evolving repertoire of the genre. Appropriation was not just a proven method of innovation, it was a professional survival strategy that can provide insights into Old Comedy's evolution over the final third of the fifth century. This form of literary exchange reveals some of the more recondite features of the comic 'animal', its biology, genes, tendencies, drives and modes of being.

The comic poet's brash and opportunistic self-promotion served his overriding aim of creating a successful career and lasting legacy in the form of either continuing prestige during his lifetime or for the benefit of his actual biological progeny. The aims of survival and replication, and the selfish disposition necessary for their achievement, were sought at the expense of his peers in comedy and other genres.[49] In these ways, his career resembled an organism struggling to survive in a quasi-Darwinian environment, much like the 'survival machine' of Dawkins's famous study.[50]

My comparison of the competitive contexts of Athenian theatre and the natural world is not the first, and is in fact anticipated in the earliest extant systematic treatment of tragedy. Aristotle's *Poetics* also conceives drama's evolution as a biological process.[51] However, the metaphorical comparison of comic and natural biology developed here has the advantage of a millennium's worth of advances in human understanding of biology and several decades of study of the economic and social dynamics of Greek drama. My understanding of the survival of comic ideas with reference to biological entities draws from Dawkins's discussion of survival and replication as the shared aims of both the gene and the 'meme', Dawkins's term for a unit of cultural transmission. In the present discussion, I define the meme as a unit of comic content – a trope, theme, signature scene – that fixes itself in the public's consciousness. Successful comic memes, like their genetic counterparts, seek to exploit their natural environment for survival. The 'evolutionarily stable' set of traits in the gene pool at any given moment has much in common with an existing pool of memes in theatrical culture. The qualities conducive to the survival of replicating genes, which multiply and confer important advantages on the organisms carrying them, are similar for memes in Old Comedy: longevity, fecundity and copying fidelity.[52] Like the gene, the meme strives to circulate itself as widely as possible in Athens's cultural ecosystem.

When a gene wins expression in an animal and that animal successfully reproduces, the gene spreads in the ecosystem. By spreading its memes into the mind of the theatre-going public, the successful comedy reproduces and gives rise to other performances of the same memes in a variety of forms and contexts: a quoted line in conversation; a song in the symposium; perhaps a reperformance of the whole comedy in a smaller venue, one of Attica's many rural Dionysia. The cumulative effect of this kind of public recognition surely increased the odds that a play would live on in the public's imagination and perhaps even help its author secure funding in subsequent festivals.

Despite my comparisons, I acknowledge the important differences between genes and comic memes. Comic competition does not begin at the cellular level, as for genes, which must overcome alleles to reach expression in the organism: comic memes compete with those from plays by other poets. In contrast to the enormous ecosystem of earth, the human brain is the natural environment in which units of comedy survive and replicate. Death for a meme, or its verse or play, did not mean the literal end of the poet's life in this competitive arena, of course. However, death is a common metaphor for describing the failure and obscurity of the comic poet whose memes lose potency. In a famous passage from the parabasis of *Knights*, Aristophanes describes a rival's popular decline in the striking terms of physical debilitation and emphasizes the importance of the memorable satirical trope – something we might label a meme but obviously not Aristophanes – for survival. Aristophanes contrasts the meteoric ascent of his thriving comedy with the decline of his elder rival, Cratinus:[53]

εἶτα Κρατίνου μεμνημένος, ὃς πολλῷ ῥεύσας ποτ' ἐπαίνῳ
διὰ τῶν ἀφελῶν πεδίων ἔρρει, καὶ τῆς στάσεως παρασύρων
ἐφόρει τὰς δρῦς καὶ τὰς πλατάνους καὶ τοὺς ἐχθροὺς προθελύμνους·
ᾆσαι δ' οὐκ ἦν ἐν συμποσίῳ πλὴν 'Δωροῖ συκοπέδιλε'.
καὶ 'τέκτονες εὐπαλάμων ὕμνων'· οὕτως ἤνθησεν ἐκεῖνος.
νυνὶ δ' ὑμεῖς αὐτὸν ὁρῶντες παραληροῦντ' οὐκ ἐλεεῖτε,
ἐκπιπτουσῶν τῶν ἠλέκτρων καὶ τοῦ τόνου οὐκέτ' ἐνόντος
τῶν θ' ἁρμονιῶν διαχασκουσῶν· ἀλλὰ γέρων ὢν περιέρρει,
ὥσπερ Κοννᾶς, 'στέφανον μὲν ἔχων αὖον, δίψῃ δ' ἀπολωλώς'.

And then he recalled Cratinus, who once rode on your great praise
and rushed through open plains, sweeping along oaks, plane trees,
and enemies uprooted. And in the symposium nothing was sung
except 'Fig-sandaled Goddess of Bribery' and 'Builders of Handy Hymns'.
Just this way did he flourish. But now you see him out babbling with

his pegs falling out, his tuning gone, and his shape disjointed, and
you don't pity him. And the old man wanders about, like Konnas,
'wearing a withered crown and dying of thirst'.

Eq. 526–534

Cratinus's period of success is described in the language of a powerful natural
event that imposed its will on the fields of comedy and politics. His popularity
was once measured in the wide circulation of his memes, specifically his lyric
poems. But now, Aristophanes claims, Cratinean poetry has declined like a
failing body, which is itself likened to a broken instrument. The poet's babbling
and aimless wandering express the meaningless, desultory effect of once-great
poetry in the present. An instructive counterpoint to this decline is the overtly
biological terms with which Aristophanes subsequently describes his own poetic
success just slightly before this passage. His transformation into Athens's pre-
eminent poet is metaphorically described as his successful courtship of comedy's
prized mate, the feminized Κωμῳδοδιδασκαλία ('Comic Production'), whose
romantic favours his comic predecessors had failed to sustain for very long
(515–517).

Because Aristophanes is the only poet whose work survives complete from
this period, this study inevitably focuses a great deal on him. Nevertheless, the
sources collectively depict an explosion of imaginative creativity by several poets
at Athens in the final third of the fifth century. This resembles a rapid evolutionary
process kicked into high gear, as a dominant cohort of superior poets
disseminated their ideas widely in Athenian festival culture at the expense of less
successful poets, not unlike the way genes competing for limited resources thrive
or decline in a gene pool. As in nature, intense competition streamlined that
pool through a period of cumulative improvement that benefited the Athenian
spectator above all, whose attentions had direct bearing on a poetic career's
survival. One very important strategy for sustaining the comic organism's life
was the growth and evolution of its repertoire through parody and appropriation,
which efficiently maximized the resources of Athenian theatre culture and
thereby amounted to what Dawkins defines as an *evolutionarily stable strategy*
(ESS) of survival.[54] Tragedy, satyr play, lyric, Aesopic fable, ethnography,
historiography and other genres provided raw material for perpetuating the
career of a poet working within a field where innovation was a proven path to
success. At least in fifth-century Athens, engaging and appropriating other texts
was a logical way for a comic poet to maintain relevance.

Comic poets do, of course, parody and attack each other, though such comic
intertextuality is not typically, as far as one can tell, woven into the deeper

structure of a play in the same way that Aristophanes tends to use tragedy.[55] An important exception to this tendency, Cratinus's *Pytinê* (423), illustrates the inherent risks of intrageneric (or 'interspecies') parody: comic poets could fight back directly and rapidly. Cratinus's response to Aristophanes' dismissive crack about his alcoholism in *Knights* (Σ *Eq.* 400), a full-scale allegorical comedy about his marriage to the personified 'Comedy' in *Pytinê*, decided this rivalry that had developed over years in favour of the older poet. In one sense, this illustration of the perpetual zero-sum conflict of comic competition aligns with competition in Dawkins's natural world. In the animal world, attacking a member of one's own species is not conducive to survival and replication because it is far safer to feed on weaker prey. As Dawkins explains, carnivorous animals that target their own species to supply dietary needs lack an evolutionarily stable strategy.[56] Lions seeking food rarely attack other lions because of the high costs of physical confrontation even for the victorious party, who risks being mauled and rendered vulnerable in a world of ubiquitous threats. The lion is better off attacking an antelope, an animal that may flee but not fight back.[57] While poets certainly fight one another, they (like lions) tend to exploit their natural advantage against weaker species by engaging in asymmetrical contests as much as possible. Aristophanes, at least, tends to do this also. Tragic and lyric poets, private citizens and individuals of marginal status are generally incapable of retaliating against comedy's superior resources, status and unique platform. In evolutionary terms, parody amounts to a form of one-sided interspecies conflict in a land of broad and varied opportunities, namely Athenian festival culture and its many forms of literary and political subject matter.[58] Athenian performance culture provided plenty of incentives for poets to look outside the fray of comedy when seeking to gain status.

The parody of other forms, thus defined as an offensive strategy of survival in the world of fifth-century Athenian performance culture, is sometimes less persuasively regarded as a defensive reaction to the gradual encroachment of other genres upon 'comic territory', as for example in Aristophanes' *Thesmophoriazusae*.[59] The paratragedy of the latter comedy rather reflects competition over territory that was new to both genres and in the sole possession of neither,[60] especially if dramatic genre in the fifth century was as fluid as it seems to have been.[61] Such content in the margins between genres has been usefully characterized by Conte as a place of *expectation* where new works or new content wait to be written and thus provide opportunities for increasing audience approval.[62] In fact, some of Aristophanes' most intriguing challenges to tragedy's cultural influence are indirect and target seemingly quotidian content that is less easily identifiable with a specific repertoire, such as aspects of daily life like sacrifice.[63] Aristophanes is especially sensitive to the potential value of such marginal content for positioning his own work. Moreover, by vigorously contesting this territory between itself and other poetic forms via parody and appropriation, Old Comedy can influence – or at least claim to influence – the range of dramatic possibilities open to other genres.

As an intrinsically competitive poetic strategy,[64] parody therefore showcases poetic craft to raise a comic poet's profile and shape his public persona. As an effective contribution to public discourse – from which tragedy is precluded, it is implied – Aristophanes' appropriation of Euripides' *Telephus* in *Acharnians* is akin to the modern marketing strategy of product branding, that is, promoting a particular product by advertising. Aristophanes was hardly the only poet to do this. A fragment of Cratinus's *Pytinê* offers compelling evidence that his rivals did the same:[65]

ἄναξ Ἄπολλον, τῶν ἐπῶν τοῦ ῥεύματος.
καναχοῦσι πηγαί· δωδεκάκρουνον <τὸ> στόμα,
Ἰλισὸς ἐν τῇ φάρυγι. τί ἂν εἴποιμ' <ἔτι>;
εἰ μὴ γὰρ ἐπιβύσει τις αὐτοῦ τὸ στόμα,
ἅπαντα ταῦτα κατακλύσει ποιήμασιν

Lord Apollo! What a flood of words,
plashing springs! A mouth of twelve fountains!
Like the Ilissus in his gullet! What can I say!?
If someone doesn't plug his mouth,
he'll overwhelm everything with his poetry!

Cratinus fr. 198

The scholiast who preserves the fragment explains that Cratinus's words here respond to Aristophanes' earlier parody of these same lines (of Cratinus) in a comedy that does not survive.[66] In other words, Cratinus's fragment reappropriates his own content that Aristophanes had earlier parodied. As an authentic specimen of Cratinus's own work, the fragment preserves the grand epic fashion in which he originally described his own poetic style, as inspired, powerful and transcendent. Whether or not such pretences to epic prestige can be taken seriously, comic poets use such grandiose statements to position themselves in a crowded, competitive field.

My use of the meme as a unit for measuring comedy's evolution is, to be clear, only a metaphor. But it is useful for conceptualizing the high-stakes competitive environment of the texts analysed in this study. To conclude this section, I will elaborate this evolutionary metaphor. Parody enabled comedy to absorb material from a diversity of poetic forms and repurpose it in various ways, as shown in Section II above. The multiplicity of comedy's 'dietary' habits is a hyperactive and extreme form of the single manner of ingestion that characterizes most living organisms. Yet like most mammals, comedy is omnivorous: it appropriates poetic and cultural forms, and really any kind of content capable of extending its life cycle in the world of Athenian festivals. The greater success of the specific work targeted for parody, the greater value it has for supporting and enhancing that life and the prestige of the specific poet. Aristophanes' parody of Euripides' *Telephus* in *Acharnians* or his various contemporaries' satire of lyric are two examples. The ragged Telephus was a desirable target of parody because he was memorable to the public. As organisms benefit from the health of the organisms they prey upon, so did the comic poets benefit from the popular success of the texts they appropriate. Old Comedy's evolving strategies for rapidly exploiting the popular success of memes from other genres – in tragedy, satyr play and lyric – amount to a long-term survival strategy of ruthless efficiency. However, the upper limits of survival for the gene and the comic meme demonstrate important differences between the competitive worlds of biology and comedy. Over time, the capacity of a specific set of genes to occupy the pool intact gradually diminishes. The meme's contribution to human culture, by contrast, has the potential to live on indefinitely and, in a sense, immortally.

IV. General overview

While the following chapters hardly exhaust the evidence for fifth-century comedy's appropriation of tragedy, satyr play and lyric, they do address much of the important evidence. Chapter 1, 'Mysian Telephus and the Aristophanic Brand', argues that the paratragedy of *Acharnians* (425 BCE) defines in programmatic fashion the long-term value of both paratragedy and the Euripidean hero Telephus to Aristophanes' specific brand of comedy. As the earliest complete evidence for parody of tragedy, *Acharnians* is the natural starting point for addressing parody's engagement with expectations shaped by Athenian theatrical and cultural norms. Dicaeopolis's transformation from rustic hero to a paratragic agent walks audiences through the mechanics of the stylistic, visual and narrative appropriation of a recognizable hero of Euripides' alleged prop-oriented, banausic style. The chapter articulates the symbolic value of Telephus for Aristophanes' new kind of self-consciously hybrid comedy, which he suggestively labels τρυγῳδία. The distinct cultural and generic hybridity of Telephus provides a template for Aristophanes' own aesthetically hybrid comedy and, moreover, advertises it as politically principled and similarly marginalized by its dramatic peers as low-status, much like the marginalization of the Euripidean Telephus.

The paratragic mechanisms of *Acharnians* furnish a conceptual basis upon which subsequent chapters build. The survey of visual evidence for parody in contemporary theatre-related Attic and South Italian vase painting (400–350 BCE) in Chapter 2 ('Visualizing the Comic') develops the visual and narrative terms of appropriation. While texts remain our most abundant evidence for comic appropriation, they are not our sole source for information about comedy's performative and narrative strategies. Most of the signature scenes analysed in this chapter likely show generic collision in the visual terms of actual performance. Such vases parallel and confirm analogous extant textual strategies of parody. The 'Würzburg Telephus', the 'Berlin Heracles' and the Lucanian 'Phaedra' furnish rare glimpses of the comic physicality of performed parody – its costumes, props and ugliness – and the visual strategies necessary for making cross-generic play understandable to the widest number of spectators. Moreover, these signature scenes are often designed to express the narrative and metonymic significance of the particular scene, and in some cases the production to which it belongs. They thus transcend their ceramic surface. Other vases engage the shared cultural knowledge of viewers in more sophisticated ways by altering key moments in traditional myth and humorously reversing expectations of recognizable stories. In my original readings of these vases, reversals of two of the most notorious episodes of the *Iliou Persis* ('Sack of Troy'), the Rape of Cassandra and the Death of Priam, reflect the kind of irreverent revisions of accepted traditions in which comedy revels. More importantly, as counterfactual exercises they offer fascinating visual testimony of Old Comedy's interest in a topic given serious attention by contemporary genres such as epic, tragedy and historiography: the obscure origins of significant historical events and chains of causality. The final vases – 'Getty Birds', 'Choregoi' and the 'New York Goose Play' – show Old Comedy's face-to-face engagement with tragedy and satyr play in actual performance and in unique and sometimes textually unparalleled ways. This contemporary visual evidence for the reception of Greek comedy reveals much about what consumers of comedy deemed memorable and significant.

Chapter 3 ('Members Only? Satyrism and Satire in Late Fifth-Century Comedy') expands upon the other, lesser-known dramatic genre appropriated by comedy, satyr play. In contrast to the variety of styles with which Old Comedy engages tragedy in the evidence of Chapters 1 and 2, the idiosyncratic appropriation of quasi-comic satyr play tends toward the *modal* and formulaic. Aristophanes, Cratinus and still more poets whose works are insufficiently preserved applied a satyric mode to expand comedy's formal and material repertoire. Satyr play's panhellenic and apolitical myth could defamiliarize and repackage comic topicality of the Athenian here-and-now with aetiological significance. Cratinus's *Dionysalexandros* (429 BCE) and Aristophanes' *Peace* (421) evoke satyr play's conventional and highly accessible themes and tropes to represent often complicated and opaque events of the Peloponnesian War as the humorously simplistic misadventures of the primitive bestial satyr chorus. An extant hypothesis shows that Cratinus reduced the war's putative instigator, the Athenian statesman Pericles, to a lecherous Dionysus surrounded by the only satyr chorus known to inhabit a comedy with certainty. Building upon recent work by Bakola and Storey, my reading suggests some hitherto unrecognized lines of interpretation, most notably the evidence for seeing *Dionysalexandros*'s parasatyric Judgment of Paris as possibly influenced by the popular narrative of the adultery plot. In *Peace*, Aristophanes compares the Greek states, which obstructed the peace process before the eventual negotiation of the short-lived peace treaty of 421 BCE, to puerile, hedonistic satyrs. Rendering his chorus of Greek *poleis* satyric in physical and emotional comportment, Aristophanes sustains his parasatyric modality much longer than previous scholars recognize.[67] After a first, unsuccessful attempt to free the eponymous goddess from her underground prison raises expectations of the generic failure associated with the childish and incompetent satyrs, the panhellene chorus overturns them to stunning effect in the successful second attempt, which liberates Peace from captivity. Such evocations of satyr play's imagery and themes position comedy in festival culture vis-à-vis the adventures of the satyrs, who were traditionally regarded as Old Comedy's putatively quasi-comic, generic relatives.

The comparison of mortals to satyrs in such large-scale parasatyrism is found in smaller, trope-oriented examples that exploit audience familiarity with a different aspect of the satyr, his notorious sexual aggression. The final section of this chapter examines character-based allusions to the aggression of these ithyphallic monsters during their inevitable encounters with vulnerable mythological females, a commonplace, if sadistic, feature of the genre's humour. In *Birds* (414 BCE) and *Thesmophoriazusae* (411 BCE), Aristophanes uses this stylized aggressiveness and the satyr's immunity from consequence as a benchmark against which the agency of the comic hero can be gauged. The hubris of these 'rape threats' and the high status of its victims inevitably raise expectations of the satyr's divine prerogative to misbehave without consequence. This misdirection, however, characterizes the very different agency of the comic heroes in question and the very different outcomes they experience.

The paratragic program of *Acharnians*, the iconography of Attic and South Italian vase painting, and the parasatyric modes of *Dionysalexandros* and other comedies develop a conceptual frame for approaching the more varied and sophisticated applications of tragedy to the social, political and cultural dilemmas of Aristophanes' *Peace* and *Thesmophoriazusae* (411) in two play-based studies that follow in the book. Four years after its introduction in *Acharnians*, τρυγῳδία drives a comic project over the whole of the plot of *Peace* (Chapter 4, 'Poetic Failure and Comic Success in Aristophanes' *Peace*'). Like Dicaeopolis, the hero Trygaeus – 'Man of τρυγῳδία' – tires of the continued bloodshed of the Peloponnesian War and enacts a drastic plan to scale the heavens and confront the Olympians. The centrality of parody to Trygaeus's comic project is hardly a new insight. Yet scholarship's overwhelming focus on the hero at the expense of other aspects of his project, namely his beetle, has hindered efforts to understand the depth of social and cultural commentary of the play's signature parodies. The cultural significance of Trygaeus's dung-beetle in the parody of Euripides' *Bellerophontes* lies in its overwhelmingly popular cultural and ideological appeal as a low-status creature who succeeds where his generic and social superiors failed. The beetle's successful transport of his master to Olympus programmatically performs, as did its parasatyric hauling-scene examined in the previous chapter, *Peace*'s overarching agenda of converting failures of other prose and poetic genres into its own success. Perhaps the most intriguing variation on the theme is a pair of moments from the alleged celebration sequence of the play's second half, which remain unrecognized as evidence for Aristophanic generic experimentation. Trygaeus's rehabilitation of civilized institutions of the polis – sacrifice and marriage – indirectly challenges tragedy by effacing two parts of its repertoire, perverted sacrifice and marriage, which symbolize violent social and cultural breakdown. Aristophanes' reinvestment of sacrifice and marriage with their positive value as rituals of social cohesion challenges tragedy's prerogative to the portrayal of such critical institutions in the theatre.

In Chapter 5 ('Old Comedy and Lyric Poetry'), I investigate comedy's relationship to its most generically diverse rival, lyric. Comic poets value the 'classic' lyric of Simonides, Pindar and others as a symbol of the culturally, socially and politically superior Athens of the Persian War era. Aristophanes, Eupolis and other comic poets evoke the declining popularity of this idealized lyric to measure Athens's present musical and ethical decline, responsibility for which rests with the artists of the highly popular contemporary movement known by its critics as the 'New Music'. The comic poets satirize the extreme and self-conscious innovation imputed to these now-fragmentary artists as ethically and socially corrosive, harmful to both the morals of the *dêmos* and the celebrated traditions of music and drama. The accuracy of those criticisms is not my concern, but rather how they effectively portray the comic poets as defenders of tradition – of the classic lyric of Archaic poets and, by extension, the virtuous Athens of that earlier era – against the musical perversions of arrogant artists such as Cinesias, Melanippides and Timotheus. Although certainly experimental and innovative, the New Musicians' explicit and ostentatious claims to originality and distinction from past poetry are not significantly different from similar claims made by those same poets of the previous generation. In a rare display of unity (in message), the comic poets exaggerate and parody such innovation for encouraging analogous innovation in everything from adventurously abusive sex and political participation to the corruption of tragedy with low-grade popular culture. The most damaging effect of the New Music, however, is its influence on choral and monodic lyric in tragedy. Extended 'deconstructive' parodies – i.e., parody of the spirit of the artist, instead of a specific model – target the transgressive and self-aggrandizing experimentation of Agathon and Euripides under this influence. This chapter's primary contribution is its demonstration that the parody of lyric is important to the comic poets' advertisement of their genre as a defender of the tradition of Greece's lyric heritage and its moral and political supremacy.

The final chapter (Chapter 6, 'The Feminine Mistake: Household Economy in Aristophanes' *Thesmophoriazusae*') treats arguably the most sophisticated parodic exercise of Old Comedy, Aristophanes' *Thesmophoriazusae* (411 BCE). This absurd thought experiment develops Aristophanes' views of Euripidean tragedy implicit in *Acharnians* and explicit in the later *Frogs* (405), namely that it taught audiences how to think (*Ran.* 954–957) and staged everyday life (958–959) in democratic fashion. Rather than devote a separate chapter to *Frogs*, which has been thoroughly studied by recent scholarship,[68] I instead apply that play's most salient and explicit insights about democratizing Euripidean tragedy to *Thesmophoriazusae* and its concern with the same question of tragedy's effect on day-to-day life in the polis. Because his Phaedras and Stheneboeas disrupt domestic life in Athens by teaching men to identify their wives with adulteress heroines, Euripides is targeted for assassination by the gathering of Athenian women at the annual Thesmophoria festival. Aristophanes' parody of Euripides' adulterous heroines and the absurd hysteria they induce in the city's men stage the problematic consequences of applying poetically formed expectations to the real world. Speeches for (466–519) and against (382–432) Euripides in the play's first half ironically critique the putative realism of his art and its heavily stylized, artificial quality by comparing it to comedy. This contest of genre between Euripides and comedy is presented in highly original terms as a dispute over competing theories of genre-specific household management (οἰκονομία): the stylized household of the Euripidean adulteress versus the exponentially more shameless household of Old Comedy, which was possibly a recent addition to the comic repertoire. Moreover, Aristophanes' comparison of Euripides' tragically stylized households to the lowbrow adultery narrative reduces the latter form's pretensions to democratic style and content to the lowest strata of popular entertainment. This fascinating glimpse of a gender-based reception of tragedy and stylized household life is every bit as illuminating as *Frogs's* famous contest between Aeschylus and Euripides. As Aristophanes' most sustained exegesis of Euripides' work, *Thesmophoriazusae* is an ideal end-point for this study on parody and appropriation as an evolutionary strategy of Old Comedy. The play's absurd but perceptive critique of the poet whose style influenced Aristophanes' branding efforts most significantly ultimately aims to establish, by mimetic demonstration, comedy as the superior alternative to tragedy, rather than its generic equal and complement, as was the case in *Acharnians* and *Peace*.

Mysian Telephus and the Aristophanic Brand

Introduction

Aristophanes' parody of Euripides' *Telephus* (438 BCE) and its famous king-in-rags in his *Acharnians* (425 BCE) is widely regarded as a signature – perhaps the signature – moment of parody in fifth-century Greek drama and a standard by which paratragedy is studied.[1] This is a programmatic moment for a poet who distinguished himself from his contemporaries by persistent and overt engagement with Greek tragedy and Euripides in particular.[2] *Telephus* is a popular account of an expatriate son of Heracles, who defends his rights and those of his adoptive people, the Mysians, against unjust Greek aggression. As a frame for *Acharnians*'s 'serious' commentary on the ongoing Peloponnesian War, *Telephus* separates Aristophanes' brand of comedy from his competitors.

Acharnians Athenocentrizes Euripides' culturally and socially ambivalent hero in its conception of the comic everyman, Dicaeopolis, an Attic farmer of modest means displaced from the countryside because of a similarly controversial war. In frustration the hero reconciles with the Peloponnesians by striking a private peace treaty, which he defends to his fellow citizens by resurrecting the ingenious and rhetorically gifted Telephus, the eponymous hero of Euripides' play from thirteen years earlier. The hero's appropriation of Euripides is achieved by physically assuming the costume and rhetoric of one of recent tragedy's most recognizable characters. This sequence of paratragedy has generated several excellent studies. Among the most noteworthy is Foley's analysis of Aristophanes' use of the biographies of Telephus and Dicaeopolis to project his own heroic quest as a principled and patriotic comic innovator. On the grounds that he too was smeared by the false charge of betraying his people in his comedy of the previous year, Aristophanes identifies himself with the wounded Telephus and his harrowing confrontation with the Argives after the Battle of Mysia. In order to make a uniquely compelling case for his comedy's value to Athens,

Aristophanes aggrandizes his (real or fictional) dispute with Cleon as a real-life analogue of Telephus's heroic defiance of his Argive kinsmen.[3]

Beyond Aristophanes' visually satisfying caricature of Euripidean hyperrealism in Dicaeopolis's visit to the prop-filled house of Euripides,[4] Telephus is central to the poet's calculated branding strategy at a critical point of his career. This chapter looks beyond the visual and audible comic pleasures of that episode to find the deeper cultural and aesthetic terms of Telephus's special value to Aristophanic comedy. In and beyond *Acharnians*, Telephus is a salient symbol of the poet's putative hybrid form of comedy that he designates *trugôidia*. By modelling the comic projects of his hero and himself on that of a popular but culturally and generically ambivalent tragic hero, Aristophanes attempts what amounts to a crude form of 'product placement' in the highly competitive festivals of Dionysus in the fifth century.[5] In emulating Telephus, Aristophanes positions himself as the heroic and victimized underdog of comedy, one whose sophisticated and politically and socially responsible product and sense of justice will inevitably win over audiences in spite of their distraction by his rivals' pandering and mediocre comedy and Athens's corrupt demagogues. Culturally marginalized and wounded, yet politically potent and even unconventionally heroic, Euripides' king-in-rags is a model for the similarly innovative and principled comedy with which Aristophanes sought to define his career as a leading figure of the 'political' comedy in the 420s.

My analysis of Aristophanes' strategic launch of his comic brand is organized in four parts. It begins with a comprehensive exegesis of the visual and audible codes of Dicaeopolis's appropriation of Telephus. Dicaeopolis's physical reconstruction of Telephus's persona at the house of Euripides offers one blueprint of the visual, linguistic and gestural levels that defined paratragic performance and its comic mechanisms, a necessary first step in assessing the socio-political terms of parody. Furthermore, the process of Dicaeopolis's appropriation of Telephus through an accumulation of physical properties affirms Telephus's unique generic significance as a hero occupying the fluid generic boundary currently separating tragedy under Euripides from contemporary comedy at this moment of the fifth century.[6] This process calibrates audience expectation so as to appeal as widely as possible to an Athenian audience of broad but stratified poetic competencies.

However, Aristophanes' reconstitution of Telephus is yet another contribution to the hero's poetic biography. With the aim of contextualizing this paratragedy within that heroic tradition, the second section surveys Telephus's larger heroic biography in the Archaic and early Classical periods. The prominent social and ethical features of the Euripidean Telephus's generic and social ambivalence as understood by Aristophanes – he is *wheedling*, a *chatterer, agile* in speech – refashion the ethnic and cultural ambivalence of this hero's earlier mythological persona. Euripides' development of a socially and aesthetically ambivalent hero, in other words, presents a further variation on the conflicting cultural affiliations that had been thematized in earlier representations of the hero in Archilochus, the Epic Cycle and ethnography. Although Euripides' version of Telephus seems to have become canonical, authors tailored the hero's problematic cultural status to serve their particular ideological aims in different generic and historical contexts.

With this deeper appreciation for Telephus's place in the Greek cultural imagination, the student of comedy is better positioned to grasp *Acharnians*'s contribution to the poetic legacy of Telephus, or rather, as I argue, Telephus's contribution to Aristophanes' legacy. While previous scholarship on *Acharnians* has analysed the place of Euripides' model in its plot, it has not examined the paradigmatic value of Telephus's hybrid identity to the Aristophanic brand more broadly. Earlier scholars note that Dicaeopolis conceives the social ambivalence of Euripides' version of the hero along generic lines: the beggarly tragic hero serves both tragic and comic purposes. This chapter demonstrates that Aristophanes, in fact, appropriates the hero's hybridity as defined in cultural terms, specifically by his bridging of wholly different, though not necessarily opposed, peoples. Telephus's divided cultural perspective, I think, drives Aristophanes' selection of this complex and unusual hero among Euripides' many other kings-in-rags. Telephus was especially attractive as a mouthpiece of paratragedy because his innate cultural hybridity could symbolize the generic and ethically hybrid comedy that Aristophanes would define as his own in *Acharnians* under the moniker *trugôidia*. This comic form is launched as Aristophanes' 'brand' under the popular and distinctive visage that audiences could recognize: Telephus. Like an ancient advertisement or marketing campaign, *Acharnians* promotes Aristophanic comedy by fashioning it after the positive aesthetic, ethical and political traits of a popular hero who had evidently resonated with the Athenian public.

Like Telephus, Aristophanic comedy will similarly negotiate cultures and competing obligations, despite its perpetual displacement by unappreciative audiences. It will persevere thanks to a Telephus-esque combination of ingenuity and grit. Telephus is a concrete symbol for Aristophanes' brand in the competitive sphere of comic business, where poets faced fierce competition from one another and allegedly the scepticism of a public reluctant to see in comedy the same 'seriousness' it identified in tragedy. In this 'discourse of genre' in fifth-century theatre, Telephus is a strategic paradigm for demonstrating comedy's similarly hybrid innovation and unyielding commitment, warts and all, to Athens's political and aesthetic edification.

I. The prop shop: *Acharnians* 395–479

In Aristophanes' earliest extant comedy, *Acharnians* (425 BCE), the Athenian farmer Dicaeopolis arranges a private peace with his city's worst enemy, the Spartans, in reaction to his fellow citizens' continued resistance to a peace treaty in the sixth year of the Peloponnesian War. After the Spartans accept his fantastic solution, Dicaeopolis remodels his household into an entirely self-sufficient, politically and economically autonomous state – hence his name, 'Just City.' Enraged by his brazen treason, the hawkish men of Acharnae, the first deme razed in the Spartan incursions into Attica starting in 431 (Thuc. 2.19), immediately confront the unknown man who dared make peace with Athens's bitter enemies. Facing death at the hands of the chorus, the hero's only hope is to persuade his critics of the justice of his choice. The problem is that lowbrow and frivolous comedy allegedly lacks the necessary public standing and cultural prestige to be taken seriously as an institution that might productively contribute to Athenian public discourse. With the aim of making himself both more persuasive and visually appealing – or pitiable (*Ach.* 384) – the hero turns to the poetic form whose claim to engaging the attention of audiences is taken for granted: tragedy. In Euripides' *Telephus* Dicaeopolis identifies a figure of considerable rhetorical facility and Odyssean resourcefulness, but one also popular enough to transcend the constraints of the dramatic medium and address the Athenian *dêmos*. First produced some thirteen years earlier at the Dionysia, *Telephus* still had significant purchase on the theatrical imagination of Athenians in 425. Dicaeopolis's present circumstances recall those of the noble expatriate Telephus, who similarly defends his actions under threat of death and boldly criticizes his adversaries' aggression as unjust. In the figure of Dicaeopolis, *Acharnians* localizes Telephus in Athenocentric terms as a comic farmer separated from his rural land and deme by war. But despite his analogous predicament, Dicaeopolis lacks the compelling gravitas of an established figure like Telephus. Fortunately, since comedy is set in contemporary Athens, the hero can simply visit the house of Telephus's creator, the tragedian Euripides.

Dicaeopolis's highly allusive visit to Euripides is the most influential extant evidence for contemporary reception of fifth-century tragedy and it has arguably shaped our understanding of Euripides' work as much as any other passage of ancient reception.[7] Seeking to fortify his dramatic *ethos* and bolster his agency, Dicaeopolis calls Euripides outside:

Δι. Δικαιόπολις καλεῖ σε Χολλήδης, ἐγώ.   406
Ευ. ἀλλ' οὐ σχολή.
Δι. ἀλλ' ἐκκυκλήθητ'.
Ευ.   ἀλλ' ἀδύνατον.
Δι.   ἀλλ' ὅμως.
Ευ. ἀλλ' ἐκκυκλήσομαι· καταβαίνειν δ' οὐ σχολή.
Δι. Εὐριπίδη –
Ευ.   τί λέλακας;
Δι.   ἀναβάδην ποιεῖς,   410
ἐξὸν καταβάδην. οὐκ ἐτὸς χωλοὺς ποιεῖς.
ἀτὰρ τί τὰ ῥάκι'; εἰς τραγῳδίας ἔχεις
ἐσθῆτ' ἐλεινήν; οὐκ ἐτὸς πτωχοὺς ποιεῖς.
ἀλλ' ἀντιβολῶ πρὸς τῶν γονάτων σ', Εὐριπίδη,
δός μοι ῥάκιόν τι τοῦ παλαιοῦ δράματος.
δεῖ γάρ με λέξαι τῷ χορῷ ῥῆσιν μακράν·
αὕτη δὲ θάνατον, ἢν κακῶς λέξω, φέρει.
Ευ. τὰ ποῖα τρύχη; μῶν ἐν οἷς Οἰνεὺς ὁδὶ
ὁ δύσποτμος γεραιὸς ἠγωνίζετο;
Δι. οὐκ Οἰνέως ἦν, ἀλλ' ἔτ' ἀθλιωτέρου.   420
Ευ. τὰ τοῦ τυφλοῦ Φοίνικος;
Δι.   οὐ Φοίνικος, οὔ·
ἀλλ' ἕτερος ἦν Φοίνικος ἀθλιώτερος.
Ευ. ποίας ποθ' ἀνὴρ λακίδας αἰτεῖται πέπλων;
ἀλλ' ἦ Φιλοκτήτου τὰ τοῦ πτωχοῦ λέγεις;
Δι. οὔκ, ἀλλὰ τούτου πολὺ πολὺ πτωχιστέρου.
Ευ. ἀλλ' ἦ τὰ δυσπινῆ θέλεις πεπλώματα,
ἃ Βελλεροφόντης εἶχ' ὁ χωλὸς οὑτοσί;
Δι. οὐ Βελλεροφόντης· ἀλλὰ κἀκεῖνος μὲν ἦν
χωλός, προσαιτῶν, στωμύλος, δεινὸς λέγειν.
Ευ. οἶδ' ἄνδρα, Μυσὸν Τήλεφον.
Δι.   ναί, Τήλεφον·   430
τούτου δός, ἀντιβολῶ σέ, μοι τὰ σπάργανα.
Ευ. ὦ παῖ, δὸς αὐτῷ Τηλέφου ῥακώματα.
κεῖται δ' ἄνωθεν τῶν Θυεστείων ῥακῶν,

μεταξὺ τῶν Ἰνοῦς. ἰδού, ταυτὶ λαβέ.
Δι. ὦ Ζεῦ διόπτα καὶ κατόπτα πανταχῇ,
ἐνσκευάσασθαί μ᾽ οἷον ἀθλιώτατον.

Di: I, Dicaeopolis of Cholleidai, call you!

Eu: I don't have time!

Di: Roll yourself out!

Eu: Impossible!

Di: But you must!

Eu: Fine, I'll roll out. But I can't come down.

Di: Euripides!

Eu: Why are you barking!

Di: You are composing raised up,   410
but you need to come down. No wonder you craft cripples!
But what's with the rags?! Are you wearing pathetic clothes
because of your tragedy? No wonder you make beggars!
Anyway, I beg you, by your knees, Euripides, to give me
some little rag from an old play. I have to address a great
speech to a chorus; it's my death if I don't do it right!

Eu: What sort of tatters? Those in which aged and
ill-starred Oineus contended?

Di: It wasn't Oineus, but one even more wretched.   420

Eu: Then those of blind Phoenix?

Di: Not Phoenix, no.
Another, more wretched than Phoenix.

Eu: Whose tatters of robing does the man seek? Those
of the beggar Philoctetes?

Di: No, but of a man much, much more beggarly than him.

Eu: Do you require the foul regalia which this
here lamed Bellerophontes wore?

Di: Not Bellerophontes. The man I mean was *lame*,
wheedling, a *chatterer*, *agile* in speech.

Eu: I know the man: Mysian Telephus.

Di: Yes! Telephus!   430
Please, I beg you, give me this man's swaddling clothes.

Eu: Boy! Give him the ragments of Telephus. They lie
above the Thyestean rags, between them and Ino's. Here, take them.

Di: Zeus, seer of things through and under, and everywhere,
fashion me as wretched as possible!

                                                        Ar. *Ach.* 406–436

This amusing exchange is an excellent demonstration of the importance of expectations in parody and appropriation. The scene as a whole is geared to arouse in the audience those expectations that will be essential to the success of the paratragic sequence, which culminates with the hero's eventual speech against the war (496). The repeated naming of Euripides, his physical appearance onstage, distinctive tragic dress and speech, and display of elements of dramatic craft (418–434) – especially the *ekkuklêma*[8] – would signal 'tragedy' to even the most inexperienced and inattentive spectator.[9] This scene kicks off the parody's 'encoding' process,[10] which describes the writer's evocation of his model as explicitly as possible for the benefit of spectators, particularly those less familiar with the model.[11]

Despite the difficulty of reconstructing parameters for audience competence with any confidence, such parameters are essential to any attempt to address the nature of successful parody in performance.[12] Gauging the cognitive experience of modern dramatic performance, let alone ancient forms now impossible to recover, is a notoriously difficult task. At best, it often amounts to arguing probabilities and even establishing 'hierarchies of interpretive likelihood'.[13] Nevertheless, I believe that this attempt is necessary, even at the risk of imposing 'historically contingent notions of theatrical perceptibility'. Without a model – however simple and crude – for contextualizing and defining basic parameters of audience perception, one runs the risk of identifying any form of allusion or intertextuality no matter how subtle and unrealistic.

It seems reasonable to assume that Athenians had some common frameworks of interpretation by virtue of shared cultural knowledge: familiarity with ritual, key historical events and a general awareness of the mythological 'meta-text' from which lyric and much drama drew their content. Revermann has identified a further source of shared knowledge: the experience of Athenian performance traditions themselves by participation.[14] His compelling treatment of the stratified nature of audience reception argues that the success of paratragedy and other forms of appropriation was contingent on the spectator's recognition of a 'defamiliarized' model. Appealing to the largest possible swathe of an audience so broad and stratified in its competence levels is a matter of designing parody in performance so that spectators with different poetic or theatrical competencies have a plethora of available clues or hints to 'get' the joke, not to mention multiple opportunities to decode. A diversity of such channels and opportunities increased the chances that a parody would provoke a desired response, laughter, but also some critical engagement. Successful parody in a genre like Old Comedy thus means offering something for everyone to enjoy by priming and playing on the audience's expectations.[15]

It is impossible to know what fraction of the citizens who had seen either the original performance of *Telephus* thirteen years previously, or perhaps a more recent reperformance at one of Athens's other venues, would recall significant details of that production while watching *Acharnians*.[16] But by 425 BCE *Telephus* would have become fully integrated into what reader-response theory would call the 'cultural horizon' of Athenians.[17] Even experienced spectators – or readers, if we think in terms of reader response – are incapable of grasping all performance codes in the first production.[18] Nevertheless, it seems fair to say that the most competent spectators, i.e., connoisseurs broadly familiar with the style and repertoire of the multiple performance genres of Athens, could understand (and enjoy) some reasonably specific literary quotation. At the other end of the competence spectrum, the least competent spectators probably needed more help, i.e., explicit, probably visual signals that would facilitate at minimum a recognition of clashing poetic registers, such as shifts between comic diction and higher registers. They might also recognize genre-specific audible cues and metrics, such as unresolved iambic trimeters. Hardest to reconstruct are the abilities of spectators falling somewhere along that wide continuum between these two extremes.

Back at the house of Euripides, Dicaeopolis identifies the hero he wants, and he sets about becoming him. The slew of performance codes communicates 'Euripidean tragedy' for the benefit of less capable members of the audience:

Δι. Εὐριπίδη, ’πειδήπερ ἐχαρίσω ταδί,
κἀκεῖνά μοι δὸς τἀκόλουθα τῶν ῥακῶν,
τὸ πιλίδιον περὶ τὴν κεφαλὴν τὸ Μύσιον.
δεῖ γάρ με δόξαι πτωχὸν εἶναι τήμερον,   440
εἶναι μὲν ὅσπερ εἰμί, φαίνεσθαι δὲ μή·
τοὺς μὲν θεατὰς εἰδέναι μ’ ὅς εἰμ’ ἐγώ,
τοὺς δ’ αὖ χορευτὰς ἠλιθίους παρεστάναι,
ὅπως ἂν αὐτοὺς ῥηματίοις σκιμαλίσω.
Ευ. δώσω· πυκνῇ γὰρ λεπτὰ μηχανᾷ φρενί.
Δι. εὐδαιμονοίης, Τηλέφῳ δ’ ἁγὼ φρονῶ.
εὖ γ’· οἷον ἤδη ῥηματίων ἐμπίμπλαμαι.
ἀτὰρ δέομαί γε πτωχικοῦ βακτηρίου.
Ευ. τουτὶ λαβὼν ἄπελθε λαΐνων σταθμῶν.

Di: Euripides, since you have been so kind to me,
please give me those things that go along with

the rags, the Mysian felt cap for my head. For
I must appear to be a beggar today, to be who   440
I am, but not seem to be; so that the spectators
must know who I am, but the *choreutai* stand
around stupidly as I can give them the finger.
Eu: I will give it; for you scheme subtle things,
with your dense brain.
Di: Bless you! And my best to Telephus!
Good. I'm already filling up with
phrases. But I do need a beggar's cane.
Eu: Take this and be gone from these marble halls.

                                        Ar. *Ach.* 437–449

Aristophanes walks the audience through the process of Dicaeopolis's visual and spiritual transformation from comic to paratragic hero of familiar expectation but of yet unknown comic trajectory.[19] The hero's request for the rags of an 'old' play (τοῦ παλαιοῦ δράματος, 415) may suggest that these heroes were resurrected in performance more often than is assumed.[20] The perceived potency of the initial items (446–447) requested by the hero facilitates an evolution of Dicaeopolis's persona from generic comic hero to something more.[21] In its ostentatious display, the scene curiously resembles a Homeric arming scene, which focalizes items individually during a hero's elaborate preparation for battle.[22] The generic provenance of the items is secondary to their distinctly demotic or 'down-market' social associations, which anticipate Dicaeopolis's later slander of Euripides' mother as a vegetable-seller (478), a favourite comic allusion to the alleged low-class, banausic background of Euripides and his tragedy.[23] Just beyond the lines quoted above, the requested objects become increasingly banal: a little basket burned through with a hole (σπυρίδιον, 453), a little cup with broken lip (κοτυλίσκιον, 459), a little bottle plugged with a sponge (χυτρίδιον, 463), dry leaves (ἰσχνά . . . φυλλεῖα, 469), and chervil (σκάνδικά, 478).[24] The gross physicality of these items is less typical of tragedy but very much at home in comedy's world,[25] especially the patently absurd dry lettuce and chervil.

Some remarks by Aristotle may help illuminate the critical thrust of Aristophanes' pageant of Euripidean stage properties. In a passage of the *Poetics* (1450b16–20), he distinguishes the kind of spectacle (ὄψις) that he considers of low importance – i.e., the manipulation of the actor's appearance using masks, costumes, props – from the true visual power of tragedy. Although emotionally potent, spectacle 'falls quite outside the art and is not integral to poetry' (ἀτεχνότατον δὲ καὶ ἥκιστα οἰκεῖον τῆς ποιητικῆς) for Aristotle because it belongs to the art of the prop-maker, a craftsman (ἡ τοῦ σκευοποιοῦ τέχνη).[26] He follows up this observation when later explaining that poets who rely on spectacle to create something sensational (τὸ τερατῶδες) have nothing at all in common with tragedy (οὐδὲν τραγῳδίᾳ κοινωνοῦσιν). Although he sees spectacle as necessary to tragedy, Aristotle here aims, as Halliwell explains, to distance the pure art of the poet from that of the craftsman responsible for creating products to enhance the spectacle of the poet's proper contribution, the *muthos* or plot. At least one ancient observer of drama viewed the physical components of the actor's appearance as banausic and not poetic products.[27] Aristotle aims to separate the genre in its true form, as something appreciated by elites reading the texts, from its enjoyment by the lower classes as performance in largely visual terms.[28]

Aristotle's differentiation of these two ways of experiencing tragedy furnishes one (admittedly biased) model for understanding the social implications of Euripides' pageant of stage properties in *Acharnians*. The joke is not just that Euripidean tragedy relies excessively on material spectacle, to the extent that its loss amounts to the loss of the poet's work. It also characterizes Euripides himself as a banausic worker of his craft like the demotic audience his tragedy appeals to the most. His house is a workshop specializing in abject 'blue-collar' heroes of socially ambivalent status whose struggle reflects contemporary Athenian social tensions between the banausic lower classes, which were increasingly empowered by the democracy, and the traditional elites managing control of them.[29] Roselli argues that Euripides' so-called 'working-class' heroes appealed to the *dêmos* as representatives of the lower class's emerging subjectivity in Athens.[30] Despite their royal and aristocratic origins, Euripides' politically disadvantaged heroes exercise this democratic subjectivity in confrontations with their putative aristocratic superiors.[31]

At some point during this reconstitution of Telephus, Dicaeopolis's model appears to cross over from the Euripidean to the comic repertoire. The process highlights a grey area between current conventions of tragedy and comedy, especially as it uniquely pertains to the character of Telephus, as well as the fluidity of these genres at this period of the fifth century. Aristophanes underscores the transfer of this hero from the tragic realm that preserved dramatic illusion, almost without exception, to his own sphere, comedy, which thematized such ruptures of the fictional and real worlds. Taplin noted that comic characters revel in the physicality of disguise, specifically its transparency and failure.[32] In Dicaeopolis's self-conscious but ridiculous attempt to disguise himself, Euripides' Telephus devolves into comedy's impression of Telephus the tragic hero. Through this process of appropriation, Dicaeopolis wishes 'to be who I am, but not seem to be' (441).[33] As an assertion of heroic agency, Dicaeopolis's control of costume expresses Aristophanes' own ability to appropriate the guise of other genres *qua* comic poet.[34]

A spectator's ability to recognize such intertextuality or paratragedy surely affected his or her rapport with the hero. Whether this was the connoisseur recalling the model and scene being parodied or the more casual spectator detecting a clash of tragic and comic registers, the dressing scene engages the mind of the spectator and cultivates an alliance with the poet analogous to that of the hero who earns his audience's sympathy by aligning with it against a shared enemy.[35] Aristophanes goes to such great lengths to make the connection between Dicaeopolis and his model text transparent and deliberate so as to maximize that portion of the audience who 'gets it'.

As an introduction to Dicaeopolis's approaching great speech to the chorus, Euripides' house serves a dramaturgical purpose that goes beyond its easily accessible physical comedy: it amounts to a sustained announcement to the audience that a scene of extensive paratragedy is near.[36] The banausic compositional habits of Euripides stress his fondness for stage properties, his tragedy's appeal to the 'working classes' and his own practical affiliations to the tradecraft of his fans. And yet the choice of Telephus, in particular, over the many other ragged heroes of the Euripidean repertoire has not been completely explained by scholarship. The next section marshals evidence for the social and cultural ideology that may explain the choice of this hero for Dicaeopolis's present purposes and for the long-term aims of Aristophanes' comic brand.

II. The biography of Telephus

Comic scholarship's limited interest in the mythological origins of the curious Telephus has meant that his broader significance to Aristophanes' long-term projection of his brand remains relatively unexplored. Recovering Aristophanes' own impression of Telephus and his value to Aristophanic comedy requires a review of the hero's Archaic and Classical biography, which will distinguish him from his helpless and pathetic tragic counterparts in Euripides' workshop in important ways. Euripides' play appears to have stressed Telephus's Odyssean resourcefulness in desperate and straitened circumstances. His rags served as a disguise (Eur. fr. 697) to gain access to Agamemnon's palace and not simply an index of wretchedness. Dicaeopolis, at least, separates Telephus from the other kings-in-rags by his rhetorical gifts: he is *wheedling*, a *chatterer*, *agile* in speech (429). Most importantly, he is 'Mysian' Telephus (430), a detail that is key to his programmatic value for *Acharnians* and Aristophanes' brand. The present section demonstrates how Archaic and early Classical sources exploited Telephus's biography to establish links between mainland Greece and foreign lands upon which the Greeks had designs.

In Greco-Roman myth, Telephus was the son of Heracles and Auge, daughter of king Aleus of Tegea, who is displaced from Greece to Mysia in Asia Minor.[37] Gantz's useful summary of his story organizes the primary sources into three main strands.[38] The Hesiodic *Catalogue of Women* and the 'new' Archilochus papyrus (see below) follow the oldest version in locating the birth of Telephus in Mysia,[39] where Heracles raped Auge. Telephus's heroic legacy in the Archaic period rests primarily on his famous repulsion of the invading Achaeans who mistakenly attacked Mysia thinking it was Troy.[40] The episode originally featured in the cyclic epic *Cypria*. During the rout, Telephus was wounded in the thigh by Achilles, either advancing or in flight.[41] Apollo revealed that the wound could be healed only by that which dealt it, i.e., the spear.[42] No source explicitly contradicts the traditional account of Telephus's parentage by Heracles and Auge, but neither does any explicitly acknowledge Telephus's Greekness. All seem rather to assume an Asiatic identity[43] and, in fact, Heracles is not mentioned in connection with Telephus before the late-sixth-century mythographer Acusilaus.

Two other traditions place Telephus's birth in Greece. The early ethnographer and historiographer Hecataeus said that Aleus learned of a prophecy that a son born from Auge would eventually kill his own sons. The king subsequently tried to preserve his daughter's virginity by making her a priestess of Athena.[44] After being raped by Heracles and giving birth secretly, she and her child were discovered and imprisoned in a chest that was then cast into the sea. Later discovered in Mysia, Auge marries king Teuthras and Telephus becomes his heir. The last tradition of Telephus' story differs from this version only in describing Aleus's arranged marriage of Auge to king Teuthras and his exposure of baby Telephus outside the city, where the latter is suckled by a hind and found by shepherds. Telephus then grows to adulthood before traveling to Mysia, either in exile for murder or in search of his mother, where he ultimately becomes Teuthras's heir.

I go to the trouble of outlining these three traditions because they collectively underscore an intriguing feature of this significant but somewhat minor hero: Telephus, though Greek, spends the better part of his life among barbarians before eventually reuniting with his original kinship group. This noble yet exotic background is elaborated in a fragmentary poem of the seventh-century iambic poet Archilochus.[45] Archilochus justifies retreat from battle using as a mythological *paradeigma* a version of the Battle of Mysia predating the *Cypria*:[46]

> If [one retreats] under the powerful compulsion of the god, one should not call it weakness or cowardice; we were right when we hastened to flee our dreadful suffering. There is a proper time for flight. Once even Telephus Arkasides put to flight the great army of the Argives, and those powerful men fled – so great was the fate of the gods that routed them – spearmen though they were. The Kaikos with its beautiful streams was crammed with the bodies as they fell and so was the Mysian plain, but the well-greaved Achaeans, slain at the hands of a pitiless man, turned away headlong toward the shore of the much-resounding sea. Gladly did they embark on their swift ships, the sons and brothers of immortals, whom Agamemnon was leading to holy Ilios to fight. But at that time they had lost their way and come to that shore; they fell upon the lovely city of Teuthras, and there, in their folly, snorting battle-might along with their horses, they were despondent in their hearts. For they thought they were quickly going up against the high-gated city of the Trojans; in vain did they tread upon wheat-bearing Mysia. And Heracles came to meet them, shouting to his brave-hearted son, Telephus, fierce and pitiless in battle, who aroused cowardly flight in the Danaans and strove in the front ranks and pleased his father.
>
> *POxy.* LXIX 4708

The 'Battle of Mysia' vividly attests to Telephus's epic legacy. Despite the poem's explicit aim of illustrating the plight of the defeated Greeks, Archilochus seems more interested in the victorious Telephus: a bold, courageous warrior of elite, epic lineage who, 'acting alone' (μ]οῦνος, 5) but with divine favour, slaughtered the Greeks and drove the Achaean demigods to flight. This impressive *aristeia* nearly changed the course of history, since Telephus almost single-handedly claimed the lives of Patroclus and Achilles, two men critical to Troy's later fall according to tradition.[47]

Archilochus's peculiar interest in Telephus's unusual lineage is key to the poem's meaning. Swift has noted Archilochus's introduction of the hero (5) as Τήλεφος Ἀρκα[σίδης, that is the descendant of Arkas, his maternal great-grandfather and the mythical founder of Arcadia. Yet after he slaughters the Greeks the poem closes by emphasizing Telephus's paternity with an epiphany of his father: Ἡρακλ]έης δ' ἤγτησ[ε] βοῶν ταλ[α]κάρδιον [υἱόν ('Heracles came to meet them, shouting to his brave-hearted son', 22). Swift convincingly explains the ring composition as indicative of Archilochus's unique appeal to the cultural affiliations of his Parian audience, either in Paros or the Parian colony of Thasos.[48] Parians traced their descent back to a legendary founder, Parios of Arcadia. Telephus's father, Heracles, had links not only with Paros, but Thasos itself: after seizing the island from its Thracian natives, Heracles allegedly awarded it to other Greeks, specifically the sons of Minos.[49] Archilochus's considerable emphasis on Telephus's lineage within such a brief span flatters his audience's sense of civic pride, but more importantly reaffirms Parian colonial claims on Thasos through mythological means: the original possession of the island by their heroic ancestor entitles them to its settlement.

While Archilochus used Telephus's Greekness to justify Parian claims to Thasos, the surrounding areas of the Troad in Mysia were of far greater interest to colonizing Greek cities, especially Athens. In fact, the increasing expression of Telephus's Hellenism likely reflects Greeks' interest in this area, to which they felt entitled since the Mysian crown passed from Teuthras to Telephus. Many of the core details of the Telephus myth and its variants – the Delphic oracle, the hero's murder of his uncles, his integration with the Mysians – are regular tropes of colonization narratives that justified imperial expansion.[50] And Mysia was close enough to the coast of Asia Minor to be conflated with one of the many Ionian states making up most of Athens's tributary allies in the mid-fifth century. Athenians justified possession of such foreign territories by myth,[51] particularly through their claim to shared ancestry with the Greek cities in the eastern Aegean as disseminated by the tradition of the Ionian migration,[52] which was promulgated from the time of Solon (fr. 4a) to the Sicilian expedition.[53]

Archaic interest in Telephus's lineage is not confined to textual sources. A bronze relief (*c.* 480) found in the northern Athenian deme of Eleutherae preserves a tableau of Heracles and baby Telephus in allegorical form: the goddess Athena aggressively confronts Heracles, who holds his son protectively in his arms as Auge stands alongside. Strauss interpreted the tableau allegorically in light of the propaganda value of the myth of baby Telephus's exposure and eventual search for his mother abroad.[54] He drew on Friedländer's hypothesis that the Medizing Spartan king Demaratus used the Telephus myth for propaganda following his exile after being (falsely) deemed illegitimate.[55] After his departure, Demaratus took refuge with the Persian King Darius I, who installed him as ruler of Teuthrania. When he later accompanied Xerxes' invasion in 480, the Medizing king took the opportunity to establish his claim to the Peloponnese: his Heraclid lineage, Athenian and Argive enemies, and royal sway over Teuthrania allowed him to fashion himself as a new Telephus returning to Greece to assume his Spartan dominion. Strauss sees the bronze relief as evidence of Athenian hostility towards Sparta over the threat of its exiled king: Athena's aggressive posture towards Heracles and baby Telephus seemingly reflects Athens's view of Sparta's ultimate responsibility (i.e., through Heracles) for their exiled king's return with the Persians in order to enslave Greece. Demaratus's use of Telephus's biography, like Archilochus's appeal to his Parian audience, uses kinship with Telephus – here metaphorical – to justify an imperial campaign.[56] Other sources exploiting Telephus's link to both Greece and Asia Minor for propaganda purposes notably include the Attalid dynasty's effort to claim him as the founder of their capital in Mysia, Pergamum.[57] In any case, it is sufficiently clear that several Archaic and early Classical sources exploited the hero's biography to bridge East and West for their own purposes. As I presently show, the Euripidean and Aristophanic versions of Telephus reconceive this aspect of the hero, his 'hybridity,' in terms that serve the unique social and generic aims of their plays.

III. Euripides' *Telephus*

Telephus's place in the epic and tragic repertoire was established by the mid-fifth century BCE. Aeschylus and Sophocles dramatized a version of his story in which he was exiled from Greece for killing his uncles, the sons of Aleus. It was Euripides' *Telephus* of 438 BCE that evidently became canonical. Aristophanes' extended parodies in *Acharnians* and *Thesmophoriazusae* (689a–761), his scattered allusions elsewhere in his corpus, and contemporary vase painting likely inspired by the play attest to the level of contemporary interest in Euripides' work.[58] This play dealt with the immediate aftermath of the Battle of Mysia, when the injured Telephus followed the Pythian oracle's advice to seek out 'the wounder' in order to be healed. Assuming that Achilles was meant, Telephus disguised himself as an Achaean warrior (frr. 697–698) and infiltrated the Greeks' assembly in Argos.[59] He found the Atreids locked in heated argument over the Greeks' next move after their Mysian setback: Agamemnon proposed aborting the invasion of Troy (frr. 722–723), while Menelaus accused his brother of betrayal. The disguised Telephus attracted suspicion by speaking in defence of the Mysians, and just about this time the assembly received word of a spy among them.[60] In an explosive sequence of events, Telephus seized the baby Orestes as a hostage and fled to an altar for refuge.[61] The evidence does not allow us to say anything very specific about the eventual reconciliation between the two sides, but it is clear that the expat son of Heracles was recognized both as a true Greek and as the man intended by Apollo's oracle to direct the Greeks to Troy.

One need not take at face value the moral terms of Aristophanes' implicit criticism of Euripides' denigration of tragic aesthetics in his presentation of Telephus to recognize its critical validity. Telephus's unusual heroic status is reinforced by several details known from the play, such as his daring escape to the altar and seizure of baby Orestes, whom he threatened to kill.[62] Telephus's questionable heroism and ailing physical condition identify him with tragedy's most vulnerable characters, women and old men, rather than valiant, heroic kings.[63] But the hero's affiliation with mutually opposed spheres – ethnic, social and even generic – truly sets him apart from most heroes in tragedy.[64] His unconventional background and heroic dilemma may reflect Euripides' interest in evolving Athenian discourse about barbarians in tragedy. The genre's creation of the uncontrollable, violent, slavish and transgressive barbarian Other in response to Persian expansion and pro-Persian tyrannies in Greece is well documented. As Athens's empire grew out of the Delian League, thus developed the profile of this multiregional barbarian as the antitype and common enemy of Greeks.

Although hardly the only tragedy to complicate and question this Greek–barbarian polarity, *Telephus* apparently privileged the perspective of its sympathetic and culturally conflicted hero in order to critique Greek chauvinism.[65] In the partially preserved prologue, Telephus underscores his long separation from putatively civilized Hellenic culture upon his return to the Peloponnese (fr. 696):

ὦ γαῖα πατρίς, ἣν Πέλοψ ὁρίζεται,
χαῖρ', ὅς τε πέτραν' Ἀρκάδων δυσχείμερον
Πὰν ἐμβατεύεις, ἔνθεν εὔχομαι γένος·
Αὔγη γὰρ Ἀλέου παῖς με τῷ Τιρυνθίῳ
τίκτει λαθραίως Ἡρακλεῖ· ξύνοιδ' ὄρος   5
Παρθένιον, ἔνθα μητέρ' ὠδίνων ἐμήν
ἔλυσεν Εἰλείθυια, γίγνομαι δ' ἐγώ.
καὶ πόλλ' ἐμόχθησ', ἀλλὰ συντεμῶ λόγον.
ἦλθον δὲ Μυσῶν πεδίον, ἔνθ' εὑρὼν ἐμήν
μητέρα κατοικῶ, καὶ δίδωσί μοι κράτη   10
Τεύθρας ὁ Μυσός, Τήλεφον δ' ἐπώνυμον
καλοῦσί μ' ἀστοὶ Μυσίαν κατὰ χθόνα·
τηλοῦ γὰρ οἰκῶν βίοτον ἐξιδρυσάμην.
Ἕλλην δὲ βαρβάροισιν ἦρχε †τεκτονων†

πολλοῖς σὺν ὅπλοις πρίν <γ᾿> Ἀχαϊκὸς μολών   15
στρατὸς τὰ Μυσῶν πεδί᾿ ἐπ[ι]στρωφῶν πατεῖ⁶⁶

Greetings, Homeland, whom Pelops divided,
and you Pan, who trod the wintry rock of the
Arcadians where I claim descent: Auge, child
of Aleus, secretly bore me to Tirynthian
Heracles. I know Mt Parthenion, where
Eileithyia released my mother from pangs,
and I was born. I have suffered much, but I
digress. I went to the Mysian land, where
I dwelt after finding my mother, and Mysian
Teuthras gave me power and the citizens of the
Mysian land called me 'Telephus', for I had
established my life far from home. And I,
though Greek, ruled barbarians ... with
mighty armaments, before the Achaean army
came and sweeping over the plain of the
Mysians trod it underfoot.⁶⁷

Eur. fr. 696

With four mentions of his Mysian identity, the fragment's *nostos* theme paradoxically stresses the returning hero's foreign affiliations.⁶⁸ Euripides replaces the traditional etymology of Telephus's name ('one connected to the teat [θήλη] of the deer [ἔλαφος]') with 'one born far away' (τηλοῦ + φύω). Such an introduction was presumably critical to *Telephus*'s representation of its hero as an outsider equally foreign to both the Greeks of his homeland and his Mysian subjects. Moreover, it evokes the key Greek cultural anxiety that informs the moral centre of the tragedy, namely the extent to which the ethical character of a Greek living abroad for years would corrode under the influence of noxious barbarian *nomoi*. The Persian Wars and the expansion of the Athenian empire had brought Athenians into greater contact with foreign peoples to the east, to the north and in Egypt, and contemporary concern about the risks of sustained contact between Greeks and such foreigners, specifically its ethically deleterious effects, is an abiding interest of both Greek tragedy and historiography.⁶⁹ Tragedy is replete with Greeks corrupted by barbarian culture and illustrations of the dangers of living among foreigners: they are softened and rendered vulnerable to flattery and other kinds of excess (Aesch. *Ag.* 918–930); they are turned into cowards by barbarian luxury (Eur. *Or.* 485); their women could develop a taste for the barbarian adulation of royalty (*Andr.* 764, 1020; *Tro.* 165).

Euripides introduces Telephus, by contrast, as a Greek hero who had *not* been corrupted, but remained true to the native values that he presumably voiced in defence of himself and the Mysian people against Greek aggression in the Argive Council. That defence was framed by Telephus's sympathy for both the Greek and Mysian peoples, if points of consistency in the Aristophanic parodies of this speech in *Acharnians* (496–556) and *Thesmophoriazusae* (466–519) reveal portions of the Euripidean original. After an *ad hominem* attack against Telephus and/or the Mysians as a kind of *captatio benevolentiae* (*Ach.* 514; *Th.* 473), Telephus questioned the basis of the Trojan War as unnecessary or unjust (*Ach.* 540–543; *Th.* 490, 496–498, 517–519) and eventually denounced the Achaean hypocrisy (frr. 712, 712a) of condemning Mysian self-defence against unprovoked attack (*Ach.* 544–554). It is difficult to gauge the originality of this argument on behalf of barbarians' right to self-defence (frr. 710–711), though it appears broadly consistent with other passages of extant Euripides that similarly contrast the barbarian capacity for nobility with the arrogance of their putative Greek superiors.[70] The defence certainly challenged Greek stereotypes of *barbaroi* as natural inferiors whose despotic, expansionist and luxurious culture rendered them fit only for servitude.[71]

While its details are unknown, the oracular identification of Telephus as an absolutely essential guide of the Achaeans to Troy eventually facilitated reconciliation between the parties. The hero's Hellenism was affirmed late in the play:

ἢ Νότ[ου ἢ] Ζεφύροιο δεινά
πέμψ[ει Τ]ρωιάδας ἀκτάς,
σύ τε π[ηδ]αλίωι παρεδρεύω[ν
φράσει[ς τῶι] κατὰ πρῶιρα[ν
εὐθὺς Ἰλ[ίο]υ πόρον
Ἀτρεῖδα[ις] ἰδέσθαι.
σὲ γὰρ Τε[γ]εᾶ τις ἡμῖν,
Ἑλλάς, οὐ[χ]ὶ Μυσία, τίκτει
ναύταν σύν τινι δὴ θεῶν
καὶ πεμπτῆρ' ἁλίων ἐρετμῶν.

mighty [gusts?] of southerly or westerly breeze will send …
to the shores of Troy; and you, stationed at the steering-oar,
will instruct the prow-man to observe a course direct for
Troy *for* the Atreidae. For a Tegean mother, Greece not
Mysia, gave you birth to be – with a god's influence,
surely – a sailor and guide of our sea-going ships.[72]

                                                        Eur. fr. 727c.25–34

The Argive chorus appears to understand Telephus's dual identity within a divine plan whereby his exile gave him the precise information needed by the Greeks, i.e., familiarity with the foreign landscape and precise location of Troy.[73] Fragment 727c's description of Telephus's mixed affiliations as something engineered by divine providence because it was essential to restarting the Trojan expedition may suggest that Euripides emphasized the priority of Telephus's native culture over links to his kinsman and father-in-law, Priam. Telephus's role as guide for the Argive forces against his Trojan in-laws makes sense within Athenian civic ideology that demanded the citizen's full allegiance to his motherland.

The fragments indicate that *Telephus* ultimately depicted Telephus's conflicted (or hybrid) identity – critical to his heroic biography since the Archaic period – as an asset. The tragedy's dramatization of the hero's critique of the Argives for their aggression and eventual reconciliation with them makes explicit what is implicit in Archilochus's poem: that Telephus was ethnically and morally Greek and the Battle of Mysia was a debacle in contrast to the just Trojan War.[74] As the ultimate insider, not only Greek but also the son of Greece's greatest hero, Telephus's rebuke of his countrymen is made with unimpeachable moral authority. Both Greek and Mysian, Telephus offers the perspective of opposed worlds, of the colonizer and the colonized (to use terms from postcolonial theory).[75]

Aristophanes made much out of the apparent generic and social tensions inherent in Euripides' version of Telephus, both socially marginalized by his post-war distress and torn between loyalty to his original kinship group and his adoptive barbarian land.[76] Subsequent poets and thinkers would reconceive the hero's hybrid identity according to their own distinctive values. Later comedy and philosophy, for example, figured Telephus as an Odysseus-like symbol of suffering and endurance.[77] By recasting Telephus's cultural affiliations in generic terms, Aristophanes makes Telephus a figure of aesthetic hybridity, a representative of the (allegedly) innovative combination of tragedy's status and comedy's topicality that defines his own brand of comedy.

IV. Telephus and *Trugôidia*

Since the Archaic period, poets were drawn to Telephus's unusual identity as a hero bridging opposed political and social spheres. This final section explores the distinctive value of this identity to Aristophanes' own comic brand. Telephus's egalitarian realism is more than a source of physical gags at the expense of

Euripides and his biography. It provides a compelling moral narrative for the fictive Dicaeopolis's own struggle. *Acharnians* assigns this moral struggle to Aristophanic comedy itself, which recasts the hero's hybrid ethnicity as generic hybridity and projects the hero as a symbol of its singular fusion of comic and tragic modes and marriage of entertainment and political efficacy. Thus, the full implications of Aristophanes' appropriation of Telephus's narrative and rhetoric for positioning his special kind of comedy at this juncture of his career have not been adequately treated. The rhetorical strategy by which poets and thinkers define themselves and their projects through heroes is well attested in Greek literature.[78] Euripides' popular hero is the focal point of a comic marketing strategy that aimed to introduce compellingly Aristophanes' blend of innovative parody and overtly political comedy, a style he terms τρυγῳδία (*trugôidia*). Exploiting the success of a Euripidean character whom he critiqued earlier in the play, Aristophanes 'piggy backs' on Telephus's popularity to advertise his work to the public.

It is now more or less the consensus that Aristophanes speaks through Dicaeopolis at several politically freighted moments of *Acharnians* that address the didactic value of his comedy and his conflict with Cleon.[79] Aristophanes claims that his conflict with Cleon was precipitated by his criticism of the city – in *Babylonians* (426 BCE) of the previous year – for its treatment of the allies in front of foreign visitors attending the Dionysia.[80] In response, Cleon sought the poet's indictment in the Council for treason (379), an indictment Aristophanes managed to escape but (he claims) nearly at the cost of his life (ὀλίγου πάνυ / ἀπωλόμην, 381–382).[81] Aristophanes' present rejection of Cleon's charge mirrors Dicaeopolis's rejection of the analogous accusation of treason levelled by the belligerent Acharnians. Lamenting the ferocity of the city's elderly men, i.e., the chorus, Dicaeopolis abruptly gives way to Aristophanes' voice, which claims that he, the poet himself, was similarly threatened by Athens's most powerful demagogue, who 'slandered' (διέβαλλε) and 'showered' him 'with lies' (ψευδῆ κατεγλώττιζέ, 380). In these places where Dicaeopolis speaks in such pointedly metatheatrical fashion it is difficult to deny that he is speaking for the poet.[82] Regardless of the actual historicity of this feud with Cleon, it allows Aristophanes to characterize himself as a solitary advocate for justice who puts the interests of the *dêmos* before his own.

The poet's claims of comedy's political efficacy here coalesce with his claims to its innovative fusion of genres with the introduction of the enigmatic term τρυγῳδία about one hundred lines later. Dicaeopolis, again speaking for Aristophanes, returns to his dispute with Cleon:

Δι. μή μοι φθονήσητ᾽, ἄνδρες οἱ θεώμενοι,
εἰ πτωχὸς ὢν ἔπειτ᾽ ἐν Ἀθηναίοις λέγειν
μέλλω περὶ τῆς πόλεως, τρυγῳδίαν ποιῶν.
τὸ γὰρ δίκαιον οἶδε καὶ τρυγῳδία.
ἐγὼ δὲ λέξω δεινὰ μέν, δίκαια δέ.
οὐ γάρ με νῦν γε διαβαλεῖ Κλέων ὅτι
ξένων παρόντων τὴν πόλιν κακῶς λέγω.

Men of the audience, don't begrudge me
if as a beggar I intend to speak about the city
among the Athenians, making *trugôidia*.
For *trugôidia* also knows what is just.
And what I say will be shocking, and right.
This time Cleon will not accuse me of
slandering the city with foreigners present.

Ach. 496–502

The sequence of Telephus's disguise and infiltration of the Argive assembly is the model of Dicaeopolis's defence before the Acharnians and at the same time the means of Aristophanic comedy's claim to political efficacy in contemporary political discourse. Similarly outclassed, outnumbered and outraged, Aristophanes is the underdog courageously fighting for justice,[83] the Telephus of Athenian festival culture. τρυγῳδία describes the totality of the poet's effort on behalf of the *dêmos* in both the poetic and political realms. For as long as he has produced 'trugedic' choruses in Athens (χοροῖσιν ἐφέστηκεν τρυγικοῖς, *Ach.* 628), he claims, Aristophanes has quietly served and been reluctant to confront the *dêmos* until now. Like Telephus, he was attacked by an enemy but ultimately survived, though wounded, after an acquittal. The poet now appears to confront his enemies head-on and question their spurious justification for continuing the war, just as Telephus challenged his Argive kinsmen for their unprovoked aggression.

Telephus's defence of himself and the Mysians is programmatic for the public mission of Aristophanic comedy in other respects as well.[84] Telephus's demand for justice despite his lowly status as a 'beggar' is a model for Aristophanes' apology for confronting his audience despite the ostensibly low status of his craft. He claims the outsider status of Telephus despite his privileged access to the *dêmos* in the dramatic festivals. Aristophanes, too, is both estranged from his poetic peers because of his unconventional comedy and targeted with unprovoked aggression by a corrupt political establishment. Recasting the narrative of Telephus's vulnerable position in the assembly of his elite Argive kinsmen, the poet claims the status of generic and political underdog. Throughout his extant corpus, Aristophanes directly and indirectly projects himself as an artist disrespected and underestimated by the status quo despite his manifest artistic and political virtue. Telephus's heroic struggle for justice provides a template for the aesthetically hybrid and politically principled comedy of *Acharnians* as well as its fusion of comedy's naturally carnivalesque drive and the political engagement or 'seriousness' commonly and uncritically imputed to tragedy.

Aristophanes' introduction of the enigmatic term τρυγῳδία in *Acharnians* is a watershed moment in comedy's advertisement of its seriousness.[85] The term's numerous appearances in the Aristophanic corpus show it to be more than an irreverent moniker.[86] τρυγῳδία conflates τραγῳδία, 'tragedy', and ἡ τρύξ, 'wine-lees', the sediment that accumulates in the bottom of a vessel of wine.[87] Aristophanes' definition of τρυγῳδία's capacities within the context of the earlier quote implicitly acknowledges tragedy: that τρυγῳδία *also* knows what is just (τὸ δίκαιον) presumes tragedy's inherent political engagement as common knowledge.[88] τρυγῳδία is prescribed to audiences as a superior alternative to tragedy 'at that point when [comedy's] alleged social function is in question'.[89] Silk describes τρυγῳδία as an 'applied theory' of comedy:

> If 'comedy *too*' implies that comedy sometimes can or does occupy tragic ground, the more fundamental corollary is that comedy normally has its own territory. Aristophanes' consciousness of tragedy presupposes a sense of difference between tragedy and his own medium, such that any comic use of tragedy opens up the possibility of new modes of comedy itself. What Dicaeopolis points us towards, then, is not merely an Aristophanic preoccupation with tragedy, but an Aristophanic interest in new alignments of comedy vis-à-vis the 'serious' drama of Euripides and his fellow-tragedians. Over his whole career, Aristophanes has, in fact, a special relationship with tragedy. In a kind of applied theory he strives to define the limits and the scope of comedy and sees in tragedy an essential point of reference. This will prove to be an immensely fruitful, exciting, if also problematic, exercise.
>
> Silk 2000: 41

This recognition of a 'special relationship' between Aristophanes and tragedy has rightfully received its due share of praise. τρυγῳδία signals a new direction for Old Comedy predicated on bridging together different genres – tragedy and comedy – as well as their naturally separate registers: the lofty and base, the serious and the funny, the political and non-political. The hybrid quality of τρυγῳδία, however, is not just predicated on enhanced political efficacy. It is generically hybrid and promises a more dynamic form of entertainment and amusement. The term thus invites audiences to connect the carnivalesque tendency scholars have long identified in Old Comedy with the (ostensibly) serious political realm from which comic business is allegedly excluded.[90]

Telephus's combination of seemingly irreconcilable positions or perspectives – Greek and Barbarian, king-in-rags, Insider and Outsider, son of Heracles yet voice of justice for the marginalized – lies latent in Aristophanes' revelation of τρυγῳδία as a form of comedy that claims to convey serious things. By evoking Telephus's combination of external humility (or weakness) and inner nobility and wisdom, Aristophanes projects a concrete representative of his comedy that will embed it in popular thinking. The poet's affected claim to offer both the funny and the serious here is a recurrent applied theory of his later comedy. While it may not be applied consistently over the corpus, τρυγῳδία frames Aristophanes' critique of political and social issues in nearly all his plays in some form or another, most obviously as a driving principle of the self-consciously literary comic project of the ostentatiously named Trygaeus in his *Peace* (421 BCE). It bookends his 'Old' corpus of comedy as a leading concern of his *Frogs* (405 BCE), when the chorus of Eleusinian initiates claims the right to say many laughable and many serious things (καὶ πολλὰ μὲν γελοῖά μ' εἰ- / πεῖν, πολλὰ δὲ σπουδαῖα, *Ran.* 389–390).[91] The far-reaching significance of Dicaeopolis's reconstitution of Telephus on comedy's own terms is therefore observable in Aristophanes' later work, as well. Aristophanic comedy claims, despite its aesthetic and political nobility, and uncommon ingenuity, to be unfairly targeted and regarded with suspicion by the Athenian political and poetic establishment. *Acharnians* underscores this in Dicaeopolis's ironic claim to require tragedy to make himself as 'pitiable as possible' (384) before the chorus. Telephus's defence of himself, the Mysians and perhaps even the Trojans furnished a *paradeigma* for Dicaeopolis's (and Aristophanes') own justification for making a deeply unpopular defence of the Spartans and taking other similarly controversial positions in later comedy. As a new form of comedy, τρυγῳδία is predicated on aesthetic and political innovation: comedy's effective combination with other poetic genres, through parody and literary appropriation, for the purposes of engaging with cultural and political topics of interest to the audience's world.

By adopting this strategic perspective on the rhetorical positioning, timing and goals of Aristophanes' introduction of τρυγῳδία through Telephus, it is possible to see the generic self-promotion of Aristophanes – and occasionally other poets – as efforts in 'branding' and 'product placement' in the classical era. I conclude this chapter by developing a line of thinking earlier presented in the Introduction's overview of the diverse and multi-layered institutional agonism of the Athenian dramatic festivals and the comic poets' explicit and self-conscious engagement with one another and the public. In his discussion of the various specialist craftsmen (e.g., in properties, instruments, costumes), poets, trainers, dancers, producers and other workers whose labours were organized and subsidized by Athens for the festivals of Dionysus, Revermann has compellingly demonstrated the great promise of applying a Western capitalist business model to the competitions of fifth-century 'comic business.'[92] By contextualizing Aristophanes' positioning of his comedy vis-à-vis tragedy as an example of competitive marketing or branding, as it is commonly known, one can better appreciate Telephus and *trugôidia*'s centrality to the communicative strategy of *Acharnians*. The enormous amount of research devoted to marketing practices since the beginning of the advertising age in the 1920s, and through the latter half of the twentieth century, has confirmed that modern advertising essentially draws on basic practices of human communication that date back to the ancient world. Marketing experts generally agree that the definition, benefits and functions of brands embrace every kind of organization and business, including – I would add – comic business. Apart from the branding strategy of *Acharnians*, a deeper appreciation of the strategic marketing that drives Aristophanes' self-presentation lends greater coherence to the poet's efforts to spin the victories and setbacks of his career in the available evidence.

As already noted, the motivations of the fifth-century poets, at least, were not profit- but prestige-driven.[93] Actors, producers and poets strove to 'make the cut' for the opportunity to win one of the coveted slots of the festival and, ideally, secure a victory. Whether they express it in the explicit rhetoric of the parabasis or the subtle (and not-so-subtle) gamesmanship of comic intertextuality, the comic poets prioritize winning and sustaining audience approval. Aristophanes strives to separate his comedy, his 'product', from that of his rivals in a poetically saturated festival environment that plied audiences with choral and dramatic performances over several days in rapid succession. The concentration of so many generically similar performances within the short span of these Dionysiac festivals replicates an experience in some ways comparable to the phenomenon described by advertisers as 'product explosion,' which refers to a situation in which the market is flooded with products of a generic kind that, at least superficially, the consumer can have trouble easily distinguishing. As in the modern capitalist marketplace, branding or product placement in comic business is much less about communicating something inherent in the dramatic product than it is about implanting ideas about that product in the mind, specifically how it improves the consumer's life. The power of a brand derives from the curious mixture of how it performs and what it stands for, and when it gets that mix right, it makes consumers feel that it adds something to their lives.[94] The competitive context of comic drama is one in which moving up the 'ladder' of the spectator's mind and positioning a product as the preferred one typically requires either directly dislodging the opponent's brand or somehow favourably relating a new product to it.[95]

At its root, 'positioning' refers to differentiating a brand from its competitors. 'You can position anything. A person, a product, a politician', state Ries and Trout in their fundamental study of marketing as basic human communication that is, in essence, comparable to that of politics or religion.[96] In Aristophanes' case, the strategic advantage of τρυγῳδία for positioning his comedy is apparent in several ways. His primary aim (at least ostensibly) is increasing his popularity in comedy. Like other service-providing organizations or companies, Aristophanes represents his service metaphorically by means of a symbol, at least in *Acharnians*. Accomplishing this involves carving out a special aesthetic category for his work that is, by his definition, transgeneric. The elegance of the conceptual category of τρυγῳδία is that it creates a new and prestigious but hitherto unrecognized corner of the comic market from which his primary comic rivals are excluded by definition.[97] The paratragedy of *Telephus* communicates the dual claims of this new subgenre in order to present a dynamic transgeneric form of comedy that challenges the political and cultural authority of the polis's dominant discourses or genres, specifically tragedy. By its name, τρυγῳδία aspires to the imputed seriousness of tragedy, but with the crucial distinction of a single well-positioned letter that steers Aristophanes' branding effort by 'relation':[98] at the same time that τρυγῳδία instils in the spectator's mind much of the prestige, pleasure and edification of τραγῳδία, it also invites the individual to reflect on the implicit promise – real or imagined – of Aristophanic comedy to offer the benefits of both poetic forms, seriousness and organic fun. The weight of Aristophanic brand positioning in τρυγῳδία thus rests on the single alteration of the alpha into upsilon, which is sufficient to indicate a new and different product that appropriates the positive attributes of a lesser rival that is already widely known.

The precise timing of τρυγῳδία's launch in 425 BCE, after Aristophanes had acquired some experience in presenting a few plays, is likely not accidental. It is a critical moment in the poet's nascent career. His ensuing production, *Knights* of 424 BCE, was apparently the first play Aristophanes himself produced, where his name only was publicly attached to the comedy. The poet takes the opportunity of that play's parabasis to explain his reasons (*Eq.* 512–516) for deferring the production of his first few plays – *Banqueters* (427 BCE), *Babylonians* (426 BCE) and, of course, *Acharnians* – and relying on a producer,[99] who is identified elsewhere as Callistratus.[100] Although scholarship generally accepts at face value the poet's claim that his caution was a show of respect (σωφρονικῶς, 545) for the comic art and his audience, the success his earlier plays achieved would seem to belie the sincerity of that modesty. Given the business aspect of comedy, it seems just as likely that the inexperienced Aristophanes availed himself of the services of a producer to reduce the risk of a potential failure to his own professional reputation: by sharing responsibility for the production with another professional, the poet had a partner who could absorb some of the blame of a possible failure. This could be construed as a strategy for limiting liability. We should not put it past these poets to seek to protect their professional reputations until they felt confident enough to produce their work independently. For it seems that when Aristophanes was satisfied that his star was on the rise after the first-prize victories for *Babylonians* and *Acharnians*, he took full credit for the success of those plays, making no mention of Callistratus in *Knights*.[101] If calculated, this reiteration of his primary role in those plays cashes in his former anonymity for optimal publicity, a strategy whose benefit marketing experts have long recognized. Premature excessive publicity can sink products that have not yet reached sufficient development, at which point they can be cashed in for maximum effect once the product has earned the consumer's trust.[102] Aristophanes shrewdly exploited the publicity generated by *Acharnians* and earlier plays by waiting until after their proven success to tie his name openly and firmly to his brand.

Moreover, the apparently fluid state of the comic marketplace in the early 420s offered rather favourable conditions for introducing an innovation like τρυγῳδία. The traditional scholarly designation of Aristophanes and his peers as the generation of comedy's 'political poets' assumes the emergence in the late 430s or early 420s of a core of new artists of shared political interests. To begin and maintain a period of success, Aristophanes needed to distinguish himself from a crop of talented and similarly politically minded rivals that included older poets like Cratinus and Hermippus and those of his own generation like Eupolis, Phrynichus and Plato. Comedy was undergoing a transition marked by the decline of less overtly political comedy – e.g., mythological burlesque, domestic humour – and the Athenian public's growing interest in more politically engaged plays. In market terms, such conditions are characterized by shifting hierarchies in which no product maintains a leading position or clear advantage and new products have the greatest chance of taking hold in the consumer's mind. Aristophanes' explicit attempts to distinguish his work from his rivals are plentiful, and scholarship has thoroughly documented them, so there is no reason for repeating them here. Let it suffice to point out how Aristophanes disparages the product of his competitors as boorish and crass (*Nub.* 537–545; *Ran.* 1–30), unimaginative and hackneyed (*Pax* 739–751), and cheap imitations (n.b. μιμούμενοι, *Nub.* 559) of his more authentic product (*Nub.* 551–559) at various moments in the 420s.

In place of the allegedly unimaginative and self-indulgent comedy of rival poets, Aristophanes offers his own entertaining and edifying τρυγῳδία with its promise of new ideas and concepts to improve the audience's life by making it laugh while cultivating its intellect.[103] We should recognize part of the impact of a hybrid concept such as τρυγῳδία through its ability to generate a buzz and shape the trajectory of the comic marketplace, or in this case, the genre. τρυγῳδία helped Aristophanes lodge his comedy in the public's mind as a new kind of comedy that offered something different, although *Acharnians* need not have been the first production to fuse parody and politics, nor the first to aspire to the status of political institution in that era.[104] This strategy need only convincingly position Aristophanes' comedy in the public's mind as the first of its kind for it to be salient and successful.

Certain points in Aristophanes' career may reflect the poet's grappling with the challenges of maintaining the prestige of his brand, for instance, his obsession with the poor reception of his first *Clouds* (423 BCE), which only survives in a revised version that the poet presumably intended for reperformance. Aristophanes' curious fixation on the failure of the play remains a point of fascination for scholars.[105] Although Aristophanes portrays it as an attempt to develop his product, his exasperated tone in the revised version of the play (*Nub.* 524–562) reveals something more akin to a kind of failure in product development that can threaten the prestige of the original product without containment of the damage.

Some might object to the apparent anachronism of my application of late twentieth-century principles of business marketing to Athens in the culturally, economically and politically distinctive Classical period. But that anachronism is only apparent. Though concepts like 'branding', 'product placement' and 'positioning' are redolent of the highly sophisticated, nuanced and expensive global marketing campaigns of international corporations nowadays, the art of advertising, even its most specialized forms, draws on basic principles of human communication and psychology. The most salient difference between branding in ancient and modern settings is the latter's scale in space, expenditure and technology. The extant evidence for self-promotion by Aristophanes and his rivals indicates an awareness of and desire for the implementation of a publicity campaign that relies on the basic tactics of self-promotion still used by advertisers today. While his 'business' lacks the infrastructure, concrete assets and revenues of a modern corporation, Aristophanes understood that the potential value of a carefully crafted brand can be greater than anything else an organization or individual has at their disposal, just as modern marketing executives do now. With Telephus, Aristophanes introduces his own brand of comedy, τρυγῳδία, which charms spectators with its innovative appropriations of other genres and, when their attention is secured, comments on cultural and political topics of greatest interest to them.

Conclusion

I began this chapter speaking about *Acharnians*'s privileged status as the earliest extended parody of Greek tragedy in Old Comedy. Since its first production, audiences and readers have delighted in its 'bottom-up' approach to Euripidean stagecraft. Like an epic hero arming himself for confrontation, Dicaeopolis's reconstitution of Telephus provided a template for the mechanisms of parody, its visual, linguistic and (certainly) gestural codes in performance. Moreover, as an effort to widen the parameters of his appeal to audiences of different competencies, Dicaeopolis's visit to Euripides demonstrates how comic poets designed parodies to be as inclusive as possible. Aristophanes' generic collision with tragedy during Dicaeopolis's extended discourse on Euripides' kings-in-rags seems geared to help the most passive spectators 'get it'.

My top-down analysis of this scene, by contrast, affirms its deeper importance for effective communication of Aristophanes' comic agenda. The poet's apparent mockery of Euripides' hyper-realistic tragic hero does not prevent him from cynically spending the cultural capital that this particular instantiation of Telephus had accrued since 438. The distinctive cultural background, plight and tragic ethics of the hero forced to defend a just but wholly unpopular view made him a salient figure for the heroic narratives of both Dicaeopolis and Aristophanes, who 'trope' *Telephus* through their own interventions in Athenian political discourse, in speeches closely modelled on the kind heard in the Athenian assembly or tragedy.[106] Using Telephus, Aristophanes fashions comedy as a superior alternative to these two significant conduits of politics in Athenian life and art. More importantly, Aristophanes uses the hybrid Telephus as a unifying symbol, much like many previous poetic and artistic representations, who brought together seemingly opposed worlds. By contextualizing Aristophanes' *Telephus* within his broader heroic biography, one gains a fresh perspective on the shared cultural knowledge audiences brought to Aristophanes' play and a sense of the deeper ideological significance of Telephus as representative of the aesthetic and political possibilities of τρυγῳδία. Aristophanes could claim that his comedy's carnivalesque exterior both amused and spoke a higher truth; that τρυγῳδία would say what is just, even if deeply unpopular; and that his comedy was more valuable than tragedy, comedy's putatively superior and more prestigious but detached rival. Only comedy, the genre hitherto marginalized in Athens, can apply itself, and the accumulated capital of tragedy, directly for Athens's benefit.

Acharnians thus presents the earliest glimpse of a self-consciously poetic approach to social and political issues that recurs throughout Aristophanes' later career. But as I trace that career in the coming chapters, tragedy less often complements and more often provides a foil for comedy's imaginative versatility and naughty critical impulses. The aggressive parodies of *Peace* and *Thesmophoriazusae* concentrate on making the aesthetic and moral 'failures' of Euripidean tragedy an engine for the comic success of Aristophanes' own heroes. It has been said that tragedy inflects myth through a complex of narrative forms that can address contemporary cultural issues.[107] Comedy's parody of satyr play and tragedy in the following chapters will show, just as *Acharnians* has, that Old Comedy inflects its own cultural, political and aesthetic concerns both through and in contrast to such dramatic rivals and associated cultural discourses. To comedy's parody of such mythological narratives in contemporary vase painting I now turn.

2

Visualizing the Comic

Introduction

Despite imminent changes to its repertoire, Old Comedy continued to enjoy enormous popularity in and beyond Attica at the end of the fifth century and into the fourth. Vases with seemingly theatre-related scenes from workshops in the Greek colonies of southern Italy confirm the export value of both Athenian comedy and tragedy. A workshop in Metapontion (modern Metaponto), which was almost certainly opened by an Athenian painter as early as the 420s, is followed a decade later by one in Taras (modern Taranto). Vases with theatrical connections begin appearing in Syracusan workshops as early as 380.[1] Of an estimated 20,000 vases catalogued, attributed and dated by Trendall, we now know of over one hundred that explicitly signal theatrical associations.

The considerable Apulian market for vases of theatre-related iconography is particularly fascinating given the dearth of similar imagery in Athens, the birthplace of theatre. Late-Archaic and Classical Athens had monopolized the pottery market of the Greek world and beyond with ceramics adorned with images of everything from the heroic labours of myth to the everyday life of the polis. Yet the most quintessentially Athenian institution of all – drama – is strikingly absent from this visual repertoire. To explain why very few pots preserve images with any clear or direct theatrical association, and even fewer with links to Old Comedy, several theories have been advanced: the particularity of the dramatic performance militated against the art form's desire to remain 'imaginatively fluid';[2] drama was too political a subject for painters who preferred the everyday and the religious;[3] painters presented only a mythological scene rather than the dramatic performance of one, and omitted the overt markers of drama in order to preserve the illusion of the stage.[4]

Nevertheless, there survives a small group of about fourteen comedy-related vases from Athens dateable to 420–390 BCE. Their unique aesthetic deviations from the beautiful, idealized figures that typically adorn Athenian vases appear all the more intriguing in light of an earlier group of approximately twenty or so pots (560–480 BCE) painted with exotically dressed komasts (with pipers) thought to be somehow connected to comedy's origins.[5] It is still actively debated whether these theatre-related Attic and South Italian vases reflect the performance of Attic tragedy and comedy, especially those originating in the colonies of Magna Graecia. The earliest studies on the interaction of images and poetry often overzealously identified dramatic models in images on thin and sometimes inconsistent evidence. But some art historians have gone to the other extreme when flatly denying that drama had any influence at all on such paintings, which (they say) drew from various, earlier traditions.[6] Other art historians approach the problem less dogmatically: while conceding the theatrical dimension of many pictures and even the rare play-specific vase, they reject most attempts to link vase and play in the absence of multiple, explicit connections to a dramatic model.[7]

When these comic vases first came to the attention of the scholarly world, eminent Hellenists could not fathom that their long-held views about the unexportability of Attic comedy might be mistaken. They believed that Old Comedy's distinctive topicality confined it to Attica, the only place where people could understand it.[8] Yet many of the grotesque characters of South Italian comic iconography are strikingly similar in type and gesture to mass-produced terracotta figures of old men, slaves, prostitutes, Heracleses and other comic characters in late fifth-century Athens and early fourth-century Apulia.[9] Clear resemblances between the costumes of painted Apulian characters and those of Attic figurines – ugly masks, fat-suits and phalloi – suggest that these figures belong to the same performance genre.

Opposition to the idea that the people of Magna Grecia were major consumers of dramatic poetry from the Greek mainland has been softening over the last three decades. Publications by Csapo, Green and Taplin have slowly built a case for the performance of tragedy and comedy in Apulia and Sicily and, moreover, that interest in the dramatic images on such pots extended much further into Italy.[10] These scholars were anticipated by Webster's visionary article of 1948, which first argued that South Italian pots reflected scenes from Attic drama. He explained that discrepancies between the details of painted mythological episodes and the tragic texts that they allegedly illustrated resulted from different mediums: painters do not reproduce every detail of a tragic myth in order to avoid cluttering up the visual field.[11] They developed a different, symbolic language for tragic tableaux that represented scenes 'their way'.

This chapter on vase painting has two aims. The first is to survey those fifth- and fourth-century comic vase paintings with rare evidence for Old Comedy's performative interaction with rival genres of the stage, including the visual expression of parodic collision. Such visual strategies are either localized on the actor's body, as in *Acharnians*, or suggested in the narrative terms of thematic incongruency and counterfactual experimentation with myth. Theatre-inspired iconography not only affirms the parodic strategies of the textual evidence of Old Comedy, it also supplements our knowledge of strategies either imperfectly preserved or altogether absent. To this end, this overview includes both theatre-inspired vases as well as those of more doubtful theatrical provenance, i.e., possibly paraiconographic scenes that parody some established and (perhaps more importantly) recognizable narratives of serious vase painting, that nonetheless preserve evidence for comedy's appropriative strategies. Iconography – both theatrical and non-theatrical – *reflects*, *confirms* and *explains* strategies Old Comedy deployed in parodying its fifth-century generic rivals.

The stage and the pot follow similar poetic codes. Like textual parody, the recognition and enjoyment of these scenes are contingent on what expectations viewers bring to them. Collisions and manipulated expectations in painting are similarly dependent on juxtaposition, ugliness, transmotivation, inversion, compression and a whole slew of other mechanisms of humour that were explored in the previous chapter. On ceramic surfaces, these strategies are also apparent at various levels: at a micro-level through materialism, physicality and reversal and substitution; at a macro-level through the defeat of expectations, counterfactual discourse and confrontational generic cross-fertilization. My approach to this iconographic evidence observes the central principle of Webster's early attempt to link South Italian material to Old Comedy. This is adopted from Aristotle's account of the humorous reversal of traditional mythical and literary narratives:[12] where those 'who are deadliest enemies in the plot, such as Orestes and Aegisthus, exit at the end as new friends, and no one dies at anyone's hands'.[13] This chapter advances Webster's insight by contextualizing these vases in their generic and (more importantly) intellectual milieus, and showing how the enjoyment of comedy's interaction with other repertoires depends significantly on what expectations the viewer brings to the images.

The first section begins with the most significant iconographic evidence for play-based comic intertextuality, the 'Würzburg Telephus'. This vase and its counterpart, the 'Berlin Heracles', furnish rare scene-specific evidence that connects the performance of Aristophanic comedy in Athens and Southern Italy. Both pots strongly emphasize costume, disguise and layered-style paratragedy – all expressive of significant, recurrent themes of their respective models, *Thesmophoriazusae* and *Frogs* – and capture the humour of those models in synecdochic fashion. A third comic vase (*c.* 400 BCE) depicting a 'respectable' comic woman likely preserves a parody of a tragic adulteress, perhaps even an Aristophanic parody of Euripides' Phaedra or, alternatively, his Stheneboea. This was produced within a decade of what were possibly the first extended treatments of respectable women in comedy, in Aristophanes' *Lysistrata* and *Thesmophoriazusae* (411 BCE).

Narrative reversal organizes the mythological burlesques of the second section. The signature scenes of these vases engage mythological tradition in a more sophisticated and counterfactual way than those of the previous group. They reverse the gendered hierarchy of war crimes ('The Rape of Ajax'), exchange the dramatic roles of established myths ('Oedipus, Creon and the Sphinx', 'Sant' Agata Antigone'), or revise antiquity's most unquestioned myths ('Priam and Neoptolemus'). These tightly focused burlesques revise traditional iconographic and/or literary narratives of momentous consequence with ruthless economy and unmatched comedic gumption.

The third and final section focuses on iconographic evidence for the primary topic of this project, comedy's cross-generic engagement expressed in direct and immediate confrontations between Old Comedy and its primary stage rivals, tragedy and satyr play. Three vases portraying Old Comedy's face-to-face engagement with these rivals confirm the visual strategies of intergeneric communication of comedy, through strict versus layered juxtaposition and (especially in the case of the 'Choregoi' vase) the investment of paratragedy and parasatyrism with topical subtexts.[14]

An important measure of the value of theatrical and paraiconographic vases for the study of fifth-century comic parody and drama is the growing frequency with which even philologically inclined scholars class such *visual* evidence with fragmentary *textual* evidence.[15] This chapter demonstrates that scene-specific vase painting can preserve a visual 'fragment' of drama that enjoys a relationship to its whole – the performance – analogous to that of a literary fragment and its text.[16]

I. Signature scenes

It makes sense to begin with the vase that changed perceptions of the relationship between vase painting, both South Italian and Athenian, and Attic drama, the 'Würzburg Telephus' (Fig. 2.1). This bell-krater from Taras (modern Taranto) and illustrated by the Schiller Painter (*c.* 380 BCE) preserves the most convincing

Fig. 2.1 Image depicting Inlaw (right) 'sacrificing' the wineskin in Aristophanes' *Thesmophoriazusae* (411 BCE).

evidence of a scene-specific illustration of fifth-century Attic comedy.[17] It contradicts two longstanding assumptions: that performance-based imagery on South Italian vases was not influenced directly by Attic drama and that the political specificity of Old Comedy precluded its marketability in other parts of the Greek world, where such features would have been obscure. Before the Aristophanic origins of the Würzburg Telephus were recognized, scholarship deemed it representative either of the so-called 'phlyax' play – a vague, native Italian performance genre whose existence is questionable – or an unidentifiable genre similar to Old Comedy.[18] These objections were substantially weakened when Csapo and Taplin demonstrated independently that the Würzburg Telephus preserved a scene-specific image at least inspired by an actual episode of extant Aristophanic comedy.[19]

Although detailed descriptions of the Würzburg Telephus and of other vases in this chapter are readily available in other publications, the following descriptions anticipate focal points of my own interpretations of the images.

Staring straight ahead from the centre-right position on the vase stands a beardless figure with stubble on his face. He wears a woman's belted *chitôn* down to his knees and a female headband, kneeling with his left leg on an altar. In his right hand is a raised sword and in his left a wineskin with two appendages curiously fitted with slippers. From the left a barefoot, ugly woman in a long robe and holding a large drinking vessel moves toward him. Her headdress (*sakkos*) hanging down the back is typical of a married woman.[20] Between the two figures in the top portion of the image floats a mirror.

In the first published analysis of the vase, Kossatz-Deissmann recognized the Würzburg Telephus's dependence on the parody of Euripides' *Telephus* (438 BCE) in Aristophanes' *Thesmophoriazusae* and that the man was none other than 'Inlaw' poised to 'sacrifice' the 'baby' of one of his female antagonists (*Thesm.* 689–691). Despite these dramatic associations, Kossatz-Deissmann maintained that such influence was indirect, and that the painter's model was a phlyax production loosely based upon the comedy.[21] The alleged absence of the headband, clearly visible on the beardless figure, from the Aristophanic text was proof enough, she reasoned, of the indirectness of Aristophanic influence. Csapo subsequently drew attention to the κεφαλὴ περίθετος provided to Inlaw by the effete Agathon in an earlier scene of the play (*Thesm.* 257–258) and moreover identified other significant points of agreement between *Thesmophoriazusae* and the image: Inlaw's refuge at the altar, the Persian shoes of the wineskin, the approaching woman with the drinking vessel, and the toiletry are all visible. The mirror and facial stubble of the figure on the vase point to the earlier toiletry scene (213–268) in which Inlaw dressed and shaved to appear as a woman.[22]

While some remain unconvinced of the Aristophanic associations of the Würzburg Telephus because of discrepancies between image and text,[23] Csapo and Taplin's strong cases for identifying the Würzburg Telephus with *Thesmophoriazusae* are generally accepted. Minor discrepancies, in fact, can be reasonably explained by the nature of visual narration and (if less favourably described) the limits of the ceramic medium. As Webster noted, the representation of a three-dimensional performance in a two-dimensional, static image demanded artists take a selective approach to detail. They can and do emphasize, de-emphasize and/or omit details of their 'models' in the interests of economy and visual coherence, to avoid confusing the viewer by crowding the field with an excess of objects and figures. Painters tell the story 'their way'.[24]

Taplin has devised a useful method for determining the dramatic associations of performance-related vases like the Würzburg Telephus. The viewer must assess the number of correspondences between details of a painting's narrative and those of the particular play upon which it may draw.[25] Yet the final adjudication of an image's origins is not simply a question of tallies, but must also take into account the placement of emphasis. The location of such correspondences between image and text, and whether knowledge of the associated drama enriches the viewing experience, are also critical questions to consider. The details of the Würzburg Telephus are particular enough that one can assume that it was painted with the aid of first-hand knowledge of a *Thesmophoriazusae* performance *at some point* in the image-production process. This knowledge need not have belonged to the painter himself but could have been conveyed by a second party, even an individual commissioning the vase. On balance, this threshold of dramatic influence is preferable to the over-rigid standards advocated by some art historians who consider anything less than 'multiple pairings' of vases to a specific text to be pure speculation.[26] Such interpretive inflexibility underappreciates the larger implications of Csapo and Taplin's findings about the Würzburg Telephus – which incidentally lacks the primary marker of theatricality, a stage – for other vases with similar indices of theatricality, such as masks, ugliness and plainly artificial costumes.[27]

The practical function of a vase is also potentially relevant to its iconography and, by extension, that iconography's generic affiliation. The Würzburg Telephus may have memorialized the favourite scene of a customer who commissioned it. Alternatively, Inlaw holding the wineskin could simply have been an attractive detail familiar to the broadest part of a painter's customer base.[28] The latter hypothesis may find support in a Corinthian clay figurine that seemingly replicates the scene's uglified female, 'Mika', who moves toward Inlaw while holding an enlarged *skyphos*. If Green is correct in his identification of the woman, the 'sacrifice' of the wineskin was indeed an 'ecplectic' moment of drama that grabbed the attention of spectators and 'had [them] talking as they walked away from the theatre'.[29]

Although it may not be possible to answer all questions concerning the production of vases such as this one, it is only by attempting to address them that one can understand the agenda that drives the 'visual poetics' that define the relation of vase painting to the stage.[30] The conflated indices of genre in the costume of Inlaw on the Würzburg Telephus visually confirm the layered juxtaposition of his appearance that received so much emphasis in Dicaeopolis's innovative fusion of comic and tragic personas in *Acharnians*. Such layered juxtaposition strategically appealed to the broadest possible portion of the audience, who could appreciate in visual terms the cross-generic play that may have otherwise eluded them in its textual form. These visual codes reinforce other visual codes (i.e., gesture, gait) and the linguistic part of performance.[31] As the parody of *Telephus* in *Acharnians* made clear, Old Comedy exploits the vast comic possibilities of costume as disguise, the metatheatricality of putting it on and taking it off and its *failure*. That failure is funny and definitive of the precise terms of comedy's engagement with other genres. The absurd and unconvincing femininity of Inlaw's disguise in this particular scene of *Thesmophoriazusae* would have been apparent to the external audience yet simultaneously (according to comic logic) imperceptible to the internal audience of festival women. An altogether different style of juxtaposition is the 'strict' kind preserved on the 'Choregoi' vase (see below): rather than combining elements of the tragic and comic on the same person, representatives of different genres are separated but contrasted with one another.[32]

Visual narrative is very different from textual narrative. Csapo and Taplin's analyses recognize at least three distinct episodes from *Thesmophoriazusae* in the Würzburg *Telephus*, which does not express time in linear, textual fashion, but rather 'hierarchically' with events arranged spatially in order of importance.[33] The painter's fusion of three distinct temporal moments in a single frame 'inflects' each of its three primary details with actions and attributes that convey its role in the narrative:[34] though not literally centred, Inlaw's imminent sacrifice of the wineskin is prioritized; the action's imminence is recognized by the approaching woman, who will attempt to catch the wine/blood that is released; the floating mirror at the centre symbolizes the earlier dressing of Inlaw and explains the relationship of the two painted figures, which is gender. These elements are comic substitutions for corresponding ones in the serious iconography of *Telephus* at the altar: baby Orestes is the wineskin; Inlaw, mid-speech, replaces Telephus as beggar; Clytemnestra, who frequently runs in terror from the altar in the serious iconography, is replaced by the alcoholic wife running toward, not away, from the sacrifice.[35] Mika's enlarged *skyphos* and the humanized wineskin symbolize the alcoholism that defines *Thesmophoriazusae*'s distinctive caricature of femininity. If Aristophanes' plays of 411 were in fact the first to dramatize femininity in any sustained way – something that seems likely although it cannot be taken for granted – the vase advertises a moment of historical significance in comedy's evolution and not just *Thesmophoriazusae*.[36]

The second vase with almost certain links to Aristophanic comedy is the so-called 'Berlin Heracles' (Fig. 2.2) of 375–350 BCE or so.[37] This now-lost Apulian bell-krater was first identified as a scene from Aristophanes' *Frogs* in 1849. A stage-naked figure in tights, stomach and rear padding and a grotesque mask, with hints of the face and head of Heracles, approaches a Doric column to

Fig. 2.2 Image depicting Dionysus (middle), dressed as Heracles, hammering on the door of Heracles in Aristophanes' *Frogs* (405 BCE).

the left.[38] With his right hand he swings a club towards the column, while his left grasps an animal skin by one of its legs. To the right and below this hand is an altar, behind which trots a donkey mounted by a second actor, who carries over his shoulder a stick at the end of which is fixed a large bundle.[39] There are several clues of theatricality:[40] both figures show the wrist and ankle seams of tights and a seam running up the donkey's right foreleg may indicate a pantomime ass.

At most points, the details of the picture are consistent with an early moment in Aristophanes' *Frogs* (405 BCE), the arrival of Dionysus and Xanthias to the house of Heracles before their journey to the Underworld (35–165).[41] Dionysus's hammering of the column, i.e., the house, corresponds to the 'centaur-style' (κενταυρικῶς, 38–39) knocking that irritates Heracles. The painter thus selected a memorable moment in the comedy: 'door-knocking' scenes are 'genre-neutral' and an especially marked form of dramatic entrance for a major character.[42] Dressed like Heracles, Dionysus has prepared for this *katabasis* by impersonating his brother, who had himself journeyed there for his own famous *katabasis* in search of Cerberus. Astride the donkey and carrying a bundle is Dionysus's slave, Xanthias. Because certain details from *Frogs* are not reproduced exactly on the vase, some question the identification of vase with play. For example, Dionysus wears none of the Dionysian elements of his appearance in this comedy or elsewhere, such as his boots, transparent gown (*krokôtos*) and thyrsus. But these omissions can be explained by the same practical concerns that motivated the Schiller painter's omissions from the Würzburg Telephus: greater accessibility.

So as not to confuse the viewer, the painter omitted the Dionysian features and added only the Heraclean attributes, slave, donkey and baggage.[43] Like the previous vase, conflation is the visual strategy, but status- rather than genre-based conflation: bravery and cowardice, divinity and mortality, and social superiority and inferiority.[44]

Though crudely depicted, the elements of this signature scene are easily identifiable and presented hierarchically to emphasize Dionysus's obnoxious hammering. When the true Heracles answers the door, doubtless dressed in the very same outfit, the audience will behold both the true and false Heracleses, staring face to face. The painter's portrayal of Xanthias as currently astride the donkey, and situated slightly to the right of centre (in the background), inflects that figure with the comic bit of the previous scene and its metatheatrical critique of the 'porter scene' that Aristophanes imputes to his hackneyed rivals. In the text, Dionysus orders Xanthias to dismount (35) when they arrive at their destination and before he begins knocking (37). Juxtaposing that earlier moment in the play with the door-knocking prompts the viewer to recall the opening argument between master and slave over carrying the luggage and its highly metatheatrical commentary on this bit.[45]

The painter thus presents a scene-specific yet still programmatic comic moment that gestures backwards at the previous porter-scene while prefiguring Dionysus's later failures of disguise: confronted by the creatures and inhabitants of the Underworld, the god soils his costume (285–308), switches identity with Xanthias (494–497) and unheroically endures a beating (640–671).[46] In this way the failure of the Berlin Heracles resembles the similarly programmatic failure of Inlaw's disguise on the Würzburg Telephus, which is re-enacted again and again as the hero attempts, and fails, to escape from the festival in *Thesmophoriazusae*.

A vase of possibly paratragic iconography of a more understated kind is preserved on a little-known bell-krater (Fig. 2.3) from about 400 BCE. Green has identified the illustration on this vase from Metapontion as a comic parody – possibly by Aristophanes himself – of a scene from one of Euripides' Hippolytus plays.[47] The tableau features two women. On the left and moving right is a slave wearing simple garment, ugly face, rough hair and large ears. While the meaning of her open and extended right hand is unknown – possibly offering aid – the left hand held to her mouth communicates dismay at a second woman's distress.[48] This second woman at the right lies or falls backward onto a bed with a pillow set at the other end. The greater elegance of her dress, headband and hairstyle, in addition to her less pronounced ugliness, suggests a comic wife. Her right hand is held back behind her head in a gesture of swooning or

Fig. 2.3 Image depicting a parody of a Euripidean adulteress (?) in distress (right) and tended by her slave (left). From an unknown comedy.

emotional distress. She appears to be using her left arm to reach out and steady herself, perhaps against a wall. The ugliness of both women suggests comedy, as does the diminutive bed.[49]

This is the only example of a potentially comedy-inspired image featuring two women at this date, as Green notes. There is no hint of the second woman's identity, but Green's argument for Phaedra seems the most likely without the benefit of any additional evidence. The ancient biographical sources explain that Euripides' second (and still extant) *Hippolytus* featured a more sympathetic Phaedra after the poor reception of *Hippolytus Veiled*. This was achieved, in part, by characterizing her as resistant to Aphrodite's malicious power. The heroine's eventual revelation of her feelings to her nurse (*Hipp.* 170–361) while stricken in bed seems like a compelling model for the present image, especially given the bed's value as a marriage symbol. However, if the depicted anguish is the frustration of romantic rejection, our comic heroine is less likely to be Phaedra and more likely to be the eponymous heroine of Euripides' lost *Stheneboea*, already mentioned in Chapter 1. The date of this 'Comic Phaedra' might suggest it marks the significant moment in comedy's history mentioned in my earlier remarks on the Würzburg Telephus: the possible introduction of the respectable woman into the repertoire in Aristophanes' plays of 411.

All three vases of this section preserve signature scenes under the influence of Old Comedy in performance. Their thematically charged moments exhibit a kind of metonymic value for their comic plots. In *Thesmophoriazusae* and *Frogs* an initial failure of absurd disguise prefigures later thematically connected failures, the emasculation of the detained Inlaw and Dionysus's unconvincing impersonation of his brother in the worlds of the living and the dead. The visual poetics of comic iconography make use of analogous strategies of the stage and, most importantly, *prioritize* rather than *interpret* the pronounced themes of their respective comic moments. This conflation of identity through layered juxtaposition of costume looks back to the Telephus parody of *Acharnians* and anticipates the generic fusions in paratragedy and parasatyrism of later chapters. The humorous effect of such absurd, transparent collocations of comedy and other generic codes facilitates a fundamental aim of appropriation in Old Comedy, its distinctive power to convert putative failure in other narratives, narratives represented in material fashion, into its own unique success.[50]

II. Epic reversals

While the previous images are more securely linked to extant or known (but now lost) comedies, the theatrical provenance of other vases with obviously comic mechanisms is less clear. Nevertheless, their distinctive iconography justifies consideration of their possible links to comic performance. In the event that they are most likely not theatre-related, their repertoire and comic mechanics are sufficiently analogous to indisputable contemporary representations of the comic stage that their exclusion would present a more misleading assessment of the pictorial record. Their comic narratives of well-known myths make the static tableaux and potential consequences of their humour more accessible to viewers. Bold revisions of critical history and the reversal of mythological tradition in four vases embody Aristotle's fascinating remarks about endings in comedy:

δευτέρα δ' ἡ πρώτη λεγομένη ὑπὸ τινῶν ἐστιν σύστασις, ἡ διπλῆν τε τὴν
σύστασιν ἔχουσα καθάπερ ἡ Ὀδύσσεια καὶ τελευτῶσα ἐξ ἐναντίας τοῖς βελτίοσι
καὶ χείροσιν. δοκεῖ δὲ εἶναι πρώτη διὰ τὴν τῶν θεάτρων ἀσθένειαν· ἀκολουθοῦσι
γὰρ οἱ ποιηταὶ κατ' εὐχὴν ποιοῦντες τοῖς θεαταῖς. ἔστιν δὲ οὐχ αὕτη ἀπὸ
τραγῳδίας ἡδονὴ ἀλλὰ μᾶλλον τῆς κωμῳδίας οἰκεία· ἐκεῖ γὰρ οἳ ἂν ἔχθιστοι
ὦσιν ἐν τῷ μύθῳ, οἷον Ὀρέστης καὶ Αἴγισθος, φίλοι γενόμενοι ἐπὶ τελευτῆς
ἐξέρχονται, καὶ ἀποθνῄσκει οὐδεὶς ὑπ' οὐδενός.

Second-best is the structure held the best by some people: the kind with a double
structure like the *Odyssey* and with opposite outcomes for good and bad
characters. It is thought to be best because of the weakness of audiences: the
poets follow, and pander to the taste of, the spectators. Yet this is not the pleasure
to expect from tragedy, but is more appropriate to comedy, where those who are
deadliest enemies in the plot, such as Orestes and Aegisthus, exit at the end as
new friends, and no one dies at anyone's hands.

*Poet.*1453a30–39. Trans. Halliwell 1995

Neither comedy nor mythological burlesque is Aristotle's primary interest, yet
his observation indirectly illustrates Greek comedy's enormous imaginative
licence to revise stories widely accepted by audiences familiar with myths of
rhapsodic, dramatic and dithyrambic poetry. In defining such endings by the
opposite fates of good and bad characters and their accommodation of audiences'
best 'moral expectations', Aristotle affirms comedy's capacity (and inclination) to
recast mythology in such radical ways.[51]

Although Aristotle appears to be speaking about comedy in his lifetime, the
scenario described is consistent with mythological burlesque found in late fifth-
and early fourth-century comedy.[52] These revisionist approaches to panhellenic
myth can be understood within the contemporary intellectual interest in
counterfactual exercises in historiography, oratory and documentary evidence
in the latter half of the fifth century. Counterfactual exercises '[pertain to, or
express] what has not in fact happened but might, could, or would happen in
different conditions'.[53] Rising interest in the subject during the fifth century is
thought to be connected to the sophists' investigations of the contradictory
nature of many myths. In its purest sense, counterfactuality is a 'mode of critical
utterance', 'an emphatic focusing device designed to draw special attention to a
hinge moment in history'.[54]

One of the cleverest counterfactual images of extant South Italian vase
painting is a mere sherd (Fig. 2.4) that was originally part of a calyx-krater
(340 BCE) illustrated by the famous Paestan painter Asteas.[55] A grotesquely ugly,
bearded male in comic mask and armour grips a Palladion, a cult statue of

Fig. 2.4 Image depicting the Trojan princess Cassandra (left) assaulting Locrian Ajax (centre). Possibly from an unknown comedy.

Athena, while an enraged female, whose figure is mostly missing, yanks him by the hair while shoving her knee into his back. Above her is inscribed '-ΣΣΑΝΔΡΗ', for 'Cassandra' the virgin daughter of Priam and priestess of Apollo. Her hairstyle, a 'tight curly mop without elegance or style' in a simple, undecorated band is characteristic of comedy's 'respectable' wife.[56] To the right stands an ugly old woman holding a super-sized temple key in her left hand and raising her right in a gesture of shock. She is evidently a priestess, for inscribed above her is 'IHPHA'.

Virtually all treatments of this sherd identify it as a parody of one of the most notorious moments of the Trojan saga, the rape of Cassandra by Locrian Ajax, son of Oileus, during the sack of Troy. Ajax's great crime was one of the most famous episodes of the *Ilioupersis*, the epic cycle's narrative of that sack.[57] When

Oilean Ajax stormed the palace of Priam, he violently seized Cassandra and raped her, either on or before an altar of Athena.[58] A popular scene of the 'Ilioupersis' type, there are countless representations of the crime preserved in Archaic black- and red-figure vase painting.[59] Two important trends that dominate the scene's evolution over the sixth and fifth centuries emphasize Ajax's barbarity: Cassandra's extension of a hand in supplication and the increasing exposure of her nude body, and the Palladion's increasing detachment.

Asteas's parody reacts to this serious iconographic tradition by switching criminal and victim and reversing the gendered expression of power. Trendall saw Cassandra inflicting physical violence on Ajax, but Webster, followed by Taplin, saw the comic potential for a more complete (and ironic) reversal if the violence were sexual.[60] The winking Palladion signals surprise or bemused interest in the events taking place, an obvious departure from the statue's increasing detachment in the serious iconography. A sexually aggressive Cassandra would seemingly respond to tragedy's distinct portrayal of the princess as a symbol of wartime's brutalized female in Aeschylus's *Agamemnon* (458 BCE) and the *Alexandros* and *Trojan Women* of Euripides' Trojan trilogy (415).[61] In the latter play (309–340), she is cruelly separated from her priestly function by her rape and perverse 'marriage' to Agamemnon, and the *agôn* makes the austere Cassandra a foil for the adulterous Helen: both are beautiful, abducted women, but Cassandra resists her violent marriages as Helen constantly acquiesces.[62]

Asteas's potential reaction to the tragic tradition of Cassandra at least raises the possibility that his scene was related to a specific Athenian comedy. While Trendall matched the facial features of both Cassandra and Ajax to three known types of comic masks, Taplin argued against paratragedy on grounds of generic decorum: the rape of Cassandra could have never been performed in tragedy, so there was no precedent for comic parody.[63] Moreover, the rich iconographic history of the scene – much of which predates extant tragedy – could have furnished sufficient inspiration for an artist of the talent of Asteas. Although I remain agnostic about the vase's link to comedy, it is very much within the realm of possibility that Asteas parodied tragedy via indirect means, such as a description of the rape in a messenger speech. The narrative expansion of messenger speeches was (after all) a favourite device of fourth-century tragedy and one frequently illustrated in contemporary South Italian vase painting.[64] Although he describes a somewhat complicated matrix of influence on the vase painter, Walsh's argument in favour of scene-specificity deserves airing. He adduces the prop-like quality of the priestess's enlarged key,[65] the implicit connection to drama possibly signalled by the Dionysiac scene on the vase's opposite side and iconographic parallels for threatened or imminent rape in other scene-specific comic vase painting.[66] It is also worth noting that Asteas's painting may invoke a common trope found in comedy, the voracious female appetite for illicit sex. Although the expression of that libido very rarely involves the physical assault of men,[67] the nature of the vase's power-reversal is consistent with comedy's approach to sexuality and mythological burlesque.

While enjoyment of the vase is not dependent on its larger mythological implications, such implications can doubtless add to an appreciation of its counterfactual exercise. Cassandra's rape had disastrous consequences for the Achaeans' return from Troy in the *Nostoi*, when a storm sent by the angry gods wiped out part of the Greek fleet. The Achaeans, enraged by the rape, decided to stone Ajax to propitiate Athena before they departed from Troy (*Ilioupersis* Arg. 16–18 Bernabé). Ajax avoided this by fleeing to Athena's altar, perhaps the same one Cassandra had occupied.[68] If Asteas's reversal of attacker and victim alludes to this story, he may be 'transmotivating' Ajax's original flight to the altar: instead of fleeing execution, he tries to escape sexual violence at the hand of his intended victim.[69] But this interpretation fails to address certain problems such as the man's facial expression, which suggests nothing of the terror we might expect given the violence looming over him. His gestures also resemble that of a man taking possession of an object rather than seeking salvation from it. Since more than one Trojan War myth involved the Palladion, one should consider the possibility that Asteas is conflating two different stories in one moment. The other story concerned the theft of the Palladion in the *Little Iliad*. The Greeks learned that Troy could not be taken without possession of the statue that magically safeguarded the city, in this instance the portable statue of Athena held in her shrine.[70] Odysseus and Diomedes infiltrated Troy through its sewer and stole the object. Though the statue of Athena that provides Cassandra refuge in the *Ilioupersis* and the purloined Palladion statuette are never conflated in tradition, Asteas is perhaps doing just that for comic effect. One could imagine, for example, a scenario involving a Greek hero accosted by the statue's protector, an aggressive Cassandra, at the moment he attempts to steal it.

A large part of enjoying a parody such as this is the suspension of the action at a moment pregnant with meaning that has the potential to alter, or rather occlude, a significant number of contingent events. The 'Rape of Ajax' engages the larger literary tradition of the Epic Cycle in even more sophisticated ways. As mentioned above, Ajax's offence against Athena provokes the goddess's anger. In retaliation, she sends a storm scattering much of the army on its departure from

Troy and so begin the *Nostoi* (the 'homecomings') of the Greek heroes. In addition to causing his own death, Ajax's crime thus had disastrous consequences for many of his comrades.[71]

The counterfactual thinking on these vases parallels textual Old Comedy in the latter half of the fifth century, which sometimes focused on the Trojan War as a paradigm of interstate conflict.[72] The war's dubious origin was a useful vehicle for satirizing the putatively trivial causes of contemporary wars to which Athens had committed. Cratinus, Aristophanes, Eupolis, Hermippus and likely many other comic poets injected mythological burlesque of the Trojan War with a dose of Old Comic topicality. Dicaeopolis's Telephus speech (496–556) used the Trojan War to denounce the ludicrous beginning of the five-year-old Peloponnesian War and Pericles' flimsy pretext for the conflict. Cratinus's *Dionysalexandros*, a key text of Chapter 3, converted the Judgment of Paris into an aetiology of the origins of the Peloponnesian War by substituting an unscrupulous and hedonistic Dionysus-Pericles for Alexandros. As tragedians and historiographers did, comic poets used the Trojan War to appeal to contemporary interest in causality and ridicule Athens's own *archai kakôn*.

Perhaps this particular image was commissioned by someone who desired to behold a moment capable of encapsulating the absurdity of the gender reversal and parody, as well as the weight of the historical alternative: Ajax's victimization negates all the events ensuing from his crime against Athena and erases an entire tradition of myth. That Cassandra's rape, like Helen's abduction, kicked off the next chapter of heroic myth lends some intellectual ballast to the parody. This assault's revision of one of the most notorious and popular moments of Troy's sack is representative of comedy's nearly limitless freedom to revise almost anything.

The Rape of Ajax is not the only vase whose humour is predicated on such brazen contradiction of historical 'fact'. An Apulian bell-krater (Berlin 3045, Fig. 2.5) of the first quarter of the fourth century shows a bearded old man sitting on an altar in a caricatured version of an oriental headdress, or Phrygian cap.[73] He speaks with his left hand raised to the right toward an ugly, younger man approaching from that direction, who is dressed in a *chitôn* and *pilos* and holding aloft in his right hand a sword. He looks poised to strike the old man with a fatal blow. The regal bearing of the old man and the threatening pose of the younger invite an identification of Priam and Neoptolemus, when the latter killed the king of Troy during the Greeks' sack of the city as narrated in both the *Little Iliad* and the *Ilioupersis*.[74] Priam's climactic death on the altar of Zeus *Herkeios*, Troy's religious focal point, was one of the most shocking moments of the Trojan saga.[75]

Fig. 2.5 Image depicting Neoptolemus (right) on the verge of striking down king Priam of Troy on an altar. From an unknown comedy.

The image's theatricality is even more pronounced than that of the Rape of Ajax: Priam and Neoptolemus wear grotesque masks, pads, body tights and phalloi. The action is frozen at a critical point in a dialogue between the two men to emphasize the comic potential of Neoptolemus's pause and careful consideration of whatever Priam is saying.[76] Like the previous vase, this Priam and Neoptolemus scene affirms Aristotle's implicit suggestion that such confrontations between mortal enemies were the 'bread-and-butter' of mythological burlesque. As with the Rape of Ajax, Taplin's scepticism of the paratragic status of Berlin 3045 is driven by the difficulty of imagining Priam's death performed onstage in tragedy. Yet the frequency of fifth-century tragic suppliant scenes, most of which presuppose an altar,[77] would seem to outweigh such caution in this particular case. Berlin 3045 merely assumes a scene of supplication, not quite sacrilegious murder. Moreover, given the prominence of the perverted sacrifice *topos* in tragedy, and Old Comedy's evident interest in parodying it (e.g., at Ar. *Ach.* 325–340, *Thesm.* 688–764, and on the Würzburg

Telephus), it seems just as likely that this vase preserves one more signature scene.

Priam and Neoptolemus may also just parody iconography. Few painted scenes of epic were more favoured than those from the 'Ilioupersis' tradition, and Priam's death was an especially popular expression of the *Ilioupersis*'s core theme:[78] the dissolution and destruction of the royal family.[79] Priam was the head of the Trojan house, and his death symbolized the death of Troy itself.[80] Though he never mentions it explicitly, Homer builds toward this moment by alluding to Priam's inevitable fate and Troy's destruction.[81] For the spectator of comedy, the historicity of Troy's fall was as certain as any known historical event,[82] and this is presumably why the painter of Berlin 3045 parodied it. It is a 'hinge moment' in myth whose alteration would have enormous consequences for subsequent history. Since visual narrative operates differently from the textual narratives of historiography and drama, vase painters concentrate on highly recognizable critical moments with a certain synecdochic value for the narratives to which they belong.[83] Homer and tragedy invest key moments or individuals of the Trojan War with the same synecdochic force to raise similar counterfactual scenarios, sometimes briefly for stylistic effect and sometimes to convey a deeper insight about causality.[84] The comic deferral or abolition of Priam's death invites the viewer to imagine the implications of such an event.[85]

The most mysterious counterfactual exercise of fourth-century vase painting is found on an Apulian oinochoe in Taranto (Fig. 2.6). This parody of the myth of the Sphinx does not switch roles, but substitutes agents: Creon, not Oedipus, attempts to solve the riddle and defeat the Sphinx.[86] Creon, identified by name, sits on a rock while wrapped in a cloak from the waist down and holding a shepherd's staff against his body. Though ugly and bearded, he wears no fat-suit and his exposed torso conforms to the male physical ideal. On the far right and perched atop a mound of boulders is a hermaphroditic sphinx smirking down at him. Her ugly physical features, sagging breasts, pronounced vulva, pot belly and phallic-shaped tail are curiously balanced by symbols of nobility and rank: a necklace, earrings, bracelets and a crown. Her hairstyle is more or less that of a 'respectable' woman. A third figure enters from the left toward Creon, who turns in that direction with a gesture of annoyance.[87] The inscribed name above the third figure has been largely lost, but '-ΔΙ-', probably for 'Oidipous', is legible. He is wrapped in a cloak, carrying a walking stick and rebuking Creon.[88] His feet are grotesquely swollen.

Though all three figures are ugly, that ugliness is restrained. Trendall was confident of the scene's dramatic provenance and assigned mask types to each

Fig. 2.6 Image of a parody of the myth of Oedipus answering the riddle of the Sphinx.

figure, but later critics have generally disagreed,[89] mainly because the figures do not actually appear to be wearing masks. But the vase's inspiration little affects its value as an exercise of comic imagination on tradition. Oedipus's meeting with the Sphinx is one of the most recognizable stories of myth. The precise circumstances of Creon's comic substitution for his future brother-in-law are irrecoverable, but the simple displacement of the future king of Thebes from one of the defining moments of his biography is bold and provocative. This parody petulantly sidesteps what is perhaps the most intractable of human fates in all of ancient mythology by reducing it to a trivial matter of timing. The inevitability of Oedipus's fate is prominently stressed in literary sources. In the second stasimon of Aeschylus's *Seven Against Thebes*, the chorus explains that Oedipus was cursed by Apollo not just before birth, but before conception, when his father Laius disobeyed the god's warning against conceiving a child (*Sept.* 745–750).[90] Sophocles' tightly constructed tragedy invests Oedipus's fate with an even crueler inevitability. These plays interpret the hero's later birth and murder of

Laius as conditions for the fulfillment of his curse, as well as the arrival of the Sphinx in Thebes. The crisis of the king's death and the presence of the Sphinx prompt the Thebans to offer the reward of kingship and marriage to the queen, Jocasta, to the individual able to rid the city of the monster. Our vase's humour lies in the absurdly simplistic and banal way that the infallable Apolline oracle's prophecy is simply derailed by another person taking Oedipus's place.

It makes little sense to speculate about how this moment came to pass in the painter's imagination.[91] The Sphinx's provocative portrayal, however, is more suggestive than previous studies have recognized. The manner in which the Sphinx's appearance seemingly anticipates the 'reward' of solving her riddle has gone largely unnoticed. Her crown, necklace and bracelet are emblems of feminine status, commonly featured in ritual imagery, funereal and athletic, but especially prominent in wedding imagery from early vase painting to that of 400 BCE.[92] The jewellery's suggestion of civilized nobility and the beast's grotesquely exaggerated anatomy point vaguely in the direction of the traditional outcome of the riddle's solution, the royal power and marriage that Oedipus goes on to acquire as ruler of Thebes. Put another way, the Sphinx seems to be less a sexually available, anthropomorphized beast than a physical embodiment of narrative prolepsis, if a crude one. She is at once the obstacle to be overcome and the hideous reward of that labour. Superimposed upon the Sphinx are the tangible rewards of overcoming it in simple, direct terms: wealth and royalty. Insofar as it anticipates the outcome of the present scene, the Sphinx herself is inflected with narrative significance, which its bemused expression suggests some awareness of. The comic scenario invites one to consider the equally unpleasant outcome of Creon's solution of the riddle, which would displace the incestuous alliance from mother and son to siblings. Creon's attempt to solve the riddle suggests that he willingly takes up the challenge: acquire the kingdom *and* his sister as his wife! The representation is such that all of these possibilities are simultaneously implied, showing that 'Creon, Oedipus and the Sphinx' presents a far more subtle comic experiment than its gritty obscenity might suggest.

The image of the next vase may parody a later episode from the same Theban cycle. An Apulian bell-krater found at Sant' Agata dei Goti (*c.* 370 BCE) and now in a private collection in Campania is one of the most intriguing theatre-related puzzles on a vase. In 1828, Panofka hypothesized that the 'Sant' Agata Antigone' (Fig. 2.7a) parodied the story of Antigone, daughter of Oedipus, and her defiance of her uncle Creon's tyrannical edict against the burial of her slain brother Polynices.[93] The grotesque mask, padding, tights and phalloi of the figures suggest theatricality. In the centre of the image stands a balding, white-haired

(a)

(b)   (c)

Figs. 2.7a, b and c Images of a parody of the tragedy of Antigone (?). From an unknown comedy.

man with a cone-shaped beard dressed in a woman's unbelted *peplos* and diaphanous undergarment extending to his feet (Fig. 2.7a). His phallus is visible underneath. His right hand grasps a (now barely perceptible) female mask, and he holds a yellowish hydria close to his body with his left. He wears an expression of surprise or alarm, for he is being roughly dragged by a figure on the right, a younger, ugly man with a beard and wearing a fur cap and animal-skin cloak (Fig. 2.7b). He holds two spears in his left hand. On the left side stands a second older man who resembles the middle figure in hair, facial features (e.g., nose, cheeks, eyes, beard) and the distinctive pattern of his garment, which he wears in a different style (Fig. 2.7c). He wears a Phrygian cap and holds a spear. His expression is one of surprise.

Trendall and Webster speculated that the old man in the centre was a clandestine substitute for the heroic Antigone from Sophocles' canonical version of her story, and that the figure on the left is Creon.[94] Taplin expanded this theory by comparing Creon and the old man to Euripides and Inlaw in Aristophanes' *Thesmophoriazusae*: just as the tragedian persuaded his reluctant relative to disguise himself and complete a perilous comic mission, so was the old man of the Sant' Agata Antigone pressured by Creon to assume the role of Antigone and bury Polynices. In this theory, the hydria would contain either the ashes of Polynices for burial or earth to sprinkle on his corpse. But the old man seems far more reluctant than Inlaw and is being dragged away by force.[95] His identity and the nature of his predicament are unclear. If Taplin is correct, the vase would expand the known parameters of the tragic repertoire targeted by Old Comedy for parody.[96] While similarly dark humour is not unparalleled in mythological burlesque, death, corpses and burial are largely unknown as subjects of paratragedy. However, the vase's possible suggestion of an unlikely partnership between ostensible enemies, Creon and the transgressor of his edict, is certainly imaginatively consistent with the vases we have seen already.

The Sant' Agata Antigone furnishes probably the finest extant visual evidence for layered-style paratragedy in a clearly metatheatrical context. The tragic female *peplos* is superimposed over an existing ugly, phallused, comic body. If nothing else, these conjectures about the Sant' Agata Antigone reinforce one of Taplin's important criteria for theatre-related imagery: one can only truly make sense of them with the aid of a 'text' of some kind. The 'Antigone', however, is exceptional in this way. Something remarkable about the other vases with counterfactual, hinge moments in this section is that their enjoyment is predicated on knowledge of a common cultural tradition and seemingly requires no familiarity with any separate literary text.

III. Cross-generic confrontations

Much as the Sant' Agata Antigone does, the vases of the third and final section of this chapter feature signature scenes that express larger narrative puzzles. Despite the obscurity of their narrative contexts, this iconography preserves tantalizing glimpses of cross-generic experimentation for which the extant texts of comedy offer limited comparisons. For some time, the best candidate for a contemporary painting of an Old Comedy from Athens was thought to be a calyx-krater datable to the end of the fifth century.[97] Currently in Naples, the vase once called the 'Getty Birds' (Fig. 2.8) preserves two fully costumed ithyphallic birdmen with large spurs, combs and small hooked beaks facing off against one another around

Fig. 2.8 Image of two bird-man chorus members (with prominent phalloi) fighting. From an unknown comedy.

a lone *aulos*-player. The performance context of the scene is clear from the *aulos* and the birdmen's chorus-like dance movements and dress. The 'satyr shorts' of both dancers (see below), moreover, show a degree of dramatic specificity that invites identification with a distinctively Athenian setting. There is disagreement about the nature of the play that is thought to inspire the image.[98] Noting the associations of these birdmen with the sole extant Aristophanic production about birds, Green argued that they belonged to the chorus of Aristophanes' *Birds* (414 BCE).[99] That theory was considerably undermined by Taplin's later observation that the roosters (ἀλεκτρυόνες) on the vase are not included among those wild species identified in the chorus's spectacular entrance in the play (229–254).[100] Moreover, that chorus's twenty-four members are also individuated (297–304). Taplin initially proposed that the two represented the Greater and Lesser Arguments from the central *agôn* of Aristophanes' *Clouds* (424 BCE) on the basis of a scholiast (Σ^VE Ar. *Nub.* 889), which claimed that the two Logoi were represented onstage as fighting cocks in cages.[101] Upon further reflection, Taplin conceded that 'two similar figures with a piper should *prima facie* be a chorus'.[102] Moreover, the birdmen's ithyphallicism is infrequent enough in the South Italian evidence to merit special attention.[103] The ithyphallicism and 'satyr shorts' (or *perizomata* shorts, noticed by Green) of the two figures may suggest that the birdmen reflect some type of comic *theriomorphosis* in which satyrs were transformed into birds.[104] Csapo's subsequent publication of an Atlanta *pelikê* (discovered in 2008), featuring a single ithyphallic birdman in the exact same costume and with another piper on the reverse, would seem to prove that the Getty Birds are at least *choreutai*.[105]

While no known comedy dramatizes 'satyriasis', such transformations are broadly consistent with the genre-fusion sometimes representative of other comic choruses, specifically Cratinus's *Dionysalexandros*, certain comic heroes like Dicaeopolis and Trygaeus in *Peace*, and the comically modified 'Pappasilenos' found on the Apulian bell-krater dubbed the 'Cleveland Dionysus' (see Fig. 3.1).[106] In any case, while the imagery on the Getty Birds remains incompletely understood, the most likely explanation is that some creative fusion of the satyric and the comic has taken place.

An even more intriguing example of concretized genres in confrontation is found on the 'New York Goose Play' (Fig. 2.9).[107] This calyx-krater (400 BCE) housed in the Metropolitan Museum was originally attributed to the Tarporley painter, but has now been credited to the Dolon painter.[108] It is the only comedy-related vase painting with an accompanying transcription of dramatic dialogue – in Attic, rather than the Doric Greek of Taras – from each of its three figures,

Fig. 2.9 Image of a confrontation between two male comic characters as an old crone (right) looks on. From an unknown comedy.

almost in the style of a single frame from a comic strip.[109] The stage, the open doors, usual indices of comedy (masks, tights, phalloi etc.), and the floating comic mask at the top of the picture all but guarantee its theatricality. At the centre, an ugly old man with a large phallus stands on tip-toe with his hands clasped above his head, as if performing a grotesque dance. Facing a figure to the left he says 'he/she has bound my hands above me' (ΚΑΤΕΔΗΣΑΝΩΤΩΧΕΙΡΕ). The left-hand figure is a younger, beardless ugly man, who is also stage-naked and extends a rod toward the old man in a 'threatening' manner.[110] The gibberish he speaks (ΝΟΡΑΡΕΤΤΕΒΛΟ) seems to represent foreign speech. Some sense of a narrative enters the picture with the right-hand figure, a clothed, ugly old woman on the left edge of a raised stage who gestures towards the old man and says 'I shall hand ... over' (ΕΓΩ ΠΑΡΕΞΩ). A collection of objects sits at her feet: a basket containing a live kid, a cloak hanging over the side of the stage and a dead goose. The old woman's statement and accompanying gesture toward the strange old man implicates him in some kind of criminal activity and may illuminate the identity of the younger man. Taplin persuasively identified him as non-Greek, probably one of the Scythian bowmen used to police Athens in the fifth century, much like the character of Aristophanes' *Thesmophoriazusae*. In other words, the left-hand man may represent the civic authorities.

Yet again *Thesmophoriazusae* may provide clues helpful for interpreting a scene from the pictorial record. The old man's predicament may parallel that of the hero from that comedy, the Inlaw who has been arrested and incapacitated by the Scythian archer. Taplin suggests the Goose Play could reveal something analogous to a scene in *Wasps* (1388–1391, 1396–1398, 1400, 1406–1408), where a similar old woman, the breadseller 'Myrtia', threatens the rampaging Philocleon with legal action after the destruction of her bread loaves. The old man's strange posture on the 'Goose Play' remains perplexing. If he is bound, as he says, it is possible that painted ropes may have since faded. Beazley suggested that he could be under the power of a spell cast by the old crone, since καταδέω/κατάδεσις was a common expression for this very thing.[111] Csapo intriguingly suggests that the missing ropes may be part of the joke: the old man mimics someone bound without actually being so.[112]

The New York Goose Play's interpretive challenges were slightly alleviated by Trendall's recognition of the same two men on an Apulian bell-krater from about 370 BCE illustrated by the McDaniel painter and now in Boston (Fig. 2.10).[113] The Boston Goose Play features the same two men standing onstage but disposed differently: on the left the younger man, the putative barbarian, balances his stick upright from the stage with a single finger; on the right is the same old man, this time pouring what appears to be oil from a flask onto his hand. At first glance, the Boston Goose Play offers even fewer hints about its performance than its New York counterpart. Taplin reasonably suggests that the oil may signal an imminent wrestling match between the two.[114] Aside from a herm positioned to the left and covered by a cloak, the only other obvious difference between the New York and Boston vases is the goose, which is now alive, although the New York vase showed it to be dead: this is presumably the root of the conflict that brought the old man to the attention of the old crone (and the law) in the first place.[115] Geese served many purposes for the ancient Greeks. In Aristophanes, they are a source of food characteristic of peacetime (*Pax* 1004) – as perhaps for the old woman of the New York vase – and could be a gift of pederastic courtship

Fig. 2.10 Image of a fight (?) about to take place between the same two male comic characters from the New York Goose Play. From an unknown comedy.

(*Av.* 707). Geese were also one of the few domesticated fowl that Greeks owned as pets (cf. *Od.* 19.536–553). Like us, Greeks were fond enough of their pets to see them as members of their households.[116]

For my purposes these details are secondary to a fourth figure in the background of the New York Goose Play. Standing apart in the upper left-hand corner of the image is a nearly naked (although not stage-naked) young male wearing neither mask nor comic costume (Fig. 2.11). A cloak hanging from his left shoulder partially covers that side of his body while from his chest juts the word 'Tragoidos'. No theory has convincingly explained the boy's identity and/or his relationship to the events taking place before him. Messerschmidt identified him as part of the current performance, the fourth actor waiting offstage to

Fig. 2.11 Detail of upper left portion of the New York Goose Play featuring a youth labelled 'Tragoidos'. From an unknown comedy.

assume the floating mask before his entrance.[117] Beazley countered that this explanation still failed to account for the inscribed name, which he understood quite literally in an occupational sense: 'Tragoidos' must be a tragic actor at the same festival watching comedy before or after his own tragic performance on that same day.[118] Csapo similarly argues that the boy could be either a tragic actor or a *choreutês*, although not, in any case, a performer.[119] While vase painting's tendency to use single figures to communicate temporality and narrative may explain the presence of 'Tragoidos', there may be a better, metatheatrical explanation for this figure, albeit one without parallel in extant Apulian vase painting.[120]

Marshall denies all three of the previous possibilities because of the age of 'Tragoidos' and argues that the figure stands apart from the action as a personification of tragedy.[121] The figure's position in the upper left-hand corner and away from the events of the foreground reveals something subtle about the image's central event: the possible paratragic modality of the episode in the foreground. If the boy did not actually appear in the play and represents an addition of the painter, the New York Goose Play may actually direct the viewer towards a more sophisticated interpretation of its tableau.

Marshall's theory can be pushed even further, I believe, if we consider the visual aesthetics of Tragoidos's youthful appearance. The figure seems to conform to pederastic iconography and, moreover, curiously lacks the hallmarks of comic ugliness. His boyish features – age, height, prepubescent body, cropped haircut (a 'bowl-cut') and, perhaps most important, small genitalia – set him apart from the pervasive ugliness of the foregrounded scene. He resembles an *erômenos*, the younger boy who is the object of the erotic advances and affections of an older male in Greek society as idealized primarily in Archaic poetry and late Archaic and early Classical art.[122] Especially representative of the *erômenos*'s appearance is Tragoidos's haircut and cloak, which is modestly draped over part of the body in an expression of the *aidôs* which *erômenoi* should ideally display.[123] If this is correct, and Tragoidos can be identified as an object of pederastic desire, the image may attempt to conceptualize generic interaction between tragedy and comedy in highly original and concrete, erotic terms.

This interpretation is inherently plausible given Old Comedy's tendency to conceptualize intergeneric relationships, whether between poet and craft, or comedy and other genres in competition, in explicitly gendered, sexual terms. Aristophanes and his contemporaries introduced feminized personifications of social, political or religious abstractions in their comedies. Many of these are, in fact, treated in earlier and subsequent chapters: Aristophanes has *Kômôidodidaskalia* ('Comic Production', *Eq.* 516), *Opôra* and *Theôria* ('Harvest' and 'Festival', *Pax* 523), *Diallagê* ('Reconciliation', *Lys.* 1114–1121), and *Penia* ('Poverty', *Plut.* 415–609); Cratinus introduced feminized 'Comedy' in his *Pytinê* and may have done the same with the 'Productions' of his *Didaskaliai*; and at some point in Pherecrates' *Cheirôn*, *Mousikê* herself appeared (fr. 155).[124] The Muse of Euripides in Aristophanes' *Frogs* (1305–1307) is especially germane to the theory I propose (building on Marshall) to explain Tragoidos. As the poet's ugly, promiscuous Muse personifies an aesthetic judgment of Euripidean tragedy, so might Tragoidos represent a 'mode' of comedy in sexual and/or romantic terms. While it is true that such metaphors in Old Comedy typically presume the poet's fundamentally heterosexual orientation and deploy the male–female relationship or marriage as a vehicle for poetic composition,[125] comic poets are represented as males in active roles, while their spheres of activity, the passive artforms, are often feminized.[126] Such metaphors of heterosexual courtship, of varying degrees of permanence and legitimacy, convey immediately and concretely the process of poetic refinement and assert superiority over romantically and sexually inferior rivals.

There is a great deal of extant evidence, then, for a gendered, and more specifically, erotic conception of intra- and intergeneric interaction in Old Comedy. Yet it remains unclear whether this kind of metaphor is operative in the New York Goose Play, if we accept that Tragoidos was a target of pederastic courtship. Was he sympathetically portrayed as a youth whose sexual integrity was threatened by the ugly middle figure? Or was he a promiscuous Timarchus-like character who exploited his own body? Was the old man a guardian or ravisher of Tragoidos? Did he fall afoul of the law through his attempted courtship? Could a pederastic courtship explain the presence of the two kids and the goose in the image?[127] The possible dramatic subtexts in the New York Goose Play seem endless. Whatever the youth's true significance in the episode that inspired the New York Goose Play, at the very least he appears to symbolize something about the generic interaction between comedy and tragedy in erotically charged terms.

The most exciting visual testimony of cross-generic activity is the Apulian bell-krater called the 'Choregoi' vase (400–380 BCE).[128] This vase's stunning depiction of an unparalleled confrontation between actors from comedy and tragedy in an actual comic performance belongs in its own class (Fig. 2.12).[129] It features three comic actors with inscribed names, two older and one younger. The rightmost dark-haired 'Choregos' rests on a walking stick, gazing attentively at a second figure to the left. A very similar figure in the middle stands on an object while gesticulating grandly with his right hand as if delivering a speech. 'Pyrrhias', a common slave name, looks directly at the viewer. The leftmost, white-haired comic figure, also named 'Choregos', is identical to the first in mask-features and name except for his white hair. With raised right hand he turns to greet a fourth figure approaching from an open door on the left. His hair, as Taplin shrewdly noticed, might identify him as the older twin of the similarly named and costumed rightmost actor. Following Trendall, Taplin reads the shared name of the two similar comic actors as indicative of their identical function as semi-chorus leaders. Their clearly aristocratic (or at least free and respectable) status – left hands in cloaks and walking sticks are common indices of respectability – differentiate them from the wildly gesticulating Pyrrhias, who is slavish in behaviour and facial features.

The figure approaching from the left is key to the puzzle. In unmistakably tragic garb, i.e., ornate clothing, boots, *pilos* and placid, attractive countenance, 'Aigisthos' seems as if he just entered from the door behind him into an unfamiliar

Fig. 2.12 'Aegisthus' wanders into the comic world of two 'Choregoi' and a slave, 'Pyrrhias'. From an unknown comedy.

world.[130] Aegisthus's confusion is amusingly captured in his 'head-scratching' gesture. As a product of incest, Aegisthus represents the ethical transgressions of tragedy's dysfunctional families. Revermann has observed that the three figures comprise an obvious unit in literary terms and reflect a 'strict' form of paratragic juxtaposition, as opposed to the layered form of previous visual and textual examples: the integrity of Aegisthus's foreign, tragic body is preserved against the 'uglified' comic body.[131]

Taplin conjectured that the comic model of the *khorêgoi* contrasted comedy and tragedy through its representatives, Pyrrhias and Aegisthus, and semi-choruses led by the *khorêgoi*.[132] Wilson developed that theory by noting the class affiliations of the *khorêgoi*, who represent the liturgical practice of *khorêgia*. He hypothesized that the scene satirized *khorêgoi* by reducing these high-status benefactors of the public to the standard, collective anonymity of a comic chorus, whose members are often fictionalized Athenians of common and even lower-class status.[133] Athens imposed the *khorêgia* on its wealthiest citizens, who were responsible for recruiting, training, maintaining and costuming *choreutai* for dithyrambic and dramatic choruses at Athenian festivals. By this interpretation, the Choregoi vase would offer a fascinating glimpse of Attic comedy's insertion into its repertoire of the *khorêgos*, who 'effected a vital material and institutional link between the theatre and those other means of social life that were the object of widespread civic attention'.[134]

By this theory, tragedy and comedy's face-to-face meeting on the Choregoi vase preserves evidence of a paradramatic world that is typically alluded to only obliquely in texts, the economic arrangements that funded the dramatic festivals. The few passages of Old Comedy to mention *khorêgoi* are generally hostile and focus in particular on the ingratitude and cheapness of bad *khorêgoi* who fail to meet their obligations to the comic choruses serving under them.[135] The vase may draw from a play that removed such public benefactors from the normal public settings in which they exercised influence – the assembly, the Council, the symposium – and placed them front-and-centre in a comic fiction that they could not directly control. Especially compelling is Wilson's reading of the economic elitism of Athenian *khorêgia* here displayed through a generic lens.[136] The field of social drama in which such privileged elites competed to aggrandize themselves is topically analogous to the conflicts of tragedy's elite, dysfunctional families. The *khorêgia* afforded aristocrats opportunities for self-promotion that could ultimately reproduce the very same issues of problematic individualism and heroism found in tragedy.[137] The Choregoi vase may capture a static moment from a comedy that thematized this comic tension between Athenian elites and the festival choruses that increasingly depended on the participation of citizens from all Athenian social strata.

Moreover, the awkward meeting between characters on the Choregoi vase may preserve comedy's association of the *khorêgos* with the distinctly antidemocratic, tyrannical figure of Aegisthus and the real-life, less attractive social inferiors over whom he grandstanded on such festival occasions. While we cannot assume this depiction of the *khorêgos* was wholly unfavourable to him, on balance such a critical and even hostile attitude conforms to the textual evidence we do have. However one reconstructs the model of the Choregoi, the vase offers an especially vivid example of parody that imaginatively situates generic archetypes from both tragedy and comedy *within* a paradramatic, institutional space that sits between the audience and the standard fiction of the stage.

Conclusion

In her wide-ranging study of adaptation, Hutcheon observes that 'the performance mode teaches us that language is not the only way to express meaning or to create stories'.[138] Theatre-related Attic and South Italian vase painting attests to the validity of this observation for classical performance culture. The vases of this chapter furnish rare, valuable evidence for the physical and visual dimension of paratragedy and parasatyrism that attended its linguistic performance in the extant texts. To the extent that these paintings show links to actual theatrical production – with more or less plausibility, depending on the vase – they furnish astonishing evidence for contemporary reception of Old Comedy and attest to the themes, tropes and scenes that seemingly made the greatest impression on audiences.

Green is doubtless correct that the images of these vases and of related items such as figurines preserve 'ecplectic' moments of plays that had people talking after the performance ended. This chapter has explored the various ways that such theatre-related images as the Berlin Heracles or Priam and Neoptolemus represent the humour of their productions synecdochically. Since these signature scenes surely aimed to appeal to a customer – whom we should assume to be a spectator of comedy although he need not necessarily be – these vases are evidence of comic audiences' critical role in the processes of reception and poetic branding. Although theatre-related vases can indirectly furnish evidence for dating a particular dramatic production or its popularity in a given period, the extent of their influence over the public's view of a given poet or one of his productions is unknown. For example, we do not know whether the Würzburg Telephus perhaps established Aristophanes' reputation as a master of comic gender or suppliant scenes late in his career. Nor can we discover whether the poet responsible for the comedy that influenced the Choregoi was forevermore associated with parodic innovations of strict juxtaposition, in the event that this scene was met with wide popularity and preserved in vase painting that advertised his particularly paradramatic ingenuity. Is the vase of Priam and Neoptolemus evidence for a specific poet's reputation for counterfactual experimentation? While these questions will probably never be answered, by raising them we are forced to recognize the various forms of reception, diverse media and shifting settings that surely affected comic advertisement – branding – in fifth- and early fourth-century theatrical culture. We cannot reconstruct the reputation of a comic poet solely from surviving written texts.

Albeit in different ways, the comic mechanics of each vase appeal to the viewer's knowledge of genre and the expectations that coalesced around it. The

Würzburg Telephus and Berlin Heracles, and perhaps also the Phaedra, exhibit strategies of generic juxtaposition and correlate visual codes with specific recurrent themes, like the comic failure of disguise that animates much of the humour in *Thesmophoriazusae* and *Frogs*. Such scenes are 'signature' because they preserve a recurring theme or trope that subsequent action in the play, or other works of the same genre, will exploit again and again. Their metonymic value lies in this subtle promise of the distinctive humour to follow.

Conversely, vases of even greater narrative sophistication tend to forego spatial arrangements of time by their careful selection of critical 'hinge' moments that *presuppose* the momentous narrative contexts for which they have greatest significance. The comic immediacy of these humorous revisions of well-known myth is funny, but our full enjoyment is largely determined by our knowledge of the larger consequences these changes entail for the sagas of Troy and Thebes. While each vase's claim to theatrical inspiration is debatable, the counterfactual experimentation that drives the humour of all four is not. To my knowledge, red-figure vase painting has yet to be recognized as an important medium for the kind of counterfactual thinking now amply documented in contemporary textual sources. And yet these vases exhibit the same counterfactual exercises we find in both the texts of Old Comedy and its contemporary, rival genres. While the visual narratives do not operate in the same way as textual narratives, comic vase painting's strategic inversions and distortions of shared cultural tradition nonetheless advance the same 'what if' intellectual exercise as its textual counterparts. While these iconographic caricatures are accessible enough to provide immediate pleasure even to those viewers unfamiliar with the production, their imagery invites further reflection on their consequences for the highly familiar mythological traditions that audiences knew.

The visual evidence also preserves a record of the kind of face-to-face generic confrontation in which Aristophanic comedy, in particular, revels. If any single group of vases is an exception to the rule that dramatic iconography *cannot* be used to reconstruct lost comic plots – an exercise rightly criticized by art historians in the past – it is this puzzling cohort of vase paintings. Unlike much of the red-figure corpus, the visual significance of these pots can only be understood and even made sense of with the help of a missing 'text'. The lost model that lies behind the provocative imagery of the New York and Boston Goose Plays demonstrates this point in compelling fashion. If one hopes to make any sense of these vases, one must attempt to understand how the iconographic repertoire shapes whatever poetic and cultural signs are offered. Scholars have made important strides in the interpretation of these pots by viewing seemingly insignificant details – fantastic metamorphoses, private disputes, the paradramatic – through the imaginative and Athenocentric prism of the comic world still available as texts. While the interpretations proposed in this and previous studies will hardly satisfy all, any debate they prompt about these pots promises to advance our understanding of the mechanisms of comedy-related parody in performance and such parody's popular circulation.

Members Only? Satyrism and Satire in Late Fifth-Century Comedy

Introduction

This study has already made clear that there is excellent evidence for the stylistic and contextual variety of Old Comedy's appropriation of tragedy. The case is different with satyr play, the other fifth-century dramatic form that comedy far less frequently, and often less explicitly, appropriated for its own ends. Our understanding of 'parasatyrism' has been hampered by the state of satyr play's evidence, which is primarily fragmentary apart from the sole surviving play, Euripides' *Cyclops*.[1] Satyr play and its peculiar appeal for Athenian audiences remain one of the great enigmas of ancient Greek performance culture. Lissarrague's concise definition (1990: 236) – 'Take one myth, add satyrs, observe the result' – summarizes best the adventures of the satyrs and their father, Silenus, as they experience the events and characters of traditional myth.[2]

Traditional conceptions of satyr play as a genre primarily comic in outlook have described it as 'playful tragedy' (τραγῳδίαν παίζουσαν), although this conflation of satyr play and comedy obscures the subtleties of comic parasatyrism.[3] An extensive pictorial record highlighting the satyr's visually grotesque mask and ithyphallic body, as well as the ugly and corpulent Silenus, has reinforced this traditional view of the two genres' affiliation. Most studies that situate satyr play midway between tragedy and comedy on the map of Athenian performance culture tend to overvalue the comic and phallic elements and overlook the subtle but distinctive peculiarities of the genre's world.[4] However, improved texts and more sophisticated theoretical approaches over the last two decades have successfully brought many distinctions to light and improved our understanding of the satyrs' place in the fifth-century dramatic repertoire.[5]

Despite the scepticism that still occasionally greets the study of Old Comedy's experimentation with satyr play,[6] there is more than enough evidence to demonstrate that this intergeneric phenomenon was both understandable for and successful with audiences of the 430s and 420s BCE. Storey, in particular, has pondered the difference between comedy's satyrs and those of satyr play proper, as well as how spectators of satyrs in Old Comedy might have balanced expectations for each genre.[7] Questions of this kind sit at the heart of this chapter's exploration of *how* comedy appropriated satyr play, specifically the mechanisms involved, and *what* the genre contributed to comedy's generic and political program.[8] What distinguishes this study from previous approaches, in part, is my treatment of parasatyrism as a *mode* of comedy, which I define not in an Aristotelian sense (i.e., narrative, dramatic etc.) but rather adjectivally, as genre critics such as Fowler and others have defined it, that is as a selective use of distinct and often abbreviated signals of one genre embedded in another.[9] Just this kind of mode, of tragedy rather than satyr play, has been convincingly identified in Aristophanes' *Clouds*, as I discuss in the following section. Second, my analysis of this strategy depends heavily on the ethical orientation and socio-psychological appeal of satyr play as advanced by Griffith in his paradigm-shifting work on the satyrs in the distinctive political and hegemonic context of Athenian theatrical culture.[10]

The evidence shows that strategies of parasatyrism were somewhat narrower and more restricted than the stylistic diversity and textual specificity characteristic of paratragedy. However, due to certain affiliations of satyr play and comedy, parasatyrism lent comedy a vehicle of greater subtlety for exploring its topical interests. Satyr play's highly formulaic and conservative character probably facilitated audiences' greater familiarity with its tropes and themes over a shorter period of time. Those expectations that accrued through experience at the theatre underpin comedy's use of satyrs no less than they do its use of tragedy. While the state of the evidence means that my analysis is at times more speculative than I would like, the breadth of the evidence considered helps me establish links between genres that previous treatments have not seen.

The earliest known instance of parasatyric play in Old Comedy is the highly fragmentary partial hypothesis to Cratinus's *Dionysalexandros*, which is usually dated to the Dionysia of 429 BCE. *Dionysalexandros*'s parasatyric stamp is just barely perceptible in the details of its plot. Cratinus's probable integration of a full satyr chorus into his comedy likely afforded him considerable possibilities for experimenting with the recognizable tropes of this alien repertoire. My analysis sheds new light on the possible parasatyric thrust of *Dionysalexandros* by bringing to bear on its evidence a few underutilized tropes of satyr play and one specific tradition of popular entertainment, the adultery narrative.

Cratinus's play-based appropriation differs in strategy and scope from the more focused parasatyrism of Aristophanes' *Peace* (421 BCE), the topic of this chapter's third section. This later comedy similarly uses its chorus to fabricate satyr play's mythological frame and produce a comic aetiology for events leading to the first sustained peace of the Peloponnesian War. Although mortal, *Peace*'s chorus of panhellenes is also undeniably satyric in speech and comportment from the *parodos* through its climactic hauling of the goddess Peace. Using the formulaic verbal and visual codes of satyr play's repertoire, Aristophanes imputes to his chorus the satyrs' feckless and puerile behaviour. I argue that this extended satyric mode allegorizes the incompetent and obstructionist policies of the major Greek states, which hindered peace initiatives early in the war. These expectations of satyresque failure are nevertheless defeated, to great effect, by the chorus's second and successful attempt to liberate Peace in a celebration of civilized collaboration.

This sustained assimilation of the comic chorus to satyrs in ethical and political terms is a complex and multilayered version of more concise, small-scale appropriations of the same genre elsewhere in Aristophanes. The final section of this chapter examines character-based allusions to the notorious sexual aggression of the ithyphallic satyrs in their inevitable encounters with vulnerable mythological females, a commonplace, if sadistic, feature of the genre's humour. The evidence (thankfully) suggests that this terrible turn of events was averted by the timely arrival of a god, hero or mortal to rescue and claim the threatened girl for a dynastic marriage. In *Birds* (414 BCE) and *Thesmophoriazusae* (411 BCE), Aristophanes deploys this trope in a different kind of critical encounter between aggressive males and feminized beings, one where the satyr's coercive and hubristic 'courtship' and his freedom from its consequences of the normal world represent a benchmark against which the subsequent agency of comic heroes is gauged. By evoking the satyrs' special brand of hubris – behaviour that was antithetical to Athenian norms of civic conduct – these 'rape threats' inevitably suggest the divine privilege that allows them to behave badly with impunity. Aristophanes raises this expectation of what satyrs do and experience in order to characterize the nature and ethics of his mortal heroes' agency.

For Aristophanes, Cratinus and probably other poets whose works unfortunately do not survive, this satyric mode is a source of formal or material variety that distances and defamiliarizes its political topicality. The satyrs' timeless and apolitical mythological world is a means of conditioning audience impressions of comedy's imaginative burlesque of mythological narrative. By swathing politically and culturally topical themes in the tropes of the satyrs and their world, comic poets presented matters of the contemporary polis in more dynamic and imaginative terms.

I. Comic modes

Before tackling parasatyrism, an illustration of my use of 'mode' as a strategy of textual engagement is in order. My chosen example is incidentally a paratragic sequence of Aristophanic comedy that has garnered some interesting commentary, the perplexing ending of *Clouds* (423–418 BCE). Given comedy's conventionally celebratory and 'closed' endings, the uncharacteristically violent destruction of the Socratic *phrontistêrion* has puzzled scholars. Facing financial ruin, domestic discord, and possible criminal charges, the unscrupulous hero, Strepsiades, accuses the Cloud-chorus of leading him astray:

Στ. ταυτὶ δι' ὑμᾶς, ὦ Νεφέλαι, πέπονθ' ἐγώ,
ὑμῖν ἀναθεὶς ἅπαντα τἀμὰ πράγματα.
Χο. αὐτὸς μὲν οὖν σαυτῷ σὺ τούτων αἴτιος,
στρέψας σεαυτὸν εἰς πονηρὰ πράγματα.
Στ. τί δῆτα ταῦτ' οὔ μοι τότ' ἠγορεύετε,
ἀλλ' ἄνδρ' ἄγροικον καὶ γέροντ' ἐπήρατε;
Χο. ἡμεῖς ποιοῦμεν ταῦθ' ἑκάστοθ', ὅντιν' ἂν
γνῶμεν πονηρῶν ὄντ' ἐραστὴν πραγμάτων,
ἕως ἂν αὐτὸν ἐμβάλωμεν εἰς κακόν,
ὅπως ἂν εἰδῇ τοὺς θεοὺς δεδοικέναι.
Στ. ὤμοι, πονηρά γ', ὦ Νεφέλαι, δίκαια δέ.

St: I have suffered these things because of you,
Clouds, who have upended my life!
Ch: You yourself are to blame for these things,
since you turned to wickedness.
St: Why didn't you warn me of this then, but
urged on an old countryman?
Ch: We do this every time we recognize someone
as a lover of evil, until we pitch him into ruin
so that he learns to fear the gods.
St: Alas, Clouds, it is harsh, surely, but just.

Nub. 1452–1462

The restrained register, neutral idiom, and absence of discontinuity, obscenity and linguistic tagging in these lines imbue this exchange with an unusual sobriety. The chorus's focus on personal responsibility, deferred punishment and 'late learning' in their response is distinctly tragic. Silk argues that the 'tragic co-presence' here exudes tragic but also non-parodic colouring.[11] Revermann identifies Strepsiades' recognition and retribution as similar to the pattern of rationalization and punishment of human error in tragedy, which deepens that sense of a tragic co-presence. He argues that the sequence resembles a traditional theomachy pattern, with the qualification that the theomachic Strepsiades is first a target and then an instrument of divine justice.[12] The generic colouring of this exchange prefigures the climactic destruction of the *phrontistêrion* (1493–1511),[13] which may have been a unique addition to the revised, extant version of our text: ancient sources claim that the incineration of the *phrontistêrion* was added in response to the original *Clouds*'s notorious failure in competition.[14]

A possible objection to this serio-comic reading is that its proponents are trying to have it both ways; in other words, the simultaneous effects of comedy and tragedy together. Yet this criticism assumes that tragedy and comedy prompt mutually exclusive responses from audiences. Instead, the mode has an effect that differs from what we think of as typical of each genre, but is hardly incompatible with either. Revermann calls it *Schadenfreude*, but this unusual co-existence of violence and humour might be more neutrally described by its depiction of a form of folk justice: the violent razing of an offender's house for special crimes. The banishment of the Socratics, who are intruders, is a generic way of dealing with undesirables in comedy. The paratragic mode complements the final outcome of Strepsiades' turn to wickedness and later redemption by adding distinctive cultural depth. *Clouds*'s abrupt conclusion when it seems headed toward tragic carnage is calculated to prevent audiences from witnessing serious injury, death or excessive moral ambiguity that would affect the comedy of the mode.[15]

II. Cratinus's *Dionysalexandros*

Clouds's paratragic closure offers a useful model for understanding the modal evocations of genre in an earlier, fragmentary comedy, Cratinus's *Dionysalexandros* (429 BCE). Cratinus was active roughly from the second quarter of the fifth century to the late 420s and reached his peak probably in the 440s. About five hundred or so fragments survive of the twenty-nine productions attributed to him.[16] Much of what is known about the man is filtered through Aristophanes, who jeered Cratinus as an incontinent drunkard of diminishing powers in the parabasis of his *Knights* (424 BCE). Grenfell and Hunt's publication in 1904 of a partial hypothesis (*POxy*. 663) to Cratinus's *Dionysalexandros*,[17] the first substantial evidence for non-Aristophanic Old Comedy and contemporary mythological burlesque, seems to confirm tradition's assessment of him as the genre's most dominant and innovative poet before Aristophanes.[18]

].	ΔΙΟΝΥΣ[ΑΛΕΞΑΝΔΡΟΣ
. . . .] ζητ( )	Ḥ [
. . . .] παν	ΚΡΑΤ[ΕΙΝΟΥ
. . . .] αυτον μη	τὸν Ἀλέξαν[δ(ρον). τὴν μ(ὲν) οὖν Ἑλένη(ν)
5 . . . . . κ]ρίσιν ὁ Ἑρμ(ῆς)	30 εἰς τάλαρον ὡς τά[χιστα
ἀπέρχ]εται κ(αὶ) οὗτοι	κρύψας, ἑαυτὸν δ' εἰς κριὸ[ν
μ(ὲν) πρ(ὸς) τοὺς θεατάς	μ(ε)τ(α)σκευάσας ὑπομένει
τινα π(ερὶ) τῶν ποιη(τῶν)[19]	τὸ μέλλον. παραγενό-
διαλέγονται κ(αὶ)	μενος δ' Ἀλέξανδ(ρος) κ(αὶ) φωρά-
10 παραφανέντα τὸν	35 σας ἑκάτερο(ν) ἄγειν ἐπὶ τὰς
Διόνυσον ἐπισκώ(πτουσι) (καὶ)	ναῦς πρ(οσ)τάττει ὡς παραδώσων
χλευάζου(σιν)· ὁ δ(ὲ) πα-	τοῖς Ἀχαιοῖ(ς). ὀκνούσης δ(ὲ) τῆς
ραγενομένων ⟨	Ἑλένη(ς) ταύτην μ(ὲν) οἰκτείρας
⟩ αὐτῶι	ὡς γυναῖχ' ἕξων ἐπικατέχ(ει),
παρὰ μ(ὲν) Ἥρα[ς] τυραννίδο(ς)	40 τὸν δ(ὲ) Διόνυ(σον) ὡς παραδοθη-
15 ἀκινήτου, πα[ρ]ὰ δ' Ἀθηνᾶς	σόμενο(ν) ἀποστέλλει, συν-
εὐψυχί(ας) κ(α)τ(ὰ) πόλεμο(ν), τῆς	ακολουθ(οῦσι) δ' οἱ σάτυ(ροι) παρακαλοῦν-
δ' Ἀφροδί(της) κάλλιστό(ν) τε κ(αὶ)	τές τε κ(αὶ) οὐκ ἂν προδώσειν
ἐπέραστον αὐτὸν ὑπάρ-	αὐτὸν φάσκοντες. κωμωι-
χειν, κρίνει ταύτην νικᾶν.	45 δεῖται δ' ἐν τῶι δράματι Πε-
20 μ(ε)τ(ὰ) δ(ὲ) ταῦτα πλεύσας εἰς	ρικλῆς μάλα πιθανῶς δι'
Λακεδαίμο(να) (καὶ) τὴν Ἑλένην	ἐμφάσεως ὡς ἐπαγηοχὼς
ἐξαγαγὼν ἐπανέρχετ(αι)	τοῖς Ἀθηναίοις τὸν πόλεμον
εἰς τὴν Ἴδην. ἀκού(ει) δ(ὲ) με-	
τ' ὀλίγον τοὺς Ἀχαιοὺς πυρ-	
25 πολ]εῖν τὴν χώ(ραν) (καὶ) [ζητεῖν	

seek ... all ... (5) judgment, Hermes leaves, while they say some things to the spectators about the poets. (10) They jeer and make fun of Dionysus when he appears [...] from Hera unshaken monarchy (15), from Athena courage in war, and from Aphrodite that he be as beautiful and sexually attractive as possible, he judges her [Aphrodite] to be the winner. (20) After this he sails to Sparta, takes Helen away, and returns to Ida. But he hears a little while later that the Greeks are ravaging the countryside (25) <and looking for Alexander>. He hides Helen very quickly (30) in a basket and changing himself into a ram awaits what happens next. Alexander appears and (35) detects each of them, and orders them to be taken to the ships and given back to the Greeks. When Helen refuses, he takes pity on her and holds on to her, to keep her as his wife, (40) but Dionysus he sends off to be handed over. And the satyrs follow him, encouraging him and insisting that they will not betray him. (45) In the play Pericles is very persuasively made fun of through innuendo for bringing war on the Athenians.

POxy. 663=Cratin. Hyp. *Dionysalexandros*

Dionysalexandros burlesqued a popular and critical event of the Trojan saga, the judgment of the three goddesses by the Trojan prince, Alexandros.[20] For Alexandros, Cratinus substituted Dionysus as the inept buffoon, although the papyrus does not explain how this happened.[21] The beginning lines in the upper left-hand column refer to Hermes' departure, a 'judgment' and a reference to an unknown 'these' (οὗτοι), the chorus.[22] The following technical diction (9–13) reveals a parabasis followed by the entrance of Dionysus and the Judgment itself. Then some interesting departures from the traditional myth follow: Dionysus escorts Helen back to Ida (not Troy) and panics at the Greek invasion of the Troad in search of Alexandros (23–33); Alexandros himself appears and discovers the culprits; he pities Helen and takes her as his wife, surrendering Dionysus to the invaders (37–41). Lines 42–44, which mention satyrs (οἱ σάτυροι), describe an *exodos*.[23] The hypothesis intriguingly ends with the statement that Pericles was satirized 'by innuendo' (δι' ἐμφάσεως) 'for bringing war upon the Athenians'.

Since publication, *POxy.* 663's mention of οἱ σάτυ(ροι) (42) has unsurprisingly attracted serious interest from scholars, for satyrs physically appear nowhere in extant Old Comedy. The possibility that another poet experimented with a genre in which Aristophanes himself appeared to take little interest was an exciting prospect. Early publications concluded that the chorus of *Dionysalexandros* was, in fact, comprised of satyrs.[24] A second camp followed Schmid's suggestion that the satyrs were subsidiary to a main chorus of shepherds, Paris's comrades.[25] Bakola's convincing argument for a chorus of satyrs has all but settled the question of the chorus's identity.[26]

It is worth reflecting on the premise of *Dionysalexandros's* cross-generic experiment, the immediate collision of visual codes normally kept separate in drama: horse-human, ithyphallic satyrs and ugly, phallused and corpulent comic bodies. One can reasonably assume that the style of juxtaposition here was the 'strict' form like that portrayed on the Choregoi vase of Chapter 2,[27] where a tragic Aegisthus found himself in the company of generically ugly comic *choreutai*. Alternatively, Cratinus's satyrs could have been 'layered' with both signs of comic ugliness, corpulence, *phalloi* and so on, and the satyr costume, as on the so-called Cleveland Dionysus vase (Fig. 3.1). Emerging from the ground – perhaps in an epiphany? – is a giant head of Dionysus, beside which stands a Silenus with distinctively comic ugliness, fat-pads and dangling phallus, and

Fig. 3.1 A Silenus with comic phallus (right) holds a bell-krater before an appearing Dionysus (centre) as his slave stands by (left).

raising an enlarged bell-krater. Typical iconography of the satyrs in mythology displays Silenus and his sons with modest phalluses in art, by contrast. On the left, picking a clump of grapes from a flourishing vine behind the god's head, is a comic slave. Clearly some kind of fusion of genre, on both the body of Silenus and in the combination of characters present, is depicted. But the broader context of this fusion is unknown.

Whichever paratragic strategy was deployed in *Dionysalexandros*, the ease with which such generic collision in visual terms could be projected front-and-centre is reasonably clear. *Dionysalexandros*'s simple inclusion of satyrs for a comic chorus takes the basic premise of satyr play, the insertion of satyrs into a mythological context where they 'have no business', to undiscovered creative territory.[28] *Dionysalexandros* drops the satyrs into the world of an entirely different genre, recasting this formulaic displacement in generic rather than mythological terms. Cratinus's modified chorus presumably exhibited the traditional hyperactivity and unique perspective of the satyrs as omnipresent, internal audience. Yet the hypothesis may hint at places where Cratinus reshaped traditional conventions of satyr play.[29] The mythological narratives of discovery, invention, divine birth and famous labours into which the satyrs are dropped always play out as expected: the Sphinx is defeated; Perseus and Danae are rescued; Apollo recaptures his cattle stolen by Hermes; and so on.[30] Evidence for the genre indicates that the satyrs' highly mimetic and 'action-oriented' lyrics differ notably from the highly politicized persona and function of comic choruses.[31] Nevertheless, the hypothesis suggests moments where the chorus functioned as a conventional chorus of comedy, specifically their address to the spectators (6–9) in a parabasis and subsequent abuse and mockery of Dionysus.[32]

This is the sum total of what one can reasonably deduce about Cratinus's chorus from the hypothesis. However, the sustained presence of Dionysus may be more significant than scholarship has recognized.[33] Lämmle makes a good case for seeing an ever-present tension between Dionysus's presence and absence in the satyrs' adventures as a theme.[34] For example, Euripides' *Cyclops* and specific fragments from other plays acknowledge the absent Dionysus's numinous spiritual presence through sympotic elements.[35] One effect of such associations was the reinforcement of the god's physical absence. While this may not outright exclude Dionysus's physical presence as a character in a play, the evidence, on balance, points to his alternating presence and absence as a fundamental aspect of the satyrs' plight. In light of this, Dionysus's apparently consistent presence in *Dionysalexandros* may have been significant.

The hypothesis's description of Dionysus's comic adventures furnishes one additional level of potential significance, the adultery narrative. Although no complete contemporary version of the adulterer's seduction of a married woman survives, its distinctive elements are indirectly attested in fifth-century popular culture, as Trenkner amply documented. The extramarital liaison is found as early as Ares' seduction of Aphrodite in Homer (*Od.* 8.266–366) and the Aesopic corpus contains its own popular variations on similar episodes.[36] Old Comedy is no exception. Inlaw's defense of Euripides (466–519) in 411's *Thesmophoriazusae* (cf. Chapter 6) draws on such popular traditions, and Aristophanes' fragmentary contemporaries show some interest in such plots.[37] The speaker of Lysias's famous *On the Murder of Eratosthenes* (early fourth century BCE) models his account of his wife's seduction on the same tradition.[38] The alleged popularity of 'adultery songs' is mentioned in a fragment of Eupolis (fr. 148).[39] Although the tradition of the adultery narrative would achieve greatest prominence as mime performance in Augustan Rome,[40] the clever adulterer's seduction of a wife seems sufficiently well known to later fifth-century audiences that several contemporary genres could appropriate it.

The hypothesis hints at places where Cratinus might have exploited certain tropes of the adultery narrative. This has the potential to reveal interesting aspects of the comedy's hybrid experiment. An adultery plot could certainly create some exceptional comedy in an already interesting cross-generic undertaking if satyr play possessed the distinctly 'romantic' outlook that Griffith has identified in it. He has shown that the fragments possess elements that ancient literary criticism deemed characteristic of this style or subgenre, including love plots, gardens of the nymphs, marriage songs and the poetry of Sappho, among other things.[41]

The Judgment of Paris's notoriously erotic subject matter, preserved especially vividly in the iconography of sixth- and fifth-century black- and red-figure vase painting,[42] made it a natural, if ironic, context for satyr play's imagination. This event opened the *Cypria*, the cycle poem apparently organized around Aphrodite's erotic patronage of Alexandros, who played Odysseus to her Athena.[43] How Cratinus staged his version of the beauty contest of the three goddesses is not clear,[44] but certain points seem to have been adjusted for maximum comic effect. Hera's 'kingship over all' (βασιλεία πάντων), Athena's 'victory in war' (πολέμου νίκη) and Aphrodite's 'union with Helen' (γάμος Ἑλένης)[45] are changed to Hera's 'unshaken monarchy' (τυραννίδο(ς) ἀκινήτου, *POxy.* 663.14), Athena's 'courage in war' (εὐψυχία κατὰ πόλεμον, 16) and Aphrodite's 'to be the most beautiful and desired' (κάλλιστος τε καὶ ἐπέραστος, 17–18). Cratinus strips out the traditional didactic terms of Alexandros's ethical failure, i.e., his choice of Aphrodite over more heroic alternatives, to present a starker illustration of Dionysus's effeminate vanity.[46] Given the chance to become heroic, Dionysus opts to beautify himself as a stereotypical comic adulterer. This is a potential key to recognizing the possible generic hybridity hinted at in the hypothesis.

When the Achaeans come 'looking for Alexandros' (23–29) after Helen's abduction, Dionysus panics, hiding her in a basket and transforming himself (μετασκευάσας) into a ram 'to await what comes' (31–33).[47] Comic manipulations of dress and appearance, and their inevitable failure,[48] are typical of Dionysus's comic persona.[49] Just when the audience expects the Achaeans to appear, Dionysus's affair is suddenly interrupted, not by Helen's returning husband, Menelaus, but by a second unrelated man, Alexandros, i.e., *the real adulterer* of the mythological model. It is remarkable to consider how easily this scene's domestic setting could have accommodated the signature comic business of the adultery narrative of popular tradition: the intruder's concealment, the wife's distraction of her husband, and finally the discovery and escape, or arrest, of the seducer.[50] When Helen 'objects' (ὀκνούσης) to Alexandros's order to surrender the adulterous pair to the Greeks, he decides 'to keep her as his wife' (ὡς γυναῖχ᾽ ἕξων ἐπικατέχει).[51] Alexandros, Helen's Trojan husband in myth, thwarted Dionysus's affair ultimately in order to steal the woman *for himself.*

In other words, Dionysus's choice of erotic beauty may have driven the comic action in *Dionysalexandros* more than scholars have realized. An often-overlooked detail is Alexandros' successful surrender of Dionysus to the Greeks, though they came looking for Alexandros (τὸν Ἀλέξαν[δ(ρον), 25–29). This discrepancy between the two characters disappears if Aphrodite's gift to Dionysus, 'to be the most beautiful and desired' (κάλλιστος τε καὶ ἐπέραστος), was his transformation into Alexandros in physical features or dress. The title of the comedy is *Dionysalexandros* after all. This qualification of Aphrodite's bribe does not just account for Alexandros's surrender of Dionysus (minus Helen) to the Greeks: it can also illuminate some potential comic business of the face-to-face encounter of the real Alexandros and Dionysus on Mount Ida. Imagine the fabulous visual effect of a meeting of the real and fake Alexandroses, which could be compared to the analogous confrontation of Dionysus-as-Heracles and Heracles (Ar. *Ran.* 37–41) in the scene of *Frogs* that succeeded the moments that were illustrated on the Berlin Heracles.[52] A good parallel for the kind of sustained comic sequence I am suggesting is the confrontation of the real and fake Sosiases in Plautus's *Amphitryo*, which are easily distinguishable by the audience thanks to a slight costume modification (*Amph.* 142–147).

While the satyrs are eventually reunited with Dionysus in *Dionysalexandros*, they are not liberated from toil and/or captivity, as normally happens. Instead, they accompany their master to the Greek ships and into bondage. If the hypothesis is taken at face value, the surrender of Dionysalexandros may have averted the Trojan War in clever counterfactual fashion. The Greeks think they have Alexandros, but the real Alexandros keeps Helen.[53] Do they simply forget Helen and leave Troy? Who knows. But that kind of ending would certainly capture of the spirit of Aristotle's description (*Poet.* 1453a36–39) of endings discussed in the previous chapter, in which enemies become new friends and no one dies.

The irony of *Dionysalexandros*'s conclusion with a second adulterous liaison, which has attracted hardly any notice,[54] seems like a calculated subversion of satyr play's concluding γάμος, a familiar *topos*.[55] Idealized aristocratic unions between heroes and virginal maidens are critical to satyr play's perceived romance and its heroic ethics:[56] marriage and its attendant sexual pleasures reward the hero for his heroism; sexual frustration rewards the childish, hedonistic and unreliable satyrs.[57] *Dionysalexandros* seemingly concluded by affirming antiquity's most notorious and accursed union and quintessential 'beginning of evils' (ἀρχὴ κακῶν) in tragedy.[58] Given the limits of the hypothesis, my reading of *Dionysalexandros* through the adultery narrative obviously cannot be pressed very far. Nevertheless, the language's similarities to the stylized and illicit adventures of adulterers in contemporary literature deserve consideration. The plot reads like an adultery tale: the vain and sex-mad Dionysus pursues a married woman; in fear of the returning husband, he attempts to conceal himself and the woman; the exposed adulterer is delivered to the Greeks (and Helen's husband) for justice.[59]

The most controversial detail of the hypothesis is its statement that the figure of Dionysus satirized the Athenian statesman Pericles for his role in bringing about the war with Sparta (44–48).[60] While subordinate to my primary concern with intergeneric engagement, the question of satire in *Dionysalexandros* is relevant to this study's larger interest in the political and social subtexts of parody and appropriation. Lively debate about the nature and extent of this satire previously divided scholars into two predominant camps: those who subordinate political topicality to the travesty of myth;[61] those who see satire, to greater or lesser degree, throughout the burlesque.[62] A third, more nuanced view sees the political satire as just one of several active and important possible discourses of *Dionysalexandros* but ultimately unknowable in specifics and scope.[63]

Whatever position one chooses to identify with, it is important to bear in mind just how easily comic performance strategies could accommodate such an attack against a high-profile figure like Pericles. Comic poets easily made their political targets accessible to audiences through masks, costumes, gestures and even tone and pitch of voice. This would be especially true of a figure as popular and physically distinctive as Pericles, as Revermann has shown.[64] Moreover, Cratinus attacks him elsewhere in his comedy, as did his contemporaries.[65] Comedy made insinuations about Pericles' lifestyle and motivations, and cruelly and viciously mocked his misshapen head.[66] In *Acharnians*, Aristophanes lampooned his aloofness and arrogance, 'thundering' oratory and the Zeus-like sexual voracity that earned him the surname 'Olympian'.[67] It is even possible that *Dionysalexandros* was staged as a public trial, a 'comic Judgment of Pericles' that satirized his carefully crafted public persona as a man of self-control, discipline and selfless subordination to the greater good of the *dêmos*.[68] A fragment of Hermippus's *Fates*, possibly produced around the same time as *Dionysalexandros*, identifies Pericles and Dionysus precisely on the basis of such putative hypocrisy and cowardice:

βασιλεῦ Σατύρων, τί ποτ' οὐκ ἐθέλεις
δόρυ βαστάζειν, ἀλλὰ λόγους μὲν
περὶ τοῦ πολέμου δεινοὺς παρέχει,
ψυχὴ δὲ Τέλητος ὕπεστιν;
κἀγχειριδίου δ' ἀκόνῃ σκληρᾷ
παραθηγομένης βρύχεις κοπίδος,
δηχθεὶς αἴθωνι Κλέωνι.

King of the satyrs, why are you unwilling
to wield a spear, but rather offer fierce words
about the war, although Teles's spirit is in you?
When a dagger is sharpened on a hard whetstone
you gnash your teeth, upset by shining Cleon.

Herm. fr. 47

The phrase 'King of satyrs' derisively alludes to Pericles' defensive strategy for conducting the Peloponnesian War, which advised remaining behind Athens's walls to avoid direct engagements in the field and using the navy to raid enemy territory.[69] The satyrs' proverbial cowardice and incompetence furnishes the subtext necessary for understanding the insult.

Finally, satyr play's particular socio-psychological dynamic might have accommodated this kind of political subtext. Griffith has argued that satyr play induced a psychological split in its spectators, who (consciously or unconsciously) may have identified simultaneously with both the constantly aroused, irresponsible, carefree satyrs and the resolute, competent, civically virtuous heroic characters who repeatedly saved them. By counterbalancing the implied social identities of these two groups, the genre was able to appeal to a conflicted Athenian subconscious. On the one hand, as guardians of Greece (and their empire) and responsible citizens, Athenians lived under the expectation that they would display the kind of confidence, assertion and ability of satyr play's mythological heroes. The stress of such obligations, on the other hand, made the life of the carefree and indulgent satyrs, who are immune from all obligation and consequences, intuitively attractive. Griffith's model is especially useful for its identification of the satyrs as nominal representatives of the *dêmos*, i.e., as a similarly dependent community looking for guidance from its own class of assertive and resourceful elites.[70] Audiences may have found it easy to identify, at least in this qualified sense, with the privileged, numinous satyrs who were licensed to enjoy a perpetual state of drunkenness and arousal at no disadvantage to themselves. The opposition and reconciliation of Dionysus-Pericles and his satyr entourage, the latter first deriding (11–12) and then pledging their loyalty (41–44), could easily refer to Pericles' rocky relationship with the *dêmos*: after the first Spartan incursion into Attica, the *dêmos* denounced Pericles but nevertheless re-elected him as *stratêgos* in 429 after stripping him of command in 430. Dionysus's (and Alexandros's) selfish lust brought the war upon Ilium just as, according to both Cratinean and Aristophanic comedy (*Ach.* 526–534), Pericles' appeasement of Aspasia initiated the hostilities of the Peloponnesian War.

Whether Cratinus applied satyr play to a political satire of Pericles will probably never be known with confidence. Nonetheless, my suggestions, if tentative, demonstrate the highly idiosyncratic yet conservative generic horizons within which Cratinus experimented. If the modal paratragedy of *Clouds* is of any value for understanding *Dionysalexandros*, we might imagine that Cratinus made his model genre's playful humour abusive, its heroism less than ideal and its marriages less than respectable. The satyrs' mythological, atopical and highly aetiological world provided Cratinus a prism through which he could refract his topical and satirical content, a frame for ironically enshrining Pericles' responsibility for the Peloponnesian War as a myth of causality to be set alongside other satyric myths such as the invention of the lyre, the discovery of fire and the rescue of Danae and Perseus from the chest. The next section, in fact, explores the deployment of this same aetiological frame in a play that fortunately survives, Aristophanes' *Peace*.

III. Aristophanes' *Peace*

The most extensive sequence of parasatyrism in extant comedy is by no means universally recognized, although a firm majority of scholars acknowledge its traces. In the so-called hauling-scene of Aristophanes' *Peace* (421 BCE), a panhellenic chorus successfully liberates the goddess 'Peace' and her two mute attendants, 'Festival' (*Theôria*) and 'Harvest' (*Opôra*). Aristophanes dramatized the return of Peace just days before the approval of the impending Peace of Nicias, the first significant pause in hostilities since the Peloponnesian War's outbreak in 431.[71] In comedy, this treaty was accomplished not by diplomatic efforts, but by a 'satyrized' comic chorus under the direction of the Athenian vine farmer, Trygaeus ('Man of τρυγῳδία'?).[72] Although not actually satyrs, this chorus was indirectly assimilated to satyrs in speech and action to raise audience expectations of the ineffectual, disorganized and feckless slaves of Dionysus. The parasatyrism of the hauling-scene, I argue, allegorizes several years of failed peace initiatives during the Archidamian War. The eventual success of the chorus's second effort to rescue the goddess overturns and disappoints the audience's theatrically conditioned expectations of the satyrs' failure in order to emphasize *Peace*'s overarching message, that panhellenic solidarity was necessary to a lasting peace.

The satyric tone of the climactic rescue of Peace was first noted in the early twentieth century. The full extent of this generic engagement and its contribution to *Peace*'s aetiology has been, however, neither fully identified nor understood.[73] The entire scene beginning with Trygaeus's arrival in Olympus reveals an extensive engagement with satyr play beyond what scholars usually confine it to: the hero's call for aid, the chorus's compulsive dancing and the choral participation of the hauling. But Aristophanes shapes the hybrid quality of *Peace*'s rescue well in advance of the actual hauling, and moreover evokes the satyr's parallel world as both a foil for the comic chorus's success and an expression of the mythologized bliss of peaceful post-war Greece. Robert originally drew attention to the hauling as a variation on the ἄνοδος ('passage up') of Mediterranean and Near Eastern myth, in which a fertility goddess returns from a deathlike place to the world above.[74] *Anodoi* are found especially in mid-fifth-century vase paintings of satyrs welcoming emerging fertility goddesses and they even structure epic (e.g., *h.Dem.*) and some late Euripidean tragedy.[75] But the miraculous revelations critical to the *anodoi* and their aetiological emphases are especially at home in satyr play's repertoire, in which satyrs stumble upon, unearth, steal or otherwise discover objects and individuals of significant cultural value.

Informed of Peace's imprisonment, Trygaeus calls for a collaborative effort to
free her. The βοή, the 'call for aid', is generally regarded as the starting point of
this cross-generic sequence:[76]

ἀλλ᾽, ὦ γεωργοὶ κἄμποροι καὶ τέκτονες
καὶ δημιουργοὶ καὶ μέτοικοι καὶ ξένοι
καὶ νησιῶται, δεῦρ᾽ ἴτ᾽, ὦ πάντες λεῴ,
ὡς τάχιστ᾽ ἅμας λαβόντες καὶ μοχλοὺς καὶ σχοινία.

You farmers and merchants and carpenters
and craftsmen and immigrants and foreigners
and islanders, come here, all you people,
as quick as you can, bringing shovels and crowbars and ropes.

Pax 296–299

A striking parallel to this call for aid is found in a fragment of Aeschylus's satyr
play, *Diktyoulkoi* (*c.* 460 BCE), about some Seriphian fishermen's rescue of
Perseus and Danae from the chest that had been set adrift in the sea by her
father, the tyrannical Acrisius. As soon as the fisherman Dictys spots the chest in
that play (fr. 46a.1–16), he likewise summons help:[77]

]πάντες γεωργοὶ δεῦτε κἀμπελοσκάφοι
    ]ε ποιμήν τ᾽ εἴ τίς ἐστ᾽ [ἐ]γχώριος
]οι τε καὶ μα[ριλ]ευτῶν ἔθνος

[come] here, all you farmers and vine-diggers, [and]
any [goatherd or oxherd] or shepherd there is in these parts,
] and you tribe of charcoal-burners

fr 46a.18–20 Radt

As in *Diktyoulkoi*, Trygaeus's call is immediately answered by a disordered
panhellenic chorus (301–308), whose entrance seemingly displayed a kind of
controlled chaos meant to evoke a chorus of satyrs:[78] distracted, scattered,
contorted, the *choreutai* run in every direction, gesture madly and collide
like 'Keystone Kops'. An approximate visual representation of this kind of
generic choreographed chaos in performance is perhaps illustrated on a krater
featuring satyrs dancing and prancing around a female divinity emerging from
below.[79] In any case, the entrance of *Peace*'s chorus may not have taken
Aristophanes' audience by surprise given the previous scene's introduction of
the personified 'Polemos' ('War'), the kind of token ogre-like villain prominent
in satyr play.[80]

From this point, satyr motifs accumulate rapidly. To avoid alerting the recently departed War to their presence, Trygaeus pleads with the excitable chorus to calm itself (309–310). The chorus's noise (voice, 318; feet, 319), absence of self-control (320–321) and compulsive dancing (324–326) – 'auto-orchestrism'[81] – are distinctively satyresque. Such displays of uncontrolled speech, gesture and movement, particularly in the face of repeated entreaties, are rare in comedy and tragedy but common in satyr play.[82] Moreover, the chorus's description of its dancing (τὸ σκέλος ῥίψαντες ἤδη λήγομεν τὸ δεξιόν, 302) is echoed in Athenaeus's later account (14.617–618) of the generic *skelos riptein*, called the 'high kick'.[83] This movement involved bringing one leg upward sharply to the side, bending the knee and then pointing the foot downward before repeating with the other leg.[84] This is the very movement practised by the single satyr in full character named 'Nikoleos' standing behind Pronomos on the famous vase bearing his name.[85]

Aristophanes' panhellenes also recall the nostalgia commonly expressed by satyrs when contrasting their present labour and enslavement to some ogre with the idealized life they previously enjoyed with Dionysus.[86] An analogous dissatisfaction characterizes the attitude of *Peace's* panhellenes, who repeatedly express their longing to escape the current hardships of war and return to the optimal conditions of peacetime life described by Trygaeus himself (337–345). Aristophanes creatively reconceives this motif of 'estrangement' from Dionysus in distinctly political terms, specifically in the chorus's expression of joy at Peace's return and her various pleasures after ten years of detestable public service as soldiers and jurymen (312, 336, 346–356) in the era of Polemos. The comic chorus thus echoes the satyrs' characteristic longing for their pleasurable past service to Dionysus.[87]

These various forms of satyric behaviour set the mode in full swing by the arrival of its focal point, namely the lyric expression of the chorus's physical exertion when hauling Peace. The hauling is highly mimetic, much like satyr play's own style of lyric: satyrs haul fishing nets, track cattle like bloodhounds, celebrate and distribute fire, etc.[88] With Hermes as foreman (429), the chorus grabs the ropes (458) that were likely attached to the front of the *ekkuklēma* (cf. 426–427), upon which sat the statue of Peace, hidden in the *skēnē*.[89] The distinctive collaboration under a character's leadership (πρὸς τάδ' ἡμῖν, εἴ τι χρὴ δρᾶν, φράζε κἀρχιτεκτόνει, 305) – a prerequisite of collective satyr action – evokes the satyrs' puerility and dependence on others in all serious endeavours. Primed by its experience of the satyrs' entrance and reaction to onstage events,[90] the comic audience was prepared to expect an analogous display of incompetence and failure.[91] Instead they eventually see – contrary to their expectations – the comic chorus overcome its dysfunction and succeed.

Though there have been various attempts to identify the specific arrangement of *choreutai*,[92] for my purposes it matters only that the chorus pulled outwards with its back to the audience, which is the accepted view.[93] The cadence of the unsuccessful hauling is distributed over two parallel segments of text (458–483, 484–507) in brief, metrically irregular exchanges (e.g., εἶα μάλα. . .ὦ, εἶα) at the beginning and midpoint of responding strophic stanzas (459–472, 486–499). The heavily spondaic anapaests underscore the chorus's physical exertion, and the pairing of physical activity and short metrically simple lyrics perhaps reflects the low-class refrains of contemporary rustic and urban work songs that may inspire satyr lyrics.[94] The ineptness of this initial effort channels the antics of the childish and incompetent satyrs.

The satyresque mode brings the topical background of *Peace* suddenly into the foreground as Trygaeus and Hermes begin singling out *choreutai* as specific cities for their obstruction of earlier peace initiatives. This struggle in the first hauling allegorizes the diplomatic efforts of the peace process since the war's outbreak and lays their failure squarely at the feet of the major city-states. It begins with the Boeotians who refused to agree to a sustainable peace:

> ἀλλ' οὐχ ἕλκουσ' ἄνδρες ὁμοίως.
> οὐ ξυλλήψεσθ'; οἶ' ὀγκύλλεσθ'·
> οἰμώξεσθ', οἱ Βοιωτοί.

> Men, won't you take hold and
> pull together?! You are too puffed up!
> You'll pay for this, Boeotians!

Pax 464–466

The Argives (475–477), Megarians (481–482, 500–502) and later the Athenians (503–505) are each singled out for the unique way they torpedoed peace:[95] the Boeotians were reluctant to cease hostilities given their territorial gains; the neutral Argives declined to get involved and remained on the side-lines to watch the spectacle; the Megarians ultimately rejected the Peace of Nicias; the Athenians were (as always) distracted by obsessive litigation. This first effort to raise Peace allegorizes the Greeks' political dysfunction by exploiting the spectators' shared familiarity with satyr play and its conventions. Like satyrs fixated upon marvels, food, wine, sex and other sybaritic pursuits of their childlike existence,[96] the

Greeks' frivolous and self-serving aims and childish animosities fritter away their opportunities to end the war as the Greek world descends deeper into violence.

Although acceptable for satyrs – protected as they are by Dionysus – such incompetence and frivolity have serious consequences for Greeks during wartime. That the audience's impressions of the panhellenes in the hauling scene would have formed along such generic lines seems especially likely given Griffith's convincing description of the perpetual adolescence of satyr life as:

> an uninterrupted continuation of infantile, pre-Oedipal desires, emblematized by the small but erect phalloi of the satyrs and their restless physical movements, and confirmed by their inability ever to grow up, learn anything useful, take care of themselves, or even fully master normal (adult) patterns of speech.
>
> Griffith 2005: 174–175

The hauling-scene transfers this perpetual irresponsibility to the Greek states and, by extension, the audience as well.[97] Unlike their mythological counterparts, the Greeks do not have the luxury of limitless self-indulgence and freedom from responsibility afforded to the satyrs because of their divine status. No heroic saviour can rescue Greece from its self-destructive political dysfunction, at least not without the Greeks' own co-operation. Satirically inept, self-serving and divided, the Greeks can only emerge from this grave situation safely with true panhellenic co-operation.

The visual immediacy of the chorus's initial failure provides a foil for the second attempt to free the goddess. The various elements of the parasatyric mode coalesce right before Peace's liberation with Trygaeus's final exhortation, this time to the farmers who have lost their very way of life (508, 512–519). A rhythmic shift from anapests to nearly pure iambic tetrameter catalectics audibly distinguishes this second, more auspicious effort.[98] Bound by a shared way of life, the farmers transcend national boundaries and petty grievances in a collaborative display of panhellenic spirit. The poetically conditioned expectations of failure that have accumulated since the appearance of Polemos are overturned in the successful rescue of Peace and her two attendants, Harvest and Festival.

> ὦ πότνια βοτρυόδωρε, τί προσείπω σ᾽ ἔπος;
> πόθεν ἂν λάβοιμι ῥῆμα μυριάμφορον
> ὅτῳ προσείπω σ᾽; οὐ γὰρ εἶχον οἴκοθεν.

> Mistress, Giver of Grapes, how should I greet you?
> Where can I find a ten-thousand-measure phrase to
> greet you with? I don't have anything that big at home.
>
> *Pax* 520–522

Trygaeus's subsequent foundation of Peace's cult in Athens enacts the permanence of the goddess's return to the world above and presents this new perpetual era of peace as a parasatyric aetiology. Although the divine Peace is very different from the fire, sport, wine or other kinds of things normally discovered by satyrs, the political stability she embodies is a prerequisite for the uninterrupted enjoyment of Dionysian pleasures defining the satyrs' existence. Just as satyrs return to their beloved former pursuits under Dionysus, so do the panhellene *choreutai* look forward to the numerous benefits of Peace – harvest, entertainment, pipes, the Dionysia, tragedies, songs of Sophocles, thrushes, Euripidean poetry (530–532) – and idealized institutions of Greek life such as farming, sacrifice and marriage.

Would the spectators have identified with *Peace*'s satirized chorus? The Athenian audience's capacity to identify with choruses in tragedy and satyr play is absolutely relevant to the present case. Griffith has made a strong case for spectators' identification with the satyrs, at least in a qualified sense, by applying Mastronarde's criteria for determining choral authority and facilitating an audience's capacity for identification.[99] Griffith argues that the satyrs' engagement with the sympathies and fantasies of the male citizen audience, who felt a combination of affection and disgust, 'fellow-feeling' and disassociation, made 'a peculiarly strong conscious or unconscious claim on the male Athenian imagination'.[100] While satyrs certainly embodied many things antithetical to Athenian ethical and civic norms, their constantly aroused, drunken and carefree existence – their lives, in essence, a perpetual *kômos* – must have seemed enviable to Athenian males living under the pressure of civic life and maintaining the empire.

Aristophanes' assimilation of his panhellenic chorus to satyrs through the latter's stylized behaviour defamiliarized that chorus in order to condition the audience's reception of the hauling-scene's success: after initially aligning the chorus's behaviour and agency with satyrs, Aristophanes overturns these pre-judgments to emphasize the success, not the failure, of choral collaboration. The parasatyric modality emphasizes the recklessness and insanity of the Greek states' frivolous behaviour just as War is preparing to grind them in a pestle. Unlike satyrs saved by Dionysus, Greece will not be saved by intervening gods for the next adventure. The effect of this modality is not unlike Strepsiades' inspired vengeance against the Socratics in *Clouds*, as a recognizable trope of comedy – choral resistance to the hero's plan – is creatively elaborated using the mood of an alien genre. Chapter 4 will show that the generic subtext of the hauling unifies the apparent randomness of cultural and political renewal in *Peace*'s second half. By assimilating a chorus drawn from various Greek states to one of satyrs in speech, gesture and thought, *Peace* visually enacts the frustrations of fifth-century diplomacy and international relations in the Archidamian War.

IV. Acting the satyr

The hauling-scene is an extended example of how satyrs could inform the ethics of a comedy by defamiliarizing cultural and political content. But what of satyric influence on comic heroes themselves, the focus of the plays? Do comic characters play the satyr and in what sense? In the very same article earlier referenced in the introduction to this chapter, Lissarrague showed how satyrs in drama and mythological vase painting were 'good to think with' as antitypes of the Athenian citizenry and thereby an excellent means of exploring human culture.[101] Hermippus's unfavourable allusion to Pericles' alleged cowardice and incompetence by referring to him as 'king of the satyrs' is predicated on the audience's ability to understand such attributes as uniquely satyresque.[102] Both Aristophanes' *Birds* and *Thesmophoriazusae* feature suggestive comparisons of comic heroes and satyrs of a similar scale to Hermippus's fragment, but in the very different terms of aggressive, sexual violence. Given Aristophanes' careful integration of threatened violence – as insulting and hubristic behaviour – into the formal and conceptual world of his comedy, his relatively brief allusions to satyrs at these moments should not be overlooked, especially because of their extreme nature.[103] Although it lacks the function of a plot point as in New Comedy, rape in Old Comedy has distinctive associations with aggressive assertions of superiority and expressions of youthful vigour by ageing but rejuvenated heroes.[104] In articulating critical information about the status and agency of their subjects, the threats of rape I will analyse are different from other examples found in Old Comedy. For one, their victims are higher status than the average target of sexual violence, who is typically a slave or, at most, a spouse. The purpose of these threats of rape is not simply the expression of superiority or rejuvenation through the experience of comic success. I see their value as establishing a clear point of reference for judging the trajectory of a hero's agency over the course of a plot. In this sense, the display of satyric sexual aggression functions not unlike the comic chorus's incompetence and obstructionism in *Peace*, which raised the expectation of a particular result, failure, for the purpose of disappointing it later.

These threats of sexual assault prompt audiences to recognize that it is mortal comic heroes claiming the licensed hubris of satyrs – more specifically, to recognize mortals displaying the kind of hubris that the satyr alone can exhibit with impunity thanks to his divine privilege. Earlier in this chapter I discussed the notorious lechery, coercion and even violence to which satyrs instinctively resort when seeking 'marriage' to the vulnerable heroines of myth. These real or imagined encounters inevitably focus on the anguish and vulnerability of helpless maidens in the face of aggression by the chorus and their sleazy father, Silenus. The suspense aroused by these conventional meetings between satyrs and a vulnerable woman is pleasurably diminished with the timely arrival of a god, hero or mortal who will rescue the maiden and claim her for a dynastic marriage of some kind. The pattern is found in the fragments of all three canonical tragedians.[105] In Aeschylus's *Netfishers*, the Argive princess Danae laments the fate of herself and her baby Perseus at the hands of the satyrs (fr. 47a.9–21 Radt);[106] a fragment (fr. 1130 Radt=*POxy.* 1083, fr. 1) from Sophocles' *Oeneus* presents the satyrs as bridegrooms making a claim to the hand of a maiden.[107] The chorus of Euripides' *Cyclops* savour their sexual prospects with Helen (175–187), imagining the gang rape of a woman they believe to be fond of being 'married to many men' (πολλοῖς ἥδεται γαμουμένη, 181).

Though perpetually unsuccessful, the satyr's routine expression of sexual desire in coercive and violent terms doubtless shaped the expectations brought by audiences not only to satyr play but also to other genres of the festivals of Dionysus. The idiosyncrasies of the satyrs' behaviour are so distinctive as to be especially recognizable when transplanted into different ethical and generic contexts, as the chorus of *Peace* illustrated. But the hauling-scene demonstrated that mortals enjoy no such immunity from the consequences of the antisocial and criminal behaviour in which it is typical for satyrs to engage. Witnessing this incompatibility of the satyr's behaviour and comedy's putatively 'real' world is the point. Much like Lissarrague's aforementioned definition of satyr play – 'Take one myth, add satyrs, observe the result' – Aristophanes adds the satyr's ethos to comic characters in the comic world for his audience to observe the result.

The first such allusion in comedy is found in Aristophanes' *Birds* (414 BCE), which follows the rapid evolution of the imperial Cloudcuckooland into an empire under the leadership of the charismatic man-bird and Athenian exile, Peisetaerus ('He who persuades his companions'). The latter mobilizes the avian tribe to colonize the sky and control all airborne traffic by spinning a yarn about the gods' theft of their primordial cosmic rule (465–635), including the sacrificial smoke that nourishes the Olympians. By starving out the Olympians with a blockade, the birds attract the attention of Zeus, who sends his messenger, Iris, with the order to desist or face destruction. In response to Peisetaerus's insolent claim that the birds, not the Olympians, are now gods, Iris threatens Zeus's thunderbolt. Peisetaerus responds with threats of gigantomachic retaliation and sexual violence against Iris herself:

ἆρ᾽ οἶσθ᾽ ὅτι Ζεὺς εἴ με λυπήσει πέρα,
μέλαθρα μὲν αὐτοῦ καὶ δόμους Ἀμφίονος
καταιθαλώσω πυρφόροισιν αἰετοῖς,
πέμψω δὲ πορφυρίωνας εἰς τὸν οὐρανὸν
ὄρνις ἐπ᾽ αὐτόν, παρδαλᾶς ἐνημμένους
πλεῖν ἑξακοσίους τὸν ἀριθμόν; καὶ δή ποτε
εἷς Πορφυρίων αὐτῷ παρέσχε πράγματα.
σὺ δ᾽ εἴ με λυπήσεις τι, τῆς διακόνου
πρώτης ἀνατείνας τὼ σκέλει διαμηριῶ
τὴν Ἶριν αὐτήν, ὥστε θαυμάζειν ὅπως
οὕτω γέρων ὢν στύομαι τριέμβολον.

Do you realize that if Zeus bothers me further,
I'll light up his palace and the halls of Amphion
with flame-throwing eagles, and I'll send against
him over six hundred *Porphyrian* birds clad in leopard
skins? I remember that he once had a hard time with
just one Porphyrion! And if you cause me any
problem, I'll bend the legs of the royal slave girl
back and plough little Iris herself, so that she'll be
amazed this old boy can give the triple ram!

Av. 1246–1256

The threat to incinerate Olympus alludes to the myth of Porphyrion, an earth-born giant who attempted to rape Hera but ultimately perished on the Phlegraean plain in the Gigantomachy. While imagined sexual violence is not unusual in Old Comedy – think of Dicaeopolis's 'Hymn to Phales' (*Ach.* 263–269) – a mortal's threat to rape a goddess is unparalleled, even though it is never carried out.[108]

Sommerstein has rightly described Peisetaerus's threat as an assertion of superiority and even an assertion of youthful vigour typical of such violence in Old Comedy.[109] In its effect, however, Peisetaerus's threat is still unlike the other examples Sommerstein collects. Most other threats of a sexual nature are made or imagined only after the hero's radically improved world and his enhanced status come into being. Although he is in the process of supplanting the Olympians, Peisetaerus has still not achieved this. Iris's task, in fact, is to inform Cloudcuckooland that the blockade is annoying the gods, who still hold power despite their vulnerability. Peisetaerus's later acquisition of Zeus's sceptre and the divine *Basileia* changes this, of course. The hero's threat against Iris is interesting precisely because he has not yet acquired cosmic power. The scene invites the spectator to consider two possibilities: either Zeus will blast Peisetaerus as a hubristic *theomachos* or the latter will avoid punishment by eclipsing the power of the Olympians. The threat, in other words, communicates or gauges the hero's *transformation* from bird-man to higher-status being by channelling the uncivilized character of the hybrid satyr.

Scharffenberger first recognized this threat of rape as an allusion to a specific mythological episode, the satyrs' attempted rape of the same Iris when she sought to disrupt the worship of their patron, Dionysus.[110] About fifteen fifth-century black- and red-figure vase paintings depict ithyphallic satyrs either menacingly advancing against Iris or taking hold of her as she attempts to interfere with a sacrifice, probably at the behest of Hera.[111] Whether or not Aristophanes drew on this specific episode in *Birds*, Scharffenberger's subtle analysis of the comic exchange persuasively demonstrates that Aristophanes uses the sexual aggression of the satyr as a point of reference.[112] The hero's satyrism reflects his new hybrid status as an 'amalgamated man-bird creature'. It is notable that the sexual terms of the hero's growing power are consistent with his original aim to re-establish the birds' right to females of other spheres. When first pitching his plan to overthrow the Olympians, the hero persuades the birds to regulate divine passages between heaven and earth in order to prevent the gods from descending to 'marry' (i.e., rape) mortal women (558–559). The hero's later marriage and sexual conquest of the divine *Basileia* brings this plan to completion.

Much like the hauling-scene, in which a satyresque chorus overcame its childish incompetence, the paradox of a hero characterized as both satyresque and successful – successful in his project, but also romantically successful – is only apparent. In evoking the satyr's libido, Peisetaerus's aggression raises the conventional failure in both practical and sexual terms that was so characteristic of the satyr's existence. Peisetaerus's ascension to the top of the cosmic hierarchy expresses, quite literally, Old Comedy's representation of sexual power as a proxy for political power.[113] This expectation is raised in order to emphasize more forcefully the cosmic and even absolute terms of Peisetaerus's later success. Far from suffering any consequences for his hubris, the hero reaches something close to invincibility upon succeeding the Olympians. He enjoys an almost satyresque immunity from consequences but with the romantic privileges always denied the satyrs. As in the earlier play, Aristophanes' comic agent is a blend of genres, satyric in ethics and even status but distinctly comic in practice and success. But where *Peace* represents satyric conduct as dysfunctional, *Birds* presents it as an ethical bar or standard for gauging the hero's rise to power.

The successful outcome of the hybrid Peisetaerus's aggressive hubris could not be more different from the fate of a similarly hubristic sexual aggressor, the Inlaw of Aristophanes' *Thesmophoriazusae* (411 BCE). Where Peisetaerus's satyrism underscores a superhuman agency that places him beyond consequences, Inlaw is an instructive example of the consequences a mortal could expect to suffer for behaving like a satyr in the ostensibly civilized society of the comic world. Inlaw's fate in *Thesmophoriazusae* actually plays out a comic variation of Lissarrague's dictum about satyr play: Aristophanes has placed a very satyresque man somewhere he is not meant to be (i.e., the Thesmophoria) and we observe the result.[114] The passivity, humiliation and suffering of Inlaw *following* his threat of rape against another character offers some measure of the difference between this character's pretence to power and his actual status. The physical abuse and humiliation of Inlaw in *Thesmophoriazusae*, which is exceptional even by the standards of Old Comedy, illustrates the spectrum of possibilities that Old Comedy could present using the expectations of other, appropriated genres.

At their annual three-day celebration of the Thesmophoria festival in honour of Demeter and Persephone, the women of Athens plot to kill the tragedian Euripides for his negative portrayals of mythological women, specifically his Phaedras and Sthenoboeas. To avert their plot, Euripides seeks one of Athens's most fashionable current tragedians, the pretentious and effeminate Agathon, who (it is hoped) can lend his expertise in the mysteries of sexuality and gender to infiltrate the festival and apply his sophistic eloquence to persuade the women to abandon their plans. Accompanied by the crass and hyper-masculine Inlaw, Euripides arrives at Agathon's house just in time to witness the poet's impromptu performance of choral lyric.[115] Agathon, probably in his thirties at the time, had a few years earlier claimed his first competitive victory in the Lenaea (416 BCE) and established himself as a leading light of tragedy.[116] The one reasonably detailed portrait of the poet to survive comes courtesy of Plato's *Symposium*, which corroborates a few well-known facts of the biographical tradition of Agathon, namely that he was youthful, attractive, effeminate[117] and had a taste for sophistic rhetoric. He probably died sometime before 399 BCE.[118]

Agathon's androgynous performance of a hymn to Apollo (101–129) as an amoebaean exchange between an *exarchos* and a maiden chorus sexually arouses the boorish Inlaw, who mockingly describes his feelings with a series of demeaning comparisons of the poet's song to the Genetyllides, women and French kisses (130–133).[119] The audience was perhaps prepared for this derisive reaction by earlier descriptions of Agathon's sexual proclivities (31–33), the Ionic rhythms of the song and his effeminate and voluptuous attire (142, 159–160, 191–192).[120] But when Agathon replies that his outward expression of gender conforms to whatever (gendered) style of poetry he is writing, Inlaw reduces this principle to its lowest sexual denominator:

Κη. οὐκοῦν κελητίζεις, ὅταν Φαίδραν ποιῇς;
Αγ. ἀνδρεῖα δ᾽ ἢν ποιῇ τις, ἐν τῷ σώματι
ἔνεσθ᾽ ὑπάρχον τοῦθ᾽. ἃ δ᾽ οὐ κεκτήμεθα,
μίμησις ἤδη ταῦτα συνθηρεύεται.
Κη. ὅταν σατύρους τοίνυν ποιῇς, καλεῖν ἐμέ,
ἵνα συμποιῶ σοὔπισθεν ἐστυκὼς ἐγώ.

Inl: So do you ride up top, when you make a *Phaedra*?
Ag: If one makes masculine drama, this feature is
in his body. But for those things we don't possess,
imitation helps to hunt them down.
Inl: So when you compose a satyr play, call me,
so that I can collaborate with you from the rear!

Thesm. 153–158

As was Peisetaerus's threat against Iris, Inlaw's threat to rape the effeminate but free citizen Agathon is somewhat abnormal for threats in comedy. I will not add here to the many attempts to explain Agathon's gender-based mimetic approach to poetry except to say that Inlaw's derisive suggestion that he 'collaborate' (συμποιῶ) with Agathon in a production of satyr play appears to compensate for what Agathon evidently lacks, a phallus. Treatments of the scene have tried to explain this reference to satyr play in various ways: it conveys Inlaw's anxieties about the poet's transvestism; it represents the style of masculinity that best appeals to his 'self-image'; Inlaw views Agathon as 'sexually insatiable, essentially lewd' and therefore naturally suited to satyr play's sexual directness.[121] Each explanation, I believe, is correct in some sense but does not sufficiently consider the genre in question. Inlaw assumes the role of the ithyphallic satyr so as to complement Agathon's own feminine disposition most generically, I believe; the poet is implicitly identified with the helpless mythical maiden typically targeted by the satyrs' sexual advances.[122] The comment does not simply depict Inlaw as a man with a deep connection to the boorish, savage and sexually entitled satyr,[123] it also prompts the audience to understand his subsequent experiences in the play within this ethical paradigm.

As was noted in the previous discussion of *Birds*, insults in Old Comedy occur at critical moments, especially in meetings between characters. Apart from Inlaw's direct threat against Agathon, his derisive quotation of one of tragedy's great *theomachoi*, Aeschylus's Lycurgus,[124] hints that the hubris he displays in his encounter with the poet will somehow redound upon his head.[125] Asking 'à la Aeschylus's *Lycurgeia*', he asks Agathon what kind of 'girly man' (ποδαπὸς ὁ γύννις, 136) he is, where his 'dick' (καὶ ποῦ πέος; 142) is, if he's a man and where, if he's a woman, his tits are (εἶτα ποῦ τὰ τιτθία; 143), among other insulting questions. While Agathon is definitely mortal and not divine, Aristophanes seems to be setting up Inlaw as a hubristic *theomachos* unaware of his imminent punishment, just like Lycurgus or Euripides' Pentheus (*Bacch.* 453–459). With a combination of naïveté and arrogance, Inlaw agrees to infiltrate the sacred Thesmophoria, from which men were strictly forbidden under penalty of death. Though humorous to Athenian audiences, Inlaw's abusive conduct in the prologue of *Thesmophoriazusae* ironically suggests his approaching humiliation with a certain quasi-tragic inevitability.

Those expectations are not disappointed. Inlaw's humiliation extends from the prologue, when he is effeminized as a female worshipper, to his arrest and torture in the second half of the play. Stripped (214), shaved (226–233), singed (236–244), dressed as a woman (253–263), strapped to 'the plank' and tortured (1001–1006), Inlaw's degradation appeals to the superiority theory of comedy, whereby the humiliation and marginalization of the target fosters feelings of solidarity and superiority in the spectating in-group.[126] The satyric conduct evoked in the prologue provides a key point of reference for understanding these tribulations. Like a satyr, Inlaw is dropped into a world where he does not belong, except that he, a standard comic *bômolochos*, lacks the satyr's immunity from consequences. The numinous satyr can act outrageously and recklessly with impunity thanks to the protection of Dionysus. The despotic Peisetaerus enjoys a similar privilege because he supplants the gods. Torture and humiliation prove that Inlaw's particular agency is inferior to both and demonstrates the real-life consequences of behaving as a satyr.

Though smaller in scale, these allusions to satyr play in *Birds* and *Thesmophoriazusae* nonetheless evoke a specific attribute of the satyr, his aggressive ithyphallicism, to measure the changing agency of mortal heroes in the comic plot. Where the parasatyrism of *Peace* compared Greeks to satyrs in numerous senses, the rape threat's momentary but highly accessible index of genre contextualizes the comic hero's assertiveness for the purpose of shaping our response to his comic trajectory.

Conclusion

The examples of parasatyrism in this chapter sufficiently demonstrate that no 'firewall' existed between comedy and satyr play, as Dobrov once argued.[127] His recognition of the city as the fundamental boundary separating Old Comedy and apolitical, ahistorical satyr play is absolutely correct, but he drew different conclusions from that insight than I have here. Satyr play's timeless and highly idiosyncratic world is, in fact, what most interested comedy, which used the ethical and political antitype of the satyr to fashion its exuberant and assertive form of heroism and defamiliarize its topicality and political satire. Satyr play's extremely formulaic and accessible tropes and conventions lent themselves well to the modal style of adaptation that I have demonstrated in the comic evidence.

The satyric chorality of *Dionysalexandros* and *Peace* treats the political subtexts of those plays in a pseudo-aetiological way that offers something more original than the typical satire confined to everyday Athens. As far as the partial hypothesis allows one to conjecture, Cratinus anchored the parasatyrism of his *Dionysalexandros* in the visual presence of his presumably hybrid chorus and its juxtaposition of separate generic codes. Although necessarily tentative, my remarks on the hypothesis's apparent social subtext, the adultery narrative, seek to bring greater attention to the comedy's potential overlaps with satyr play through one of the latter's organic themes, its romantic liaisons. At the very least, my analysis has identified a fundamental mechanism of *Dionysalexandros*'s burlesque of satyr play, the visual assimilation of 'Dionysalexandros' to the real mythological adulterer, Alexandros. If *Dionysalexandros* did, in fact, satirize Pericles, the distancing effect of the parasatyrism ironically committed the statesman's putative responsibility for the Peloponnesian War to panhellenic cultural memory.

Peace evokes the stylized hyperactivity, dance, incompetence and nostalgia of the satyrs to condition the audience to expect the rescue of Peace to fail. The chorus's sustained resemblance to satyrs is not just amusing comic business. The mode builds a narrative trajectory whose sudden reversal communicates with vivid immediacy the panhellenic and collaborative effort needed to end the Peloponnesian War and initiate a lasting peace. *Peace* deploys the conventions of satyr play to emphasize Greece's need to transcend its satyresque cycle of dysfunction and self-destruction if that lasting peace is to be achieved. This parasatyrism, like *Peace*'s broader engagement with poetry, exploits the failure of other genres for its own comic success.

Dionysalexandros and *Peace* perform large-scale appropriations of satyr play using the chorus to raise expectations around the plot and contextualize the project of the comic hero within contemporary political events. But when the heroes themselves become satyrs, comedy prompts expectations about their agency and eventual trajectory within the plot. The hubristic threats of sexual violence by Peisetaerus and Inlaw channel in a more abbreviated fashion the satyr's familiar behaviour to characterize the broader narrative implications of antisocial, theomachic behaviour for the later comic trajectories of these heroes in the real world. Their implicit claim to the numinous satyr's divine privilege to act outrageously and recklessly with impunity evokes a generic frame within which the spectator can measure the extremes of comic agency. The significance of Peisetaerus's threat to rape Iris is that it measures the hero's incredible agency: he meets with no consequences for threatening a goddess because his power eventually eclipses hers. For Inlaw, parasatyrism illustrates the opposite. His humiliation, harassment and torture in *Thesmophoriazusae* are entertainment for the audience. But they also illustrate the immense gulf between a generic comic buffoon and the divinely privileged follower of Dionysus, free to behave according to his basest instincts.

If more evidence of such parasatyric experiments of the 430s and 420s survived – if more evidence of satyr play itself survived – we might find a more detailed record of cross-pollination between these comic but nonetheless highly distinct forms of drama. The parasatyrism examined in this chapter expands comedy's repertoire but also imbues the conventions of satyr play with a certain political and ethical depth. Therein may lie a clue to satyr play's value to the comic poets' efforts to position their comedy in the Athenian marketplace. Since so little parasatyrism survives, and what does survive is not explicitly signalled but rather subtle and implicit in its appropriation, it is difficult to detect how – or even whether – Old Comedy used satyr play to advertise itself. Although satyr play's hallowed status at the festivals was assured, the comic poets may very well have perceived it as a rival. It was, after all, the *other* genre that sought to make audiences laugh. Moreover, it was produced by tragedians. In Athenocentrizing satyr play, Cratinus, Aristophanes, Hermippus and other poets may have made a pretence of staging satyr play that was, in fact, better than satyr play itself, the product of the tragedians. The satyr play of comedy was political, topical and relevant to the Athenian spectator's life. Parasatyrism, in other words, showcases comedy's most unique feature, that which no other poetic genre possesses to the same extent: the capacity to do another genre (allegedly) better than that genre.

Poetic Failure and Comic Success in Aristophanes' *Peace*

Introduction

My analysis of Aristophanes' *Acharnians* in Chapter 1 demonstrated the formal and thematic diversity, social and political ambition, and inherently parasitic approach of Aristophanic paratragedy. After Dicaeopolis's successful defence of his controversial peace treaty, his paratragic alter ego recedes into the background, as does *Acharnians*'s engagement with *Telephus*, which is only sporadic from that point onward in the play. Aristophanes' next sustained engagement with tragedy and other genres evolves in strategy and perspective. In *Peace* of 421 BCE, *trugôidia* is the driving force of the action and this is seemingly reflected in the very name of the play's hero, Trygaeus. Usually derived from 'τρυγάω' ('to gather in the vintage, harvest'), 'Trygaeus' is normally translated as something like 'Grape-Harvester' *vel sim.*[1] Alternatively, Hall finds the etymology of the hero's name in the concept of *trugôidia* itself, translating it as 'son of "Trugedian"'.[2] But perhaps the name has an additional meaning, one which does not necessarily deny the validity of previous interpretations but rather complements them. This additional meaning derives from the ambiguity of the word τρύξ.[3] τρύξ can refer to 'must',[4] that is the juice of the grape before or during the fermentation process, and to the Greeks often means 'new wine' (οἶνος νέος). This is wine produced from the recent grape harvest, the drinking of which is associated with harvest time. Yet τρύξ also refers to 'wine-lees' or 'dregs', i.e., the grape-fragments or sediment remaining at the bottom of a jar.[5] This is the 'old' part of the wine, that is the remnants of the grape from which the juice was extracted.

Such a combination – or co-existence – of 'new' and 'old' that the term τρύξ can suggest may be implied in *Peace*'s portrayal of its hero, 'Trygaeus', an old man whom the chorus perceives as youthful thanks to his heroic achievements:[6]

Χο. ζηλωτὸς ἔσει γέρων,
αὖθις νέος ὢν πάλιν,
μύρῳ κατάλειπτος.

Chor: You'll be an enviable codger,
being young once again,
Anointed with scent.

Pax 860–862

Moreover, the driving principle of Trygaeus's comic project, *trugôidia*, is itself predicated on the co-existence of old and new: older literary models from tragedy and other genres are rejuvenated in the plot and almost acquire a new agency or political efficacy, as tragedy and *Telephus* in particular acquired in *Acharnians* a few years earlier.

Like the heroes of *Acharnians* and the third 'peace play' with which *Peace* is often classed, *Lysistrata* (411 BCE), Trygaeus is driven to act by the continuing crisis of the Peloponnesian War. However, the specific historical developments of springtime in 421 that contextualize *Peace*'s comic fantasy in truly unparalleled fashion separate this remarkable play from those two more popular productions. As the previous chapter explained, Trygaeus's quest to end the Peloponnesian War was underway as negotiations leading to the approval of the Peace of Nicias, the first significant break from hostilities between Athens and Sparta since the beginning of the Archidamian War, were proceeding in real life.[7] *Peace*'s unique topicality has helped it escape the historically poor reception it has suffered because of its allegedly lacklustre conception and execution. The play currently enjoys respectable status thanks to growing scholarly interest in the past two decades.[8] This interest was anticipated to some degree by modern theatrical appreciation of the play's exceptional physical and visual treats and an enduring topicality that naturally appealed to twentieth-century stage directors, particularly in war-ravaged Western Europe.[9]

Like *Acharnians*, *Peace* is fundamental to Aristophanes' evolving effort to position his comedy – and his brand – as an institution essential to the polis.[10] While its extensive poetic and literary agenda has received a few good book- and article-length studies, none have shown much interest in what this chapter identifies as its unifying principle, the conversion of 'failure' in other poetic forms into comedy's own poetic and political agency. This is achieved by exploiting audience expectations of these genres. This conversion of other texts' failures begins with the opening parody of Euripides' well-known but now lost *Bellerophontes*, the point of departure for Trygaeus's admittedly short but poetically rich comic project. My focal point is the provocative conception of the hero's 'horse', the dung-beetle, as an embodiment of Old Comedy's generic and social hybridity. While the beetle is the dramaturgical means of comic success, its status and function reflect the overwhelmingly popular cultural and ideological thrust of Aristophanic appropriation: although tragic in purpose, the beetle's literary biography in fable and *iambos* invests it with an unparalleled practical agency among animals and a popular form and ethos. The cultural and class prejudices of Greek attitudes toward such genres are projected partly through the Aristophanic beetle's clear equine associations. The focal point of the Bellerophontes parody, the beetle economically captures the multilayered strategy of *trugôidia*, which consistently invests its literary targets with broader social and cultural relevance, the same relevance that Aristophanes claims for his brand.

The hauling-scene's subtle and effective evocation of satyr play and its notions of failure were treated already in Chapter 3. I will only reiterate that this scene's effectiveness as a political allegory was similarly predicated upon the successful manipulation of an audience familiar with satyr play's highly formulaic elements. That sequence bridges the opening paratragedy of Bellerophontes and the continuing intergeneric engagement of *Peace*'s second half, where failure is similarly converted to success but by a different strategy. There the targets are Athenian cultural rather than dramatic institutions. *Peace*'s ostensibly celebratory frame, the initiation of the post-war era, keeps the focus squarely on Old Comedy and its representative hero, who gradually rehabilitates the traditional institutions of the polis and the hallmarks of Greek civilization since the time of Hesiod: agriculture, sacrifice and marriage.[11] Trygaeus's renewal of the latter rituals – sacrifice and marriage – through public performance certainly presents memorable occasions for 'bread-and-butter' comic business, with props, slapstick and *busyness*. However, as far as they correct or rectify highly popular metaphorical representations of sacrifice and marriage at that time commonplace in one particular genre, tragedy, these sequences amount to competitive gestures against comedy's primary rival. Aristophanes' competing versions of sacrifice and marriage efface the perversions of sacrifice and marriage that in tragedy symbolize violent social and cultural breakdown. The intended effect of these comic rituals is, I argue, to create a sense of 'aesthetic distance' between them and the perverted tragic model. Aesthetic distance, as defined by Jauss, refers to the difference between the given horizon of expectation established by previous texts and the degree of difference concerning that same topic   or motif, or theme, or trope, etc. – in a new work. The aesthetics of reader response measure the impact of such a literary event chiefly by its potential to affect the horizon of expectations. By renewing an old or commonplace theme, an innovative text changes the way an audience approaches that theme or even its genre.[12] Applied to the rituals of *Peace*, the aesthetic distance inhabits the space between the trope as commonly known from tragedy, i.e., a *corrupted* sacrifice, and Trygaeus's proper and idealized 'bloodless' sacrifice (*Pax* 1019–1022). While we lack the evidence to gauge the full effects of an ancient text on subsequent literary history in all but the most exceptional cases, what matters most in the present study is that Aristophanes *attempts* to create a degree of aesthetic distance with his idealized sacrifice and marriage in *Peace*. As an indirect challenge to a rival genre's dominant cultural influence, these rituals represent shifts in comic strategy: instead of parodying head-on, Aristophanes treats – or, rather, disputes – content and *topoi* of a more marginal kind but shared by both tragedy's mythological world and Old Comedy's contemporary setting. Aristophanes plays ritual 'straight' through proper performance. By reinvesting these rituals with their positive connotations, specifically as public ceremonies to cultivate civic cohesion, Aristophanes offers something familiar from everyday life yet uncommon to the stage and his audience's acquired expectations.

I. Openings

Unlike tragic poets, who draw their content from a large and well-known network of myth, comic poets must reinvent the wheel each time they produce a play. Tragedians could be confident that their myths are familiar enough that they need only name their heroes and audiences would remember at least some details of their stories. If Oedipus is named, they immediately recall his parents, children and sufferings. When poets run out of things to say, they simply use the *deus ex machina* to round it all off. Comic poets, by contrast, have to start from scratch, and if they leave out any formulaic element, they are booed off the stage. These are the starkly different challenges faced by the poets of each genre, at least according to the obviously biased point of view of the character speaking in a fragment (fr. 198) of *Poetry* by the early fourth-century comic poet Antiphanes.[13] While this perspective on these respective genres is skewed,[14] it certainly seems true that laying the foundations for a new story as quickly and as early as possible is a unique challenge of writing comedy and would explain why its prologues are on average three to four times greater than tragedy's.[15]

Peace's prologue is an instructive example of one such comic beginning. An opening 'warm-up' of slaves engaged in some secret activity that only gradually, teasingly, becomes known arouses the audience's interest. Slave A swiftly ferries away 'cakes' of an unknown kind prepared by Slave B to feed an unknown animal offstage. The gradual revelation of the recipe – for 'shit-cakes' – would naturally arouse the audience's curiosity about what kind of god-awful animal would consume shit-cakes. We soon learn that this is a giant dung-beetle and that Aristophanes invites his audience to interpret it metaphorically. Slave B imagines that interpretation in the audience at this very moment:

Οι.ᵝ οὐκοῦν ἂν ἤδη τῶν θεατῶν τις λέγοι
νεανίας δοκησίσοφος, 'τόδε πρᾶγμα τί;
ὁ κάνθαρος δὲ πρὸς τί;'
Οι.ᴬ   κᾆτ' αὐτῷ γ' ἀνὴρ
Ἰωνικός τίς φησι παρακαθήμενος·
'δοκέω μέν, ἐς Κλέωνα τοῦτ' αἰνίσσεται,
ὡς κεῖνος ἐν Ἀΐδεω σπατίλην ἐσθίει.'

Sl.B: Won't some young buck, some clever-dick
sitting in the audience say, 'What's the deal?
What's the beetle for?'
Sl.A: And then some Ionian
sitting next to him will say, 'I think he's alluding
to Cleon, since that guy is eating shit in Hades!'

                                        Pax 43–48

The Ionian thinks his own cultural heritage of iambic invective from Ionia, a popular form that occasionally featured dung-beetles, affords him special insight into Aristophanes' insect.[16] While the beetle's deeper meaning is never made explicit, this imaginary exchange between spectators nonetheless encourages the audience to consider the insect's literal and even metaphorical place in the play. In this first part of the present chapter, I show how and why the beetle is vital to *Peace*'s comic project and moreover that it is even symbolic of *trugôidia* itself. Conceived as a hybrid of genre and class, the beetle elicits popular sympathy and succeeds where tragedy has failed.

Slave B then explains (τὸν λόγον) what is happening: their master is mad (μαίνεται) in a 'novel way' (καινὸν τρόπον).[17]

ὁ δεσπότης μου μαίνεται καινὸν τρόπον
οὐχ ὅνπερ ὑμεῖς, ἀλλ' ἕτερον καινὸν πάνυ.

δι' ἡμέρας γὰρ εἰς τὸν οὐρανὸν βλέπων
ὡδὶ κεχηνὼς λοιδορεῖται τῷ Διὶ
καί φησιν, 'ὦ Ζεῦ, τί ποτε βουλεύει ποιεῖν;
κατάθου τὸ κόρημα· μὴ 'κκόρει τὴν Ἑλλάδα.'
ἔα ἔα·   60
σιγήσαθ', ὡς φωνῆς ἀκούειν μοι δοκῶ.
Τρ. ὦ Ζεῦ, τί δρασείεις ποθ' ἡμῶν τὸν λεών;
λήσεις σεαυτὸν τὰς πόλεις ἐκκοκκίσας.
Οι.ᵝ τοῦτ' ἐστὶ τουτὶ τὸ κακὸν αὖθ' οὑγὼ 'λεγον·
τὸ γὰρ παράδειγμα τῶν μανιῶν ἀκούετε·
ἃ δ' εἶπε πρῶτον ἡνίκ' ἤρχεθ' ἡ χολή,
πεύσεσθ'. ἔφασκε γὰρ πρὸς αὐτὸν ἐνθαδί·
'πῶς ἄν ποτ' ἀφικοίμην ἂν εὐθὺ τοῦ Διός;'
ἔπειτα λεπτὰ κλιμάκια ποιούμενος,
πρὸς ταῦτ' ἀνηρριχᾶτ' ἂν εἰς τὸν οὐρανόν,   70
ἕως ξυνετρίβη τῆς κεφαλῆς καταρρυείς.

Sl.B: The master is mad, in a new way, not in the
way you all are, but in a much different 'new' way.
Staring all day at the sky, he gapes like this
and abuses Zeus, saying, 'Zeus! What are you planning
to do?! Put down the broom, don't sweep Hellas away!'
Oh! Oh!   60
Quiet! I think I hear his voice.
Tr: (within) Zeus! What are you doing to our people!?
Before you know it, you'll wreck our cities!
Sl.B: This! This is the evil I was just talking about!
You hear this symptom of his delusions.
You'll hear the things he first said when the bile
took hold. He was saying this to himself: 'How
could I get straight to Zeus?' Then, after constructing
light ladders, he would scramble up these to heaven,   70
till tumbling down he bashed his head.

Pax 54–71

This linguistic and metrical paratragedy was assuredly supplemented with gestures and vocal effects, such as the repetition and pitch of the hero's offstage cries (ὦ Ζεῦ, τί ποτε βουλεύει ποιεῖν; 58; ὦ Ζεῦ, τί δρασείεις ποθ' ἡμῶν τὸν λεών; 62; πῶς ἄν ποτ' ἀφικοίμην ..., 68).[18] In Trygaeus's mad outbursts (54, 65), Wilkins recognized the tragic νόσος theme perhaps best known from Euripidean heroines like Medea (*Med.* 96-97) and Phaedra (*Hipp.* 205, 269), whose 'disease' (νόσος and cognates) eventually leads to rash decisions and destructive outcomes for them and their houses.[19] Given expectations associated with the νόσος trope, the audience probably awaited the hero's entrance and lament of his present condition.[20] However, this is not what happens. The slave continues:

ἐχθὲς δὲ μετὰ ταῦτ' ἐκφθαρεὶς οὐκ οἶδ' ὅποι
εἰσήγαγ' Αἰτναῖον μέγιστον κάνθαρον,
κἄπειτα τοῦτον ἱπποκομεῖν μ' ἠνάγκασεν,
καὐτὸς καταψῶν αὐτὸν ὥσπερ πωλίον,
'ὦ Πηγάσιόν μοι,' φησί, 'γενναῖον πτερόν,
ὅπως πετήσει μ' εὐθὺ τοῦ Διὸς λαβών.'
ἀλλ' ὅ τι ποιεῖ τῃδὶ διακύψας ὄψομαι.
οἴμοι τάλας· ἴτε δεῦρο δεῦρ', ὦ γείτονες·
ὁ δεσπότης γάρ μου μετέωρος αἴρεται   80
ἱππηδὸν εἰς τὸν ἀέρ' ἐπὶ τοῦ κανθάρου.

Then yesterday disappearing to I don't know where
he brought back an enormous Etnian beetle,
and he made me be its groom, and he himself caresses it
just like a colt, saying 'My little Pegasus, my thoroughbred
wings, you must pick me up and fly me straight to Zeus.'
I'll peek in and take a look at what he's doing.
Holy shit! Neighbours, get over here! My master
is raised aloft up in the air, astride his beetle   80
like a horse!

Pax 72–81

The paratragedy evolves abruptly from the generic to the specific in a virtuoso imitation of Euripides' famous but now fragmentary *Bellerophontes* (c. 455–425 BCE).[21] Suddenly swinging into view from behind the *skênê*, Trygaeus hovers aloft before his astonished household and treats the audience to a dextrous recitation of the very same anapaests (82–101) chanted by Bellerophontes (cf. frr. 307–308), but does so while being suspended in the air.

The fragmentary state of Euripides' tragedy obviously limits what can be said about Trygaeus's performance as Bellerophontes. Although Homer and the Archaic poets allude to the Argive hero's involvement in a 'Potiphar's Wife' plot with Proetus's wife, Anteia,[22] the first extended treatments of the major events from Bellerophontes' life come courtesy of Euripides' *Stheneboea* – the tragedian's name for Homer's Anteia – and *Bellerophontes*. *Stheneboea* dealt with the hero's ruthless killing of Stheneboea by throwing her from Pegasus in flight.[23] As to

Bellerophontes, there was a time when scholars felt certain only that the play concluded with the hero's hubristic flight to Olympus for the purpose of confronting the gods for their injustice and his fatal fall from Pegasus.[24] The significant piece of evidence for this 'hubris' theory was the notoriously atheistic fr. 286:

φῆσίν τις εἶναι δῆτ' ἐν οὐρανῶι θεούς;
οὐκ εἰσίν, οὐκ εἴσ', εἴ τις ἀνθρώπων θέλει
μὴ τῷ παλαιῷ μῶρος ὢν χρῆσθαι λόγῳ.

Does someone say there are indeed gods in heaven?
There are not, there are not, if a man is unwilling
to rely foolishly on antiquated reasoning.

Eur. fr. 286.1–3

While certainly not the only Euripidean hero to criticize the gods directly and passionately, Bellerophontes was thought to have done so with unparalleled vehemence in this fragment.[25]

However, there is some inconsistency between the sentiments of fr. 286 and the words ascribed with near certainty to the dying Bellerophontes in a different fragment connected to the play's final scene, where the hero describes his heart as 'reverent towards the gods' (εἰς θεοὺς μὲν εὐσεβής, fr. 310.1). Pointing to this apparent inconsistency, Dixon argues that the hero of *Bellerophontes* did not, in fact, seek Olympus out of hubris but ventured too close to the gods by mistake.[26] The speaker of frr. 307–308a, who is almost certainly Bellerophontes, expresses optimism and even excitement in the moments before taking a flight. But if an embittered hero overcome by suffering sought the heavens to challenge the gods, as is the conventional interpretation, we would rather expect some indication of disillusionment, bitterness and anger.

If Dixon's pious but tragically errant Bellerophontes is the correct version, it alters our conception of precisely what is Euripidean and what is Aristophanic about Trygaeus's paratragic flight. *Peace* 54–71 specifies that Trygaeus is driven by bitterness and insanity: he is mad (χολή, 66), resents the gods (62–63, 107–108) and isolates himself within his household (cf. Eur. fr. 285). Although Bellerophontes' motives are irrecoverable, Trygaeus's intentions are explicit: seek heaven, interrogate Zeus and, if necessary, indict him on charges of Medism (107–108). The hero's madness, which paradoxically enables his comic success, is thus probably an original contribution to the Euripidean model rather than something inherited from it.

Despite the importance of the hero's role and the many performative challenges of the comedy's opening paratragedy,[27] the true ethos of *Peace*'s comic appropriation is the comic 'Pegasus' that is the focus of the action from the prologue onward (43–45). The dung-beetle is more than a grotesque joke.[28] It is an emblem of Old Comedy's parasitic relationship to other genres and, more specifically, *Peace*'s specific agenda of converting poetic failure to comic success. Aristophanes' replacement of myth's most noble creature, Pegasus, with a vile, biological inferior – remember that the beetle's defining activity is eating dung – is loaded with ideological meaning.[29] His unique literary agency is noted in the paratragic stichomythia (114–148) between Trygaeus and his child, who initially questions her father's insane plan.[30] Instead of pleading with her father, as Bellerophontes' child is believed to have done in the analogous scene of the tragic model,[31] Trygaeus's unnamed daughter questions the beetle's comic agency. Aristophanes takes this opportunity to establish the beetle's popular generic credentials:

Πα. καὶ τίς πόρος σοι τῆς ὁδοῦ γενήσεται;
ναῦς μὲν γὰρ οὐκ ἄξει σε τήνδε τὴν ὁδόν.
Τρ. πτηνὸς πορεύσει πῶλος· οὐ ναυσθλώσομαι.
Πα. τίς δ' ἡ 'πίνοιά σοὐστὶν ὥστε κάνθαρον
ζεύξαντ' ἐλαύνειν εἰς θεούς, ὦ παππία;
Τρ. ἐν τοῖσιν Αἰσώπου λόγοις ἐξηυρέθη
μόνος πετηνῶν εἰς θεοὺς ἀφιγμένος.   130
Πα. ἄπιστον εἶπας μῦθον, ὦ πάτερ πάτερ,
ὅπως κάκοσμον ζῷον ἦλθεν εἰς θεούς.
Τρ. ἦλθεν κατ' ἔχθραν αἰετοῦ πάλαι ποτέ,
ᾧ' ἐκκυλίνδων κἀντιτιμωρούμενος.
Πα. οὔκουν ἐχρῆν σε Πηγάσου ζεῦξαι πτερόν,
ὅπως ἐφαίνου τοῖς θεοῖς τραγικώτερος;
Τρ. ἀλλ', ὦ μέλ', ἂν μοι σιτίων διπλῶν ἔδει·
νῦν δ' ἅττ' ἂν αὐτὸς καταφάγω τὰ σιτία,
τούτοισι τοῖς αὐτοῖσι τοῦτον χορτάσω.

Ch: By what means will you make the journey?
A ship certainly won't take you on it.
Tr: A winged colt will take me; I won't go by sea.
Ch: What is your aim in yoking a beetle and riding
it to the gods, daddy?
Tr: In Aesop's works he was the only winged thing
I could find that reached the gods.   130

Ch: Father, father, you've told an incredible story,
that such a rank creature reached the gods.
Tr: Once upon a time it went bearing a grudge against
the eagle and avenged itself by rolling eggs from its nest.
Ch: Well, you should have saddled the wings of Pegasus
so that you'd appear more tragic to the gods.
Tr: Then I would need food for two, my dear.
Now, I'll fodder this thing by reusing whatever food
I eat.

Pax 124–139

This justification of the beetle as a superior alternative to the tragic Pegasus articulates *Peace*'s unifying principle of parody and literary appropriation: other genres' failures furnish the means to comedy's success. Unlike Pegasus, the beetle has actually made it to the gods (130), specifically in the famous Aesopic fable in which it exacted vengeance against the eagle (133–134).[32] Aesop's beetle confronted the eagle on Olympus just as the humble farmer Trygaeus seeks to confront the gods themselves for their responsibility for Greece's continuous war. The fable of the eagle and the beetle (*Fab.* 3 Perry) tells of the powerful eagle's crime against the lowly dung-beetle, either eating its young, destroying its eggs or killing its suppliant, depending on the version. With the angry beetle in pursuit, the bird of Zeus fled to Olympus and sought refuge in Zeus's lap, where he nested. Accounts differ as to what happened then: either the beetle dropped a ball of dung on Zeus (*Fab.* 3 Perry) or buzzed around his head (Σ^{RV} 130), compelling Zeus to leap up in disgust, eject the eagle's eggs and thereby destroy them. The moral is that divine favour does the wicked no good, even when their enemy is a creature of the lowest status.[33] It is worth noting that the fable is especially significant to the corpus because of its place in the account of Aesop's death within the biographical tradition.[34] According to the legend, Aesop recited this very fable to the Delphians who led him to his execution after falsely accusing him of stealing from Apollo's temple. The beetle, as Aesop will, ultimately triumphs over his biological (and social) superior, the eagle, who wronged him.

By means of the fable, or *ainos*, the Aesopic beetle also belonged to iambic poetry's repertoire as a character in its own right, as the extradramatic discussion between spectators earlier in *Peace* confirms.[35] These popular, sub-literary associations give the beetle a kind of folk-hero status and the pretence to greater accessibility to audiences. Trygaeus's comic project then acquires a certain social abjectness that conditions the audience to expect that comedy will outperform its allegedly superior tragic model.[36] The insect is generically, socially, and even biologically representative of parody in Old Comedy, defined broadly. In fact, Aristophanes' construction of the beetle is analogous to his appropriation of Telephus to characterize comic hero and poet as wronged and downtrodden but ultimately noble heroes. *Peace* implements a similar strategy using the Aesopic beetle as the quintessential underdog seeking a more narrowly defined justice. As an agent for the powerless against the powerful, the generic status of the beetle is inversely proportional to its popular renown in pedestrian fable. The comic substitution thus exploits the cultural currency of the beetle's literary biography and particularly its proven track record of success; as the only literary creature to reach heaven (129–130), Aesop's beetle had succeeded where his loftier tragic counterpart, Pegasus, failed.

The demotic appeal of the beetle extends deeper than its popular literary status as folk hero. The quasi-equid character imputed to it throughout the episode conceptualizes the beast within the culture of public display and status that determined ancient Greek social hierarchy. Note the hero's orders to his steed as it takes flight:

ἀλλ' ἄγε, Πήγασε, χώρει χαίρων,
χρυσοχάλινον πάταγον ψαλίων
διακινήσας φαιδροῖς ὠσίν.
τί ποιεῖς, τί ποιεῖς; ποῖ παρακλίνεις
τοὺς μυκτῆρας; πρὸς τὰς λαύρας;
ἵει σαυτὸν θαρρῶν ἀπὸ γῆς,
κᾆτα δρομαίαν πτέρυγ' ἐκτείνων   160
ὀρθὸς χώρει Διὸς εἰς αὐλάς,
ἀπὸ μὲν κάκκης τὴν ῥῖν' ἀπέχων,
ἀπό θ' ἡμερίων σίτων πάντων.
ἄνθρωπε, τί δρᾷς, οὗτος ὁ χέζων
ἐν Πειραιεῖ παρὰ ταῖς πόρναις;
ἀπολεῖς μ', ἀπολεῖς. οὐ κατορύξεις
κἀπιφορήσεις τῆς γῆς πολλήν,
κἀπιφυτεύσεις ἕρπυλλον ἄνω
καὶ μύρον ἐπιχεῖς; ὡς ἤν τι πεσὼν
ἐνθένδε πάθω, τοὐμοῦ θανάτου
πέντε τάλανθ' ἡ πόλις ἡ Χίων
διὰ τὸν σὸν πρωκτὸν ὀφλήσει.

Now, giddy up, Pegasus, and bon voyage;
strike up the rattle of curb chains
on your golden bit, with ears laid back.

What are you doing!? What are you doing!? Where
are you pointing those nostrils? Toward the latrines?
Hurl yourself bravely away from the ground,
then spread your racing pinions
and head straight to the halls of Zeus,   160
averting your nose from poop
and from all mortal foods.
Man! Man in Piraeus, the one shitting
in the whores' quarter: what are you doing?
You'll get me killed, killed! Do cover it up,
pile plenty of dirt on top,
and plant thyme over it,
and pour on perfume! Because if I fall
from here and suffer any harm, for my death
the Chian state will be fined five talents,
all because of your arsehole![37]

Pax 154–172

The incongruity of the beetle's outward markers of equine status – 'golden bit',
'ears laid back' and 'racing pinions' – and its hopeless indiscipline and appetite
for the most low-quality fare are conceived for comic and ideological effect.
Griffith has argued that horses, donkeys and mules were subject to the same
cultural prejudices applied to the various social strata in the Greek imagination.[38]
Like their aristocratic owners, horses were bred only for battle, racing, elite
transportation and display, and never for the menial tasks of labour and basic
transportation commonly reserved for lower-class equines such as donkeys and
mules.[39] The beetle's contradictory equine qualities situate the beast somewhere
in the middle of this spectrum, though it definitely aspires to the status of a
superior equid. The slave complains about serving as a groom (ἱπποκομεῖν, 74),
in which capacity he must treat the beetle as a pony (πωλίον, 75, 126), when it is
really more like a 'pack ass' (κάνθων, 82). To Trygaeus, the beetle is a 'Pegasus' (76,
154) with a certain heroic grandeur (ἱπποκάνθαρος, 181) despite its 'grazing' on
dung (βουκολήσεται, 153). The hero's order for the beast to begin its flight slowly
(ἠρέμα, 82) and not too insolently (σοβαρὸς, 83) utilizes the specialized
vocabulary of horse-training and maintenance (Xen. *Eq.* 7.10; 10.17).[40]

Hippotrophia – the breeding, training and riding of horses – was the most
distinctive marker of 'wealth, brilliance, and style' to Archaic and Classical
Greeks.[41] It taught horses strict discipline through training, maintained their
superior health with high-quality feed, and cultivated their appearance with

luxurious accessories.[42] While *hippotrophia* was the domain of the wealthy aristocracy, to 'less aristocratically-minded' Athenian citizens such as Trygaeus it represented excess, waste and even 'antidemocratic tendencies'.[43] Equine themes are common in tragedy's aristocratic world, where horses are ubiquitous and donkeys almost non-existent. The latter, by contrast, are confined to lower genres such as comedy.[44]

The beetle's absurd pretensions to 'horsiness' actually have the effect of associating it with the inferior donkey, who occupied the opposite pole of the ideological spectrum from the horse and was largely perceived as a graceless and incorrigible beast suited to little more than hard labour. The slave's explicit identification of the beetle as a κάνθων ('pack ass', 85) agrees with the scholiast's derivation of κάνθαρος ('beetle') from the same term.[45] The beast's appalling diet takes to comic extremes the different and specific dietary needs along the equid spectrum: horses enjoyed better feed, water and rest than donkeys, who subsisted on lower-quality fare like thistles, straw and weeds.[46] Whereas noble Pegasus threw his rider out of fear – behaviour for which horses were notorious – the voracious and undisciplined beetle's attraction to food on the ground (157–158) nearly dooms his rider. This is typical behaviour for a donkey, an animal with a reputation for stupidity, laziness, greed and excessive curiosity.[47] Moreover, the beetle's absurd fastidiousness and refusal to eat anything except the most finely rounded dung cake is reminiscent of the donkey's tendency in literary sources to aspire for higher things than it deserves.[48]

At one level, the beetle's blend of high and low – he is a ἱπποκάνθαρος (181) – is typical of paratragedy's appeal to the broadest possible swathe of the *dêmos* by coupling heroic aspirations and lowbrow humour. In other words, the beetle's equine hybridity reflects the generic hybridity of τρυγῳδία. Since traditional prejudices about equids informed Greek ideas of human nature, the breeding, education, and class and gender differentiation of humans are frequently viewed through an equid prism in our sources;[49] the identity of the equid reflects that of its owner. The beetle of *Peace* projects the status of both its rider and his comic project. Furthermore, the generic agency and amalgamation of (equine) attributes in the beetle are analogous to Old Comedy's own character as a genre of parody, particularly with reference to the evolutionary terms discussed in the Introduction. The beetle is a survival machine that outperforms other poetic species; unlike Euripides' Pegasus, whose fright dooms Bellerophontes, the beetle reaches Olympus and is later appropriately immortalized for his achievement (ὑφ' ἅρματ' ἐλθὼν Ζηνὸς ἀστραπηφορεῖ, 722). Moreover, the beetle's unique dietary preference for the diverse yet freely available waste-products of other organisms profoundly resembles the parasitic nature of Old Comedy's appropriation, which is a recycling of both the literary and non-literary. The beetle is thus emblematic of *Peace*'s comic agenda of converting poetic failure to comic success.

One final dimension of the beetle may contribute to the parody of *Bellerophontes*, the visual impression of the hero's flight on the *mêchanê* (μηχανή) or 'crane'.[50] Did it have some special impact on this particular parody that has gone unrecognized? This 'derrick which simulated unassisted flight of the gods, or of heroes like Perseus ... or Bellerophon' lifted an actor in a harness or some kind of trapeze-like structure from beyond the stage-building and up and over it, where he either remained suspended in the air or alighted on the roof.[51] The machine was an effective way to overturn the spatial and kinetic expectations of the audience. Though comedy acknowledges its operation, most famously in this very scene of *Peace* (174–176), there is no description of its mechanics until later prose writers like Pollux (IV 128). It is typical to understand comedy's deployment of the crane, much like that of the *ekkuklêma*, as a pointed satire of a contemporary tragic convention, which in principle sought to offer audiences a degree of realism but in practice may have seemed rather slow, clumsy and artificial.[52] Much of the responsibility for creating this impression rests with comic poets like Antiphanes (in the fragment above) and ancient critics like Aristotle, who disparage the device's most common application as a *deus ex machina* ('god from the machine'), a divine epiphany that (in his view) concludes plays through the least skilful kind of dramatic resolution (*Poet.* 1454a37–b6).[53] Aristotle implies that the crane was primarily associated with introducing divinities in closing scenes,[54] for it allowed a producer to insert gods or goddesses with the swiftness and abruptness with which they were imagined to move.[55]

Peace's deployment of the *mêchanê* may react to the intended visual effect of tragic convention as Mastronarde defines it in his theory of the gods' privileged position and movement above stage level.[56] The god's elevated position on the roof of the stage-building and above mortals below visually reinforced the distinction between divine and mortal that is fundamental to Greek thought. Moreover, the speed and invisibility of the divine epiphany in that elevated location – by means of either the *mêchanê* or internal/external staircases to the roof – perform a style of locomotion characteristic of the gods and their status. This spatial arrangement and kinetic movement in the upper portion of the performance area maintained the social, ethical and psychological distinctions between gods and mortals. Apart from notable exceptions, gods and mortals typically do not appear alongside one another in tragedy, and in fact occupy distinctly different spaces when simultaneously present.

Such idealized distinctions of space and movement may help one better visualize the genre-bending impact of Trygaeus's Bellerophontean flight, which took him up to the regions of the stage normally reserved for the divine. Where tragedy's crane assigns and enforces the cosmic barrier between divine and human, comedy's *mêchanê* expands the range of mortal agency by permitting the hero access to the divine world normally forbidden to heroes like Bellerophontes. Trygaeus's flight seemingly reconceives the tragic ignorance of Bellerophontes' errant journey as an insane but inspired and audacious rejection of mortal limitation. Such a conjunction of mortal and divine worlds using the *mêchanê* could reinforce the aesthetic and political agency of *trugôidia* in strikingly immediate terms for an audience.

By employing tragedy's convention of the epiphany at the outset of the play – this timing is key for distinguishing the effect of Trygaeus's flight from his tragic model's – and appropriating its divine authority successfully, Aristophanes endows his hero and comic project with the mandate of a tragic divinity from its outset. The crane's common application as the *deus ex machina* identified it with dramatic resolutions, particularly in Euripides. Nine of his plays conclude with a god resolving an impasse, at least in a dramaturgical sense, and communicating future events.[57] This primarily communicative function of the *deus* provides privileged knowledge reinforced by the larger Olympian order.[58] Trygaeus's flight, by contrast, challenges the intellectual basis of the crane as an affirmation of Olympian authority and sovereignty by its successful achievement of the heavenly summit, where the hero can reject the gods' reasoning for continuing the Peloponnesian War. As the means of Trygaeus's access to the gods and divine knowledge, which is otherwise unavailable to mortals, the comic crane provides a means to overcome the cosmic limits represented by the same effect in tragedy.

II. Comic renewal

Aristophanes' use of the crane in the opening paratragedy is not the only important epiphanic moment of *Peace*. After the parasatyric rescue of the eponymous goddess, Trygaeus initiates the foundation of Peace's new cult in Athens. While *Eirênê* belonged to the Olympic pantheon since at least Hesiod, and is mentioned a handful of times in extant tragedy, she did not receive cult status at Athens until it defeated Sparta at Alyzia in 375.[59] It is possible that Aristophanes' dramatization of her rescue in 421 was the first physical representation of the goddess in the fifth century.[60] The sole evidence for this representation comes courtesy of a scholiast on Plato's *Apology* (19c), who says that Aristophanes' comic rivals Eupolis and Plato Comicus mocked the statue (κωμῳδεῖται δὲ ὅτι καὶ τὸ τῆς εἰρήνης κολοσσικὸν ἐξῆρεν ἄγαλμα).[61] Whatever quality of the statue struck these poets as absurd, the text indicates that Peace sat at centre stage as an ἄγαλμα, an object of talismanic power, for the rest of the play.[62]

This front-and-centre position of the goddess is fundamental to Aristophanes' representation of the *process* of peace in the play's second half through a handful of critical cultural institutions. Since almost two-thirds of the play's length is devoted to this enactment of Peace's social, political and cultural blessings, scholars have usually deemed *Peace* a 'celebration' play.[63] Nevertheless, *Peace* keeps attention focused on its literary rivals and continues to affirm the aesthetic and political value of *trugôidia*. Instead of parodying or appropriating specific textual models, Aristophanes engages Greek tragedy by 'playing straight' and effacing two of tragedy's preferred *topoi*, its parodies of sacrifice and marriage as perversions. In tragedy, perverted sacrifice and the 'tragic wedding' became generic metaphors for the breakdown of civil society through uncontrolled and politically destabilizing violence, especially of an intrafamilial kind.

While not exactly rare, sacrifice and marriage – specifically the wedding – are sufficiently infrequent in the extant evidence of Old Comedy to merit concentrated analysis. *Peace* preserves the earliest instances of these ritual ceremonies in the comic corpus. In the case of marriage, the available evidence suggests that Old Comedy had only begun exploring the topic in the last quarter of the fifth century. Given their infrequency in Aristophanes, it is worth asking whether Trygaeus's sacrifice and marriage could be more than just generic tropes of celebration, which is (after all) what marriage in comedy at least comes to represent as it increases in prominence over the next hundred years. I believe the performance of these rituals continues *Peace*'s strategy of intergeneric engagement by offering competing versions of dramatized ritual that challenge Greek tragedy's popular claim to them as critical parts of its traditional repertoire. Aristophanes shifts from the comic distortion of motifs, themes and subplots to a less direct approach, one that challenges comedy's great rival on more neutral terms. In these positive treatments of ritual, Trygaeus dramatizes the rectification of the distorted and perverted sacrifices and marriages of Greek tragedy. Evoking audience expectations is central to this alternate strategy to create comic success from tragic failure. Aristophanes' 'straight' take on these institutions reverses tragedy's original distortion and parody and in so doing challenges its cultural supremacy.

Comic sacrifice

Peace's unique emphasis on panhellenic solidarity is expressed throughout, in everything from the panhellenic choral rescue to the socially indistinct person of the hero.[64] The creation and celebration of social and political cohesion in *Peace* begin with the chorus's immediate return to the countryside and the agrarian life it enjoyed before the war. Like satyrs released back into the service of Dionysus, the farmers of the panhellenic chorus return to their quasi-utopian world of rustic labour and agricultural abundance, as the repeated refrain εἰς ἀγρόν emphasizes.[65] *Peace*'s pastoral, utopian imagery draws on Hesiod's famous description of the conditions of Golden Age life in *Works and Days*, in which 'the grain-giving field bore crops / of its own accord, much and unstinting' (καρπὸν δ' ἔφερε ζείδωρος ἄρουρα / αὐτομάτη πολλόν τε καὶ ἄφθονον, *Op.* 117–118).[66] But in contrast to the Hesiodic view of work as hardship, *Peace* figures labour in more positive terms, as the *sine qua non* of natural abundance and communal solidarity.[67] This impression is bolstered by the play's uniquely altruistic outlook, specifically Trygaeus's extension of the benefits of his victory to the whole Greek world, in contrast to *Acharnians*'s Dicaeopolis, who notoriously hoards his blessings from others.

Sacrifice too is a fundamental cultural institution, one which situates humanity between the beasts and the gods, at least in Hesiod's cosmos (*Op.* 42–105).[68] The stages of the sacrificial process create community – e.g., the washing of hands, the drawing of the sacred circle, the throwing of the barley – as do the distinct roles of its participants (basket carrier, herder, priest etc.). Anthropologists such as Durkheim, Radcliffe-Brown and Malinowski imputed to such religious ritual the function of maintaining society, specifically regulating it, adjusting its interactions, maintaining its communal identity and aiding its restoration following crises.[69] For Burkert, the shared aggression and guilt of the culminating act of violence against a domesticated animal within the community created a sense of solidarity among sacrificial participants, whose violence is authorized by the public sanction of the city at peace.[70] Thus sacrifice, when correctly performed, provides an ultimate standard for judging the health of a community through its containment of violence, fair distribution of goods and formalized rules of consumption.[71]

The positive social effects of proper sacrifice explain why, upon his successful return to Athens with Peace and her two mute female attendants, 'Festival' (*Theôria*) and 'Harvest' (*Opôra*), Trygaeus orders his slave to prepare the necessary sacrifice (*Pax* 923) for the foundation of Peace's new cult. Apart from the hauling itself, Trygaeus's sacrifice is one of the play's most curiously ostentatious moments. The only other extended sacrifice of extant fifth-century comedy, Peisetaerus's foundation sacrifice in *Birds* (848–1469), is primarily comic in its aims: that sacrifice is constantly interrupted by a series of intruders in search of some share of Cloudcuckooland's good fortune. Aristophanes similarly prolongs Trygaeus's sacrifice of a sheep to Peace's cult for almost a hundred lines, ostensibly to incorporate a healthy dose of slapstick and comic busyness: the conspicuous collection of necessities (altar [942], basket, barley meal, garland, knife, kindling [947–949], victim [956]), the characters running on and off stage and yelling, and even an amusing prayer to the goddess by master and slave (974–1016). There are, in other words, ample reasons to believe a sacrifice is imminent at this point in the play. As readers, it is all too easy for us to miss the effectiveness of this scene's comedy, which uses ostentatious onstage hi-jinks to frustrate audience expectations that have been building for some time. Instead, sacrifice is continually deferred.

> Τρ. λαβὲ τὴν μάχαιραν· εἶθ' ὅπως μαγειρικῶς
> σφάξεις τὸν οἶν.
> Οι.   ἀλλ' οὐ θέμις.
> Τρ.   τιὴ τί δή;
> Οι. οὐχ ἥδεται δήπουθεν Εἰρήνη σφαγαῖς,
> οὐδ' αἱματοῦται βωμός.
> Τρ.   ἀλλ' εἴσω φέρων   1020
> θύσας τὰ μηρί' ἐξελὼν δεῦρ' ἔκφερε,
> χοὕτω τὸ πρόβατον τῷ χορηγῷ σῴζεται.

> *Tr*: Take the knife, and be sure to slaughter
> the sheep like a master-chef.
> *Sl*:   That's not proper.
> *Tr*: And why not?
> *Sl*:   Peace takes no pleasure in slaughter,
> nor is her altar bloodied.
> *Tr*:   Well, take it inside and sacrifice   1020
> it there, then remove the thigh pieces and bring them out
> here. That way the sheep is saved for the *Khorêgos*.

> *Pax* 1017–1022

The distinctive vocabulary here is notable. Olson comments that σφαγαῖς (1019), 'slaughterings', does not simply refer to animals, but the 'violent deaths (of men)'.[72] The word appears nowhere else in the extant corpus of Aristophanes or his major rivals but is fairly common in tragedy.[73] Moreover, αἱματοῦται ('be soaked in blood,' 1020) is certainly tragic diction.[74] The slave's contention that Peace naturally disapproves of all violence, even sacrificial violence in her honour, prompts the hero to rethink his decision and suggest a compromise: the sacrifice will take place, but the audience will not see it. The characters' motivations combine the ethical and the practical. Violence is not only abhorrent to Peace, the honorand, but also expensive. To save the *khorêgos* money, the hero opts only to pretend to sacrifice so that when the play takes first prize the liturgist will be spared the added expense of a second sheep for the celebratory dinner.[75] Aristophanes thus has it both ways: violence that potentially contradicts the spirit of the play is avoided while the ritual's distinctly positive benefits, namely social solidarity and cohesion, are exploited. And the *khorêgos* saves some money.

Though necessary for the installation of Peace, the sacrificial violence is inconsistent with the new post-war ethos of total and uncompromising peace, and its representation is thus excluded. However, this exclusion might be understood at a second, poetic level in light of sacrifice's significance as a primary, if not the primary, vehicle for the metaphorical expression of exceptional violence and brutality in tragedy. Under the pretence of Trygaeus's sacrificial discretion, Aristophanes alludes to parody in contemporary tragedy. Surviving tragedy's corruption of the sacrificial ritual is an especially potent means of describing moral or social disorder at moments of crisis when violence, particularly between members of the same household, spirals out of control.[76] This occurs in various ways. Frequently humans are substituted for animals, as in Clytemnestra's killing of Agamemnon in the play of his name. She memorably describes her three fatal blows as a sacrifice to *Dikê* in retribution for her husband's earlier sacrifice of their child, Iphigenia (Aesch. *Ag.* 1384–1392). The audience is prepared for this outcome by the queen's earlier mention of the sheep awaiting sacrifice to Zeus, protector of the household (*Ag.* 1037–1038, 1056–1057), upon the king's return. Perverted sacrifice can also have an aetiological function, as in Euripides' *Bacchae* (405 BCE). The *sparagmos* of Pentheus initiates a new institution. Alternatively, the specific perversity of the sacrifice might be located in procedural impropriety, such as the compromised state of the sacrificer and the impurity of the participants.[77] The Sophoclean Ajax slaughters the Greeks' livestock as if they were his enemies and without regard for the proper rites, for example. The oath of the Seven over a slaughtered bull prefigures the carnage and fratricide that will shortly engulf Thebes (Aesch. *Sept.* 43–44). In this instance, as in so many others, sacrifice presages violence between kin. Impiety is incurred by the avenger's poor timing and/or manner of killing, as in

Euripides' *Electra* (undated). Although Aegisthus is certainly culpable for his participation in Agamemnon's murder and the seduction of Clytemnestra, his killing by Orestes is grotesque: he dies in the process of sacrificing, at the hands of those whom he graciously invited into his home.[78]

>   ... τοῦ δὲ νεύοντος κάτω
> ὄνυχας ἔπ' ἄκρους στὰς κασίγνητος σέθεν
> ἐς σφονδύλους ἔπαισε, νωτιαῖα δὲ
> ἔρρηξεν ἄρθρα· πᾶν δὲ σῶμ' ἄνω κάτω
> ἤσπαιρεν ἠλέλιζε δυσθνήισκων φόνωι.

> ... And standing on his tip-toes over the
> man bending down, your brother struck
> him on the spine, and smashed his vertebrae.
> And his whole body from head to toe convulsed
> as he shrieked dying in bloody agony.

Eur. El. 839–843

The presentation of the guest's murder of his host as continuation of the animal sacrifice and ritual feast is intended to shock and appal.

Perverted household rites in tragedy frequently express not only the death of members of that kin group but also the house's self-destruction.[79] An important corollary to such destruction, at least according to Seaford, is the foundation of an altogether new ritual that can restore the polis to proper ritual health. In this theory, the benefits of household and polis are mutually exclusive, and the annihilation of an elite family facilitates the foundation of a new cult whose future rituals will ensure social cohesion.[80] Tragedy identifies the controlled killing of sacrifice with uncontrolled violence in deteriorating households, which threatens the very social cohesion whose promotion was the original purpose of the ritual. By rectifying tragedy's parody of sacrifice, Aristophanic comedy aspires to a status equal to that of tragedy.

Trygaeus's sacrifice provides no explicit signal that it is reacting to the perverted sacrifice of tragedy. It hints indirectly, first through diction, when the slave uses vocabulary preferred by tragedy to describe the kind of sacrifice to be avoided. Such an ostentatious performance of ritual in a comedy which, before and after this scene, is as self-consciously concerned with parodying other genres as *Peace* is ought not to be overlooked when interpreting this scene. Tragedy, satyr play, dithyramb, epic and sympotic lyric are each appropriated in the course of *Peace*, a comedy driven by the creative engagement of other poetic forms. It cannot be assumed, therefore, that all such engagements will be explicit and direct.

Schechner's understanding of the relationship between ritual and theatre provides some context for understanding these performed rituals as a locus of competition between Aristophanes and tragedy. The transformation of real behaviour in the form of ritual into symbolic behaviour is at the core of drama, Schechner argues.[81] Such transformation has two fundamental types: either anti-social, violent or disruptive behaviour is displaced by ritualized gesture and display *or* characters who act out fictional events are invented or real events are fictionalized. The bottom line is that drama is in a dialectical relationship with ritual. All performances – ritual and theatrical – contain some amount of both social efficacy, which is the function of ritual, and entertainment; but one or the other is dominant in any given instance.

The comic sacrifice of *Peace* ostensibly acknowledges this dialectic between the real ritual and its social function and how that ritual is fictionalized onstage. In the devotedly panhellenic and anti-violent plot of this particular comedy, Aristophanes opportunistically critiques a significant aspect of the theatrical repertoire: sacrifice. Trygaeus's 'bloodless' sacrifice makes a pretence of restoring the social efficacy of fictionalized ritual (in drama) from the excesses of tragedy, from sacrifice as murder, into a non-violent act of commensality. Despite the poet's self-serving promotion of *trugôidia*, the bloodless sacrifice nonetheless acknowledges the social utility of this topic when represented in purely aesthetic terms.

Aristophanes' conscious departure from this culturally dominant representation of sacrifice as slaughter, his correction of tragedy's perverted ritual, amounts to a parody of a parody, albeit one performed offstage. For once, Aristophanes essentially plays tragedy straight, alluding to a legitimate properly performed act conducted in place of a distorted one. In normalizing the sacrificial trope, the poet serves *Peace*'s agenda of τρυγῳδία, converting tragedy's perverted sacrifices into controlled and concealed violence to reaffirm its original, functional purpose of communal cohesion. Amid all this onstage comic busyness, the concrete and stationary statue of Peace projected an attitude of permanence and stability hitherto missing from the spectacular violence plaguing the Greek world. Reified, immediate and even attractive, the new goddess reassured the imminence of the treaty desired for so long.

Comic marriage

Like Hesiod's Aphrodite (*Theog.* 201–202) rising from the ocean foam and flanked by her attendants, *Erôs* and *Himeros* ('Desire'), Aristophanes' Peace is pulled from her underground prison with her eroticized attendants *Theôria* and *Opôra*.[82] *Theôria*, 'Festival', is portrayed as a prostitute. In one of the many gestures toward theatricality scattered throughout *Peace*,[83] *Theôria* is handed over to the Athenian *boulê* (878) as represented by the theatre audience. Festival is the earliest extant representation of a term for which no precise modern equivalent exists,[84] but generally means attendance of sacred religious festivals at major panhellenic gatherings like Olympia, Delphi, Nemea and the Isthmus of Corinth, as well as events at smaller local and regional sanctuaries like Eleusis and Brauron.[85] Athenians and the citizens of nearby *poleis* undertook *theôriai* all over Attica.[86] *Theôroi* ('festival-goers') travelled either in an official capacity, i.e., as state representatives, or as private citizens, and participated in festival activities, whether ritual (i.e., sacrifice), athletic or poetic. In general, Aristophanes characterizes *theôria* more as an experience, the colloquial 'good times' (888), than the ritual observance of a complex institution.

Opôra, 'Harvest', however, is betrothed and married to Trygaeus himself in *Peace*'s climactic wedding procession. This procession expresses the transcendent quality of their sacred marriage. As the embodiment of vegetable and human fertility, Harvest enacts the long-awaited post-war recovery and transformation that *Peace* fetishizes and which is predicated on prosperity at both the human and agricultural levels. The marriage of Trygaeus, synecdochic hero and representative of the farming class, and 'the harvest' personified allegorizes the permanent reconnection of the hero and his supporters to the soil. The transformation of post-war society is structured through this wedding ritual. *Opôra* is identified with the soil at Peace's resurrection by Hermes' parody of the *enguê*, the contractual formula by which a male guardian betrothed a maiden to her new husband. Here it is comically rendered as '... you may take *Opôra* as your wife; and then set up a house with her in the countryside and make for yourself a cluster of grapes ...' (706–708).[87] The wedding feast completes a thorough economic reorganization of the polis through its guest list, which excludes the war-profiteers (1210–1264), whose wares Trygaeus either outright rejects (1221–1223) or insultingly refashions for various crude uses (1226–1264). Correlative with this economic change is a cultural or ethical shift represented by the replacement of martial poetry with the didactic and symposiastic kind for entertainment at the wedding feast: the heroic epic recitations of the son of Lamachus earn him an ejection from the celebration (1270–1297). By contrast, invitations are extended to the hero's peace-loving allies, sickle-makers, who supply their products as wedding gifts (1191–1209).[88]

The conflation of human and agricultural fertility culminates with the opening lines of the hymeneal, which directly equate Trygaeus's bride-to-be with fertility and life-giving agriculture:

Ὑμὴν Ὑμέναι᾽ ὤ.
Ὑμὴν Ὑμέναι᾽ ὤ.
ὦ τρὶς μάκαρ ὡς δικαί-
ως τἀγαθὰ νῦν ἔχεις.
Ὑμὴν Ὑμέναι᾽ ὤ.
Ὑμὴν Ὑμέναι᾽ ὤ.
τί δράσομεν αὐτήν;
τί δράσομεν αὐτήν;
τρυγήσομεν αὐτήν,
τρυγήσομεν αὐτήν.

Hymen, Hymenaios!
Hymen, Hymenaios!
Triple-blessed man,
well-deserved are your
luxuries!
What will we do to her?
What will we do to her?
We'll pick her crop!
We'll pick her crop!

Pax 1332–1340

The words and meter of the song communicate the transformative power of the marriage allegory as an agricultural windfall for Greece (πάλιν εἰς τὸν ἀγρὸν, 1318) and a golden age of plant and human production for all (τρυγήσομεν αὐτὴν, 1339). The imagery of the hymeneal is anticipated by the agricultural abundance of the second parabasis, with its ripening vines (1161–1163) and alternation of winter planting (1140–1158) and summer harvesting (1159–1171).[89] The comic wedding song concretizes typical hymeneal tropes, such as the comparison of the bride to fertile soil and its harvest in the chorus's declaration of its intention 'to pluck' (τρυγάω) the bride, a *double entendre* and obvious play on the hero's name.[90] The bridal pair's genitals are compared to figs (1351–1352),[91] big and ripe (μέγα καὶ παχύ) and sweet (ἡδύ), in a parody of the conventional praise comparing the bride to various plants.[92]

Though Trygaeus, as *Opôra*'s husband, is the explicit beneficiary of these blessings, *Peace* describes these rewards as benefitting all. For the marriage symbolizes a renewal of the Greeks' relationship to the land and their rural way of life. The couple is settled in the countryside by a choral escort in the *nymphagôgê*, which also returns their partisans – including the panhellenic chorus – to their rustic homes.[93] This rural golden-age simplicity is described as a collective flight from the crowded,[94] diseased and depraved city to an older, purer, better way of life in the countryside (εἰς τὸν ἀγρὸν, 1318).[95] The wedding thus frames a comic aetiology of this new era of perpetual spring, with liaisons of mortals and divinities,[96] and reverses the belligerent Iron Age of War. The hymeneal's intrinsically inclusive choral form,[97] the groom's repeated encouragements to the chorus to participate, and the latter's invitations to the audience create an optimal level of audience integration.[98] The permanent peacetime and agricultural prosperity of Trygaeus's marriage frees Greeks from the threats of enemy invasion, loss of their land and the hardships of poverty.

As with sacrifice, the generic self-consciousness of *Peace*'s comic marriage is every bit as important as its allegorical meaning. Because *erôs* in the (admittedly limited) extant evidence for Old Comedy is conceived in emphatically carnal and sexual terms, and often with little sense of legitimacy or permanence,[99] the legitimacy and permanence of Trygaeus's marriage are noteworthy. The positive terms of *Opôra*'s sexual transition as the embodiment of prosperous, life-sustaining, agricultural harvest supersedes the cultural conception of the maiden's transition to wife in Greek marriage as a form of death. The contemporary genre that especially emphasized this negative principle of marriage, specifically its potential for creating or reflecting destabilizing violence in the polis, was tragedy.[100] Seaford has shown that tragedy is intensely interested in the associations of marriage and death, particularly the 'profoundly anomic' failure of the maiden to complete the transition to wife, which it conveys in various ways.[101] Aeschylus's Clytemnestra envisions her revenge against Agamemnon as his wedding to his mistress, Cassandra, in death (*Ag.* 1440–1447). Sophocles' *Antigone* presents a marriage *in death* after the eponymous heroine and her betrothed each kill themselves in the tomb where she is imprisoned, which is itself likened to a bridal chamber (781–786).[102]

Often the death of a maiden just come to marriageable age occurs within the context of an actual or feigned wedding in tragedy. In Euripides' *Medea*, Jason's bride-to-be, Glauce, is incinerated by the robe and crown offered as deadly wedding gifts by Medea (1156–1202).[103] A faked marriage arrangement is critical to the deception of Euripides' *Iphigenia at Aulis*. Under the false pretence of marriage to Achilles, Iphigenia is lured to Aulis where she will be sacrificed. The wedding ritual's various stages are grimly parodied as the maiden is readied for death.[104] Tragic marriage, like perverted sacrifice, expresses or signals the self-destruction of the family and society.[105]

The lyrics of *Peace*'s hymeneal, by contrast, efface the negative associations of the destruction of the maiden and her body so problematic in tragedy's 'marriage to death'.[106] Unlike the violent couplings of tragedy, the marriage of Trygaeus and Harvest and the hero's return to his previous life as farmer are an auspicious and festive occasion and one of many positive outcomes in post-war Greece. Comedy restores the positive status of this social institution, but also dissolves tragedy's ritual antagonism between specific households and the polis, where ritual normality and social cohesion are sometimes restored with the foundation of a new civic cult resulting from the violent implosion of a heroic family.[107]

In sum, *Peace*'s second half shows that the 'old' things, which Trygaeus performs in fresh ways, can also include aspects of the theatrical repertoire of all three forms of drama, not just specific textual models. The first half's program of converting failure to success continues, but now with the reversal of parody. Properly performed sacrifice and marriage, two rituals with deep homologies,[108] reflect and facilitate the play's political and generic renewal of comedy's repertoire: by 'playing straight' tragedy's parodies of sacrifice and marriage, Aristophanes creates 'aesthetic distance' between his rituals and those of tragedy and challenges the latter's cultural prestige using some of its favourite tropes.

Conclusion

Peace marks a significant development in the strategy and perspective of *trugôidia* since *Acharnians* four years earlier. The concept moves beyond Dicaeopolis's use of tragedy for political agency and assumes a life of its own as the driving principle of *Peace*'s action. In *Peace*, parody and appropriation display comedy's poetic potency and agency by converting failure in other genres into its own success. This is most elegantly, if grotesquely, represented by the dung-beetle of the Bellerophontes parody rather than the traditional focus of this sequence, the hero. The beetle's amalgamation of different genres and relevant, popular content embodies the agency of *trugôidia* and its very biology is analogous to comedy's creation of poetic success from other genres' failure. Much like its rider, who makes 'old' things new again, the dung-beetle's mode of life – the consumption of dung – is a metaphor for *trugôidia*'s appropriation of old and used-up material from its natural competitors. The beetle's transgression of the upper air above the stage challenges tragedy's conception of the cosmos in perhaps the most immediate expression of comedy's aspiration to tragedy's revered status.

Insofar as it rejects tragedy's organization of the world, Trygaeus's use of the crane to cross the conventional boundaries of mortal travel in tragic theatre anticipates the intergeneric spirit of *Peace*'s second half. Moreover, the co-operative panhellenic virtues displayed in the hauling-scene, which has already been treated in Chapter 3, establish the egalitarian values of the second half's renewal of the traditional institutions of sacrifice and marriage. Aristophanes' focus on these institutions signifies a shift (or evolution) in his strategy of intergeneric engagement from the direct confrontation of performative rivals to indirect challenges to tragedy through a pair of its own parodies, the popular *topoi* of perverted sacrifice and marriage. By renewing the positive connotations of these fundamental rituals and challenging tragedy's dominant cultural narrative of corrupted sacrifices and weddings, Aristophanes demonstrates comedy's potential to efface tragedy's popular representation of these practices. Trygaeus's sacrifice and wedding are rare occasions where Old Comedy is not the genre doing the parodying but rather playing things 'straight' and reversing the parody of a rival text. In place of tragedy's perverted sacrifices, the bloodless sacrifice to install Peace's cult promotes ideas of communal solidarity and peaceful reconciliation which anthropological thought has identified as the established traditional intent of this hallowed practice. The simultaneous renewal of city and household symbolized in the comic wedding typifies comedy's attempt to have things both ways. While a return to health for the polis in tragedy can require the destruction of an elite household, comedy's restoration of both spheres of Greek life presents them rather as complementary. Trygaeus's marriage, which structures the social, economic and political reorganization of post-war society's recovery, expresses the joy, security and hope of a future world at peace. It may have captured the high hopes that Greeks placed in the Peace of Nicias as a long-term solution to the ubiquitous total war that afflicted the fifth century.[109]

The pervasive panhellenism of *Peace*'s cross-generic program, especially in the second half, is symptomatic of its historical context. Dover describes best how this must have determined its final shape: 'Trygaeus is not the mouthpiece of a far-sighted minority lamenting the continuation of an apparently unending war, but a man who performs on a level of comic fantasy a task to which the Athenian people had already addressed itself on the mundane level ... [and this] made the play more of a celebration than a protest.'[110] Aristophanes' task in 421 BCE became much less a question of devising a plot of pure comic wish-fulfilment than of furnishing an aetiological account to explain the recent turn of events, which must have seemed nothing short of miraculous after ten years of war. The innovation and experimentation of *Peace* could thus be said to parallel, at a literary level, the welcome, if short-lived, changes taking place in the Greek world at large.

Old Comedy and Lyric Poetry

Introduction

The potential rewards of studying comedy's parody of lyric are greater than ever given the robust growth in scholarship on various aspects of ancient Greek 'song culture' and Greek drama's interest in it.[1] Most work on the latter topic focuses on tragedy, whose structural and metrical flexibility allows it to adopt genres as various as dirge, hymn, heroic, epinician, hymeneal, curse and others.[2] However, lyric and tragedy's natural overlap in style and even theme, as well as the inherent challenges of defining lyric in terms of genre, poses particular hermeneutic challenges to articulating the precise effect of lyric in the songs of tragic drama.[3] Fifth-century comedy does not have this problem – or at least not to the extent that tragedy does – since high-register poetry always stands out within its popular idiom.

This chapter focuses on allusions to and appropriations of lyric in fifth-century comedy, but its approach differs somewhat from that of the previous chapters. The patchy nature of the evidence requires that I shift my focus frequently between the different genres of lyric and between fragmentary and complete texts. Moreover, my primary interest is in the response of Old Comedy as a whole rather than any single poet or play. I argue that Old Comedy primarily evokes lyric to position itself against a specific kind of music, the so-called New Music, mainly for the purpose of characterizing itself as a defender of tradition, specifically of 'classic' forms of lyric poetry.[4] Comic poets parody the highly innovative and popular musicians of contemporary lyric as excessive and self-indulgent, but also as harmful and pernicious to Athenian norms, especially in morality and politics. Worst of all, the wild popularity of artists like Timotheus, Cinesias, Philoxenus and others throughout the Greek world allegedly threatens the cultural status and preservation of Pindar, Simonides and others who have (allegedly) fallen out of popular favour.

As a formal element of fifth-century comedy,[5] lyric has been amply studied: in the affiliation of *iambos* and comedy's satirical posture and invective,[6] in the biographical content of the parabasis,[7] and in the multiple categories of comic allusion to lyric, among other topics.[8] The comedians exploit the cultural prestige of lyric genres with which audiences were apparently very familiar, judging by the sheer volume of lyric tropes found in tragedy.[9] Although not in direct competition with lyric poets in quite the same way as it is with tragic poets, Old Comedy makes contemporary music central to its self-definition in the poetic marketplace of Athens, which was everywhere dominated by the performance of lyric in the latter half of the fifth century BCE. Unlike drama, lyric poetry was performed in multiple settings and on multiple occasions both inside the festivals of Dionysus and elsewhere in Attica and the larger Greek world.

Although the New Musicians were demonstrably innovative and exerted considerable influence over musical practice in the concert hall and on the stage, especially in tragedy, Old Comedy exaggerates and distorts its innovations and their effects on the ethics and politics of Athenian society so as to better promote itself as a saviour or protector of culture. To repeat, I do not deny that the New Music was unquestionably innovative. But in claiming innovation self-consciously and distinguishing themselves from more conservative predecessors and their styles, Timotheus, Cinesias, Philoxenus and other artists of the movement were, at least in this sense, not much different from the previous generation of poets, who had themselves made similar claims.[10] The comic poets are a major source of the specific criticism that, as LeVen has described it, 'depicts the late fifth-century New Music as *the* New Music revolution, when in fact it was only the latest, and best documented, in a series of revolutions'.[11] As it was wont to do, Old Comedy exaggerated and distorted the scope and ethics of New Music's innovations, implicating its style and popular appeal in the degeneration and corruption of the aesthetic, ethical and social health of Athens. Aristophanes and his comic peers couch their criticisms in an idiom of moral transgression, 'filtering' the lyric corpus of this transitional period between the song culture of the Archaic poets and the book culture of the later Hellenistic period, as part of an effort to brand Old Comedy as a defender of tradition and the privileged status of Pindar and others.[12] In an era when the preservation and survival of poetry was largely contingent on reperformance, there was legitimate concern that declining public interest in Archaic lyric could consign it to oblivion. Although comedy's concern that the New Music's popularity threatened to efface cultural memory of the superior lyric tradition of the past was perhaps merited, its apparent exaggeration of the social and political threat of the movement enables individual poets to position their own ostensibly traditional style and morally edifying content more favourably before an impressionable Athenian public. Old Comedy's conservative turn at these moments is deliciously ironic given its artists' constant, self-promoting and formulaic efforts to style *themselves* as poetic innovators whose pioneering ideas frequently pass unappreciated by the Athenian public.

The first section of this chapter examines a handful of citations and allusions to classic lyric by poets probably dead by the last quarter of the fifth century.[13] Because Stesichorus, Pindar or Simonides represent a bygone age of a panhellenic Athens before the radical democracy, their decline in popular favour is construed as a decline in Athenian poetics and politics.[14] Moreover, the stylistic and moral transgressions of contemporary (late-classical) lyric represent much of the poetic and political corruption of the present.[15] Parodies reflective of the aesthetic and cultural innovations of the New Musicians are the topic of the middle portion of this chapter (Section II).[16] Such innovations are pilloried for divesting song of its religious and social function and reducing it to mere entertainment. This divorce of song from context facilitated the creation of hybrid generic forms, which inspired the poets' intensive self-promotion.[17] Much like the comic poets' own strategic branding, contemporary lyric advertised itself with explicit commentary and in more indirect ways, such as virtuoso combinations of sound and gesture. This may explain why Old Comedy viewed musicians as rivals for public prestige, especially given lyric's clear influence on the choral and monodic lyric of tragedy – especially Euripides – Aristophanes' primary rival. I analyse several comic parodies of the structural, acoustic and mimetic dimensions of tragedy's lyric under the influence of New Music that reflect the standard conservative criticisms of innovation, i.e., excessive emphasis on musical virtuosity over dramatic *logos* and the confusion of distinct aesthetic categories. Such criticisms are concretized in the confusions of gender in both the song and body of Agathon in Aristophanes' parody of his hymn (*Thesm.* 101–129). The famous deconstruction of Euripidean choral lyric in Aristophanes' *Frogs* (1309–1322) imputes to Euripides a love of New Music commonplaces and of virtuosity over dramatic *logos* and coherence: human and animal worlds are conflated and 'democratized' with the parlous and demotic outlook of Euripidean style explored in Chapter 1.

The final section (Section III) treats Aristophanes' parody of a key development of late fifth-century tragedy and particular tendency of Euripides, the growth of actors' songs and their encroachment on the prestige of the chorus. Aristophanes' send-ups of the Andromeda monody in *Thesmophoriazusae* (1015–1055) and the peasant's lament for her rooster in *Frogs* (1331–1363) exaggerate the stylistic and rhythmic features, over-the-top emotiveness, and popularizing realism of the New Music that, as conservative critics suggest, corrupted the tragic art. Inlaw's 'marketplace monody' travesties these collocations of emotional outpouring and popular, demotic content by substituting characters of the *agora* for exotic figures of myth, as does the lament for the rooster of *Frogs* (*Ran.* 1331–1363), which combines low-class banality and domestic scandal.

Innovation results in change and cultural loss.[18] The preservation of 'classical' musical and poetic works for posterity was only assured by their reperformance in large-scale public and official occasions first established in the sixth century BCE.[19] With the wild popularity of poets such as Phrynis, Cinesias, Timotheus and Philoxenus, 'old-fashioned' poets such as Pindar presumably risked being gradually squeezed out of public and private performance. The poor survival of the enormous corpus of lyric that had been publicly performed starting in the seventh century seemingly attests to the difficulties of preservation in a society where literacy was not common. The comic poets seized the opportunity of this (alleged) cultural crisis to portray themselves as the defenders of traditional lyric and culture, resisting New Music's allegedly pernicious influence and triggering of widespread cultural amnesia.[20]

I. The decline of 'classic lyric'

A good starting point for understanding Old Comedy's attitude to lyric of the past and present is a fragment of Eupolis, one of Athens's most prominent comic poets alongside Cratinus and Aristophanes. In fr. 148, currently ascribed to his *Heilôtes* (*Helots*),[21] a character says:

> τὰ Στησιχόρου τε καὶ Ἀλκμᾶνος Σιμωνίδου τε
> ἀρχαῖον ἀείδειν, ὁ δὲ Γνήσιππος ἔστ᾽ ἀκούειν.
> κεῖνος νυκτερίν᾽ ηὗρε μοιχοῖς ἀείσματ᾽ ἐκκαλεῖσθαι
> γυναῖκας ἔχοντας ἰαμβύκην τε καὶ τρίγωνον.

> It's old-fashioned to sing Stesichorus and Alcman
> and Simonides. But now one only hears Gnesippos.
> That guy invented nocturnal songs for adulterers to
> entice women outside with the *iambykê* and *trigônon*.

> Eup. fr. 148

Meter and content suggest that the fragment belongs to a parabatic address to the audience. For reasons unclear, the comedy's chorus laments the fact that celebrated lyric poets such as the Sicilian Stesichorus, the Spartan Alcman and the Cean Simonides are regarded as 'old-fashioned' (ἀρχαῖον), while poetically and morally bankrupt artists like Gnesippus are celebrated.[22] Since the term ἀρχαῖος is pejorative in Old Comedy and suggests something outdated and irrelevant, Stesichorus, Alcman and Simonides clearly represent both musical excellence and an earlier and putatively idealized panhellenic era, which has devolved into a musically and ethically debased present. The speaker's conflation of contemporary musical innovation and moral decline and even sexual perversity is typical of the conservative criticisms of music by Old Comedy and Plato,[23] who implicate fashionably radical styles of art with analogous, pernicious 'innovations' in culture and society.[24]

An illustration of the New Music's transgressive and pernicious influence in action is found in Aristophanes' *Clouds* (423–418 BCE). When explaining how his son, Pheidippides, came to assault him, the conservative but unscrupulous Strepsiades explains that he urged his boy to take up the lyre and sing some Simonides at a small symposium in celebration of his graduation from the Socratic *Phrontistêrion*. Pheidippides not only boldly refuses this request of a citharodic performance: he dismissively belittles it as old-fashioned (ἀρχαῖον) and derisively compares it to a woman 'hulling barley' (κάχρυς...ἀλοῦσαν, *Nub.* 1358), i.e., ponderous and monotonous like a work song.[25] The song in question, 'How 'the Ram' was shorn', memorialized the humiliation or 'shearing' of an Aeginetan aristocrat and Medizer (491 BCE) named Crius ('Ram'), who was held in captivity by the Athenians. Rawles has explained Strepsiades' natural affinities for this piece's Athenian chauvinism, which recalled the past glories of Athens around the time of the Persian Wars.[26] So, both the author and the overtly conservative ideology of 'How 'the Ram' was shorn' establish its classic status and appeal for conservative Athenians nostalgic for an older, more aristocratic Athens.

Pheidippides' rejection of both the aesthetics and political ideology of Simonidean poetry is meant to reveal the extent of his corruption by the intellectual innovations of the Socratics, as does his subsequent preference for a *rhêsis* from the *Aeolus* of Euripides, tragedy's most well-known proponent of the New Music. The *rhêsis* in question is a notorious defence of incest by the mythological youth, Macareus, who fell in passionate love with and impregnated his own sister. It thus exemplifies the amorality imputed to the New Music. The ensuing dispute between father and son illustrates the ethically and socially destabilizing values of contemporary drama and music more provocatively than Eupolis fr. 148. Pheidippides' musical tastes prompt his father's overdue recognition of the severity of the threat to ethical and social order posed by sophistic education and Socrates. An often overlooked aspect of this scene is that the diminished status of Simonides and Aeschylus is precisely a consequence of the growing popularity of the fashionable poetics of the New Music.

Both Eupolis and Aristophanes suggest that rejection of these celebrated poets is tantamount to the rejection of the older, poetically and politically superior Athens of the Persian Wars. Even when it is ironic, the recollection of these poets in Aristophanic comedy is frequently coloured with nostalgia for that earlier era – for example, in the sole Aristophanic citation of classic dithyramb from the parabasis of *Acharnians*.[27] Speaking through the chorus, Aristophanes demands public gratitude for the didacticism of his 'trugedic' choruses, which prevented the *dêmos*'s deception (ἐξαπατᾶσθαι) by the self-serving appeals and flattery (θωπευομένους) of representatives from foreign states:

πρότερον δ' ὑμᾶς ἀπὸ τῶν πόλεων οἱ πρέσβεις ἐξαπατῶντες
πρῶτον μὲν 'ἰοστεφάνους' ἐκάλουν· κἀπειδὴ τοῦτό τις εἴποι,
εὐθὺς διὰ τοὺς στεφάνους ἐπ' ἄκρων τῶν πυγιδίων ἐκάθησθε.
εἰ δέ τις ὑμᾶς ὑποθωπεύσας 'λιπαρὰς' καλέσειεν 'Ἀθήνας',
ηὕρετο πᾶν ἂν διὰ τὰς 'λιπαράς', ἀφύων τιμὴν περιάψας.

Before ambassadors from the allies deceived you, first calling
you 'violet crowned'. And whenever anyone says this you
immediately sit up on the tips of your butt, because of the crown
part. And if someone flattering should call you 'sleek Athens',
he would get everything, because of the 'sleek' part, praising you
with an honour fit for sardines.

Ach. 636–640

The phrase αἱ λιπαραὶ καὶ ἰοστεφάνοι Ἀθῆναι alludes to a famous and well-received dithyramb of Pindar honouring Athens.[28] Pindar addressed the honorands as ὦ ταὶ λιπαραὶ ἰοστέφανοι καὶ ἀοίδιμοι, / Ἑλλάδος ἔρεισμα, κλειναὶ Ἀθᾶναι, δαιμόνιον πτολίεθρον (fr. 76) in commemoration of Athens's naval victory at Artemisium, one of several achievements upon which Athenians constructed their identity as defenders of Greek liberty against the barbarians:[29] ὅθι παῖδες Ἀθαναίων ἐβάλοντο φαενάν / κρηπῖδ' ἐλευθερίας, 'when the sons of the Athenians laid the shining foundation of freedom' (fr. 77). The quoted epithets exemplify the high register of civic lyric that commemorates the city and is now appropriated by outsiders seeking to exploit Athenians' collective memory of their achievement and the exceptional status and goodwill they previously enjoyed among fellow Greeks.[30]

The same epithets used to describe an older and putatively nobler Athens in *Acharnians* are again ironically deployed to characterize a new and improved Athenian *dêmos* in the following year's *Knights* (424 BCE): 'Demos', the people personified as a crotchety Athenian householder, is returned to his former glorious self, the 'violet-crowned' (ἰοστεφάνοις) version 'of old' (ἀρχαίαισιν). Greeted by the chorus in Pindaric fashion as ὦ ταὶ λιπαραὶ καὶ ἰοστέφανοι καὶ ἀριζήλωται Ἀθῆναι (1329), Demos dons the golden-cricket brooch of his old costume, smelling of treaties and worthy of his trophy of Marathon (1331–1334). However, only moments earlier the new Demos admitted to being the same dysfunctional Demos of recent decades (1121–1130). So the lyric tropes that ostensibly herald old Demos's renewal are probably as ironic as those deployed in the parabasis of *Acharnians*. Much like the previous examples of Eupolis and *Clouds*, the classic lyrical associations of 'sleek' and 'violet-crowned' Athens are evoked as a measure of present decline.

Aristophanes seemingly attempts to show this decline of classical lyric in Athens from a different and perhaps more sympathetic perspective when introducing an itinerant bard of old lyric in *Birds* (414 BCE). One of the series of intruders who continually interrupt Peisetaerus's performance of a foundation sacrifice for Cloudcuckooland is a dithyrambist seeking patronage:

Πο. Νεφελοκοκκυγίαν   905
τὰν εὐδαίμονα κλῇσον, ὦ
Μοῦσα, τεαῖς ἐν ὕμνων
ἀοιδαῖς.
Πε. τουτὶ τὸ πρᾶγμα ποδαπόν; εἰπέ μοι, τίς εἶ;
Πο. ἐγὼ μελιγλώσσων ἐπέων ἰεὶς ἀοιδὰν
Μουσάων θεράπων ὀτρη-
ρός, κατὰ τὸν Ὅμηρον.
Πε. ἔπειτα δῆτα δοῦλος ὢν κόμην ἔχεις;
Πο. οὔκ, ἀλλὰ πάντες ἐσμὲν οἱ διδάσκαλοι
Μουσάων θεράποντες ὀτρη-
ροί, κατὰ τὸν Ὅμηρον.
Πε. οὐκ ἐτὸς ὀτρηρὸν καὶ τὸ ληδάριον ἔχεις.   915
ἀτάρ, ὦ ποιητά, κατὰ τί δεῦρ' ἀνεφθάρης;
Πο. μέλη πεποίηκ' εἰς τὰς Νεφελοκοκκυγίας
τὰς ἡμετέρας κύκλιά τε πολλὰ καὶ καλὰ
καὶ παρθένεια καὶ κατὰ τὰ Σιμωνίδου.

Πε. ταυτὶ σὺ πότ᾽ ἐποίησας; ἀπὸ ποίου χρόνου;

Πο. πάλαι πάλαι δὴ τήνδ᾽ ἐγὼ κλῄζω πόλιν.

Πε. οὐκ ἄρτι θύω τὴν δεκάτην ταύτης ἐγώ,

καὶ τοὔνομ᾽ ὥσπερ παιδίῳ νῦν δὴ ᾽θέμην;

Πο. ἀλλά τις ὠκεῖα Μουσάων φάτις

οἷάπερ ἵππων ἀμαρυγά.   925

σὺ δὲ πάτερ, κτίστορ Αἴτνας,

ζαθέων ἱερῶν ὁμώνυμε,

δὸς ἐμὶν ὅ τι περ τεᾷ κεφαλᾷ θέλῃς

πρόφρων δόμεν {ἐμὶν τεῖν}.

Po: Celebrate blessed *Nephelokokkugia* in your songs   905
of hymns, Muse!

Pe: Where'd this business come from? Who are you?!

Po: A devoted servant of the Muses, expounding song
of honey-sweet words, to quote Homer.

Pe: So, are you a slave? I see long hair …

Po: No, but we professionals are eager vassals of
the Muses, to quote Homer.

Pe: No wonder your outfit is meagre.
Really, Poet, why have you come here!?   915

Po: I've made songs for your *Nephelokokkugia*,
dithyrambs numerous and fair, Partheneia, and numbers
à la Simonides.

Pe: When did you write these? Starting when?

Po: I praised this city a long, long time ago.

Pe: But I only just now began its tenth-day sacrifice,
and named it just like a baby!

Po: A swift voice of the Muses,
like the flashing of horses.   925
And you, father, founder of Etna,
namesake of the holy rites,
give to us whatever you are willing to grant by your nod.

Av. 905–930

The comic mechanism juxtaposes the pretentious but inept Pindarist and the
short-tempered and practical man-bird hero. In dactylo-epitrites mixed with
lines of Aeolic and iambic trimeter,[31] the dithyrambist speaks in a pastiche of
Doric forms (τεαῖς, 907), epic and lyric diction (Μουσάων θεράπων, 911),[32] lyric
phraseology and two citations of Pindar.[33] Σ 926 identifies the source of lines
926–930 as a Pindaric *hyporchêma* (fr. 105a), i.e., song accompanied by lively

dancing, in honour of Hieron I, tyrant of Sicily, on the occasion of his foundation of Etna (476/475 BCE). The poetaster revises Pindar by deferring his famous opening line (σύνες ὅ τοι λέγω, 'mark what I say') all the way down to line 945, (see below), reversing lines 2–3, and making a few other minor alterations.[34]

The hack poet's poverty seems to imply that classic lyric is so unpopular in the present, so ἀρχαῖος, that only the most destitute and desperate will turn to it to earn their livelihood. This inept bard's proposed foundation song for a city still being founded is an awkward pastiche of different models from an absurd repertoire (e.g., κύκλια, dithyrambs; παρθένεια, maiden songs; and Simonidean compositions). However, he still earns a slave's vest (σπολάς) and cloak (χιτών) for his troubles, not the standard beating meted out to other intruders by comic heroes. The popularity of contemporary lyric has reduced formerly great lyric and its artists – men like Ibycus, Anacreon, Simonides, Pindar and Bacchylides – to impoverished buffoons and parasites.[35] The poet's second request to Peisetaerus (*Av.* 941–945), which he describes as a 'Pindaric saying' (τεᾷ φρενὶ μάθε Πινδάρειον ἔπος, 939), may put a finer point on this marginalization. The Pindarist begs for a cloak (τὸν χιτωνίσκον) by comparing himself to an outcast Scythian nomad, who is similarly marginalized from his tribe for lacking a cloak. Although the context of Pindar's ethnographic observation on the Scythians in the original is unknown,[36] thanks to Herodotus (Hdt. 4.1–142) we know the Greeks saw Scythian culture as completely antithetical to their own, in part because of its nomadic existence.[37] This ethnographic subtext that emphasizes the poet's social marginalization may be underscoring the cultural marginalization of the poet's craft, classic dithyramb, in the age of the New Music.[38] This context makes Peisetairus's modest patronage of the bard that much more noteworthy.

While I lack the space to explore additional citations of classic lyric in Old Comedy's corpus,[39] the previous examples are sufficient to show that the comic poets invoke so-called classic lyric poets to illustrate the poetic, moral and social decline of the present. This insight is not especially new. What is new, rather, is my argument that a significant aim of Old Comedy's satirical critique of the New Music for its contribution to the decline and loss of this essential poetry is the projection of itself as a defender of tradition. As I have made clear, this is not to claim that the innovation of this movement was a fiction concocted by comedy. This music was innovative, but the comic poets – as they do – distort and misrepresent that innovation for their own aggrandizement. In the case of the dithyrambist, his incompetence is both funny and indicative of the decline of popular interest in and preservation of poets such as Pindar. In the next section

I will contrast this reasonably favourable portrayal of the poet, who is at most a benign nuisance, with the violent hostility shown Cinesias, a representative of the New Music.

II. The New Music and Greek tragedy

Innovation and self-promotion

Direct portrayal of poets of the New Music is less common than one might imagine given the movement's popularity, although parodies that do survive present its musical innovation in the social and ethical terms previously described. A few hundred lines after the Pindaric poet exits from *Birds*, the Athenian citharode Cinesias (active *c.* 425–390 BCE) enters as an intruder in search of the wings given to new citizens of Cloudcuckooland. Nothing of Cinesias's work survives apart from some testimonia and the title of a single *nome*.[40] Old Comedy several times attacks his poetry and frail, sickly appearance.[41] While the present parody (*Av.* 1372–1404) targets Cinesias's preference for some of the same features mocked in the Pindaric poet's work – bold compounds, redundant accumulation of adjectives and associations with 'airiness'[42] – his aspirations are much less benign than the dithyrambist's. His obsessive fantasy of flying over the sea,[43] his aggressive assertion and his egotistical solo performance of what is normally a circular dance reveal a kind of hubristic φιλονικία.[44] His self-aggrandizing desire to master aerial space is especially transgressive in the colonial context of the play. Cinesias describes his flight using the vocabulary of innovation: to traverse the air, walk on winds and cleave the air. His errant paths appear to allegorize the narrative, metrical and syntactic unpredictability, and privileging of music over sense or *logos*, which critics imputed to the New Music.[45] These airy 'paths of song' can be contrasted with the pedestrian wanderings of the Pindaric poet.

Elsewhere Cinesias's musical transgressions are measured according to the smaller scale of the human body. A fragment from the *Cheiron* (*c.* 415 BCE)[46] by Aristophanes' elder rival, Pherecrates,[47] introduces *Mousikê* ('Music') personified and 'in the dress of a woman whose whole person has been brutally mauled'.[48] In fr. 155 *Mousikê* explains her mistreatment at the hands of several prominent contemporary musicians to a personified *Dikaiosynê* ('Justice'). Degrading, abusive and unnatural sex (or rape) suffered by *Mousikê* is the conceptual vehicle through which Pherecrates graphically satirized his musical innovation.

Mousikê's evils began when the Melian dithyrambist Melanippides (active 440–415) 'stretched' (ἀνῆκέ) and 'loosened her up' (χαλαρωτέραν) with a dozen strings.[49] He was still better than her next lover, Cinesias:

Μο. Κινησίας δέ <μ᾿> ὁ κατάρατος ᾿Αττικός,
ἐξαρμονίους καμπὰς ποιῶν ἐν ταῖς στροφαῖς
ἀπολώλεχ᾿ οὕτως, ὥστε τῆς ποιήσεως   10
τῶν διθυράμβων, καθάπερ ἐν ταῖς ἀσπίσιν,
ἀριστέρ᾿ αὐτοῦ φαίνεται τὰ δεξιά.
ἀλλ᾿ οὖν ἀνεκτὸς οὗτος ἦν ὅμως ἐμοί.

Mu: Kinesias, that damned Athenian,
making exharmonic bendings in my strophes,
wrecked me so much that the right side of his dithyrambs   10
appeared to be the left, as if reflected in a shield.
Yet nevertheless this man was endurable to me.

Pherecrates fr. 155.8–13

Cinesias 'destroyed completely' (ἀπολώλεχ᾿ οὕτως) *Mousikê* by introducing dissonant modes (καμπὰς, 'bendings,' i.e., modulations)[50] into his dithyrambs and reversing the strophes like reflections in a polished shield. *Mousikê*'s next assailant, Phrynis, a Mytilenean citharode who triumphed in the dithyrambic competition of the Panathenaea of 446 BCE, shoved into *Mousikê* a στρόβιλον, i.e. a 'whirlwind'. This may refer to a flurry of notes at different scales.[51] Such rapid modulations in mid-performance violently bend and twist (κάμπτων με καὶ στρέφων) *Mousikê* in every which way.[52] Finally, Timotheus of Miletus, in this fragment described as a rapist, took hold of *Mousikê* when she was out walking alone, dug in (κατορώρυχε), and ground her down (διακέκναικ᾿) shamefully.

Although Pherecrates provides a minimum of corporeal specificity, the self-indulgent and self-conscious musical innovations of Cinesias (and his peers) correspond to (allegedly) deplorably sensuous and erotic rhythms, innovation in modes and meters, physical alterations to instruments to achieve these innovations, and a self-aggrandizing virtuosity. The violation of *Mousikê* also seemingly alludes to the New Music's penchant for mixing (κεραννύντες) previously fixed and even antithetical modes, genres and sounds, i.e., manly (i.e., Dorian) and effeminate (i.e., Phrygian) scales.[53] Fr. 155 represents the dismantling of musical hierarchies that appealed to popular tastes (Pl. *Leg.* 700e)[54] – sound over *logos* and musician over actors and chorus – as a violation of sexual mores and the female body.[55]

Birds 1372–1404 and Pherecrates fr. 155 satirize the New Music's provocative innovation and disregard for musical and poetic convention with macro- and microcosmic metaphors that stress its social and ethical corruption. These imaginative parodies utilize the language of metaphor to suggest and humorously exaggerate many of the same critiques levelled directly by other opponents of the New Music. Plato, for example, blames the *polychordia* of the New Music for corrupting an earlier, superior era of pre-democratic political and artistic simplicity (*oligochordia*) and order, when the *dêmos* obeyed the *nomoi* (*Leg.* 699c, 700a–701d) and before the victories in the Persian Wars made them arrogant and intent on extreme freedom in all things (699e), music included.[56] In implicating the poetic movement in Athens's moral, social and political decline, Plato was perhaps influenced by the comic poets' hostility to the New Music's encroachment upon the status of classic lyric and the pernicious effects of its innovation: adultery, parricide, hubris, sexual perversion and the excesses of radical democracy. These cultural and political consequences of the New Music help us better understand Old Comedy's reaction to the same lyrical developments in tragedy.

Hymn in tragedy: Little oxen and manly shouts

Parody of choral lyric embedded in tragedy appeals to audiences differently from the allusions to classic lyric surveyed earlier. Its deconstruction of lyric style appeals more directly to spectators' accumulated experience of theatre, i.e., their expectations of a poet's style and personality. The parodies of the present section may reflect comedy's view of what genres were most familiar to spectators: hymn, prayer and choral ode. Exposure to the lyric repertoires of Athenian public and private cult over the course of their lives increased the likelihood that audiences might easily recognize parodies of hymn and prayer. Moreover, many in Aristophanes' audiences would have seen the choral lyric of leading poets like Euripides and Agathon in performance.

Hymns are a common part of the dramatic repertoire of fifth-century drama and in fact comprise the most common kind of lyric in comedy.[57] While defining hymn has proven challenging given the inconsistencies of the ancient sources themselves,[58] this study defines it as a song addressed to a divinity or divinities with greater formality than a prayer but sufficiently flexible to accommodate other related forms such as paean, dithyramb and prosodion. Full-length hymns are recognizably tripartite in structure, with *invocation*, *argument* and finally *petition*.[59] Major poetic forms like epic and drama shape the recognizable formulae of such prayers and hymns to their specific needs.[60]

The most extensive parody of hymn in extant Old Comedy is the Hymn to Apollo (101–129) in Aristophanes' *Thesmophoriazusae* (411 BCE) by the effeminate and pompous tragedian Agathon. The parody belongs to the same scene in which Inlaw threatened Agathon with rape. Euripides and Inlaw appear before Agathon's house in search of help to avert the plot against the poet.[61] Agathon emerges and performs a hymnic amoebaean exchange between an *exarchos* and a chorus of maidens:

Αγ. ἱερὰν Χθονίαιν
δεξάμεναι λαμπάδα, κοῦραι, ξὺν ἐλευθέρᾳ
πραπίδι χορεύσασθε βοάν.
– τίνι δαιμόνων ὁ κῶμος;
λέγε νιν· εὐπείστως δὲ τοὐμὸν
δαίμονας ἔχει σεβίσαι.
– ἄγε νῦν ὄλβιζε Μούσᾳ
χρυσέων ῥύτορα τόξων
Φοῖβον, ὃς ἱδρύσατο χώρας
γύαλα Σιμουντίδι γᾷ.   110
– χαῖρε καλλίσταις ἀοιδαῖς
Φοῖβ', ἐν εὐμούσοισι τιμαῖς
γέρας ἱερὸν προφέρων.
– τάν τ' ἐν ὄρεσι δρυογόνοισιν
κόραν ἀείσατ' Ἄρτεμιν ἀγροτέραν.
– ἕπομαι κλήζουσα σεμνὰν
γόνον ὀλβίαν τε Λατοῦς
Ἄρτεμιν ἀπειρολεχῆ.
– Λατώ τε κρούματά τ' Ἀσιάδος   120
ποδὶ παράρυθμ' εὔρυθμα Φρυγίων
διὰ νεύματα Χαρίτων.
– σέβομαι Λατώ τ' ἄνασσαν
κίθαρίν τε ματέρ' ὕμνων
ἄρσενι βοᾷ δόκιμον,
τᾷ φάος ἔσσυτο δαιμονίοις
ὄμμασιν, ἁμετέρας τε δι' αἰφνιδίου ὀπός. ὧν χάριν
ἄνακτ' ἀγάλλετε Φοῖβον.
χαῖρ', ὄλβιε παῖ Λατοῦς.

Ag: Welcome, maidens, the sacred torch of
the Two Chthonic goddesses and dance a
shout with liberated heart.
– For which god is our *komos*?

Tell us his name: I am ready to
revere the gods.
– Come, with the Muse give
joy to Phoebus, stretcher of the
golden bow, who founded the
hollows of the country in the
land of the Simoeis.
– In such beautiful songs, rejoice, Phoebus,
extolling this sacred prize in well-disposed honours.
– Hymn also the wild maiden Artemis
on oak-birthing hills.
– I follow praising, blessing
the solemn offspring and blessing of Leto,
virgin Artemis.
– And Leto the beating of the Asian land,
keeping time with the dance against the
rhythm, by the nods of the Phrygian graces.
– I revere mistress Leto and the cithara,
mother of hymns, esteemed in her manly shout,
by which, and by our sudden voice, the light has
shone in divine eyes. For this, exalt lord Phoebus.
Rejoice, blessed son of Leto.

Thesm. 101–129

The song's hymnic and devotional orientation is evident from the petition (χορεύσασθε, 103), vocative address (112), χαῖρε (111, 129), relative clause (109), epithets (ἀγροτέραν, 115; ἄνασσαν, 123) and multiple hymnic verbs.[62] New Music features of the song include a chorus of foreign females, 'projection' of choral song, music and dance, lavish descriptions of music and instruments (e.g., κίθαρις), expression of heightened emotion, emphasis on sound over sense, and mention of divinities from the Dionysiac sphere.[63] The 'hollows' (γύαλα) of the land of Simoeis (110) and the Phrygian Graces (121) identify the setting and female chorus as Trojan, and the chorus's thanks for the salvation of their city (102–103) refers to the Trojans' mistaken impression of the Greeks' false departure from Ilium and eventual discovery of the horse.[64]

This subtle parody is only just perceptible at the linguistic level. The greater part of its effect was the androgynous appearance of the singer himself, which was seemingly complemented by the shifting gender of the hymn's perspective.[65] Agathon's subsequent identification with classic Ionic poets and Inlaw's confused reaction to his appearance indicate that he was dressed androgynously,[66] donning the pale beardless mask of stage femininity and something akin to the female wardrobe he later bequeaths to Inlaw (219–265),[67] but without comic phallus (142).[68] The song corroborates this gender mixing: it is καλλίσταις in an eastern style (κρούματα…Ἀσιάδος / ποδὶ παράρυθμ᾽ εὔρυθμα Φρυγίων) and its cithara is the 'mother of hymns' (ματέρ᾽ ὕμνων).[69] His vocal shifts between the roles of male *exarchos* and maiden chorus, his Ionic rhythms and the possibly high and feminized pitch of his delivery in falsetto (cf. the feminine lyre's 'manly shout', 125) parallel his hybrid appearance.[70]

Agathon's song stands out from most other parodied lyric of Old Comedy by the unexpectedly tragic consequences it anticipates.[71] Though the hymn prefaces the humorous outcome of Euripides' misguided plan to infiltrate the Thesmophoria, the effect of its juxtaposition of hymnic thanksgiving and the impending catastrophe of Inlaw's foolish impiety is quasi-tragic in its irony. Contemporary tragedy deploys hymnal celebrations of victory and prayers with the aim of averting unforeseen disasters. But these are often then subverted by sudden, subsequent misfortune,[72] as Swift's treatment of tragedy's ironic use of the paean has shown.[73] Agathon's hymn elegantly furnishes some context for Inlaw's heedless, quasi-tragic march towards disaster. More importantly, its effort to connect the aesthetic excess and perversion of Agathon's poetry under the influence of the genre-bending New Music to the poet's own confused gender and (it is implied) deviant sexuality conveys the antinomianism of the New Music in Old Comedy.

To be fair, not all hymnic parody of Old Comedy is as viciously satirical as Agathon's hymn. Surprisingly playful is Aristophanes' parody of a fragment of a hymn from Euripides' *Cresphontes* (*c.* 424 BCE). In his ruminations on poetic descriptions of peacetime, the fifth-century CE writer Stobaeus preserves part of a Euripidean ode from *Cresphontes*, as well as Aristophanes' parody of that ode. *Cresphontes* dealt with the return of Cresphontes, youngest son of king Cresphontes of Messenia, and his revenge against the usurper Polyphontes, who had killed the king and married the queen Merope by force.[74] Fr. 453 belonged to a hymn to the goddess Peace that stretches over a strophe and the first three lines of the antistrophe of an ode delivered by a chorus of old war-weary Messenians:

Εἰρήνα βαθύπλουτε καὶ
καλλίστα μακάρων θεῶν,
ζῆλός μοι σέθεν, ὡς χρονίζεις.
δέδια δὲ μὴ πρὶν πόνοις
    ὑπερβάλῃ με γῆρας,

πρὶν σὰν προσιδεῖν χαρίεσσαν ὥραν
καὶ καλλιχόρους ἀοιδάς
φιλοστεφάνους τε κώμους
⟨ἴθ'⟩ ἴθι μοι, πότνια, πόλιν.

τὰν δ' ἐχθρὰν Στάσιν εἶργ' ἀπ' οἴ-
κων τὰν μαινομέναν τ' Ἔριν
θηκτῷ τερπομέναν σιδάρῳ.

Peace, of deep wealth and
fairest of the blessed gods,
I pine for you, long in coming.
I fear old age will overcome me
with hardships before I can look
upon your graceful beauty, your
songs adorned with dancing and
garlanded revels. Come, mistress,
to my city!

Force from our homes hateful Stasis
and insane Strife,
delighting in whetted iron.

Eur. fr. 453

Apparently sung just after the protagonist lays a plot against Polyphantes' life, this ode has standard cletic features:[75] the *invocation* (1–3) in praise of the goddess with epithets (βαθύπλουτε, καλλίστα, πότνια); the *argument* (4–8) pleading with the goddess to hasten her arrival while the chorus still lives; and the *petition* (9–12) that she drive out Stasis and Strife (εἶργε) and come (ἴθι) with her songs accompanied by dances (καλλιχόρους, 7) and garland-loving (φιλοστεφάνους, 8) revels. Despite identifying itself in the singular (με), the chorus is a communal one, whose plea reflects the formal elaboration and occasion of a civic event. Euripides' hymn evidently impressed contemporary audiences,[76] including Aristophanes, who parodied it in his lost peace-play, *Farmers* (*c.* 424–422 BCE):

Εἰρήνη βαθύπλουτε καὶ ζευγάριον βοεικόν,
εἰ γὰρ ἐμοὶ παυσαμένῳ τοῦ πολέμου γένοιτο
σκάψαι τ' ἀποκλάσαι ⟨τε⟩ καὶ λουσαμένῳ διελκύσαι
τῆς τρυγός, ἄρτον λιπαρὸν καὶ ῥάφανον φαγόντι.

Peace, of deep wealth and little team of oxen,
would that it were mine to have an end of war, and dig
and dress the vines, and after a bath to swig the new
wine after eating some hearty bread and cabbage.

Ar. fr. 111

Aristophanes' alterations of the model are subtle.[77] Although metrically elaborated,[78] the hymnic register of the original is diminished but not parodied: Euripides' goddess and her epithet ('of deep wealth'), as well as the petition, are retained but followed by the comic diminutive 'little team of oxen'. The imperatives (εἶργε, ἴθι) are replaced with a less direct optative of bare wish ('would it were mine').[79] The urban setting of the tragic chorus is recast as the simple pleasures of the farmer's rustic, self-sufficient and productive life, now familiar from Aristophanes' *Peace* discussed in Chapter 4. Aristophanes also removes the dread of impending old age and the threat of Stasis and Strife. However, Aristophanes' modest personal prayer does not disparage the model, as previous scholars argue,[80] so much as amusingly redefine the goddess's realm by altering her generic and social orientation at a time when she had no official civic cult in Athens. Aristophanes fr. 111's relocation of the goddess from urban to country life as patroness of modest rural pleasures is less parodic than quaintly rustic. The chorus's anticipation of the blessings of peace is uniquely playful in its adaptation of the original.

Choral lyric: Bee governesses, babbling birds, and a caterpillar chorus

A more vivid record of the aesthetic and cultural impact of late-classical lyric's influence on tragedy is found in Aeschylus and Euripides' deconstructions of one another's work in Aristophanes' *Frogs* (405 BCE). Since my space is limited and my focus is Euripidean lyric's expression of that poet's claim earlier in *Frogs* (959) to have introduced οἰκεῖα πράγματα into tragedy, I am unable to treat the finer points of the parodied Aeschylean lyric. The latter will simply serve as a basis for comparing the subsequent parody of Euripides. Aristophanes reduces Aeschylean choral poetry (*Ran.* 1264–1277) to a patchwork of heroic, genealogical and cultic content, targeting about a half dozen ethical and rhythmic features of Aeschylus here and in the following parody (1284–1295).[81] Diction (πελάθεις), compounds (ἀνδροδάικτον, πολυκοίρανε, μελισσονόμοι) and an archaic refrain – ἰὴ κόπον οὐ πελάθεις ἐπ᾽ ἀρωγάν; – humorously distort Aeschylus's martial archaic style in exaggerated and monotonous form. The opening lines' refrain Φθιῶτ᾽ Ἀχιλ- / λεῦ, τί ποτ᾽ ἀνδροδάικτον ἀκούων (from *Myrmidons,* fr. 132) is absurdly paired in each subsequent iteration with text from entirely different plays. These bizarre pairings, nonsensical terms ('bee governesses', 1273), repetitive dactylic rhythm, and inarticulate cries and violent choppings produce 'a ludicrous impression of rhythmical and repetitive violence, devoid of sense, predictable and ponderous'.[82] The comic mechanism of the second parody is even more straightforward, exaggerating the sound of Aeschylus's combinations of rough consonants and compounds by capping each dactylic line with the nonsensical phrase φλαττοθραττοφλαττοθρατ (*Ran.* 1284–1295).

Aeschylus's monotonous style and content, and the incoherence of his diction and narrative, underscore the 'parlous' nature of Euripidean lyric and that poet's aversion to traditional choral performance in *Frogs.* Hunter helpfully underscores the comic Euripides' specific complaint (919–920) that the audience sitting through Aeschylus's choral lyric was constantly wondering when the real talking would begin.[83] To my knowledge, the prominence of talking – babbling, rather – as the unifying theme of the disparate vignettes of Aristophanes' parody of Euripidean lyric has not previously been noted:

Αι. ἀλκυόνες, αἳ παρ᾽ ἀενάοις θαλάσσης
κύμασι στωμύλλετε,   1310
τέγγουσαι νοτίοις πτερῶν
ῥανίσι χρόα δροσιζόμεναι·
αἵ θ᾽ ὑπωρόφιοι κατὰ γωνίας
εἱειειειειειλίσσετε δακτύλοις φάλαγγες
ἱστότονα πηνίσματα,
κερκίδος ἀοιδοῦ μελέτας,
ἵν᾽ ὁ φίλαυλος ἔπαλλε δελ-
φὶς πρῴραις κυανεμβόλοις
μαντεῖα καὶ σταδίους,
οἰνάνθας γάνος ἀμπέλου,   1320
βότρυος ἕλικα παυσίπονον.
περίβαλ᾽, ὦ τέκνον, ὠλένας.

Ae: Halcyons, who chatter on the everflowing
swells of the sea,   1310
moistened by the rainy dews of wings,
besprinkled on the skin.
And the rafter-dwelling spiders in the corners
you wiyiyiyiyind spoolings-of-thread,

stretching-across-the-loom,
practicings of the singer shuttle,
where the aulos-loving dolphin
at dark prows shakes oracles and stades,
sheen of the vine bloom,   1320
pain-easing tendril of the grape.
Embrace me, child!

Ran. 1309–1322

The paratactic arrangement of strikingly different tableaux from the natural world – in some cases drawn from several different tragedies[84] – distorts an apparent Euripidean tendency of interest even in antiquity, the irrelevance of his odes to the dramatic action.[85] The influence of the New Music's imagery and its tendency to privilege sound and music over sense and *logos* is apparent throughout the parody.[86] Also typical of the New Music is the opening 'hanging invocation', here addressed to the halcyon.[87] But where we might expect a verb of singing or grandiloquence (e.g., ἀείδετε, κελαδεῖτε etc.) to connect the halcyon's shrill cries with stylized lamentation,[88] the halcyon 'chatters' (στωμύλλετε) in the typical fashion of Euripides and sophistic ideas in comedy.[89] As Telephus's Euripidean cast was partly reflected in his skill as a στωμύλος (Ar. *Ach.* 429), a 'chatterer', the chattering halcyon is similarly the quintessential Euripidean bird, dexterously applying its mouth as a versatile tool.[90] This opening allusion to the oral craftsmanship, or 'mouthwork', repeatedly imputed to Euripides and his work evokes the babbling of his characters and preference for talk over choral song.

To the Greek ear, the sound of the halcyon's nest-making resembled the sound of the beam of the loom (*Anth. Pal.* 6.160.2). This nicely segues into the following vignette of 'spiders lurking under the rafters' (ὑπωρόφιοι…φάλαγγες, *Ran.* 1313–1314), winding their 'taut' woofs (ἱστότονα πηνίσματα).[91] The apposition of the arachnid's weaving to the 'shuttle singer' (κερκίδος ἀοιδοῦ) links animal and mortal spheres through shared craft.[92] As early as Homer,[93] weaving is likened to poetic narration as well as deception and subtlety.[94] The *melisma* of ειειειειειειλίσσετε ('Wiyiyiyiyiyiyind') mocks Euripidean stylistic innovation and the delicacy of arachnid weaving as it simultaneously alludes to the complicated and pretentious discourses of Euripides and the sophists.[95] Comedy denigrates all such subtle thinking as στωμυλλεῖν and λαλία.[96]

The ode tips into nonsense somewhere between the spider and the 'aulos-loving' dolphin, who 'shakes' (1317–1319) 'oracles' according to its association with Apollo and, by extension, Delphi.[97] The vicious zeugma of oracles and 'stades' is nonsensical,[98] although it may evoke Euripides' interest in precise measurement,[99] which is parodied in his claim (also in *Frogs*) to have taught audiences 'to apply rulers (κανόνας) and set-squares (γωνιασμούς) of delicate (λεπτῶν) words' (*Ran.* 956).[100] The absence of any discernible link between the dolphin and the next lines in apposition, οἰνάνθας γάνος ἀμπέλου and βότρυος ἕλικα παυσίπονον,[101] prepares for the absurd abruptness of the recognition.[102] Instead of narrowing its horizons and gradually leading the spectator or reader back to the dramatic present, the ode concludes with a recognition, περίβαλ', ὦ τέκνον, ὠλένας, 'embrace me, child!' (1322). The emotional charge of an imagined reunion mocks Euripides' tendency to defer melodramatic and insufficiently motivated recognitions in ostentatious fashion, which I explained in the introductory chapter.[103]

The halcyon's babbling, the arachnid's weaving and perhaps also the dolphin's shaking are οἰκεῖα πράγματα, everyday things, put through the imaginative machine of Euripidean chorality. The song's repeated emphasis on varieties of 'talking' by animals and insects is perfectly appropriate for a poet who swears his oath to 'tongue' (*Ran.* 892–894) and prefers talk to odes. Euripides' juxtapositions of anthropomorphized and 'talking' nature flatten the traditional cosmic hierarchy to reflect his 'democratized' tragedy. A similar portrait of democratized nature in Euripidean song by another comic contemporary has fortunately survived.[104] Strattis fr. 71 (from *Macedonians*) amusingly pokes fun at the influence of dithyramb on Euripidean lyric by anthropomorphizing caterpillars as traversing gardens 'in fifty-foot steps' (πεντήκοντα ποδῶν ἴχνεσι βαίνετ') and 'twirling choruses' (χοροὺς ἑλίσσουσαι) in basil plants and parsley.[105] The anthropomorphism of Strattis's conception of insect locomotion as a circular dithyrambic chorus is like that of Aristophanes' parody, and both seem to take aim at the radically democratizing tendency of Euripidean tragedy that is such a focus of *Frogs*.[106] Under Euripides, comedy implies, tragic lyric's panoramic views of nature are distorted by the poet's insertion of the banal and everyday into the genre's lofty mythological world.

III. Tragic monody

When listing tragedy's basic formal elements, Aristotle identifies actors' songs (τὰ ἀπὸ τῆς σκηνῆς) and *kommoi* as 'special (ἴδια) to some [tragedians]' (1452b17–18). He describes actors' songs as gradually encroaching on the chorus's conventional responsibility for dramatic song as tragedy evolved over time. Where choral odes deepen our conception of events by turning to panoramic views separate from the dramatic here-and-now, the actor's monody focuses on the singer's emotional experience of the moment. All fifth-century tragedians made use of such songs, though they are sometimes difficult to distinguish with certainty.[107] Monody's narrow and focused perspective made it an excellent vehicle for concentrating extreme grief or fear in virtuoso performances of speech, music, mimesis and even props.[108] Tragic characters sing in several types of lyric, but lament has an undeniably special place in tragedy's outlook.[109] Much like the marriage and sacrificial rituals explored in the previous chapter, heavily stylized tragic lamentation perverts proper practice by undermining its culturally assigned function of comforting the afflicted with emotional release and a measure of closure. Tragedy's ritual laments recreate a style of mourning that would be illegal in an Athens that restricted public lamentation.

Before analysing comedy's parody of such monodies, one should bear in mind the sociological constraints on who can and cannot lament in tragedy. Apart from a few exceptions, women and foreigners, rather than men of 'respectable' status, almost always lament. In comedy, by contrast, citizen males are the *only* monodists. They, like their tragic counterparts, break out in song at moments of intense emotional and physical distress, although unlike tragedy's nobler and often innocent characters, comic figures lament the unpleasant consequences of their own transgressions. For example, the gluttonous poetaster Melanthius recites anapaests from his *Medea* – Ὀλόμαν, ὀλόμαν ἀποχηρωθεὶς / τᾶς ἐν τεύτλοισι λοχευομένας ('I'm done for, done for! Bereft / of her that lay in amid beets!' (*Pax* 1013–1014) – when the market has sold out of eels. The banal τεύτλοισι ('beets') shatters the emotive repetition, poetic diction and Doricism of this lament of Medea's murder of Jason's new bride.[110]

Andromeda of the marketplace: *Thesmophoriazusae* 1015–1055

One of the most dynamic comic monodies is Inlaw's parody of the title character's song of Euripides' *Andromeda* (412 BCE) in *Thesmophoriazusae* (411). Euripides dramatized the sudden rescue of the princess Andromeda by the Argive hero, Perseus. To appease divine anger at his wife, Cassiopeia, king Cepheus of Ethiopia ordered that his daughter Andromeda be bound to the coastline as an offering to a sea monster sent by Poseidon. Euripides' tragedy began with the innocent, helpless heroine alone on the seashore and chanting the introductory anapaests of a lament for her cruel fate.[111] By opening with a chained and immobilized Andromeda on the Ethiopian seashore at night (fr. 114),[112] as opposed to a prologue or similarly informative beginning, Euripides attempted a significant theatrical innovation, possibly even departing from the influential Sophoclean *Andromeda* of roughly forty years earlier.[113] The extreme spatial and emotional isolation of the heroine cruelly denied her any degree of relief or comfort apart from her own power to lament. By focusing attention on this single aspect of her performance and reducing performative codes to a single verbal channel, Euripides conveyed the heroine's isolation with striking originality.[114] Andromeda's opening address to Night (ὦ νὺξ ἱερά, fr. 114.1) must have captured this sense of isolation effectively before her amoebaean exchange (fr. 116) with a chorus of Ethiopian maidens (fr. 117), who were drawn to the seaside by her cries.

Similarly incapacitated and in drag, Aristophanes' Inlaw is condemned to die a similarly gruesome death by the process referred to as *apotympanismos*, while the Scythian archer stands guard.[115] When comic Euripides somehow signals his intention to play the part of Perseus from the previous year's *Andromeda*, Inlaw assumes the role of the distressed heroine and accordingly recites that lament:

φίλαι παρθένοι, φίλαι,
πῶς ἂν ἀπέλθοιμι καὶ
τὸν Σκύθην λάθοιμι;
κλύεις, ὦ προσᾴδουσ᾽ ἀϋτὰς ἐν ἄντροις;
κατάνευσον, ἔασον ὡς   1020
τὴν γυναῖκά μ᾽ ἐλθεῖν.
ἄνοικτος ὅς μ᾽ ἔδησε, τὸν
πολυστονώτατον βροτῶν·
μόλις δὲ γραῖαν ἀποφυγὼν
σαπρὰν ἀπωλόμην ὅμως.   1025
ὅδε γὰρ ὁ Σκύθης πάλαι <δὴ> φύλαξ
ἐφέστηκε κῶλον ἄφιλον ἐκρέμα–
σέ <με> κόραξι δεῖπνον.
ὁρᾷς; οὐ χοροῖσιν οὐδ᾽ ὑφ᾽ ἡλίκων νεανίδων   1030
κημὸν ἕστηκ᾽ ἔχουσ᾽,
ἀλλ᾽ ἐν πυκνοῖς δεσμοῖσιν ἐμπεπλεγμένη
κήτει βορὰ Γλαυκέτῃ πρόκειμαι.
γαμηλίῳ μὲν οὐ ξὺν
παιῶνι, δεσμίῳ δέ,   1035
γοᾶσθέ μ᾽, ὦ γυναῖκες, ὡς
μέλεα μὲν πέπονθα μέλε–
ος, ὦ τάλας ἐγώ, τάλας,
ἀπὸ δὲ συγγόνων ἄνομ᾽ ἄνομα πάθεα,

φῶτα λιτομένα, 1040
πολυδάκρυτον Ἀίδα γόον φλέγουσα,
αἰαῖ αἰαῖ ἒ ἔ,
ὃς ἔμ᾽ ἀπεξύρησε πρῶτον,
ὃς ἐμὲ κροκόεντ᾽ ἀμφέδυσεν·
ἐπὶ δὲ τοῖσδε τόδ᾽ ἀνέπεμψεν 1045
ἱερόν, ἔνθα γυναῖκες.
ἰώ μοι μοίρας
ἂν ἔτικτε δαίμων·
ὦ κατάρατος ἐγώ·
τίς ἐμὸν οὐκ ἐπόψεται
πάθος ἀμέγαρτον ἐπὶ κακῶν παρουσίᾳ; 1050
εἴθε με πυρφόρος αἰθέρος ἀστὴρ –
τὸν βάρβαρον ἐξολέσειεν.
οὐ γὰρ ἔτ᾽ ἀθανάταν φλόγα λεύσσειν
ἐστὶν ἐμοὶ φίλον, ὡς ἐκρεμάσθην,
λαιμότμητ᾽ ἄχη δαιμόνι᾽, αἰόλαν
νέκυσιν ἐπὶ πορείαν.

Dear, dear Maidens,
how could I flee
and escape this Scythian?
Do you hear me, you singing your cries in the caves?
Permit, let me, the most mournful of mortals, 1020
to go home to my wife.
Pitiless is the man who bound me, saddest of mortals.
Barely escaping the rotten old hag,
I'm nonetheless finished.
But here the Scythian sat long ago as my
guard, and he hung me up, cursed, friendless
dinner for the crows.
Do you see? Neither in dances nor with my age-mates 1030
do I stand holding a voting funnel,
but pressed by these tight bonds I remain food
for the whale Glaucetes.
Mourn me, ladies, not with a hymn of marriage
but with one of jail,
as I, wretched, have suffered
wretchedly from my relations, sufferings unspeakable,
although I begged the man, 1040
blazing teary groans of Hades,

Aaaah … Aaaah, Eeeee! Eeeee!
You who first shaved me,
who draped me in saffron,
and on top of all these sent me to
this festival, where there are women.
Oh my! My fate!
which a god brought forth!
Oh my, I'm cursed!
Who will not see my sufferings,
wretched me fraught with evils?!
If only a fiery celestial star –   1050
would obliterate this barbarian!
I can't even gaze at the immortal flame
so dear to me, because I'm hung up,
neck-severing divine curse, on a shimmering journey
to the dead.

Thesm. 1015–1055

Inlaw's song is primarily iambic with a mix of other meters and chock-full of the rhetoric and *topoi* of tragic threnody. The text appears to bear out the scholiast's claim that Aristophanes holds reasonably close to his model.[116] However, the *para prosdokian* style of humour inserts banalities to clash with the original's specific *topoi*, converting its horror and pity into comic degradation and humiliation. In the first section (1015–1028), the typically high-register wish for escape, which is common enough in tragic lament, is reduced by the banality of Inlaw's considerably less heroic wish to go home to his wife.[117] While the maiden chorus of the original denounced Cepheus's cruelty (fr. 120), Inlaw curses his immediate tormentor, the Scythian archer.[118] Furthermore, Inlaw imagines his death at the hands of the Athenian glutton Glaucetes (1033) rather than at the hands of the sea monster. Finally, the traditional theme of 'marriage to death', or the doomed maiden's lament for her fate of eternal maidenhood, is in the second section (1029–1041) recast as Inlaw's comic indignation for his earlier emasculation by shaving, pubic depilation and transvestism (1037–1041, 1043–1046). When Inlaw voices the standard wish for death or some similarly radical event by a tragic character given over to despair (1050), he pleads instead that a lightning bolt obliterate the Scythian.

This monody *twice* overturns expectations of the tragedy's proper sequence of events that was still fresh in the audience's mind from the previous year's performance. When Inlaw glimpses his 'Perseus' (1010–1011), i.e., Euripides, he starts lamenting instead of following the correct order of events in the model, which introduced Perseus after the heroine had delivered much of her lament. A second and more explosive surprise is Aristophanes' response to one of Euripides' more innovative and perhaps controversial imaginative choices in the play, namely his introduction of the nymph Echo as a disembodied voice. The tragic Andromeda's pathetic plea for silence so that she might lament her coming death with the chorus (fr. 118) and avail herself of its comfort may indicate that the nymph was drawn to the sound of the dirge and stood just outside the audience's vision. Euripides' introduction of this rare figure of poetic tradition as an invisible entity ingeniously emphasized the 'lonely horror of Andromeda's night chained to the rocks'.[119] In both Sophocles and Euripides, Echo is the voice of cruel abandonment, taunting isolated mortals most in need of human contact. She is a fixture of Lemnos's desolate landscape traversed by the chorus of Greek sailors as they poignantly imagine the marooned and suffering Philoctetes in the play of his name (409 BCE). She is a 'babbler' (ἀθυρόστομος), hearing and responding to the hero's pained cries (πικραῖς οἰμωγαῖς).[120] In *Andromeda*, Euripides developed the mythological conceit of the disembodied Echo by giving an audible existence to her babbling and maddening repetition of the maiden's cries. This repetition deepened the sense of pathos by cruelly obstructing the maiden's dirge.

It is interesting to try to imagine what members of Aristophanes' audience, specifically those who had seen *Andromeda* the previous year, were expecting in the lead-up to this scene in *Thesmophoriazusae*. Were they relishing Aristophanes' inevitable response to Euripides' hyper-realistic and perhaps over-the-top portrayal of Echo? Or would the model's ancient special effect have even registered as particularly innovative to the average spectator in the theatre? Perhaps it is safe to say that few if any spectators expected a fully embodied Echo – played by comic Euripides himself? – to appear in the flesh before the incapacitated Inlaw:

Ηχ. χαῖρ', ὦ φίλη παῖ· τὸν δὲ πατέρα Κηφέα
ὅς σ' ἐξέθηκεν, ἀπολέσειαν οἱ θεοί.
Κη. σὺ δ' εἶ τίς, ἥτις τοὐμὸν ᾤκτιρας πάθος;
Ηχ. Ἠχώ, λόγων ἀντῳδὸς ἐπικοκκάστρια,
ἥπερ πέρυσιν ἐν τῷδε ταὐτῷ χωρίῳ
Εὐριπίδῃ καὐτὴ ξυνηγωνιζόμην.
ἀλλ', ὦ τέκνον, σὲ μὲν τὸ σαυτῆς χρὴ ποιεῖν,
κλαίειν ἐλεινῶς.

Echo: Greetings, dear child. Your father Cepheus
who reared you, may the gods destroy him!

Inlaw: Who are you, who pity my suffering?

Echo: Echo, the crone who babbles back your words,
who last year in this very place shared in the
struggle with Euripides in the dramatic contest.
Anyway, child, you must do your part and wail piteously.

Thesm. 1056–1063

The entrance of Aristophanes' obnoxious (and likely ugly and cronish) Echo just as the audience is led to expect 'Perseus' hilariously impedes the plot's forward progress.[121] The comic Echo is an ἀντῳδός ('one who sings in response') who 'shared the struggle' (ξυνηγωνίζομην) with Euripides in the previous year's festival. Use of this technical term for choral sympathy in tragedy suggests comic Echo's aspiration to one of the chorus's common roles as sympathetic observer and partner in the dirge.[122] Inlaw manages to recite only six lines (1065–1072) of *Andromeda* (frr. 114–115) before losing his patience with the crone's repetition of his final word in each line. The Scythian bowman, returning from offstage, is similarly drawn into an exchange with the babbling (λαλῖς, i.e., λαλεῖς) Echo.[123] The scene's comic effectiveness derives from Aristophanes' imaginative one-upmanship of his model with a concrete and Athenocentrized hag of the comic marketplace. Her identification as a γραῦς (old woman) στωμυλλομένη ('chattering') with λαλία ('babbling') seemingly identifies her with a figure of comedy's world, the obnoxious and aggressively outspoken older women who serve as market-sellers, nurses, brothel-managers and inn-keepers.[124] Aristophanes reduces Euripides' moving scene of innocent suffering into antagonistic bantering between low-class figures of the Athenian marketplace.

In its parodies, comedy edits tragic laments to maximize the collision of the singer's absurd and embarrassing comic situation and the deadly, cruel and often unjust circumstances faced by the lamenting tragic monodist. Monody is the sole outlet for tragic characters suffering extreme emotional and physical duress in situations that have arisen through no fault of their own. Although Inlaw's situation is certainly dire – he is strapped to the plank for execution – his Andromedan monody detaches the song from its ethical moorings in tragedy. Instead of inducing the sympathetic reaction an audience might feel for an innocent tragic heroine, Inlaw's song communicates his well-deserved humiliation for shameless and hubristic behaviour. The song's transposition of lines from the original and inclusion of banal details from the comic present, including Inlaw's separation from his wife, drive home the consequences of his satyresque hubris in the Athenian world. By grafting an established tragic convention onto a completely alien comic world, Old Comedy is able to produce a very different dramatic effect.

Fowl play: *Frogs* 1331–1363

Extant Old Comedy's most famous monody conveys the intensely personal perspective of a peasant lamenting the ludicrously trivial theft of a rooster in Aristophanes' *Frogs*. By approaching this song with greater awareness of the established comic repertoire on women and roosters, one can perhaps detect a different kind of theft than the one scholarship has long assumed.

ὦ νυκτὸς κελαινοφαὴς ὄρφνα,
τίνα μοι δύστανον ὄνειρον
πέμπεις, ἀφανοῦς Ἀίδα πρόμολον,
ψυχὰν ἄψυχον ἔχοντα,
Νυκτὸς παῖδα μελαίνας,
φρικώδη δεινὰν ὄψιν,
μελανονεκυείμονα,
φόνια φόνια δερκόμενον,
μεγάλους ὄνυχας ἔχοντα;
ἀλλά μοι, ἀμφίπολοι, λύχνον ἅψατε
κάλπισί τ᾽ ἐκ ποταμῶν δρόσον ἄρατε, θέρμετε δ᾽ ὕδωρ,
ὡς ἂν θεῖον ὄνειρον ἀποκλύσω.   1340
ἰὼ πόντιε δαῖμον,
τοῦτ᾽ ἐκεῖν᾽· ἰ-
ὼ ξύνοικοι, τάδε τέρα θεάσασθε· τὸν ἀλεκτρυόνα
μου ξυναρπά-
σασα φρούδη Γλύκη.
Νύμφαι ὀρεσσίγονοι.
ὦ Μανία, ξύλλαβε.
ἐγὼ δ᾽ ἁ τάλαινα
προσέχουσ᾽ ἔτυχον ἐμαυτῆς
ἔργοισι, λίνου μεστὸν ἄτρακτον
εἰειειλίσσουσα χεροῖν,
κλωστῆρα ποιοῦσ᾽, ὅπως
κνεφαῖος εἰς ἀγορὰν   1350
φέρουσ᾽ ἀποδοίμαν·
ὁ δ᾽ ἀνέπτατ᾽ ἀνέπτατ᾽ ἐς αἰθέρα
        κουφοτάταις πτερύγων ἀκμαῖς·
ἐμοὶ δ᾽ ἄχε᾽ ἄχεα κατέλιπε,

δάκρυα δάκρυά τ' ἀπ' ὀμμάτων
ἔβαλον ἔβαλον ἁ τλάμων.
ἀλλ' ὦ Κρῆτες, Ἴδας τέκνα, τὰ τόξα <τε> λαβόντες
    ἐπαμύνατε, τὰ κῶλά τ' ἀμπάλλετε κυ-
κλούμενοι τὴν οἰκίαν.
ἅμα δὲ Δίκτυννα παῖς ἁ καλά,
τὰς κυνίσκας ἔχουσ' ἐλθέτω διὰ δόμων πανταχῇ,   1360
σὺ δ', ὦ Διός, διπύρους ἀνέχουσα
λαμπάδας ὀξυτάτας χεροῖν Ἑκάτα, παράφηνον
εἰς Γλύκης, ὅπως ἂν εἰσελ-
θοῦσα φωράσω.

O darkly shining Darkness of Night,
what baleful dream do you send me,
approach of unseen Hades, with life
that is not life, child of black Night
visage horrifying, terrible,
black-corpse-shrouded,
glaring murder ... murder ...
with huge claws?
Light a lamp for me, maids,
and draw up dew from the river in pitchers, and heat it,
so that I may wash away this portent.   1340
Oho, god of the deep,
it's come to pass! Oho, fellow lodgers,
behold these marvels: snatched my rooster
and vanished, has Glyke.
Nymphs of the mountains,
and you, Mania, help me!
I, poor thing, happened to be seeing
to my own chores,
wiyiyiyinding in my hands
a full spindle of flax,
and making my cloth,
so that I could get to the
market before sunrise and   1350
sell it. But he flew, he flew,
up to the sky on the lightest of wingtips.
And he left pain, pain to me,
and from my eyes, poor me, fell tears, tears.
O Cretans, children of Ida, snatch up your

bows and assist me! Urge on your limbs, circling
her house, and let the fair child, Dictynna,
with her bitchlets, run all through her halls.   1360
And you, daughter of Zeus, Hecate, raising in your hands double torches
shining brightly, light the way to the house of Glyke
so that I may search her house.

Ran. 1331–1363

An unidentified singer is awoken early in the morning by an ill-omened dream, which she attempts to neutralize with a purifying bath. Suddenly recognizing the portent's meaning, the theft of her 'rooster' by her slave, Glyke ('Sweetie'), she bewails her misfortune and prays for aid in the recovery of her pet. The singer calls down punishment on the guilty party and requests that Artemis and Hecate accompany her to the culprit's house.

As parody typically does, the monody exaggerates the author's recognizable features of content and style, particularly with oxymora, repetition, cries, extravagant compounds (μελανονεκυείμονα, 'black-corpse-shrouded')[125] and even Euripides' demonstrable interest in the shifting effects of light.[126] Although this song's interruption of high style with bathetic elements is a common parodic mechanism, its effect is considerably subtler than the Andromeda monody. Aristophanes fluidly weaves into the overwrought imagery many tropes of monody that are not typically combined: the visit of a frightening dream, the sudden recognition, the call for help and the prayer or request for aid. While the song is permeated with bathetic elements of the singer's lower-class world – e.g., λύχνος ('lamp'), κάλπις ('pitcher'),[127] φωράω,[128] the colloquialism τοῦτ᾽ ἐκεῖν᾽ – the shifting meter complements the song's emotional fluctuations well.[129] Introductory short, anapaestic cola (1334–1337) build to the rising alarm of the Aeolic rhythm (1341a) with trochees and dochmiacs of the calls for help at peak distress (1341b–1345; 1346–1354). Cretic-dochmiac combinations (1356–1363) convey the singer's galvanized resolve to seek vengeance with the help of Dictynna, Hecate and 'Cretans', i.e., Cretan archers. The command to shake their limbs, i.e., dance around the thief's house as a dithyrambic (circular) chorus might (κυκλούμενοι τὴν οἰκίαν) [1358], alludes humorously to New Music.[130]

Nothing quite like the lament for the rooster survives in fifth-century texts, though it may recall the New York Goose Play discussed in Chapter 2 and its similar conflict over a domestic animal. A better parallel is a twenty-four-line mime preserved on two papyri from the first century BCE.[131] Though much later than Old Comedy, mimes draw upon earlier popular traditions which comedy itself exploits. The mime's twelve well-preserved lines parody the lament for a

dead friend or soldier in order to eulogize a fighting cock – possibly named
'Truphôn' – who has abandoned his master for a hen. The singer's pathetic
reflection on the childhood of the deceased, the consolation of his surviving
children (τὸ ἑρνίον, τροφὴν αὐτοῦ, 17), and the loss of the honour he brought to
the family are standard tropes. Exclamations of grief – 'my ship is wrecked!' (ἡ
ναῦς μου ἐρράγη, 15), 'I'm fighting to live!' (ψυχομαχῶ, 21) – for this dead warrior
(τοῦ μ[αχ]ίμου, 18), who has not actually died, underscore the absurdity. A
closing vow 'to be still' (καθ[η]συχάσομαι, 24) may signal the intention to commit
suicide.[132]

The mime represents one kind of popular tradition Aristophanes could
plausibly borrow from in conceiving a peasant's melodramatic lament for a pet
rooster. What value would a rooster have for a slave, the culprit? Roosters ensure
a food supply (i.e., eggs and more chickens) and occasionally serve as alarm
clocks in our sources.[133] Cockfighting is certainly a Greek pastime, but one
pursued by aristocratic youth, not peasants and slaves. A slave could sell a stolen
rooster and pocket the money, of course.

Even though the distinctly demotic character of a lament for a rooster by a
peasant is perfectly appropriate for a parody of Euripides, it is nonetheless worth
asking whether the song might instead provide an example of the adulterous
scandals of tragic households that so greatly interest the comic Euripides in
Thesmophoriazusae and *Frogs*. Could the rooster lamented by the female singer,
in fact, be a man? Roosters symbolized ideal masculinity, sexual and martial, in
Greek thought. Their demeanour and appearance mirror the good hoplite, their
virility the idealized sexual potency of the citizen. Greek ideology drew close
connections between roosters, especially fighting cocks, and male martial and
sexual prowess,[134] a link that the Getty Birds of Chapter 2 may convey visually.
The rooster's distinctive crow signals sexual arousal and potency, and comedy
dwells upon this in part through emphasizing the wing's phallic symbolism.[135]
We should think of the icon of the famous 'phallic birds' found on some extant
South Italian vase paintings.[136] The victorious rooster's swollen, fluttering and
raised posture was a visual embodiment of phallicity.[137]

Given this cultural subtext, it is at least possible that the slave, Glyke, ran off
with the singer's husband or lover – her 'rooster' – instead of an actual fowl. The
adultery theory can account for certain oddities in the song. The cretic meter
of the singer's call for vengeance may allude to Euripides' 'Cretan monodies'
criticized by Aeschylus, earlier in the play (*Ran.* 849–850), as one of his opponent's
perverse innovations in tragedy, along with 'unholy unions' (γάμους...ἀνοσίους).
Cretan monody is a shorthand for arias sung by Cretan royal women (e.g.,

Pasiphae, Phaedra and Aërope) who were paradigmatic of the immoral Euripidean heroine. Such Cretan monodies lamented illicit, destructive love affairs and in some cases even openly defended such sexual immorality.[138] The scholiast at *Frogs* 1356 (ὦ Κρῆτες), the final and heavily cretic section of the monody, in fact notes an allusion to Euripides' *Cretans* (fr. 472). Adultery might also explain the singer's invocation of Dictynna, the Cretan persona of Artemis, whose task was policing the sexual conduct of women, most often her female hunting companions.[139] Several myths show that policing the sexual boundaries between mortals and gods was Artemis's special concern as early as the *Odyssey*, where Calypso cites the goddess's killing of the huntsman Orion when complaining of the gods' jealousy of mortals who consort with goddesses (*Od.* 5.121–124). Elsewhere Odysseus tells of Ariadne's death at the hands of Artemis acting on the request of the girl's lover, Dionysus (*Od.* 11.321–325), and Artemis kills Coronis for Apollo in Pindar (*Pyth.* 3), and in other myths the giant Otus (*Od.* 11.305–310; Hyg. §28). Hubbard has shown how these various victims of the goddess affirm her task of enforcing mortal and divine sexual boundaries.[140]

While the evidence is certainly not explicit, the unusual content and style of the monody may support the idea that the singer seeks vengeance not for the theft of a rooster but for the theft of a husband by one of her slave girls. The frequency of male sexual exploitation of household slaves – real or imagined – makes this scenario inherently plausible. It might also explain why a rooster that has been stolen is for some reason described as flying away (ἀνέπτατ[ο], 1352). Whether the rooster is a fowl or man, Aristophanes' parody of Euripidean monody is an unquestionably funny and original expression of his critique that Euripides steeped his tragedy in οἰκεῖα πράγματα.

Conclusion

Old Comedy understood song's importance in creating and sustaining a poet's legacy. Smaller logistical demands and a greater number of performance contexts would have made lyric more accessible to the public than drama. Lyric compositions extracted from plays added to an already robust repertoire of songs and numbers, which could survive in circulation long after the original dramatic performance. It is generally believed that songs by Aristophanes and other comic poets were, in fact, written to be detached and circulated as short performance pieces in informal contexts like symposia and *kômoi*, where they could continue to entertain audiences beyond the poet's lifetime.[141] It is telling that when Aristophanes describes the earlier successful period of his rival Cratinus's career, he recalls it in terms of such songs, which filled symposia with hymnic evocations of 'fig-sandalled Bribery' and 'craftsmen of handy hymns' (Δωροῖ συκοπέδιλε…τέκτονες εὐπαλάμων ὕμνων).[142]

The comic poets' use of lyric poetry to project themselves as defenders of an imagined canon of classical song from the depredations of the New Music is one of the very few examples of the comedians' unified presentation of a collective identity. Old Comedy makes poets like Pindar and Simonides the standard-bearers of old-fashioned poetic and moral sensibilities, recalling an earlier period of Athenian musical and political greatness that has fallen into decline thanks to the mutually reinforcing movements of the New Music and radical democracy. As I have noted throughout this chapter, the self-conscious innovation of the New Music was not an invention of Old Comedy. These musicians mixed genres and modes, privileged sound over *logos*, altered their instruments and appealed to the populace. The extant evidence absolutely indicates that they undertook and encouraged many of the aesthetic, ethical and political innovations deplored by conservative critics such as the comic poets and Plato. However, we can safely assume that these critics, especially the comedians, exaggerated these innovations and their broader impact. And the New Music was certainly not the first movement to claim innovation as a means of distinguishing and distancing itself explicitly from earlier tradition. Scholars such as LeVen, Prauscello and others have shown that such claims to innovation by late fifth-century musicians are not radically new but rather continue a much earlier tradition that includes poets of the previous generation, of the classic kind.[143] Pindar and others made the very same effort to break with the past, even ostentatiously.

While the defence of classic and contemporary lyric by Eupolis, Aristophanes and other comic poets may be driven by earnest concern for the preservation of this celebrated canon – a canon thought to be representative of an idealized era – Old Comedy's satire of late fifth-century lyric was neither altruistic nor selfless. Old Comedy's aggressive attacks against artists like Timotheus and Cinesias likely attempt to counteract the wide popularity of these musicians and, most especially, their growing influence over the realm of theatre. Old Comedy consistently characterizes this influence as a corruption of norms in all aspects of life: a gendered conflation of modes and cultures of East and West on the body of Agathon; exhibitionist and dehumanizing sex with Lady Music herself (Pherecr. fr. 155); a radically democratizing flattening of tragedy's formerly noble ethical and natural worlds in Euripidean lyric (*Ran.* 1309–1322).

The New Music's influence over the theatre, comedy's own realm, naturally inspires the most comprehensive and sustained examples of extant parody. Aristophanes' collocations of exaggerated high style and popular content travesty the over-the-top emotion of late-Euripidean monody, as in Inlaw's 'marketplace monody' (*Thesm.* 1015–1055) and the theft of the rooster (*Ran.* 1331–1363). The comic Aeschylus's summoning of Euripides' grotesque Muse, the embodiment of all that is popular and corrupt in his lyric, conveys in wildly exaggerated terms the tragedian's shameless integration of elements both foreign and undignified into hallowed tragedy: 'whore songs' (πορνῳδιῶν), drinking songs by Meletus, Carian pipe tunes, laments (θρήνων) and dances (*Ran.* 1301–1303). The many parodies of tragedians who were heavily influenced by the New Music's style and thought might suggest that the comic poets' greater concern was neutralizing any popular advantage their loftier tragic rival derived from contemporary lyric, and commandeering that movement for itself – to produce laughs – rather than preserving lyric greats like Pindar and Simonides. The comic poets set themselves at the vanguard of this reaction to the New Music by mounting a collective attack against its allegedly pernicious innovations in society, education, ethics, politics and other spheres of life.

Aristophanes and his generic peers use old and new lyric to negotiate their place in the poetic landscape of Athens and to promote comedy as the only genre capable of safeguarding poetic tradition from the New Music and the fawning, impressionable public. As long as Cinesias, Timotheus and Melanippides continue occupying those Athenian performance contexts and occasions that play such a critical role in textual preservation by reperformance, the older poets will be slowly squeezed out of public and private repertoires until they are simply forgotten. Blaming the poets allegedly responsible for this cultural crisis was, of course, wiser than directly attacking the popular audiences who gave these popular performers such applause, wealth and prestige. However, these audiences will finally be censured, if indirectly, in the comprehensive critique of Euripidean tragedy in Aristophanes' *Thesmophoriazusae* (411 BCE), the play to which I now turn in the final chapter of this study.

The Feminine Mistake: Household Economy in Aristophanes' *Thesmophoriazusae*

Introduction

The year 411 BCE was an exceptional one for the Western tradition of comedy. This is the year that the 'respectable woman' may have been welcomed into the repertoire of Greek comedy. Aristophanes' *Lysistrata* and *Thesmophoriazusae*, produced at the Lenaea and Great Dionysia respectively, portrayed the citizen wife *at length* possibly for the first time in the history of comic theatre. The extant corpus of complete and fragmentary comedy before 411 offers only occasional glimpses of the wife: standing on the roof during a festival (Ar. *Ach.* 262); in her husband's nightmares (Ar. *Nub.* 41–55, 60–70); or emerging abruptly to wed the comic hero (Ar. *Pax* 706–708). However, in *Lysistrata* and *Thesmophoriazusae* she is both front-and-centre and an effective political agent against the civic and domestic mismanagement of her husband. Despite its innovative synthesis of sexual and generic issues, *Thesmophoriazusae* has always been overshadowed by *Lysistrata* as the preferred choice of late twentieth-century readers seeking empowered women and/or mobilized political action.[1] Those seeking sophisticated Aristophanic parody gravitate towards the comprehensive, multi-layered and flashier representations of the tragedians in *Frogs* (405). Even theatre directors have foregone *Thesmophoriazusae*'s rich social, material and literary themes because of its persistent topicality and pervasive misogyny.[2] Only by the final decades of the twentieth century did classical scholarship begin to acknowledge *Thesmophoriazusae*'s highly original treatment of gender and genre.[3] While many of its comic strategies will be familiar from earlier chapters – inversion, compression, comic biography and even remediation – these are creatively combined in a *tour de force* of parody within a fictionalized day in the life of the tragedian Euripides. It is perhaps a measure of this comedy's imaginative sophistication that scholars occasionally draw from its clever metafictional parody to illuminate obscure theatre-related images in South Italian vase painting and plastic art.⁴ But beneath this sophisticated plot structure, *Thesmophoriazusae* is a discursive examination of dramatic realism organized around tragedy and comedy's respective depictions of woman. By the time of *Thesmophoriazusae*'s production, female characters of mythology had been a fixture of tragedy and satyr play for as long as a hundred years. In his second comedy of 411, Aristophanes throws comedy's hat in the ring in the competition for female representation. In his earliest extant sustained comic portrayal of one of the most guarded figures of Athenian life, Aristophanes fleshes her out against the most familiar woman of contemporary theatre, the ethically compromised wife of Euripides.

After hearing the women of Athens plot his demise at the autumn Thesmophoria festival for 'slandering them' (κακῶς αὐτὰς λέγω, 182) with his adulterous and shameless heroines, the tragedian Euripides persuades his nameless Inlaw to impersonate a wife, infiltrate the festival and defend him before Athens's angry female mob.⁵ But the latter's lurid account of the hitherto unknown depths of female depravity enrages the women further and arouses their suspicions of Inlaw, who is forced to take refuge as a suppliant on the festival altar. His subsequent escape attempts are modelled on a trio of recent Euripidean productions: *Palamedes* (415 BCE), *Helen* (412), and *Andromeda* (412).⁶ While this crowd-pleasing sequence of Euripidean paratragedy has generated the most published research on *Thesmophoriazusae*, it is not my focus here. This chapter limits itself instead to the comedy's first half, the intergeneric heart of the comedy where Euripides and his putatively misogynistic tragedy are publicly tried by Athens's women. Since Zeitlin's important 1996 study, *Thesmophoriazusae*'s novel blending of the mimetic challenges of representing gender and genre has often been taken for granted.⁷ However, the mechanisms deployed by Aristophanes to critique tragedy's mimetic practices, and their implications for Aristophanes' continuing effort to define comedy's political and social relevance, remain insufficiently explored.

Aristophanes' comic exegesis of Euripidean misogyny and its deleterious effects takes Euripides' 'democratizing' didacticism – mentioned several times already in this study – to its natural and absurd conclusion. The first part of this chapter explores the female account of the pernicious effects of Euripides' realism, which convinces husbands that their wives are as shameless and dangerous as his tragic heroines. By cultivating his audience's critical faculties and making familiar aspects of everyday life the subject of his tragedy, Euripides redirects the aggressively litigious temperament that Athenians notoriously exercised in public affairs toward the private sphere of their households. Inspired by Euripides' Phaedras and Stheneboeas, men apply tragedy's expectations of female corruption to their home lives with disastrous results. Aristophanes' paratragic presentation of male oppression under Euripidean influence upends the practices of the household idealized by extant poetic and prose sources: the partnership between spouses, proper domestic order and the household's relationship with the larger community. Aristophanes' humorous depiction of the domestic discord wrought by Euripides satirizes the latter's highly conventional and artificial brand of realism and its 'democratizing' project.

The second part of this chapter focuses on the second speech, Inlaw's lurid description of the parallel domestic world of women's secret, sexual debauchery, which is unknown to their husbands. I show that this speech exposes the uselessness of poetically conditioned expectations to address and prevent women's misbehaviour. In this continuation of the comedy's almost clinical deconstruction of tragic realism, Inlaw's ostensible defence of Euripides sets the record straight about the true scope of female depravity. My primary – but not exclusive – focus is women's skilful exploitation of the practical and spatial precepts of proper οἰκονομία and its larger ethical and ideological purposes in the polis to serve their insatiable lust. While this demonstration of what Euripides *did not* reveal about women does not strive for realism as we would define it, i.e., the faithful and accurate representation of reality, Inlaw's exaggerations detail those things that Euripides *cannot* reveal within the constraints of his genre. *Thesmophoriazusae* thereby exposes the limits of the comic Euripides' claim to represent the world, or at least women's world, realistically.

A corollary of Aristophanes' extended critique of tragic realism is comedy's own limitless capacity to represent and expose these same topics. Comedy can present women as they truly are in their varieties of shamelessness. *Thesmophoriazusae* casts its intergeneric debate about the true nature of women as a presentation of competing theories of dysfunctional οἰκονομία: the oppressive, masculine, Euripidean kind and the popular, female-oriented version that only comedy can represent. The significant novelty of this portion of *Thesmophoriazusae* is its critique of dramatic realism through the ideals of household management. Though direct evidence for this late fifth-century discourse of household management is patchy, its principles inform the ideology of domestic life throughout the tradition of Greek literature. Moreover, certain sophists developed an interest in its theory, specifically Protagoras of Abdera, who (in Plato) described his specialization as teaching others how best to run their households.[8] Xenophon's *Oeconomicus*, whose dramatic date is (at least) the late fifth century (*c.* 420–410 BCE),[9] is devoted entirely to the practices of οἰκονομία as well as the larger political ideals such practices expressed: the partnership and co-operation of husband and wife, a sense of parity between them, and order (τάξις) that ensured optimal household productivity and protected against the 'promiscuous chaos' (9.2–10) that threatened ethical and economic stability.

The third section of this chapter is the payoff of the earlier analyses, specifically *how* Aristophanes uses women as the ultimate test case for demonstrating the limitations of the putatively superior genre and extolling the capabilities of his own. Comedy's own contribution to the discourse of household management is a corrupted female brand of οἰκονομία with which women exploit household resources entrusted to them for development of the οἶκος and apply them for gastronomic and sexual gratification at odds with the financial and biological integrity of their husbands' estates. The complexity, scope and unpredictability of female mischief demands, Inlaw implies, strategies that create meaning on stage in analogous ways: openness, accumulation and multiplicity. Comedy's stylistic and topical promiscuity make it the only genre suited to address the multiplicity and unpredictability of female promiscuity. In a concentrated display of comedy's diversity of action, property and movement in Inlaw's speech, Aristophanes lobbies for his comedy's status as the genre uniquely capable of coming to terms with the practical and ethical ambit of female sexual agency.

Thesmophoriazusae is not retaliation against Euripides for some perceived trespass of comedy's rightful territory, i.e., women and the household, as a number of prominent studies have argued. A more fruitful approach to this comic exegesis of Euripides is to view it as an example of opportunistic positioning in the theatrical marketplace. Aristophanes' ridicule of the expectations that tragic realism cultivated in audiences for over a century does not just target Euripides:[10] it parodies the so-called competent spectator of tragedy, the fan whose intellect Euripidean tragedy flatters. This astute and informed consumer of drama, whom this study has periodically referenced, is finally introduced as a leading character of comedy.

I. Democratizing tragedies

Thesmophoriazusae preserves the most extensive depiction of the Aristophanic Euripides as an allegedly pretentious, hair-splitting intellectual of fashionable ideas and lower-class, demotic origins. *Thesmophoriazusae's* version of the man sits at roughly the midpoint between the earlier, curmudgeonly poet of

Acharnians and the pompous shade of *Frogs*. The comedy's treatment of Euripides and his work in some ways anticipates the extensive look at his philosophy of tragedy in *Frogs*, when he squares off against the representative of tragedy's earlier era, Aeschylus. Because its overt and explicit exegesis of Euripides illuminates tacit features of his tragedy that are merely implied in *Thesmophoriazusae*, *Frogs* supplies the critical idiom that can unpack the presentation of the poet six years earlier. When the hero Dionysus arrives in the Underworld seeking to resurrect the newly deceased Euripides in 405, he learns of the disturbance caused by the poet's recent arrival:

Οι. ὅτε δὴ κατῆλθ᾽ Εὐριπίδης, ἐπεδείκνυτο
τοῖς λωποδύταις καὶ τοῖσι βαλλαντιοτόμοις
καὶ τοῖσι πατραλοίαισι καὶ τοιχωρύχοις,
ὅπερ ἔστ᾽ ἐν Ἅιδου πλῆθος, οἱ δ᾽ ἀκροώμενοι
τῶν ἀντιλογιῶν καὶ λυγισμῶν καὶ στροφῶν
ὑπερεμάνησαν κἀνόμισαν σοφώτατον·
κἄπειτ᾽ ἐπαρθεὶς ἀντελάβετο τοῦ θρόνου,
ἵν᾽ Αἰσχύλος καθῆστο.

Sl: When Euripides came down, he started
performing for the muggers and purse-snatchers
and father-beaters and burglars, of which there
are a horde in Hades. And when they heard
his disputations and twists and turns, they
went mad for him and deemed him the smartest.
Then, fired up, he commandeered the chair
where Aeschylus sat.

Ran. 771–778

Evidently, Hades has a standing policy that the most excellent (τὸν ἄριστον) artist of any esteemed craft is awarded an official chair next to Pluto himself. Euripides' sophistic performances for a depraved mob of muggers, purse-snatchers, father-beaters and burglars in Hades humorously describe the ethical and social makeup of the poet's fanbase and the viral spread of his popularity. There ensues a furious contest over which tragedian had the greater claim to the 'chair of tragedy' in Hades, the usurper Euripides or its current occupant, Aeschylus. The dispute is resolved through a poetic *agôn* stretching over several hundred lines. I would like to focus on just a few critical points. In response to Aeschylus's demand to hear from his opponent the criteria by which a good poet is deserving of admiration (*Ran.* 1008), Euripides answers that a poet's didacticism, skill and good counsel are the basis of poetic greatness. We learn that Aeschylus's claim to such admiration is his grand style, hieratic voice and larger-than-life heroes and demigods that made the audience into nobler and better soldiers by inspiring them with 'lust to be warlike' (*Ran.* 1021–1022). Euripides, by contrast, adduces his egalitarian characters, intellectualizing didacticism and realistic focus on elements of everyday life – i.e., its people, objects, conduct and actions – as the basis of his own claim to that same admiration. First, he claims to have given a voice to the socially marginalized: the wife, the slave, the maiden and the granny – and not just the master – all speak in his work (948–950). Because he 'democratized' tragedy:[11]

Ευ. δημοκρατικὸν γὰρ αὖτ' ἔδρων.
Δι.   τοῦτο μὲν ἔασον, ὦ τᾶν.
οὐ σοὶ γάρ ἐστι περίπατος κάλλιστα περί γε τούτου.
Ευ. ἔπειτα τουτουσὶ λαλεῖν ἐδίδαξα –
Αι.   φημὶ κἀγώ.
ὡς πρὶν διδάξαι γ' ὤφελες μέσος διαρραγῆναι.
Ευ. λεπτῶν τε κανόνας εἰσβολῶν ἐπῶν τε γωνιασμούς,
νοεῖν, ὁρᾶν, ξυνιέναι, στρέφειν †ἐρᾶν† τεχνάζειν,
κάχ' ὑποτοπεῖσθαι, περινοεῖν ἅπαντα –
Αι.   φημὶ κἀγώ.
Ευ. οἰκεῖα πράγματ' εἰσάγων, οἷς χρώμεθ', οἷς ξύνεσμεν,
ἐξ ὧν γ' ἂν ἐξηλεγχόμην· ξυνειδότες γὰρ οὗτοι   960
ἤλεγχον ἄν μου τὴν τέχνην· ἀλλ' οὐκ ἐκομπολάκουν
ἀπὸ τοῦ φρονεῖν ἀποσπάσας…

Eu: I was doing something democratic.
Di: Leave this alone, sir;
it isn't the best topic, coming from you.
Eu: Then I taught them how to talk …
Ae: I'll say!
If only you'd have burst apart first!
Eu: … and apply subtle rulers and squared-off words,
to think, to see, to understand, to twist, to love (?)
to scheme, to be suspicious of others, to think of all
aspects of everything …
Ae: I'll say!
Eu: … by staging everyday scenes, things we're used to,
which we live with, of which I would be grilled about,   960
because these spectators knew them as I do and could

have exposed my art. But I never distracted their minds
with bombastic bluster…

Ran. 952–962

This rich source of evidence for Aristophanes' reception of Euripides' mimetic philosophy, as Stanford observed, pokes fun at the 'suspicious and hypercritical temper of contemporary Athenians'.[12] The words ὑποτοπεῖσθαι ('to be suspicious'), a common term for the detection of deception or intrigue, and περινοεῖν ἅπαντα ('to think of all aspects of everything') evoke the πολυπραγμοσύνη of the radical democracy and its rancorous debates and partisanship.[13] Euripidean tragedy allegedly injects this aggressively interrogative approach to politics into citizens' private households. By mimicking the democracy's meticulous and litigious approach to public affairs, men learn to govern their domestic affairs, which Greek culture kept from the public eye and entrusted to the female members of the family. Euripides' claim seemingly satirizes the fairly common late fifth-century *topos* that οἰκονομία and political participation utilized the very same skill-set.[14]

Euripides' plain language, regular people, straightforward presentation of moral conundra and other οἰκεῖα πράγματα (*Ran.* 959) fostered a sense of confidence and intimacy between poet and audience – criminals in the Underworld and low-status, banausic craftsmen – who see him as a counsellor in their affairs and his plays a dialogue with them.[15] These too developed their own pretensions to being arbiters of Euripides' art and adjudicating its relevance to day-to-day life.

Frogs's characterization of the increased critical agency of the *dêmos* as spectators as a threat to peace and stability finds parallels in analogous explorations of the *dêmos*'s empowerment as a cause of political decline in other contemporary texts. The *locus classicus* is Thucydides' account of the second Mytilenean Debate (427 BCE), when Cleon lambasts the Assembly as victims of its own pleasure in listening to clever arguments in rhetorical contests (Thuc. 3.38.4–5). Athenians disadvantage themselves and their empire, he maintains, by acting as spectators (θεαταί), enchanted by novel argument (καινότητος … λόγου) and slaves to every paradox (τῶν αἰεὶ ἀτόπων). Slightly more germane to the dramatic subject at hand is Plato's account of Athenian θεατροκρατία and its contempt for established laws (*Leg.* 659b–c, esp. 659d).[16] Plato blames this ethical decline on the public's growing estimation of its own powers of discernment in musical performance, alleging that audiences of an earlier time respected the boundaries of genre by remaining composed and refraining from voicing their feelings by 'catcalls' (ἄμουσοι βοαί, 700c) and outbursts (θόρυβοι, 700d) during performances. Then the New Music began blending genres and melodies, encouraged by the positive response of the audience:

> By compositions of such a kind and discourse to the same effect, they inspired the masses with contempt of musical law and an arrogance in their own competence as judges. Thus once silent audiences found a voice, in the belief that they understand what is good and bad in art; and in place of old rule of the best in that sphere arose an evil sovereignty of the audience. If democracy was the only thing to come out of this, the outcome would not have been very bad. But now a general conceit of universal knowledge and contempt for law resulted from music, and liberty followed after. Fear was cast out by confidence in supposed knowledge, and loss of such fear gave birth to impudence. Dismissiveness of the opinion of one's betters that comes from shameless excess of liberty is basically a deplorable shamelessness.
>
> *Leg.* 700e–701a

This music's pernicious effect on audiences illustrates the larger ethical and political effects of declining cultural institutions that should ideally educate the public: contempt for the traditional laws of music brings about contempt for traditional ethical and political norms. Plato's reconstruction (or revision) of the history of Athenian festival culture identifies the principles of aesthetic judgment as ultimately indistinguishable from those of moral and political deliberation.[17]

Although not without their biases, Thucydides and Plato's accounts of Athenian 'rule of the spectator' (θεατροκρατία) are useful hermeneutics for understanding Euripidean tragedy's effect on audiences in *Frogs* and *Thesmophoriazusae*. Both plays attribute Euripidean tragedy's distinctly popular appeal to its very similar cultivation and encouragement of the public's own critical impulses. And Aristophanes humorously suggests that such exercises in judgment lead to dysfunction in public institutions. What concerns me here is Aristophanes' interest in the adverse effects of Euripidean θεατροκρατία in private, rather than public, business. Shortly after boasting of the didactic and democratic aims of his tragedy in *Frogs*, Euripides describes the private context in which his spectators applied the intellectual refinements of his tragedy:

> τοιαῦτα μέντοὐγὼ φρονεῖν
> τούτοισιν εἰσηγησάμην,
> λογισμὸν ἐνθεὶς τῇ τέχνῃ
> καὶ σκέψιν, ὥστ' ἤδη νοεῖν
> ἅπαντα καὶ διειδέναι

τά τ᾽ ἄλλα καὶ τὰς οἰκίας
οἰκεῖν ἄμεινον ἢ πρὸ τοῦ
κἀνασκοπεῖν, ‘πῶς τοῦτ᾽ ἔχει;
ποῦ μοι τοδί; τίς τόδ᾽ ἔλαβεν;’

That's how I encouraged these
people to think, by putting rationality
and critical thinking into my art, so that
now they grasp and really understand
everything, *especially* how to run their
households better than they used to,
and how to keep an eye on things:
‘How's this going?’ ‘Where'd that get to?’
‘Who took that?’

Ran. 971–979

By staging their day-to-day lives, Euripides claims to sharpen his audience's intellect, teaching them to apply critical thinking to everything around them: tragedy, politics and especially their own private lives. The core of this didactic program in *Frogs* is the proper way of running one's household. This ‘domestic realism’ is a collaboration between poet and his audience that cultivated the same aggressive and hypercritical judgment identified by Thucydides and Plato as the source of the *dêmos*'s intellectual and ethical decline in artistic and political spheres.[18] Yet *Frogs*'s derision of Euripidean tragedy's effort to encourage Athenian ‘busybodies and skinflints’ to question each other and authority is anticipated in Aristophanes’ mockery of the ‘chatter’ (λαλία) and quibbling of Telephus in *Acharnians*.[19] Nor is Euripides’ encouragement of Athenian πολυπραγμοσύνη in private life in the same play an entirely new contribution to comic discourse on Euripides. As I proceed to show, the infection of the domestic world by the didactic realism of Euripidean tragedy is anticipated in *Thesmophoriazusae* six years earlier. The satiric program in the latter play, however, calls into question both the nature of that realism and its claim to political efficacy.

II. At home with Euripides

The personal and domestic destruction wrought by Euripides’ notorious heroines – his Melanippes, Phaedras and Stheneboeas – have educated Athenian spectators with a curriculum of misogyny and made them suspicious of their own wives.[20] The alleged realism of his stylized mythological heroines has encouraged Athens's men to run their households very differently. For this reason, Athens's wives plan to retaliate against the poet on the occasion of the all-female gathering of the Thesmophoria, the annual festival to Demeter in celebration of the Athenian wife's contribution to the city and its prosperity.[21] As one of the few occasions when the politically excluded female community congregated, the festival furnished a rare opportunity for respectable women to worship, socialize and even gossip about everything from their home lives to their personal grievances. Aristophanes configures his Thesmophoria as a parallel female world, complete with its own political assembly,[22] whose sole order of business on this occasion is eliminating Euripides for slandering them consistently as keepers of lovers (μοιχοτρόφους), man-chasers (ἀνδρεραστρίας), wine-oglers (οἰνοπίπας), traitors (προδότιδας), chatterboxes (λάλους), pernicious (οὐδὲν ὑγιές) and the great bane (κακόν) of men's lives (*Thesm.* 383–432). The worshipper Mika's account of Euripides' influence confirms the psychological impact of this particular aspect of his tragedy:

> ὥστ᾽ εὐθὺς εἰσιόντες ἀπὸ τῶν ἰκρίων
> ὑποβλέπουσ᾽ ἡμᾶς σκοποῦνταί τ᾽ εὐθέως
> μὴ μοιχὸς ἔνδον ᾖ τις ἀποκεκρυμμένος.
> δρᾶσαι δ᾽ ἔθ᾽ ἡμῖν οὐδὲν ὥσπερ καὶ πρὸ τοῦ
> ἔξεστι· τοιαῦθ᾽ οὗτος ἐδίδαξεν κακὰ
> τοὺς ἄνδρας ἡμῶν· ὥστ᾽ ἐάν τίς <καὶ> πλέκῃ   400
> γυνὴ στέφανον, ἐρᾶν δοκεῖ· κἂν ἐκβάλῃ
> σκεῦός τι κατὰ τὴν οἰκίαν πλανωμένη,
> ἀνὴρ ἐρωτᾷ· ᾽τῷ κατέαγεν ἡ χύτρα;
> οὐκ ἔσθ᾽ ὅπως οὐ τῷ Κορινθίῳ ξένῳ;᾽
> κάμνει κόρη τις, εὐθὺς ἀδελφὸς λέγει·
> ᾽τὸ χρῶμα τοῦτό μ᾽ οὐκ ἀρέσκει τῆς κόρης.᾽
> εἶέν. γυνή τις ὑποβαλέσθαι βούλεται
> ἀποροῦσα παίδων, οὐδὲ τοῦτ᾽ ἔστιν λαθεῖν.
> ἄνδρες γὰρ ἤδη παρακάθηνται πλησίον·
> πρὸς τοὺς γέροντάς θ᾽, οἳ πρὸ τοῦ τὰς μείρακας
> ἤγοντο, διαβέβληκεν, ὥστ᾽ οὐδεὶς γέρων
> γαμεῖν ἐθέλει γυναῖκα διὰ τοὔπος τοδί·
> ᾽δέσποινα γὰρ γέροντι νυμφίῳ γυνή.᾽

As soon as our men get home from the stands,
they begin immediately glowering at us suspiciously
and searching the house for a hidden lover. We can
no longer do anything as we used to do before,

so terrible are the things this man has taught our
husbands about us. If a wife so much as weaves a   400
garland, she's suspected of being in love, and if she
drops some utensil as she moves around the house,
her husband asks, 'Who's the pot being broken for?
It's surely in honour of the Corinthian guest!' Say a
girl doesn't feel well; right away her brother says,
'This maiden's colour pleases me not at all!' There's
more. A wife without children wants to pass off another's
baby as her own but can't even get away with that,
since now our husbands plant themselves nearby. He's
slandered us to the old men too, who used to marry
young girls; now no old man wants to get married
because of the line, 'The elderly bridegroom gets
a boss.'

Th. 395–413

This humorous account of spectators applying the rules of genre to real life lays particular stress on the way men interpret physical and concrete signs within the household as indices of female psychology. Honed by Euripides' pernicious didacticism, men take swift and aggressive measures to avert the tragic 'narrative inevitability' that ensnares their less vigilant tragic counterparts.[23] Because their expectations about women have formed over the time they have spent in the theatre, even the most innocuous items and occurrences of everyday life trigger their fear of impending female corruption and disaster.[24] Since they watched the adulterous heroine of Euripides' *Stheneboea* (*c.* 430 BCE) pleat garlands for the sake of Bellerophontes, her husband's houseguest, the men believe their own wives have similarly fallen in love when they see them pleating garlands (400–401), one of women's many religious responsibilities. Commentators suggest Stheneboea's garland aimed to secure the hero's well-being during his labours.[25] An extant fragment of that play's prologue verbalizes the fear that grips the male mind: 'many men proud of their wealth and birth are disgraced by a foolish wife in their home' (fr. 661.5). Similarly, Bellerophontes is the putative 'Corinthian guest' whom men believe their wives are actually toasting whenever they drop a dish in the house.[26] Furthermore, women cannot even be sick without arousing suspicion of the illicit love-sickness or pregnancy (405–406), which Euripides has shown to be the herald of adultery.[27] Since the destruction of house and family is the expected outcome of the adultery of Stheneboea and the two other Euripidean heroines criticized by the Thesmophoriazusae (i.e., Phaedra and

Melanippe),[28] the fear of divine retribution – as much as the disgrace of their households – drives men's paranoia.[29]

Aristophanes makes effective comedy out of the dissonance arising from men's poetically conditioned expectations and the banality of day-to-day life in their households, where ordinary, commonplace and accidental events are freighted with dire consequences. Women's persecution in their own homes is the consequence of taking Euripides' putatively realistic and tendentious depiction of women as a model for interpreting the banalities of everyday life. Euripides' conventional portrayals of female biology and psychology furnish his poetically competent audience with a misleading template for identifying the signs of female corruption.

The indignities women suffer go beyond mere suspicion. Their men impose extreme restrictions on their movements in the house.

> εἶτα διὰ τοῦτον ταῖς γυναικωνίτισιν
> σφραγῖδας ἐπιβάλλουσιν ἤδη καὶ μοχλοὺς
> τηροῦντες ἡμᾶς, καὶ προσέτι Μολοττικοὺς
> τρέφουσι μορμολυκεῖα τοῖς μοιχοῖς κύνας.
> καὶ ταῦτα μὲν ξυγγνώσθ᾽· ἃ δ᾽ ἦν ἡμῖν πρὸ τοῦ
> αὐταῖς ταμιεῦσαι καὶ προαιρούσαις λαθεῖν,
> ἄλφιτον, ἔλαιον, οἶνον, οὐδὲ τοῦτ᾽ ἔτι
> ἔξεστιν. οἱ γὰρ ἄνδρες ἤδη κλείδια
> αὐτοὶ φοροῦσι κρυπτά, κακοηθέστατα,
> Λακωνίκ᾽ ἄττα, τρεῖς ἔχοντα γομφίους.
> πρὸ τοῦ μὲν οὖν ἦν ἀλλ᾽ ὑποῖξαι τὴν θύραν
> ποιησαμέναισι δακτύλιον τριωβόλου . . .

> Then, because of this man, they install seals and bolts
> on the women's doors to guard them, and not only that,
> they raise Molossic hounds to spook lovers. All that is
> forgivable. But we're not even allowed to do what used
> to be our own jobs: keeping household inventory and
> removing supplies on our own, like flour, oil and wine,
> because our husbands now carry the house keys with them,
> complicated nasty things with triple teeth, imported from
> Sparta. Before, we had no trouble opening the door with
> just a signet ring ordered for three obols . . .

Thesm. 414–425

Locks and doorbars (μοχλοί) are used to confine the mad within the house or keep out aggressors.[30] Here they reduce the residents to prisoners. The introduction of vicious dog breeds into the household would be especially problematic because Molossians were not house dogs but large ferocious mastiffs used for shepherding and hunting.[31] Given the openness of Greek houses, which were commonly organized around a central courtyard, the presence of an aggressive rural dog would prohibit even visits from approved friends and relatives, including symposia and, for example, rituals for the introduction and integration of children into the community. One might recall how the vicious herding-dogs of the swineherd Eumaeus nearly tear the disguised Odysseus to pieces when they do not recognize him.[32] Nasty Laconian locks exclude women from the food stores (418–423) and alienate them from what is arguably their most important domestic role, preparing and serving food. The special feature of the 'Spartan key' is that it locked doors from the outside. It may have acquired its moniker for its association with the Lacedaimonians' civic policy of excluding foreigners.[33]

The totalitarian rule that men have imposed on the household magnifies the traditional domestic hierarchy to the point where it impedes the house's proper functioning. Such extreme and self-defeating measures evoke the natal family's fruitless attempts to control (typically unmarried) females in Greek tragedy.[34] Seaford has shown how all three tragedians dramatize the extreme and oppressive measures of tyrannical male figures to preserve a maiden's chastity and prevent her marriage or rape by an outsider or god. This distortion of a female's natal bonds, usually through her confinement, consigns the maiden to a lonely and unnatural maidenhood in perpetuity.[35] My survey of the Telephus myth in Chapter 1 showed how Aleus attempted to preserve Auge's chastity by forcing her to serve as priestess of Athena. Chapter 3 mentioned Danae's confinement in a bronze tower and then a *larnax*. Extant and fragmentary Greek tragedy, including many plays of Euripides, preserves numerous examples of this imprisonment theme.[36]

In Aristophanes' comedification of this *topos*, Athens's men create problems as severe as those they attempt to prevent, disrupting the gender-based division of labour in the οἶκος, whose health and prosperity is idealized as an affectionate partnership between husband and wife in contemporary sources. Women become common domestic assets, stripped of their roles within the house, isolated from their extended family and presumably excluded from the broader community. *Thesmophoriazusae*'s distinctive parabasis, where Athens's wives demand recognition for the good as well as the bad they do, provides a helpful picture of this public participation: wives celebrate festivals together (795–796), loan each other household items and pay back what they take (811–813), and give birth to the city's best men (832–835). Apart from the economic disadvantages they incur from such aggressive micromanagement of their homes, men are prevented from doing their own work, either in the fields or the Assembly, if they sit at home guarding their wives like sedentary, banausic craftsmen, whom our elite sources consider shameful (Xen. *Oec.* 7.30).

While plenty of amusement is provided by the various tableaux in which clueless Athenian spectators attempt to pre-empt tragic inevitability, their authentic significance lies in the irony that such civic upheaval is caused by artificial, Euripidean conventions that make a pretence of realism. As early as *Acharnians*, the Aristophanic Euripides identifies this egalitarian realism as a promise to his audience of an increasingly greater role in shaping the genre. While the Athenian women of *Thesmophoriazusae* are hardly innocent, as the next section shows, the Euripidean heroine is a hopelessly inadequate measure for assessing female psychology and behaviour.

III. My two dads

Despite such mistreatment in their own homes, Athens's women – by their own admission – are not as blameless as their mythological counterparts in tragedy. They curse anyone who exposes a supposititious child (Ar. *Thesm.* 339–340), any slave who reveals that she has served as a procurer (340–341), any adulterer who lies (343–344) and all others who inhibit or expose their illicit behaviour. They protest that the infertile wife cannot even pass off a supposititious child as her own thanks to men's close attendance of the birthing process (407–409).[37]

These scattered and understated claims are brought to life in Inlaw's ensuing defence of Euripides (466–519). Contrary to what women claim, he explains, Euripides' restrained profiles of evil women in fact understate female wickedness. Like Dicaeopolis, Inlaw models his speech on that of Euripides' *Telephus*, but with the key difference that the opposition between speaker and audience is defined by gender, not nation or culture.[38] Inlaw's narrative of sexual deviancy emphasizes female exploitation of the principles of οἰκονομία with which women were meant to sustain and preserve their households in Greek thought. It plays on the powerful anxiety that drove Greek society's criminalization of adultery, namely that a husband would unknowingly support a child sired by an adulterer in his household. Aristophanes fashions Inlaw's narrative of women's secret sexual lives around the (ridiculous) assumption that the child in any given household has two fathers: the man believed to be the father, the legitimate husband, and its true biological father, a μοιχός.[39] Note especially the speech's repeated characterization of female crime as unpredictable and completely resistant to the rules and principles that, by contrast, governed Euripidean aesthetics of the same topic. Inlaw begins with an account of his own 'wifely' indiscretion:

> ἐγὼ γὰρ αὐτὴ πρῶτον, ἵνα μάλλην λέγω,
> ξύνοιδ' ἐμαυτῇ πολλὰ <δείν'·> ἐκεῖνο δ' οὖν
> δεινότατον, ὅτε νύμφη μὲν ἦν τρεῖς ἡμέρας,
> ὁ δ' ἀνὴρ παρ' ἐμοὶ καθηῦδεν. ἦν δέ μοι φίλος,
> ὅσπερ με διεκόρευσεν οὖσαν ἑπτέτιν.   480
> οὗτος πόθῳ μου 'κνυεν ἐλθὼν τὴν θύραν·
> κἀγὼ εὐθὺς ἔγνων· εἶτα καταβαίνω λάθρα.
> ὁ δ' ἀνὴρ ἐρωτᾷ· 'ποῖ σὺ καταβαίνεις;' 'ὅποι;
> στρόφος μ' ἔχει τὴν γαστέρ', ὦνερ, κὠδύνη·
> εἰς τὸν κοπρῶν' οὖν ἔρχομαι.' 'βάδιζέ νυν.'
> κᾆθ' ὁ μὲν ἔτριβε κεδρίδας, ἄννηθον, σφάκον·
> ἐγὼ δὲ καταχέασα τοῦ στροφέως ὕδωρ
> ἐξῆλθον ὡς τὸν μοιχόν· εἶτ' ἠρειδόμην
> παρὰ τὸν Ἀγυιᾶ κύβδ', ἐχομένη τῆς δάφνης.
> ταῦτ' οὐδεπώποτ' εἶφ' – ὁρᾶτ'; – Εὐριπίδης ...   490

To begin with, I myself, not to mention anyone else,
have a lot of awful things on my conscience. I'll tell
you maybe the worst. I'd been married only three days,
and my husband was sleeping beside me. But I had a
boyfriend who'd deflowered me when I was seven.
And he still had the hots for me, and he came scratching
at my door and I knew right away who it was. I start to
steal downstairs, and my husband asks, 'Where are you
going downstairs?' 'Where? I've got colic and achiness
in my stomach, husband, so I'm going to the can.' 'Go
on then.' And he starts grinding up juniper berries,
dillweed and sage, while I pour water into the door
socket and go out to meet my lover. Then I bend over,
holding onto the laurel tree by Apollo's Pillar, and get
pounded. Euripides has never said anything about
that, see what I mean?

Thesm. 476–490

This opening tableau subverts the primary criterion of marriageability for a woman, the sexual purity that enabled her to pass on her husband's blood. Though an adulteress after a mere three days married, 'she' had long been corrupted and was a 'sexual prodigy' by age seven.[40] Her rendezvous with an adulterer rehearses a sequence of common tropes: the signal of the lover; sudden withdrawal under pretence of illness; the hapless husband's humiliation; the cunning escape from the house undetected; and shameless copulation.[41] The wife's sexual liaison with her lover, in which she sacrilegiously grips the statue of Apollo and his laurel branch for dear life,[42] presents a variation of a familiar trope of illicit sexual encounters in temples and sacred spaces in contemporary genres.[43] Deserving of special note is the rendezvous's subtle but marked reversal of gender-based domestic norms: each spouse does/gets their 'pounding', the young wife asserting the typically male prerogative of seeking out extramarital sexual outlets (ἠρειδόμην: 'getting pounded'), while her emasculated husband assumes the more traditionally feminine and domestic task of preparing (ἔτριβε) a cordial.[44]

Such clever inversions of the approved functions of household economy drive the humour of the speech. It is not only that wives repeatedly outsmart and humiliate their hapless husbands to live out secret sexual lives, but that they do so by exploiting the skills and aptitudes acquired through οἰκονομία:

οὐδ' ὡς ὑπὸ τῶν δούλων τε κὠρεωκόμων
σποδούμεθ', ἢν μὴ 'χωμεν ἕτερον, οὐ λέγει·
οὐδ' ὡς ὅταν μάλισθ' ὑπό του ληκώμεθα
τὴν νύχθ', ἕωθεν σκόροδα διαμασώμεθα,
ἵν' ὀσφρόμενος ἀνὴρ ἀπὸ τείχους εἰσιὼν
μηδὲν κακὸν δρᾶν ὑποτοπῆται.

Nor does he mention how we get pounded by the
slaves and mule-grooms, if we don't have anyone
else; nor how we chew garlic in the morning after
we've been really shagged by someone all night, so
that when the husband coming home from the wall gets
a whiff he won't suspect we've been doing anything
naughty.

Thesm. 491–496

Since Greek wives were tasked with supervising servants and other workers around the house while their husbands were away working, household slaves and labourers likely had an unusual amount of access to them.[45] Months earlier

Aristophanes made a similar joke in his *Lysistrata*, when one of the male adversaries of Athens's sex-striking wives explains how men unwittingly enable (ξυμπονηρευώμεθα, 404) their wives' corruption. Foolishly, he explains, they arrange for the young cobbler with a large penis (πέος ἔχοντ' οὐ παιδικόν, 415) to visit the house, while they themselves are away, and 'loosen up' her sandal, 'so that she's got a little more room in there' (χάλασον, ὅπως ἂν εὐρυτέρως ἔχῃ, *Lys.* 419).

With a similarly mundane household item, garlic, wives forestall suspicion that they have welcomed lovers in their own bed by chewing it in the morning: husbands returning from guard duty on the wall will never suspect they have been with anyone else.[46] Inlaw's ensuing remarks may parody a specific text known to his audience:

> … εἰ δὲ Φαίδραν λοιδορεῖ,
> ἡμῖν τί τοῦτ' ἔστ'; οὐδ' ἐκεῖν' εἴρηκέ πω,
> ὡς ἡ γυνὴ δεικνῦσα τἀνδρὶ τοὔγκυκλον
> ὑπαυγάσ' οἷόν ἐστιν, ἐγκεκαλυμμένον[47]   500
> τὸν μοιχὸν ἐξέπεμψεν, οὐκ εἴρηκέ πω.

> … if he abuses Phaedra,
> what's that to us? He hasn't yet told that one,
> the one about the woman showing the weaving
> to her husband, stretching it out under the sun's
> light as her lover, all muffled up, bolted out,   500
> no he hasn't.

Thesm. 497–501

The term τὸ ἔγκυκλον refers to the purple border of a woman's *himation*, which was specifically used to veil the appearance and conceal the physical form.[48] A husband's unexpected return from work has trapped an adulterer in the house. To distract her husband, the wife has spread out her weaving in the light as proof of her devotion and productivity while obscuring his view of the escaping lover. As many others have noted, the joke perverts weaving as a sign of proper female industriousness since Homer.[49] Although myths with prominently featured textiles often attend and symbolize a high degree of female agency, such domestic agency undermines the home's integrity.

Though the vignette is clear in overall thrust, the detail of the 'muffled' (ἐγκεκαλυμμένον) adulterer has troubled scholars, who are uncertain of the value of a swathed head for an adulterer if he were seen.[50] However, Seager observed that an obscured appearance would protect the adulterer's identity if he were seen but not caught, since the husband would be unable to identify him.[51] Building on Seager, Cowan has persuasively argued for the scene's possible inversion of a detail in Euripides' earlier controversial Phaedra play, *Hippolytus Kaluptomenos* ('Hippolytus Veiled'). The title is generally but not universally believed to refer to the doomed youth's concealment of his face in an expression of shame (αἰδώς) at his stepmother's direct sexual advance.[52] If Cowan is correct, the parody of *Hippolytus Kaluptomenos* pivots on the discrepancy between tragedy's highly stylized and, in Aristophanes' view, considerably less realistic representation of female wrongdoing and the true reality Inlaw presents: in the comic world, 'real' youths do not veil themselves out of shame in the face of a sexual advance, as the noble and chaste Hippolytus, but in order to avoid *being identified* by the husband they have just cuckolded. While the wife uses τὸ ἔγκυκλον to distract her husband and obscure his vision, the adulterer flees with a second fabric around his face.

The precise setting of this meeting between husband and wife within the spatial organization of the house strengthens Cowan's case but also provides a more expansive look at women using οἰκονομία to capitalize on their natural environment. The display of the garment in the sunlight may be set in the street before the house.[53] But there are hints that it occurs within the household. Among the shared architectural features of contemporary houses reconstructed from extant ruins in Attica, Olynthus and elsewhere is their centripetal organization around an open space or courtyard. The roofless courtyard, which divided the (single) street entrance from the separate rooms at the rear, provided a work-area in which activity and movement could be monitored from most points within. This specific arrangement accommodates the action proposed by Seager and Cowan: the wife, mid-coitus in one of the rear rooms, hears her husband's entrance from the street door, rushes to the courtyard, picks up the ἔγκυκλον and meets him before he reaches the back of the house.[54] Colonnades bordering the courtyard on the side facing the separate rooms would help obscure the fleeing intruder.

This specific design of the house to control contact between visitors and the family's female members can provide some sense of the adulterous wife's transgressions. Like the deceptive trip to the toilet, the weaving adulteress exploits household architecture to undercut the norms it was designed to enforce. In Inlaw's speech, true female iniquity does not simply contravene the generic patterns of tragedy: its very deceptions make use of the practical and organizational features of the house intended to restrict women's movements. The climax of Inlaw's narrative is a duplicitous wife's introduction of a purchased illegitimate baby into the household.

ἑτέραν δ᾽ ἐγῷδ᾽ ἣ ᾽φασκεν ὠδίνειν γυνὴ
δέχ᾽ ἡμέρας, ἕως ἐπρίατο παιδίον·
ὁ δ᾽ ἀνὴρ περιήρχετ᾽ ὠκυτόκι᾽ ὠνούμενος·
τὸ δ᾽ εἰσέφερε γραῦς ἐν χύτρᾳ, τὸ παιδίον,
ἵνα μὴ βοῴη, κηρίῳ βεβυσμένον.
εἶθ᾽ ὡς ἔνευσεν ἡ φέρους᾽, εὐθὺς βοᾷ,
᾽ἄπελθ᾽ ἄπελθ᾽, ἤδη γάρ, ὦνέρ, μοι δοκῶ
τέξειν.᾽ τὸ γὰρ ἦτρον τῆς χύτρας ἐλάκτισεν.
χὠ μὲν γεγηθὼς ἔτρεχεν, ἡ δ᾽ ἐξέσπασεν   510
ἐκ τοῦ στόματος τοῦ παιδίου, τὸ δ᾽ ἀνέκραγεν.
εἶθ᾽ ἡ μιαρὰ γραῦς, ἣ ᾽φερεν τὸ παιδίον,
θεῖ μειδιῶσα πρὸς τὸν ἄνδρα καὶ λέγει·
᾽λέων λέων σοι γέγονεν, αὐτέκμαγμα σόν,
τά τ᾽ ἄλλ᾽ ἀπαξάπαντα καὶ τὸ ποσθίον
τῷ σῷ προσόμοιον, στρεβλὸν ὥσπερ κύτταρος.᾽
ταῦτ᾽ οὐ ποιοῦμεν τὰ κακά; νὴ τὴν Ἄρτεμιν
ἡμεῖς γε.

And I know another wife who pretended to be in
labour for ten days, until she could buy a baby, while
her husband was running all over town buying medicine
to quicken birth. An old woman brought it in a pot,
the baby I mean, its mouth stuffed with a honeycomb
so it wouldn't cry. Then the old woman gave the signal
and the wife yells, 'Out you go, husband, out you go;
this time I think I'm giving birth!' Yes, the baby had
kicked the pot's belly! He ran out joyous, she unplugged   510
the child's mouth, and it raised a shout. Then the dirty
old lady who'd brought the baby runs out to the husband
smiling and says, 'You've got a lion, sir, a lion, the very
image of yourself, sir, with everything a perfect match,
its little dick too, curled over like an acorn!' Don't we
commit these misdeeds? By Artemis, we do indeed!

Thesm. 502–518

A wife fakes labour long enough for her old nurse to purchase a substitute while the husband degrades himself with the slavish labour of buying drugs in the market. The old nurse, a common enough character in tragedy, facilitates the fraud by purchasing what was doubtless the unwanted child of a slave and introducing it into the household as legitimate.[55] The household pot, a χύτρα, comically represents a false womb, at which the baby kicks from within.[56] The pot underscores the irony of the plot to introduce an otherwise unwanted child. Wide-mouthed pots were commonly used for the burial (or exposure) of dead (or unwanted) infants in order to protect the body from scavenging animals. This tour de force of deception manipulates the full resources at the wife's disposal as household manager: the unfettered movement of her aged female slave; the common household χύτρα; the unmonitored privacy of the birthing process. The crowning insult is the crone's deception of the simple-minded husband with the well-established trope of recognition between separated kin in epic and tragedy. In loftier genres like tragedy, the token used is normally a scar, piece of embroidery or some other object that preserves and commemorates an important event in the family history. In this case, the comic recognition is facilitated by what is (at least in comedy) the *least distinctive* part of the male anatomy in comic costume, the penis.[57] The basis of affiliation between father and son, who lacks any biological connection to either parent, is their shared endowments.[58] Like the Echo who appears later in the play, the old crone is a standard comic substitution for a maternal figure. This disgusting Eileithuia suddenly appears to facilitate the 'birth' of the baby whom she compares to a lion. A comic Heracles, the child has two fathers: the sap who believes he is the father and the unknown, biological father.[59] In comedy's world, every wife in Athens is a potential Alcmene, whose child might be fathered by one of two potential men, her husband or an adulterer.

Inlaw's virtuoso narrative of female sexual escapades prompts questions about its generic affiliation. Their rapid and abbreviated form suggests that they were familiar to audiences, and scholars usually ascribe them to comedy.[60] Yet extant comedy before 411 BCE offers little evidence for the wife as part of the established repertoire.[61] Alternatively, Inlaw's speech may draw from a more lowbrow, popular genre. Chapter 3's discussion of the adultery narrative in the context of *Dionysalexandros* raised a number of possible sources for these vignettes.[62] Yet their generic provenance is less important than their multiplicity and variety, which define female sexual agency in the play's first half. The wives exploit principles of οἰκονομία for their own sexual gratification. As it is for Inlaw's new bride, who was deflowered at the age of seven, sexual transgression is a *condition* of comic femininity, which shapes and exploits οἰκονομία and the domestic world in service to the comic woman's baser condition. The typical μοιχός is never a high-status male but simply an available one, i.e., slaves, labourers and tradesmen. Because comic sex and sexual deception occur inside, outside and frankly everywhere, they operate outside known literary and cultural expectations. The partnership of husband and wife in the house's division of labour, the order (τάξις) and transparency of space and resources, and that order's expression of the family's ethical propriety, ideally maximized the resources of the οἶκος but also restrained women's innate potential for excess and subversion of order.[63] The perverse comic brand of οἰκονομία described by Inlaw exploits those household resources assigned to women for development. Water, garlic, fabric, pots, money and even servants are misapplied to sustain women's secret sex lives. This cacophonous mixing of objects and the abuse of their proper uses threaten the biological integrity of the household and muddle the organizational categories – function, placement, gender – of domestic life.

IV. Comedy exceeding expectations

It is difficult to believe that Athenian spectators actually saw Euripides' morally compromised heroines or Inlaw's shameless women in their own wives and daughters. Femininity is rather an amusing pretext for exploring a different issue, one of the key concerns of this study: how genres engage the expectations that spectators brought to performances. The speeches for and against Euripides who, as Silk writes, has not misstated the case against women so much as understated it: tragedy, with its conventional and stylized portrayal of human behaviour and psychology, not to mention its stricter standards of decorum, lacks the repertoire and imaginative flexibility to represent the agency and ingenuity of female deception to a satisfactory degree.[64] Though Greeks would not use the term, we would describe this as a problem of realism. Nor are Euripides and his realism the only targets of *Thesmophoriazusae*. The spectators themselves are lampooned for their complicity in that realism and invasive promotion of it in their homes.

Like the play's later parodies of *Palamedes, Helen* and *Andromeda*, its portrayal of Athens's men absurdly organizing their lives by the artificial dictates of tragedy invites ancient spectators and modern readers to consider what is actually 'real' about the realism claimed by the Aristophanic Euripides of *Thesmophoriazusae* and *Frogs*. Ruffell argues that the paratragic escape attempts of *Thesmophoriazusae*, as well as Dicaeopolis's Telephean persona in *Acharnians* and Trygaeus's Bellerophontean flight in *Peace*, call into question Euripides' 'mapping' between fictional tragic worlds and the ostensibly real world of comedy.[65] While they certainly underscore the thoroughly conventional and stylized aspect of Euripides' allegedly realist content – its empirical impossibility, limited emotional realism and over-reliance on artificial devices – do these comedies all critique Euripides' work as 'hyper-realistic', and even in the same way, as Ruffell describes it?[66] While certainly prepared to agree that *Acharnians* and *Peace* lampoon such hyper-realism, I believe *Thesmophoriazusae*, at least those parts examined in this study, makes a very different point about realism as it pertains to representing women: though the Athenian public widely assumes it to be realistic, Euripidean tragedy – at least when representing women – is anything but.

We enjoy Mika's description of the way Euripides has made life for the Athenian woman tense and unpleasant because it is so absurd. Euripides' paranoid and pretentious fans run their households on principles derived from the fictional world of the stage. Their 'reading' of the real world as one that operates according to tragic conventions and probability produces the same collision found in this study's previous analyses of paratragedy. Tragic convention and the banality of life collide in the opposing interpretations, the 'discrepant decoding', of the tragic indices of adultery by husbands and wives.[67]

Mika's eyewitness account is an 'experiencing' focalization that aims to increase its emotional effect, and it privileges consistency in space, time and milieu.[68] Events are arranged hierarchically and developed with a certain probability: upon their return from the performance, men's innate suspicions of women lead to interrogation followed by radical change in domestic life. Their behaviour accordingly arouses certain expectations in audiences, as they proceed to interpret various trivial household events as evidence of wrongdoing (*Thesm.* 414) and begin imposing harsher household measures: confinement, seals and bars, dogs, and Spartan locks. These benighted efforts are amusing because they are ultimately self-defeating and merely provide false security against the true nature of female crime. The speech's strategic repetition of specific Euripidean elements satirizes popular enthusiasm for Euripides by portraying what Rosen describes as the phenomenon of 'fandom',[69] one of Athenian culture's 'mechanisms of iterability' through which a poet's work and reputation became 'classicized' as something more concrete and fixed after its original performance.[70] Like the Underworld audience's passion for Euripides' public displays in *Frogs*, men's psychological investment in the accuracy of the Euripidean woman reflects the *dêmos*'s fanatic enthusiasm for the poet.

The focal point of male delusions is the intersection of Euripidean stagecraft and its distinctive dramatic illusion, or realism. Although notional as opposed to physical, the properties highlighted in Inlaw's description nonetheless evoke thematic patterns which the spectators have learned to internalize because of their experience of tragedy. The crux of the satire emphasizes the fans' perception of a necessary relationship between these otherwise common and everyday objects and female character, a relationship stressed by the prominence of the physical and material as an accurate or realistic reflection of emotion or intention, or human psychology.[71] As visual elements of a universally or near universally decodable kind, props are an important component of the everyday that Euripides, and to a lesser extent Aeschylus and Sophocles, inserts into his work to bolster a greater sense of realism. As Revermann explains, props:

> often bring a history to a play, apart from acquiring such while dramatic attention in being lavished on them. Like all theatrical signs, props can, to use semiotic jargon, be polyfunctional as indexical, iconic and symbolic signs (possibly all three at the same time). They are also mobile signs, meaning that they are capable of replacing any other sign system: the waving of a handkerchief, for example, can replace a farewell speech; a Christmas tree on stage may replace any other indication (verbal or non-verbal) that the action takes place during Christmas time, and so forth.[72]

The excessive credence given by men to such slight and dubious evidence of female wrongdoing exaggerates tragedy's tendency to invest those minimal properties and movements it did deploy with clear and distinctive significance.[73] The men's singling out and erroneous decoding of the wreaths, dishes and female complexion exaggerate the conventional way by which a significant prop with distinctive associations can focalize stage action in a particular way.[74] In tragedy, such props put the spectator inside the fictive mind of the character and inspire a general expectation – often as soon as they appear to the spectator – that their bearer will act in specific ways.[75] Because of their powerful stage biographies, the properties noted by Mika possess their own generic mini-narratives, which imbue the otherwise insignificant and banal occurrences of women's everyday life with a pernicious significance, and implicate women in the clandestine schemes of sexual transgression by tragic heroines. In reality, those items belong to no broader pattern of tragic action and consequence any more than any other common household item. As symbols of those plots, the objects appeal to the spectator's imagination, cultural background and theatrical knowledge, supplanting the neutral and everyday application of the same properties in the household, i.e., their denotative value, to become evidence of 'plausible intentionality'. This expression from Poe describes a prop that, when manipulated, connotes a character's status or state of mind, and thus their intention in the dramatic action.[76]

Although ostensibly arguing for the limitations of Euripides' understanding and portrayal of household matters, Inlaw offers a competing pattern of adultery as an example of comedy's own tendentious standard of realism. This proceeds by a different dramatic logic, one with a much higher tolerance for illogicality and improbability than tragedy has. In effect, it demonstrates that Old Comedy's openness and multiplicity, its principles for the creation of meaning in performance, are uniquely compatible with the openness and unpredictability of the present topic of the play, female agency. The speech narrates in concentrated form those practices that lend a distinctive openness and multiplicity of meaning to comic stagecraft. Where Mika's account presents several static moments in a hierarchy – homecoming, interrogation and restriction – Inlaw's accumulated tableaux privilege the openness, multiplicity and improbability of female crime. The lengthy opening episode with the νύμφη is followed by several paratactic scenes: wives sleeping with slaves and labourers, wives chewing garlic, wives distracting with weaving and, finally, the supposititious child. The variety and rapidity of presented objects emphasize not the 'plausible intentionality' like that of tragedy, but the way comic props defy any reasonable expectations they might evoke for an informed audience. The latrine, the garlic, the cloth and the pot lack the plausible intentionality that is definitive of tragedy.[77] The variety of women's improbable and outrageous deployment of numerous pretences and properties poses a much greater hermeneutic challenge whose decoding requires a more astute and informed spectator, the comic spectator.

The prop of *Thesmophoriazusae* is the most economic means of representing the superior realism of a handful of comic strategies of making meaning, such as the 'openness' represented by the accumulated action of Inlaw's narrative. His paratactic arrangement of different adulterous scenarios – as opposed to the successive narration of Mika's speech – describes multiple entries and exits of characters as opposed to the strongly motivated movements identified by Taplin and others as essential to tragedy's structure.[78] The unbounded scope of the faithless woman's movements, inside and outside the house and everything in between, lacks such unity of space and time. Comic adultery is defined by such openness and discontinuity of accumulated action and object. Audience expectations formed by any other genre, even comedy, are obsolete.

In essence, *Thesmophoriazusae* implies that sexual infidelity can only be represented by generic and performative infidelity, or promiscuity rather. The play's critical exercise at Euripides' expense is an advertisement for comedy's near unlimited capacity for representation, which is bound by no law. Inlaw's affirmation of comedy's status as the only genre capable of truly and effectively treating something as ethically and psychologically complex as woman is arguably the strongest promotion of Aristophanes' brand vis-à-vis tragedy.[79]

Only this genre has the requisite freedom from logical and ethical constraints and near limitless repertoire to dramatize the variety and sheer unpredictability of female agency for which the narrower and idealized strictures of other forms prove inadequate in *Thesmophoriazusae*. Comparison of Inlaw's critique of tragedy to Dicaeopolis's earlier metapoetic argument for the social and political value of comedy in *Acharnians* makes this point more emphatically. Insofar as it asserts Euripides' mimetic inferiority by demonstrating the compatibility of women's secret lives and comedy's narrative and dramatic style, Inlaw's speech amounts to the claim that 'comedy knows women, too' (cf. *Ach.* 500). This is *how* Euripides' version of the wife and her life is exposed as an inferior analogue to what has been described as the 'more relevant and useful comic anecdote.'[80] However, this is not quite the same as concluding, as some scholars have, that *Thesmophoriauzusae* claims women and their domestic world as the natural 'territory' upon which Euripides has transgressed.[81] It seems no more true to describe *Thesmophoriazusae*'s analysis of gender as retaliation for Euripides' trespass of the comic repertoire than it is to describe Aristophanes' claim of justice in *Acharnians* as retaliation for tragedy's interest in notions of justice. *Thesmophoriazusae* seems to suggest that tragedy, which has portrayed women for generations, has not delivered the level of accuracy that both its own prestige and woman herself merit.

More than any other Aristophanic comedy, *Thesmophoriazusae* bespeaks the poetic efficacy of parody and appropriation in Old Comedy, which absorbs material from all conceivable poetic and cultural sources as the premier survival machine of Athenian literary culture. Only comedy can stage such a public and sustained exegesis of poetry and art of this scale. By using Euripidean fandom as a conduit for the process of his reception, Aristophanes attempts to claim that his comedy does not just arrogate other poets and their work, it influences their subsequent receptions. While Aristophanes obviously exaggerates and perverts the nature of what we might call Euripidean realism, his provocative exegesis raises fundamental questions about dramatic poetry's capacity to influence its audience's perception of the world.

Conclusion

A prominent scholar of Greek religion describes the Thesmophoria as an absolute ritual expression of the ideological division of labour between the sexes.[82] Given the festival's purpose of honouring and celebrating women's contribution to fertility and the household, Aristophanes' selection of this setting for his humorous exploration of the *male* contribution to representing women and their lives is ironic. *Thesmophoriazusae* makes light of this opportunity for Athens's marginalized female community to reaffirm its essential but strictly defined and regulated role in the city by exposing women's true priority, which is maintaining the secret status quo of their salacious private lives by eliminating Euripides, its greatest threat.

Treatments of Old Comedy's imaginative exuberance typically focus on its grandest and most fantastic expressions of escapism: the private peace; the flight to heaven on the beetle; the creation of an avian empire to rival the Olympians. *Thesmophoriazusae*'s innovative exploration of genre directs this imaginative drive inward, into the private life of the household, the female domain, which the genre seems to have refrained from representing at length before 411 BCE. Inlaw's demonstration of the unpredictability of female behaviour and psychology is a potent example of Old Comedy's creative representation of the improbable. Its aesthetic is not escapist, but rather conservative, aiming to expose the mimetic limitations of Euripidean realism under the pretence of women's ethical shortcomings. Though *Thesmophoriazusae*'s links between gender and genre have long been recognized, the comedy's ostensible focus on Euripidean tragedy and its allegedly negative portrayals of women primarily serve Aristophanes' underlying interest in tragedy and comedy's competing notions of dramatic realism. The comedy's prefatory interest in tragedy's contemporary reception beyond the theatre of Dionysus and into the average Athenian household is a frame within which Aristophanes can address realism as it pertains to a specific subject of drama: women. In comparing the different ways each genre brings its style and repertoire to bear on the idealized paradigm of domestic life and undermines it, Aristophanes entertains the audience while drawing its attention to a subject whose dramatic representation tragedy cannot convey with comedy's (albeit tendentious) precision. Inlaw's revelation of the truth about women is obviously a gross exaggeration and not meant to be taken at face value. However, that distortion can at least draw upon the realia of household life and its principles of οἰκονομία found in the audience's world, which did not adhere to tragedy's heavily stylized laws of characterization and probability. Dramatic poetry, like all literature, is incapable of representing the psychological complexities of gender with any precision. *Thesmophoriazusae*'s point is that Old Comedy, through its principles of openness and multiplicity, is the *only* genre capable of coming to grips with that complexity to any satisfactory degree in performance.

Thesmophoriazusae continues *Acharnians*'s critique of the true extent of tragedy's practical value to the public and comedy's sense of its own value *vis-à-vis* its superior rival, but in the household's more immediate and familiar terms. Aristophanes does not claim parity with tragedy in the representation of women, and mimesis generally, but superiority. Given that Euripides and Aristophanes shared audiences, *Thesmophoriazusae*'s satire of Euripides' pretentious yet naïve acolytes amounts to mocking his own spectators. The unpredictability of the comic woman that Euripides *did not show* is comedy's argument against the restricted expectations of other genres. And this is why Aristophanes seems to be above all claiming for comedy a greater capacity to represent the world accurately, rather than propose a model of human behaviour, as the comic Euripides claims to provide throughout the Aristophanic corpus. Unlike tragedy, Old Comedy did not mould audiences' expectations in specific ways. It rewarded them for keeping their expectations a certain way: concentrated on current cultural and literary topics of interest, yet spacious enough to accommodate whatever imaginative delights the comic poets had in store for them.

Conclusion

τίς δὲ σύ; κομψός τις ἔροιτο θεατής.
ὑπολεπτολόγος, γνωμιδιώκτης, εὐριπιδαριστοφανίζων

'Who are you?' Some pompous spectator
would ask. A logic-chopper, maxim-chaser, Euripidaristophanizer

Cratinus fr. 342

This testimonium of Aristophanes' special interest in Euripides presents an alternative, if tendentious, view of Aristophanic branding as essentially one poet's cheap imitation of something generic about a second, trendy artist.[1] That an active manager of his brand, Aristophanes, has been branded unfavourably by a rival attests to the vital importance of controlling public narratives about one's work in fifth-century theatre. Cratinus's derision of his younger rival confirms that Aristophanes projected his work, his *trugôdia*, as sophisticated and innovative, and that his appropriation of tragedy was sufficiently well known to be publicly derided and distorted. There may be a certain irony in Cratinus's ridicule of another poet for fashioning his work in the mould of another, since there is some evidence that he modelled his own style and persona on that of Aeschylus. However, if evidence for Old Comedy attests to anything, it is that these poets were not prevented by a sense of honesty or shame from seizing any advantage in the competitive marketplace of fifth-century theatre. If more of Cratinus's own work had survived we might have less reason to believe that Aristophanes was distinctive in his parody and appropriation of tragedy and other forms.

The available evidence tells us little about all fifth-century comic poets except Aristophanes, and indicates that parody and appropriation informed his 'brand' during the fifth century, at least more than any other single topic, and that its evolution follows a reasonably coherent trajectory. The originality of *Acharnians's* contribution to the established tradition of Telephus is Aristophanes' reconception of the hero's hybridity along generic and social instead of ethnic and cultural lines. Dynamic, memorable and recognizable, the Euripidean Telephus reflects the kind of cross-cultural and cross-generic attributes that best suit the analogous attributes of τρυγῳδία around which Aristophanic comedy forges its brand personality. Just a few years later, *Peace* affirms the development of τρυγῳδία into an exemplary subgenre of Old Comedy. Most treatments focus on the comedy's appropriately named hero, but it is the dung-beetle whose generic hybridity, popular status and unique biology best symbolize the meaning of τρυγῳδία in 421. Feeding on the waste of other organisms, the dung-beetle is the biological counterpart of the parasitic comedy of Aristophanes, a survival machine of the poetic ecosystem and recycler of the old in an effort to spread its genes. In *Peace*, τρυγῳδία is defined above all by the creation of comic success from poetic 'failures', failures of plot and failures of culture, such as tragedy's corrupted sacrifices and weddings. These poetic conversions of failure are performed at a historical moment when Greece seemed as if it would overcome its many recent political failures, i.e., negotiations for peace. This political promise of τρυγῳδία to affect political change, or at least reflect upon political affairs publicly, is equally apparent in Aristophanes and Cratinus's appropriation of satyr play in *Peace* and *Dionysalexandros*. The evidence shows that several comic poets, by evoking the conventions of this other dramatic rival, attempted to defamiliarize conventional political satire in their genre, recontextualizing the Athenian present within the mythological world of the slaves of Dionysus.

Thesmophoriazusae is a fitting conclusion to this study. Much of its parody targets the political and social consequences of Euripides' adept brand management, specifically his creation of a brand personality around radical democratizing and the development of that brand through active exchange with his fans, the consumers. The basis of the Athenian choice of Euripidean tragedy, that it aligns with one's actual or preferred self and improves or adds something to one's life, is the same basis for a modern consumer's choice of one brand over its competitors. The fanatical loyalty that inspires Athenians to apply the norms of Euripides throughout their lives is the driving force of *Thesmophoriazusae*'s conflict between the poet and women. Given Aristophanes' portrayal of a banausic Euripides conceiving his craft-based tragedy from *Acharnians* onward, my conception of Euripidean tragedy as a marketed product is especially appropriate to the parody of *Thesmophoriazusae*.

Thesmophoriazusae's exegesis of Euripides is extant Old Comedy's most discursive reflection on each genre's different approach to reality and thereby anticipates Aristophanes' position of overall aesthetic independence from

Euripides in *Frogs*. The authentic significance of Inlaw's narrative of what Euripides 'did not say' and, thus, its inferior realism, is its indirect demonstration of comedy's more nuanced and capacious repertoire, i.e., its mimetic superiority. As Dionysus presides over the contest for tragedy's greatest poet in *Frogs*, Aristophanes seemingly implies that comedy belongs in its own category, which its mastery of parody and appropriation – for the salvation of the city – has afforded it as the ultimate arbiter of tragedy and other genres. Aristophanes' decision in this comedy to leave Euripides behind in Hades – dead – seemingly announces his creative independence from an artist who influenced him for so long. Despite the passing of that poetic organism, the survival machine of Aristophanic comedy, continuing to thrive, carries on some of its genes.

Given the nature of the evidence, this study has inevitably focused on Aristophanic comedy. Yet for all we know, Aristophanes' corpus may have been just one of many bodies of work that drove Old Comedy's evolution through parody and appropriation in the late fifth century. Glimpses of such evidence for parody outside the Aristophanic corpus were examined in the visual fragments of comedy-related vase painting in Chapter 2. Painters and/or their clients who commissioned vases evidently found the parody of genres, myths and institutions an excellent way to capture the essence of a given play's humour within the narrower expressive parameters of visual art. It is especially revealing that, more often than not, this essence of parody is conveyed in static images that are utterly pregnant with expectation, expectation being so critical to the comic effect of distorting a model text.

We cannot say for certain what role (if any) such theatre-related vases had in advertising a specific comic poet's brand, but such vases confirm another medium, outside the stage, in which spectators could participate in the process of 'feedback' that steered comic innovation. As plausible 'contexts of iterability' around which fans of theatre could recall, discuss and even promote specific productions and their poets, these vases may have shaped the legacies of specific comedies and even their style of humour as part of the classicizing process. The potential value of vases in this respect is enormous. Like printed playbills advertising signature scenes from their productions, could theatre-related vases have functioned as notices for other performances, i.e., a 'second run', after premiering at major festivals such as the Dionysia and the Lenaea? Less prestigious venues such as deme theatres in rural Attica were certainly an option for producers and poets who desired the continued performance of a play. Moreover, the ever-expanding number of cities that were importing Athenian drama throughout the Greek world naturally increased the possible venues for performance. The comic visuals of these paintings could generate interest and create a 'buzz' in advance of scheduled productions. If such vases *could* prolong the cultural life of the productions they featured, not unlike lyric poems' survival of their original performance by later recitation in various other contexts, they would function as an important conduit for the survival of the comic meme and the poet's legacy, maintaining the comic brand.

Despite the self-aggrandizing and polemical tendencies of comic poets like Aristophanes and Cratinus – especially in the passage quoted above – Old Comedy occasionally spoke in one voice and with some consistency on certain topics. The comic poets are unified in their hostility to the innovative, populist performers of the New Music. Perhaps threatened by the immense popularity of men like Timotheus, Cinesias and Philoxenus and, even more likely, their influence on contemporary tragedy, the poets of Old Comedy conduct a sustained PR battle against these rivals for popular favour. It is deeply ironic when poets of a genre, a genre in which shameless self-promotion and constant claims to innovation are *de rigueur*, suddenly become guardians of conservative tradition. Chapter 5 analysed the many passages in which comic poets directly or indirectly act as guardians of the 'classic' lyric, whose existence is allegedly under threat by the New Music, and guardians of the traditional musical and ethical norms represented by such classic artists as Pindar, Simonides and other lyricists of the Archaic period. Aristophanes, Eupolis and other poets who go to great lengths to characterize their brand as innovative within comedy shift to a more conservative message in order to compete with flamboyant artists outside drama and their pervasive influence over art and society. Like vase painting, lyric as a target of parody had the added attraction of easy circulation, something Old Comedy repeatedly acknowledges. The comic poets surely intended their parodies of specific lyric to enter public circulation just as these models had. It is easy to imagine some Athenians in the Assembly cynically whispering 'sleek and violet-crowned Athenians' (αἱ λιπαραὶ καὶ ἰοστέφανοι Ἀθῆναι) to one another as the majority was being taken in by flattery from foreign representatives. Perhaps Timotheus was derided as the 'rapist of *Mousikê*' for a time thanks to Pherecrates. I have a feeling at least one symposiast in Athens imitated Cinesias being pummelled while demanding to 'cleave a harbourless furrow of sky' (*Av.* 1400) in the days following the production of *Birds* in 414 BCE.

Despite its challenging and sometimes patchy evidence, this study has shown that parody and appropriation were evolutionarily stable strategies for Old Comedy in the competitive marketplace of fifth-century theatre. Although Old Comedy reigned for just a brief moment in the great span of Western comic drama, the originality and ingenuity of these poets who figured out how to prolong and advance their own careers by appropriating from their generic superiors can still be observed in the present: in the sometimes brilliant parody of contemporary sketch comedy; in the boundary-pushing crudity of the comic 'roast'; and, most especially, in that rare lampoon that is so successful that we are unable to remember the 'serious' work it appropriated.

Notes

Introduction

1 Politics: The comedian Tina Fey repeatedly parodied the brash and polarizing US Republican vice-presidential candidate Sarah Palin on *Saturday Night Live* leading up to the 2008 presidential election, which she and her running mate, John McCain, would eventually lose. The parody was so effective that many Americans were unaware that one of its memorable lines, that Palin claimed she could see Russia from her house (in Alaska), was never in fact spoken by her. Ruined lives: Noted Miami dermatologist of the stars Fredric Brandt spiralled into depression and eventually committed suicide in April 2015 after he was parodied on the Tina Fey-produced comedy, *Invincible Kimmy Schmidt*. Violence: In retaliation for satirical caricatures of the prophet Muhammad by the French satirical magazine *Charlie Hebdo*, two Al-Qaeda terrorists stormed the Paris headquarters of the magazine on 7 January 2015. They killed ten employees, including five cartoonists and two editors.

2 Monograph: Platter 2007; Biles 2011: 134–166; Ruffell 2011; Zogg 2014; Farmer 2017. Volume: Medda et al. 2005. Articles/chapters: Taplin 1983; 1986; 1993: 79–88; Foley 1988; 2008; Silk 1993; 2000: 42–97; Dobrov 2001; Revermann 2006a: *passim*; 2006b; Bakola 2010: 118–179; Silk 2013.

3 Theatre: Revermann 2006a; 2006b; Bosher 2012; Csapo and Miller 2007; Csapo et al. 2014. *Khorêgia*: Wilson 2000; 2007b. Music: West 1992; Murray and Wilson 2004; Power 2010. Acting: Easterling and Hall 2002; Csapo 2010.

4 Rau 1967: 1–18; cf. Silk 1993: 478–479

5 Important studies of satyr plays include Griffith 2002, 2005, 2008; O'Sullivan and Collard 2013; Lämmle 2013 and Shaw 2014. For comedy's adaptation of satyr play, see Dobrov 2001: 101–104, Storey 2005 and Bakola 2005, 2010.

6 Silk 1993: 480.

7 The meshing of a theme in parody (or appropriation) with the larger thematic agenda of a comedy is drawn from Swift's model (2010: 26–31) of tragedy's use of lyric tropes.

8 See also Rose (1993: 31) on the incongruity or discrepancy between the model and parody. In a further elaboration, Silk (1993: 480) adds that paratragedy in Aristophanes must involve *either* the presence of positively tragic features commonly absent in Aristophanes *or* the absence of non-tragic features commonly present in Aristophanes *or* both.

9   As analysed by Silk 1993: 480–481

10 The translation is Silk 1993. Unless stated otherwise, all translations of Greek are my own, all texts of Aristophanes are from N. Wilson 2007 and all comic fragments from Kassel and Austin 1983–2001.

11 Silk 1993: 481.

12 The apostrophe to the heart is typical of self-addresses in tragedy, e.g., Eur. *Med.*1056; *Alc.* 837 (καρδία).

13 On paralinguistic devices in drama, see Elam 2002 [1980]: 70–75.

14 As Swift 2010: 27–31 notes, more sustained allusion of particular lyric genres through motifs, *topoi* or stylistic features can affect an audience's perception of episode (medium) and play as a whole (high-level).

15 For comedy's nearly exclusive use of προσέρχεται to refer to arriving characters, see Austin and Olson 2004: *ad loc.* (with references).

16 Σ (Ar. *Th.* 871) claims that Euripides here donned the mask (τὸ πρόσωπον) of Menelaus.

17 Foley 2008: 23–24. This deferred recognition is parodied in the Euripidean choral lyric of *Frogs* (1309–1322).

18 On this, see the discussion of Allan 2008: 47–48.

19 Foley 2008: 24: '… [the scene] enables comedy to engage both verbally and performatively with the complex question of dramatic representation and imitation'.

20 For an assessment of the evidence, see Bakola 2010: 135, 141, 174–176.

21 See Bakola's convincing reading (2005; 2010: 81–102) of the play's hypothesis.

22 On modes, see Fowler 1982: 106–111; also Frow 2006: 63–67.

23 Garner 1990 and Bagordo 2003 explore specific allusions in tragedy.

24 E.g., Elam 2002; Pfister 1988. See also Roselli 2011: 3–6.

25 Fowler 1982; Frow 2006. For its application to Greek drama, see Silk 2013.

26 Bevis 2013: 4.

27 Each scholar was influenced by the earlier work of Michael Riffaterre and Roland Barthes; cf. Fish 1980.

28 Jauss 1982: 21.

29 Iser 1978 [1976]: 112.

30 Jauss 1982: 142–143; Iser 1978. On expectation in parody, see Rose 1993: 170–177.

31 Jauss inherited the concept of the horizon from his teacher, Hans-Georg Gadamer, who used the term to denote the historical perspective that was a hermeneutic precondition of traditional texts. To Gadamer (2013: 302–318), an analyst must understand a text on its own terms (or its true dimensions) by transposing himself into its different historical context and acquiring the perspective within which the author had formed his/her own views. By projecting himself into this historically specific horizon and acquiring this historical consciousness, he sees the text from a

superior perspective as part of a larger whole. Bringing together the circumstances of these two horizons of past and present constitutes understanding.

32 See esp. Bennett 1997: 38–39, 50–54.

33 Rose 1993: 170–177 (esp. 171); cf. Hutcheon's (1985: 20) more minimalist definition of parody as repetition with critical distance.

34 See Elam 2002: 85; Bennett 1997.

35 Gomme 1938; de Ste Croix (1972) goes on to articulate his dubious standard for identifying evidence for the poet's own views as those places in the text that express serious opinions *and* are not funny in themselves.

36 Henderson 1990. Subsequent studies of the poetic, social, and cultural forces driving comic satire have challenged this prevailing view of Old Comedy's real influence over Athenian politics by arguing for a more sceptical approach to Aristophanic satire: Halliwell 1984; 1993; Heath 1987; Rosen 1988; 2003; 2015. Yet even those disinclined to take Aristophanes at face value agree that certain passages appear to express the poet's own political views, for example the political recommendations of *Frogs*'s famous parabasis (*Ran.* 686–705; cf. Heath 1987; Silk 2000: 305–306); cf. *Nub.* 298–313.

37 Silk (2000: 301–349) is the first to locate poetic concerns and their social and political implications within a conception of the serious.

38 I identify with the majority's view that the theatre audience consisted of women, slaves and other social minorities, but that comedy notionally defines its audience as a male and Athenian citizen community.

39 Burian 1997: 191.

40 De Ste Croix 1972: 357.

41 Roselli (2011: 28–29) argues that comedy presents the spectators and judges' views as equal in value.

42 Roselli 2011: 44–47.

43 For summaries of this dynamic, see Revermann 2006a: 6, 20–21; Wilson 2000, 2007a; Biles 2011.

44 Revermann 2006a: 94.

45 Roselli 2011: 22 (on ancient testimonies comparing the large sums of festival expenditure in Athens with other expenses, i.e., political and military).

46 For changes to the payment of actors and poets at the end of the fifth century, see Revermann 2006a: 22. The increasing specialization of actors and musicians is discussed by Csapo 2010: 83–116.

47 The number of program slots for comedy is usually regarded as five, with a reduction to three during the Peloponnesian War. The eponymus archôn was tasked with selecting the poets whose plays would receive funding (Csapo and Slater 1995: 105).

48 The actor's prize was instituted at the City Dionysia in 449 and at the Lenaea in 432.

49 For theatrical families, see Sutton 1987; Csapo 2010: 88–89; and Roselli 2011: 136.

50 Dawkins 2006: 62.

51 Halliwell 1998: 49–51.

52 Dawkins 2006: 194.

53 Note also how Cratinus passes away (ἀπέθανεν) at *Pax* 700.

54 The idea was first introduced by Maynard Smith and Price 1973.

55 On intrageneric conflict, see Rosen 2000; Biles 2002; Ruffell 2002.

56 See Dawkins's (2006: 69–86) discussion of this term.

57 Dawkins 2006: 83.

58 Cf. Foley 2008: 28–33, who argues that Aristophanes' influence can be seen in Euripides' special use of comic self-consciousness and distancing, specifically his continued use of ragged heroes following *Acharnians*.

59 Cf. e.g., Zeitlin's (1996: 398) claim that the paratragedy of *Thesmophoriazusae* is retaliation for Euripidean transgressions against social (and aesthetic) norms in his *Helen* and *Andromeda*; cf. Taaffe 1993: 98; Bowie 1993: 219–220.

60 See Gibert 1999–2000: 89–90.

61 Mastronarde's (1999–2000: 25; 2010: 47) comparison of dramatic genre to a slowly moving target; cf. Fowler's (1982: 37) understanding of genre as less a pigeonhole and more like a pigeon.

62 Conte 1992: 111.

63 The Russian formalist Shklovsky (2008: 14) discusses the value of such non-art elements to generic renewal; cf. Silk 2013: 32.

64 Hutcheon 1985: 97.

65 Bakola argues (2010: 24–29 and *passim*), at least, that Cratinus branded his comedy as affiliated with Aeschylus and Dionysus.

66 Σ Ar. *Eq.* 526a: ὁ γὰρ Κρατῖνος οὕτω πως ἑαυτὸν ἐπήνεσεν ἐν τῇ Πυτίνῃν...; cf. Ar. *Eq.* 526–528 (a very similar description of Cratinus). For commentary, see Olson 2007: 86–87; Bakola 2010: 21–24.

67 Dobrov 2001, 2007; Hall 2006.

68 Rosen 2003, 2006, 2008; Griffith 2013. Aristophanes' two latest plays, *Assemblywomen* (391 BCE) and *Wealth* (388 BCE), are omitted because they were produced after Old Comedy began the gradual stylistic and topical transformation of the early fourth century. For practical reasons, I also exclude the paratragic fragments of the comic poet Strattis (but see Farmer 2017) because he merits a full-length study.

Chapter 1: Mysian Telephus and the Aristophanic Brand

1 *Telephus*'s popularity can be assumed given the large number of visual representations it seemingly inspired (see Taplin 2007: 205), as well as Aristophanes' frequent reference to the play in subsequent decades. Critical studies include Rostagni 1956: 134–152; Rau 1967: 19–42; Foley 1988.

2   On Aristophanes' special interest in Euripides, see Foley 1988: 34; Silk 2000: *passim*; Revermann 2006a: 102–103, 188; Farmer 2017: 1–3 and *passim*. Although Bakola (2010: 178–179) has demonstrated Cratinus's interest in tragedy, the evidence does not support her claim that comic poets showed considerable interest in tragedy before Aristophanes.

3   While the majority of scholars take Aristophanes' account of his conflict with Cleon at face value, I belong to the minority of those who are sceptical.

4   In this study, 'realism' refers to an egalitarian perspective that especially informed Euripidean tragedy, according to Aristophanes. As I later discuss at length, the Aristophanic Euripides defines his work as 'democratic' (*Ran.* 952) for its inclusion of everyday and lower-class characters (*Ran.* 948–949) and its engagement of that same segment of the population in performance (*Ran.* 971–979). For a discussion of this egalitarian realism, see Wohl 2015: 63–64.

5   Revermann (2006a: 23) applied the phrase 'product placement' to the self-promotion typical of the poets of Old Comedy.

6   Foley 2008.

7   Silk (2000: 39) shows that allusions to *Telephus* actually pervade the comedy from the start (*Ach.* 8 = Eur. fr. 720) to finish (1188 = Eur. fr. 705a).

8   Use of the *ekkuklêma*, the low, wheeled platform designed to introduce interior tableaux emerging from the *skênê* in tragedy, is suggested here by Dicaeopolis's request that Euripides 'roll himself out', ἐκκυκλήθητ' (408). The scholiast's remark on this line is the *locus classicus* of ancient descriptions of the device: ἐκκύκλημα δὲ λέγεται μηχάνημα ξύλινον τροχοὺς ἔχον, ὅπερ περιστρεφόμενον τὰ ἔνδον ὡς ἐν οἰκίᾳ δοκοῦντα διαπράττεσθαι καὶ τοῖς ἔξω ἐδείκνυε, λέγω δὴ τοῖς θεαταῖς ('The wooden machine with wheels that when revealed presents things that appear to be happening within to those outside, i.e., the spectators, is called the *ekkuklêma*.'). See Dearden 1976: 50–74; Taplin 1977: 442–443; cf. Pickard-Cambridge 1927: 100.

9   Moreover, if the exchange between hero and tragedian is modelled on a scene type found several times in Euripides, the so-called 'guessing game' (Fantuzzi and Konstan 2013: 256), then the very design of the scene evokes a prominent pattern of Euripidean tragedy (e.g., Eur. *Alc.* 512–521, 803–821; *Med.* 1306–1313; *Hipp.* 790–800; *Hec.* 667–682; also [Eur.] *Rhes.* 164–183).

10 Rose 1993: 39.

11 Aelian's anecdote (*VH* 2.13) about Socrates silently standing up in the audience for the benefit of foreigners who did not know him at the performance of *Clouds* (423 BCE) illustrates the value of hints within or outside the play to keep different members of an audience sufficiently informed. See also Aristotle's (*Pol.* 1342a19–21) division of the theatre audiences into the 'free and educated' (ἐλεύθερος καὶ πεπαιδευμένος) and the other 'boorish and composed of vulgar craftsmen, hired laborers, and other people of that kind' (φορτικὸς ἐκ βαναύσων καὶ θητῶν καὶ ἄλλων τοιούτων συγκείμενος).

12 See Csapo and Slater 1995: 286–305; Hardwick 2013 (esp. 12–13).

13 This and the ensuing quote are drawn from Telò 2015: 12.

14 Revermann 2006a: 115.

15 Obviously not everyone would enjoy Old Comedy (see 'Old Oligarch' 2.18). My point is that Old Comedy hedges with its humour in order to appeal to the largest possible part of the audience.

16 MacDowell (1995: 58) is one of the few to consider reperformance as a possible explanation for Aristophanes' apparent confidence in his audience's continued familiarity with the hero in 425.

17 'Cultural horizon' is an expression of Gadamer 2013; see also Hardwick 2013: 12.

18 Elam 2002: 85.

19 See Biles 2011: 68.

20 Inscriptional records of Athenian performance indicate that παλαιός means something more like 'performed at a previous festival' or a revival performance than a play from an earlier part of the poet's career. See Olson 2002: *ad* 414–415 and Biles 2011: 68.

21 On topical invention as one of several possible strategies of generic transformation, see Fowler 1982: 170–190.

22 For the Homeric warrior's achievement of a new state after donning immortal armour, see Collins 1998. Dicaeopolis's experience of 'filling up with phrases' (*Ach.* 447–448), and thus agency, recalls for us Hector filling with the power of Ares after donning the armor of Achilles (*Il.* 17.210–212).

23 Roselli 2005.

24 Cf. Olson (2002: 192), who notes the sudden drop in register with the use of σκευάριον (450) to describe the items; Rutherford (2012: 59): 'the dignity and pathos of the sordid robes are dissipated by the detailed apparatus of a poor beggar's props.' Cf. Dover 1972: 80; Wyles 2011: 63.

25 For comedy's love of props, especially outsized ones, see Revermann 2006a: *passim*.

26 Translations of terms from the *Poetics* belong to Halliwell 1995.

27 Halliwell 1998: 337–343 (esp. 340 n. 11); Roselli 2011: 53.

28 Roselli 2011: 53.

29 In this case, Aristophanes jokes (*Ran.* 1063–1068) that the pernicious influence of kings-in-rags like Telephus was the way he taught wealthy citizens to pretend to be poor to avoid assuming the financial onus of public liturgies.

30 Admittedly 'working-class' in relation to ancient society might be misleading because it seemingly includes anyone who works for a living and does not distinguish Dicaeopolis, an independent farmer with some assets, from a destitute labourer.

31 Roselli (forthcoming) maintains that the misrecognition of these ultimately successful characters as 'lower-class' – i.e., Telephus the beggar – naturally appealed to the lower classes because it disassociated virtue and merit from the fundamental nobility of citizen birth and their membership in the 'noble demos'.

32 Taplin 1986: 170.

33 The scene is reinforced by its opposite, the swift exposure and humiliation of the cross-dressing Inlaw in the parallel episode of *Thesmophoriazusae* (411).

34 Compton-Engle (2015: 91) describes the manipulation of disguise as 'status enhancing' (2015: 11–12), linking it to the agonistic spirit of 'gear manipulation' in Homer.

35 For this emotional collusion of hero and audience as fundamental to comic heroism, see Rosen 2014, who reconsiders the seminal (but problematic) work of Whitman 1964.

36 It may even parallel an analogous prologue of Euripides' *Telephus*, in which the hero prepared himself to enter the palace of Agamemnon (Cropp 1995c: 19–20).

37 There is a consensus that Telephus was originally a local Mysian hero slowly adopted by the Greeks beginning in the Archaic period.

38 Gantz 1993: 431.

39 See [Hes.] fr. 165.8–17 MW. The earliest extant mention of Telephus is *Od.* 11.519–521; cf. *Little Iliad* (*Pl*) Arg. 12–13 Bernabé with West 2013.

40 Telephus routs the 'valiant Danaoi' (Pind. *Ol.* 9.70–73); cf. *Isth.* 5.41. *Cyp.* Arg. 36–40 Bernabé with West 2013: 106–107.

41 Apollod. 3.17–20; Σ^A *Il.* 1.59.

42 *Cyp.* Arg 41–42; [Hes.] fr. 165.

43 Scheer 1993: 71–75.

44 *FGrHist* 1 F29a preserved at Paus. 8.48.7. Holley (1949: 39–40) discusses this example as a variant of the mythological pattern of the child sealed in a chest and cast into the sea.

45 Obbink 2005; 2006.

46 Since those sections of the text relevant to my argument are not in dispute, I quote only a translation.

47 Stewart (1997: 117) argues that Dionysus's interference by tripping up Telephus in combat averted the deaths of Achilles and Patroclus and thus preserved the plan of Zeus.

48 Swift 2014: 439. For Archilochus's use of the myth, see also Aloni and Iannucci 2007: 231–236.

49 Graham (1978: 94) explains that the possession of Thasos by Minos's sons would have adequately justified Parian colonization.

50 Graham 1964: 145.

51 See, e.g., Aesch. *Eum.* 397–402; Hdt. 5.94–95 (Sigeum); Hdt. 6.137–140 (Lemnos).

52 The myth says that the sons of the mythical Athenian king Codrus arrived in Anatolia as part of single colonization effort sometime after the Trojan and Theban Wars and founded Ionian cities to rule over the native inhabitants (Paus. 7.2.1–4).

53 Graham 1964: 11, 63, 183, 213; Mac Sweeney 2013: 162–163; Hdt. 1.56; 1.143; Thuc. 2.15.4; 7.57.2.

54 Strauss 1990.

55 Friedländer 1907: 161 n.1. For Demaratus's Amphitryonesque conception, see Hdt. 6.68–69 and Burkert 1965: 174–175.

56 See Hall's (2002: 15) distinction between genealogies of descent and 'metaphorical' genealogies.

57 Eumenes II built the city's Great Altar (168 BCE) with an inner frieze depicting the hero's life.

58 E.g., Ar. *Ran.* 853–855 (with Dover 1993: *ad loc.*).

59 Telephus seemingly gained access to the palace with Clytemnestra's help (cf. fr. 699). See Cropp 1995c: 44 (fr. 699); cf. Preiser 2000: 401–402.

60 See Handley and Rea 1957: 35. Fr. 727a hints at the search for the intruder.

61 Fifth- and fourth-century depictions of Telephus on Attic and South Italian vases showing him threatening the baby while propped on the altar attest to the impact of the scene. See Taplin 2007: 205–210.

62 While Aeschylus's earlier *Mysians* also featured a suppliant scene involving Orestes, the threat to kill the baby seems to have been added by Euripides (Preiser 2000: 53–59, 90).

63 Mastronarde 2010: 261.

64 As recognized by Handley and Rea 1957: 33.

65 For barbarous conduct of Greeks who complicate this polarity, see Hall 1989: 211; Cropp 2000: 48–50.

66 Obbink (2006: 9) recognizes an echo of the Archilochus poem (9–10, 21) in Eur. fr. 696.16.

67 The text of all Euripidean fragments is Kannicht 2004.

68 On the *nostos* plot, see Taplin 1977: 124–127; Hall 1997: 107–109.

69 Greeks infamously seduced by Persian culture include Pausanias (Thuc. 1.94–95; 1.130–134) and Themistocles (1.135–138).

70 For this conclusion, see Rau 1967: 23; Preiser 2000: 87–88.

71 Euripides' portrayal of this conflict between Greeks may have been influenced by suspicion of expatriate Greeks (like Telephus) in contemporary Athens and the passage of Pericles' Citizenship Law (451/450 BCE), which restricted citizenship to those born of two citizen parents, just twelve years before *Telephus* was produced (cf. Hall 1989: 175). A significant number of Athenians lived abroad where they would have developed attachments to foreign women and possibly had children (Griffith 2011: 187–190).

72 This translation is from Cropp 1995c with very slight modifications.

73 See Preiser 2000: 517.

74 See Mayer 2006.

75 For migrant literature and hybridity, see Smith 2004.

76 *Telephus* need not accurately represent the experience of a Greek exile in Mysia to facilitate the literary and/or artistic renewal to which migrant perspectives can aspire according to postcolonial theory.

77 E.g., Timocles fr. 6 (esp. 5–11, 17–19). The affiliation of Telephus and Odysseus possibly began with Eur. fr. 715, which describes Telephus as a 'wheedler' (αἱμύλος) who, like Odysseus, learned to be clever (σοφός) through need.

78 Pindar compares himself to the victorious athlete. Cratinus stressed his affinities with Dionysus by presenting himself as a 'Dionysiac' poet inspired by alcoholic intoxication (Biles 2011: 138–144). For Herodotus and later historians' use of Odysseus as a model of their craft, see Marincola 2007. The New Musicians of the late fifth century may have consciously presented themselves as adherents of the mythological kitharode Thamyris (Wilson 2009).

79 Sceptical treatments include Whitman 1964: 22; Forrest 1963; and Bowie 1993: 28–32. See also Goldhill 1991: 191–201 for the issues.

80 For extant evidence of the play (Ar. frr. 67–100), see Henderson 2007: 141–143.

81 Foley 1988; Goldhill 1991: 188–196; Hubbard 1991: 41–47; Biles 2011: 56.

82 For nuanced treatments of Aristophanes' alleged conflict with Cleon, see especially Pelling 1999: 145–150; Sommerstein 2004: 145–174.

83 For his projection of the underdog here, see Rosen 2014: 233.

84 The earliest identification of Dicaeopolis as a mouthpiece for the genre appears to be Dover 1963: 15.

85 See Taplin 1983; Silk 2000: 41; Robson 2009: 173–175; Wright 2012: 11.

86 See, e.g., Ar. *Ach.* 628, 886; *Vesp.* 650, 1537; fr. 156.9 (cf. *Nub.* 296); Eup. fr. 99.29.

87 Taplin 1983; see also Ruffell 2011: 347.

88 Taplin 1983: 333. Alan Sommerstein suggests to me that if τρυγῳδία is an Aristophanic coinage, it must have been coined before *Acharnians*, where it is mentioned (499) as if spectators should already understand its meaning.

89 Wright 2012: 18, 20–21.

90 The pretence to the disrespected status of an outsider beset by socially superior rivals is one commonly adopted by satirists in Western literature; see Rosen and Baines 2002.

91 Foley (2008: 25) draws attention to the operative principle of τρυγῳδία in the chorus's sporting and mocking (*Ran.* 390–394).

92 This is not to deny that non-capitalist economies have their own markets.

93 I.e., competition was not prestige-driven for poets. The many craftsmen and labourers contracted to work for the festivals understandably had financial reasons for doing so.

94 Olins 2004: 16.

95 For the 'ladder' of the consumer's mind, see Ries and Trout 2001: 36–38.

96 Ries and Trout 2001: 159.

97 For adopting a completely new approach to a current market, see Miller and Muir 2005: 107–108.

98 On such 'relational' brand positioning, see Ries and Trout 2001: 77–88; Olins 2004: 190–191.

99 Specifically, Aristophanes relates that he is asked why he did not 'ask for a chorus' (χορὸν αἰτοίη) for himself (*Eq.* 513), a reference to the official procedure of applying to the *archôn eponymous* for a place in a festival program; see Csapo and Slater 1995: 105.

100 Callistratus as producer: Suda σ 77 (*Babylonians*), *Ach.* Hyp. I.38; cf. *Nub.* 528–530; *Vesp.* 1018–1022 (with Biles and Olson 2015: *ad loc.*).

101 Aristophanes' sole propriety over *Knights* might also be explained by others' reluctance to risk being associated with such a vitriolic attack against Cleon.

102 Ries and Trout 2001: 125–126.

103 *Vesp.* 1044, 1051–1060.

104 As Wright (2012: 11, 17–20) notes, the tone of τρυγῳδία in *Acharnians* is largely aspirational, a statement of comedy's ambitions rather than one of empirical fact concerning its relation to politics.

105 Biles 2011: 167–210; Silk 2013. Telò 2015 presents the most advanced case.

106 For 'trope' as a precise style of allusion, see Hinds 1998: 9.

107 Burian 1997: 191.

Chapter 2: Visualizing the Comic

1 On the Athenian links of early Metapontine workshops, see Nafissi 1997; Csapo 2010: 98; Green 2014: 101. For evidence for dramatic performance in Apulia and Sicily and the popularity of Euripides (from the early fifth century BCE; cf. Plut. *Vit. Nic.* 29; *POxy.* 1176, fr. 39), see Csapo 2010: 97–98.

2 Osborne 2008: 411–413.

3 Taplin 1997: 89.

4 Csapo and Slater 1995: 53.

5 Csapo and Miller 2007: 8–18.

6 E.g., Giuliani 1996. Taplin (2007: 9) discusses the debate.

7 Small 2003: 40–78.

8 Webster 1948: 19; Körte 1893: 62 (followed by Pickard-Cambridge 1927: 268; Small 2003: 53).

9 Hughes (2012: 4–5) singles out the 'New York group' (in the New York Metropolitan Museum) from Athens; see also Csapo 2010: 101–102.

10 Green 1991; Csapo 1986, 2010; Taplin 1993: 6–11; 1997; 2007.

11 Webster 1948: *passim*.

12 Webster 1948: 23.

13 *Poetics* 1453a36–39.

14 Revermann 2006a: 155–156.

15 Kassel and Austin (vol. 8) cites the 'New York Goose Play' vase as textual evidence because it preserves the inscribed speech of the characters depicted (*Adespota* fr. 57). Moreover, in his Loeb edition of Greek epic fragments, West (2003) includes, as a legitimate fragment of epic, Pausanius's description (frr. 15–27 [frr. 10–18 Bernabé]=10.25.5–27.2) of Polygnotus's murals in the Cnidian *leschê* at Delphi, allegedly based on the *Little Iliad*.

16 Most 1997: VI–VIII.

17 *RVAp* 65 (4a).

18 See Taplin (1993: 48–54) for the term 'phlyax.'

19 Csapo 1986; Taplin 1987; 1993: 36–41; Austin and Olson (2004: lxxvi) and Walsh (2009: 74) present overviews of the scholarship.

20 Lee (2015: 72–74, 158–160) distinguishes different types of head coverings.

21 Kossatz-Deissmann 1980: 290.

22 Csapo 1986: 384–387; Taplin 1993: 36–40.

23 Austin and Olson (2004: lxxvii) argue that the absence of Inlaw's shoes and phallus, and the brush set around the altar by the women, suggest something other than a simple depiction of a South Italian performance.

24 Revermann 2005: 8; 2010a: 69–78; Csapo 2010: 'the Berlin Heracles demonstrates that vase painters are generally less interested in accurately documenting every detail of a performance than in producing an attractive, clear and recognizable image.'

25 Taplin 2007: 35–37.

26 To clarify, I share Small's scepticism of attempts to link vases to lost plays, especially for the purpose of reconstructing the latter (Small 2003: 37 and *passim*).

27 Cf. Small 2003: 68.

28 Though primarily concerned with the dramatic provenance of iconography, I acknowledge that the popular and evolving serious iconographic traditions, such as that of the tragic Telephus at the altar, potentially informed the artist's – and comic poet's – rendering of the scene. Taplin (1993: 37) counts over twenty surviving versions of Telephus in vase painting. For the levels of competency required for recognizing the dramatic models that influence the iconography (at some point in the production process), see Revermann 2006b: 116–117.

29 Green 2015: 62. Athens, National Museum, inv. 12556.

30 The expression belongs to Lissarrague 2010: 54.

31 Revermann 2006b: 102–104.

32 Revermann 2006a: 102, 155.

33 Small 1999: 564; Snodgrass (1998: 57) describes this arrangement as 'synoptic.'

34 For 'inflection', see Small 1999: 566.

35 Taplin 1993: 39–40.

36 For the introduction of female characters in Old Comedy, see esp. Henderson 2002; Stroup 2004.

37 *PhV* 22.

38 Csapo (2010: 59) credits Richard Green with noticing the detail of the lion skin near the figure's head.

39 Csapo (2010: 60) observes a small section of this barely visible behind the rider's chin.

40 Csapo 2010: 58–61.

41 Panofka 1849b was followed by Webster 1970: 102; (mostly) *PhV* 22; Gigante 1971: 37; then Taplin 1993: 46 and Csapo 2010: 60; sceptics include Körte 1893; Pickard-Cambridge 1927: 268; and Bieber 1961: 133.

42 On comic door-knocking, see Revermann 2006a: 184–185.

43 Csapo 2010: 60.

44 Stone 1981: 418; Compton-Engle 2003: 525.

45 Ruffell (2011: 370–373) understands the textual scene as representative of the principle mode of comic intertextuality.

46 Moreover, the generic hybridity of 'Heracleioxanthias' (*Ran.* 499) is analogous to that of the Greco-Mysian, beggar-king Telephus in *Acharnians*.

47 Green 2014: 99.

48 Cf. Hughes (2012: Fig. 38 [f]) for the uncertainty of the gesture.

49 Green 2014: 129.

50 The titles and fragments of lost comedies such as Ar.'s *Aeolosikon* and Strattis's *Anthoporestes* and *Lemnomeda* imply that such visual strategies were important to comic appropriation.

51 I follow Halliwell's analysis (1998: 271–272). For application of Aristotle's comments to the vases in question, see Taplin 1993: 82; Walsh 2009: 95.

52 See esp. Nesselrath 1995; Konstantakos 2014.

53 For this definition, see Wright 2007: 417–418. On counterfactual thinking in the late fifth century, see Tordoff 2014: 109; cf. Wohl 2014: 1–14. Modern historical examples are discussed by Ferguson 1999.

54 Hornblower 2011: 8 (emphasis mine).

55 *PhV* 86 (Villa Giulia, inv. 50279). For discussion, see Trendall 1936: 28–29; Taplin 1993: 81–82; Mitchell 2009: 153.

56 On hairstyle in comic vase paintings, see Green 2014: 105.

57 See *Ilioupersis* Arg. 15–16 Bernabé with West 2013: 235–237. Gantz (1993: 650–655) summarizes different versions of the story.

58 Homer does not include the scene but may allude to it at *Od.* 4.499–511.

59 For the development of Athena's posture from 'promachos' to lifeless, see Beazley 1963: 64–65; Connelly 1993: 89; Gantz 1993: 655.

60 Taplin 1993: 81 n. 9; Walsh 2009: 81–85.

61 Connelly 1993: 121.

62 Note also Cassandra's erasure of her religious status by symbolically 'undressing' at Aesch. *Ag.* 1264–1274, Eur. *Tro.* 451–454.

63 Taplin 1993: 81–82.

64 See Green's (2000) study of such narrated, unperformed tableaux in vase painting.

65 Walsh 2009: 84 and n. 42. See Revermann (2006a: 244–246) for outsized props.

66 Walsh (2009: 85–86) points specifically to the Sicilian red-figure calyx-krater (340–330 BCE) in Leontini illustrating Heracles' attempted rape of Auge (Museo Archeologico, Ht. 49) as a parallel.

67 The important exception is obviously Ar. *Eccl.* 1098–1111 (392 BCE).

68 West 2013: 237. Sutton (1984: 7–9) summarizes the available evidence.

69 For transmotivation, see Genette 1997: 330–335.

70 Several dramatic portrayals of the theft of the Palladion are attested, including Sophocles' *Lakainai* (Arist. *Poet.* 23.1459b6).

71 *Nost.* Arg. 12–13 Bernabé. In Homer's account (*Od.* 4.499–511), Ajax himself initially escaped the onslaught with the help of Poseidon, who washed him up onto the cliffs of Gyrae. He drowned when the enraged god struck the rock with his trident.

72 Wright 2007: 412–414, 418.

73 For discussions, see Trendall and Webster 1971: IV 29; Taplin 1993: 82; Walsh 2009: 94–96.

74 *Ilioupersis* Arg. 13–14 Bernabé; cf. *Little Iliad* fr. 27.25 West (based on Paus. 10.27.25), where Priam is dragged from the altar and killed at the doors of his house.

75 Anderson 1997: 28–38.

76 Perhaps a tragic speech (Walsh 2009: 94) or an oration (Bieber 1961: 135).

77 Rehm (1988: 264) notes that over a third of surviving Greek tragedies require an altar (or a tomb) for scenes of supplication and refuge.

78 By 'Ilioupersis tradition' I refer to the oral tradition predating the story in written form, *Ilioupersis*.

79 Anderson (1997: 27): 'the Fall of Troy is in essence the fall of its ruling family'. See Wiencke 1954 and Hedreen 2001: 64–80 for the scene's evolution. For the South Italian evidence, see Moret 1975: 45–50.

80 Anderson 1997: 37, 194.

81 Anderson 1997: 44–45; such allusions to Priam's death in the later books of the *Iliad* highlight its significance for the entire Cycle.

82 The birth of Helen, another critical moment of the origins of the Trojan War, was the subject of Cratinus's *Nemesis* (*c.* 430 BCE) and at least one other comedy that inspired a depiction of the myth of her birth from an egg on an Apulian bell-krater in Bari (inv. 3899, *c.* 350 BCE; see Taplin 1993: 82–83).

83 Lear and Cantarella (2009: 26) explain that synecdochic elements are present in every type of vase painting, detached from their original scene type or subject.

84   E.g., *Il.* 11.310–312; cf., Thuc. 8.86.4–5, 8.87.4, 8.96.4 (with Flory 1988).

85   It is not out of the question that the comedy upon which this illustration may have been based also featured the assault of Ajax on the Asteas sherd.

86   *PhV* 62 (115).

87   For the gesture, see Hughes 2012: Fig. 38(c).

88   See Hughes 2012: Fig. 38(d).

89   Sceptical is Taplin 1993: 80–81; leaning towards performance is Walsh 2009: 208.

90   Sommerstein 1996b: 85.

91   Walsh (2009: 208) suggests that Creon and Oedipus are haggling over the reward for solving the riddle.

92   Lee 2015: 142–145.

93   Panofka 1849a: 216–221.

94   Trendall and Webster 1971: 141–142.

95   Taplin 1993: 83–88; cf. Walsh 2009: 222, whose interpretation is more in line with Trendall and Webster's suggestion that the old man was Antigone's co-conspirator.

96   Though the Trendall-Webster-Taplin theory cannot supply answers to many important questions about the scene, there is currently no better explanation of the vase. Alternative theories are possible, but invite different problems. For example, the old man's female archetype could be Sophocles' Electra, who memorably lamented her supposedly dead brother, Orestes, as she grasped an urn thought to contain his ashes (Soph. *El.* 1117–1122).

97   Taplin 1993: 101.

98   Small (2003: 45–47) is sceptical of dramatic associations.

99   Green 1994: 29–32.

100 See the detailed comments of Dunbar 1995: *ad loc.*

101 Taplin 1987: 95.

102 Taplin 1993: 103.

103 Taplin 1993: 103; cf. Figure 13.10 (in Taplin 1993) with an old woman turning away from an old man rising from a stool with his erect or semi-erect (?) phallos.

104 Taplin 1993: 103; Revermann (2006a: 217–219) suggests that the dots on the costume might be of Persian origin, which might identify the figures as 'Persian Birds' (farmyard cocks).

105 Csapo 2010: 10.

106 Taplin's theory is adopted by Revermann 2006a: 218–219, Rothwell 2007: 57–58, and Bakola 2010: 105–106; cf. Csapo 2010: 11.

107 See e.g., Rosen 2000; Biles 2002; Ruffell 2002; Sommerstein 2005.

108 *RFVAp* 46, *PhV* 53–4 (84). On the attribution to the Dolon painter, see Denoyelle and Silvestrelli 2013.

109 Marshall 2001: 62; Csapo (2010: 46–47) compares it to a film clip 'in which the characters speak, interact, and move'.

110 This is Taplin's (1993: 30) adjective.

111 Beazley 1952: 193.

112 Csapo 2010: 46.

113 *RVAp* 99 (257).

114 Taplin 1993: 32.

115 Taplin (1993: 32) credits the recognition of this detail to Eric Csapo.

116 A pet rooster, slain by a cat, is memorialized at *Anth. Pal.* VII 202.

117 Messerschmidt 1932.

118 Beazley 1952: 195.

119 Csapo 2010: 46.

120 Although the Bari pipers and the Choregoi vase preserve signature scenes of unique metatheatricality – the former conjoins the world of the play with that of the audience and the latter juxtaposes figures symbolic of tragedy and comedy onstage at the same time – to my knowledge there exists no parallel for such offstage spectatorship of the fictional comic world by a representative of its rival genre.

121 Marshall 2001: 56, 66.

122 In general, see Dover 1989, the contributions to Hubbard 2000a, and Hubbard 2003. See Hubbard 2006 for pederasty in literature; see Lear and Cantarella 2009 for art. For the restriction of pederastic themes in popular culture over the fifth century, see Hubbard 2000b; 2015.

123 Lear and Cantarella 2009: 27, 40.

124 See Sommerstein 2005; Hall 2006: 172.

125 Dover 1989: 148.

126 Hall 2006: 177. In the few examples of 'Tragedy' (τραγῳδία) in the serious iconographic tradition, she is usually a maenad in the company of a *thiasos* of Dionysus. *LIMC* s.v. 'Tragoidia' (A. Kossatz-Deissmann): 48–50.

127 Geese are (admittedly) not well-attested courting gifts for the *erômenos* in extant vase painting, despite the testimony of Ar. *Av.* 707.

128 *RVAp* suppl. 7–8, 1/124.

129 The Fleischman estate bequeathed the vase to the J. Paul Getty Museum (inv. 96.AE.29), which sent it to Naples (inv. 248778).

130 *RFVAp* suppl. 46, 3/7.

131 Revermann 2006a: 102, 147, 155.

132 Taplin 1993: 60. Gilula's (1995: 9–10) argument that χορηγός refers to the Roman 'choragus', or prop/costume man, ignores the common thematization of *khorêgia* in Old Comedy. On Taplin's theory, see also Wilson 2000: 260.

133 Wilson 2000: 261. Also discussed by Taplin 1993: 58.

134 Wilson 2000: 137.

135 See Ar. *Ach.* 1150–1161 with the comments of Wilson 2007a: 275–276.

136 But not completely Athenian. Evidence that an Apulian audience could have understood a comedy about *khorêgoi* is presented by Wilson 2007b.

137 Wilson 2000: 111; cf. Biles and Thorn's (2014: 296) interpretation of the scene as shorthand for a full dramatic festival.

138 Hutcheon 2006: 23.

Chapter 3: Members Only? Satyrism and Satire in Late Fifth-Century Comedy

1 *Cyclops* is usually dated to the latest phase of Euripides' career. Studies of comedy's relationship to satyr play include Scharffenberger 1995; Dobrov 2001: 101; Bakola 2005; 2010: 81–117; Storey 2005; Hall 2006: 340–341, 351–352; Lämmle 2013: 35–50; Shaw 2014. See Dobrov 2007 for a sceptical position.

2 Lissarrague 1990: 236. On this, see esp. Seidensticker 2003.

3 Demetr. *Eloc.* 169. For comments on the statement, see Griffith 2008: 76–77; Shaw 2014: 13–14.

4 Griffith 2005: 163.

5 For example, Conrad 1997; Krumeich, Pechstein, and Seidensticker 1999 (hereafter cited as *KPS*); Griffith 2002, 2005, 2008, 2010; Lämmle 2013; Shaw 2014. Earlier studies include Guggisberg 1947; Sutton 1980. A classic treatment of satyrs in art is Lissarrague 1990.

6 Dobrov (2007: 258) describes the sum of satyr play in Old Comedy as little more than a single allusion in Aristophanes, a few bare titles, and Hermippus fr. 47.

7 Storey 2005, in response to Marshall 2000.

8 I.e., how parasatyrism serves comedy's interest apart from enriching its repertoire.

9 Fowler 1982: 106–111; see also Frow 2006: 63–67.

10 Griffith 2002; 2005; 2008.

11 Silk 2000: 352–356.

12 Revermann (2006a: 226–235) identifies Socrates' striking entrance with the crane, 'walking on air' (223–227), as an early signal of the theomachy pattern.

13 If it evoked for ancient audiences the ancient punitive practice of 'razing the house' of those guilty of exceptional crimes, the burning of the *phrontistêrion* was even more at odds with conventional comic endings. On this punishment, see Connor 1985; Forsdyke 2005: 296. The historical precedent for the incineration of an esoteric philosophical community, the destruction of a Pythagorean school in Croton (*c.* 450 BCE), is worth mentioning.

14 Hyp. I Dover (= hyp. 6 Wilson); cf. Σ *Nub.* 543a (see Revermann 2006a: 228).

15 On closure in comedy and tragedy compared, see Taplin 1996.

16 See Bakola (2010: 2 n. 3) for ancient references.

17 Before this discovery, scholars knew so little about the comedy that Meineke (1839: vol. 1, 56–57) mistook the 'Alexandros' of the title as Alexander the Great, and its author as Cratinus the Younger.

18 For burlesque in general, see Casolari 2003; Konstantakos 2014; Nesselrath 1995.

19 I print Körte's more accepted reading (followed by Olson 2007: 71), instead of KA's π(ερὶ) υῶν ποιή(σεως), 'about the creation of sons.'

20 The Judgment was narrated in the *Cypria* of the Epic Cycle (*Cyp.* Arg 5–11 Bernabé). On the *Cypria*, see Currie 2015. An ivory comb (Athens National Museum, inv. 15368) depicting the Judgment proves the story dates to at least *c.* 620 BCE (Burgess 2001: 183).

21 For the theory that Hermes, looking for a substitute judge after Paris went missing, enlisted Dionysus, see Storey 2006: 111–112; also Bakola 2005: 52.

22 See Bakola 2005; 2010: 82–88.

23 For the phrasing, see Bakola 2010: 83–87.

24 Grenfell and Hunt 1904: 70; Croiset 1904: 299; Körte 1904: 483–484; see also Storey 2005: 211; 2006: 119–122; Bakola 2005: 46.

25 Schmid 1946: 77 n. 8, followed by Luppe 1966: 184–192; Rosen 1988: 55 n. 59; Casolari 2003: 100–101.

26 Bakola 2005; 2010: 82–88; Storey 2005: 209–215; Revermann 2006a: 302. My debt to Bakola's analysis of *Dionysalexandros* will be obvious throughout this section.

27 On visual juxtaposition, see Revermann 2006a: 102.

28 See esp. Lissarrague 1990: 235; Seidensticker 2003: 106–107; see also Sutton 1980: 137; Seaford 1984: 44.

29 Also rightly prioritized by Shaw 2014: 94.

30 For Aeschylus's *Sphinx* (frr. 235–237), see *KPS*: 189–196; O'Sullivan and Collard 2013: 504. For Aeschylus's *Netfishers* (esp. frr. 46a–47a), on Danae and Perseus, see later in the present chapter. For Sophocles' *Trackers* (frr. 314–318), see *KPS*: 280–312; O'Sullivan and Collard 2013: 336–343.

31 Also noted by Shaw 2014: 91. For the mimetic style of satyr lyric, see Griffith 2005: 168.

32 The distinctive vocabulary of ἐπισκώ(πτουσι) and χλευάζου(σιν) (11–12) has no clear parallel in the evidence of satyr play.

33 For the god 'out of his element,' see Storey 2003: 250–257; cf. Eup. frr. 271, 275.

34 Lämmle 2013: 111–153.

35 On Dionysus's spirit, see Griffith 2002: 207.

36 E.g., Aesop 420 Perry; cf. Babrius 116.

37 E.g., Ameipsias's *Adulterers*: frr. 12–13 (with Orth 2013: *ad loc.* and esp. 256–257 for the adulterer's profile); cf. Xen. *Mem.* 2.1.5; Xenarch. fr. 4.10–12.

38 See Porter 1997.

39 For Eup. fr. 148, see also Chapter 5.

40 Though scholars are rightly sceptical of its accuracy, one tradition suggests that mime was known in Athens by the late fifth and early fourth century. A fragment of Duris of Samos (*FGrHist* 76 F 72) mentions that Plato admired the mimes of Sophron, the Syracusan poet; cf. Hordern 2004: 26–27; Prauscello 2006.

41 These are Demetrius's (fourth century BCE?) *topoi* (*Eloc.* 132). Griffith 2008.

42 This erotic content likely explains Homer's reluctance to acknowledge the story directly, despite its importance. However, cf. *Il.* 24.23–30.

43 Hedreen (2001: 208–211) argues that the iconography of Alexandros as an amorous shepherd sought to account for his preference for Aphrodite's bribe over the other two in the literary tradition.

44 The bribes are mentioned at Apollod. 3.2. Bakola (2010: 285–294) attractively suggests that Athena and Hera did not appear but were represented by female personifications of their bribes.

45 For Athena and Hera's bribes as post-*Cypria* developments, see Gantz 1993: 570–571.

46 Sophocles' *Krisis* presented it along these lines, with Aphrodite and Athena as symbolic representations of pleasure (ἡδωνή) and virtue or discipline (ἀρετή), respectively. See Stinton 1965: 8; *KPS*: 358–362.

47 Although Bakola argues (2005; 2010: 95) that this scene and fr. 45 suggest the 'trickery and fraud' of satyr play, such deception is not exclusive to that genre and can be found in both comedy and (to some extent) tragedy.

48 Compton-Engle (2003: 509) shows that comic characters frequently describe disguises of themselves or others with terms such as '(ἐν)σκευάζω'. Revermann (2006a: 300) has compared this scene to an image on an Apulian bell-krater from *c.* 370 BCE now in the Getty (inv. 96.AE.112); a hybrid figure in the centre has the head of a ram but a human body.

49 Bakola 2010: 253. For failure of disguise, see Taplin 1986: 170.

50 The adulterer's concealment in a chest (or basket) in the bedroom at the husband's abrupt return is standard in Roman adultery mime, for example (e.g., Hor. *Sat.* 2.7.56–67; Juv. 6.42–44). For a sense of the chaos that ensued upon the adulterer's discovery, see Hor. *Sat.* 1.2.128–134 (*c.* 35 BCE).

51 I follow Bakola's translation. The phrasing may allude to Helen's traditional character when it records that she 'objected' to being surrendered with Dionysus. Whether 'ὀκνέω' conveys 'fear' or 'cowardice' (*LSJ*), some notion of guilt seems to be implied.

52 See also discussion in Chapter 2 of the Berlin Heracles.

53 See Wright's (2007) analysis of counterfactual exercises in *Dionysalexandros* and elsewhere in comedy.

54 Shaw 2014: 83.

55 This is a *topos* in over half of extant plays, e.g., Poseidon and Amymone (Soph. *Amymone.*), Dictys and Danae (Aesch. *Dictyoulkoi.*), a Sophoclean(?) play featuring the marriage contest of Oeneus (*POxy.* 1083 fr. 1), and even Menelaus and Helen (*Helenês Gamos*). See also the γάμος of Dionysus and Ariadne represented on the Pronomos Vase (Museo Archeologico Nazionale, inv. 81673, H3240).

56 Seaford 1984: 39 (and n. 111 for references), 105; Krumeich 1999: 28–32; Griffith 2002: 231–233; 2006; 2008; 2010: 53; Bakola 2005: 55.

57 Griffith 2002: 203.

58 For the ἀρχὴ κακῶν in tragedy, see Hose 1990: vol. 2, 103; Allan 2000: 205–209.

59 Potentially noteworthy in this respect is the repeated *failure* of Cratinus's heroic protagonist, which may invert the typical success of satyr drama's heroes.

60 Storey (2006: 118) sees the Alexandros/Pericles identification as a better fit for the Samian War, perhaps more likely undertaken to gratify the Milesian Aspasia (see Plut. *Vit. Per.* 24). For a balanced discussion of the possibilities, see Olson 2007: 87.

61 Körte 1904: 491; Norwood 1931: 122. For Alexandros, rather than Dionysus, as Pericles, see Storey 2005: 214.

62 Schwarze 1971: 11–24; Rosen 1988: 52–53; Heath 1990: 147; McGlew 2002: 47–48; for wholehearted support of the Periclean satire, but complete denial of the parasatyrism of *Dionysalexandros*, see Dobrov 2007: 257. Schwarze's exhaustive, often unbelievable, but occasionally ingenious conjectures deserve special acknowledgment. Although his reading has been justly criticized, it provides useful parameters for thinking allegorically about comedy.

63 Revermann 1997; Olson 2007: 87. Slightly more sceptical positions on the allegory are found in Bowie (2000: 325) and Bakola (2010: 180–208); cf. Shaw (2014: 92), who makes the valuable point that the satire was obvious enough that it was recognized centuries after the original production.

64 Revermann (1997) suggests that Dionysus was identified as Pericles through the use of a special mask.

65 Cratinus's *Plutoi* (c. 430/429 BCE) and *Cheirones* both allegorized the public career of Pericles with the Succession Myth's narrative of decline, dramatizing the arrival in Athens of mythological beings, 'wealth gods' and miniature(?) Cheirones seeking the indictment of Pericles and his partisans for destroying former golden ages of Athenian abundance by enriching themselves. For the possible identity of the 'Plutoi,' see Bakola 2010: 49 (but cf. Revermann 2006a: 307).

66 Plutarch (*Vit. Per.* 3) explains this as the common reason for the representation of Pericles in visual art wearing a helmet; cf. Cratin. fr. 73.1–2 (*Thrattai*): ὦ σχινοκέφαλος Ζεύς ('Squill-headed Zeus').

67 See *Ach.* 509–556, *Pax* 605–648. Cratinus's *Nemesis* (*c.* 431) allegorized his precipitation of the war using the myth of Zeus's seduction of the goddess Nemesis, 'righteous indignation' (*LIMC* iv [1994] 4–9 s.v. *Nemesis* [I. Krauskopf]).

68 McGlew 2002: 48. Thucydides' Funeral Oration (2.34–46) and Plutarch's biography attest to Pericles' cultivation of this public persona.

69 The fragment may allude to *Dionysalexandros* (Olson 2007: 87, 209–210, 411 [Hermippus's biography]).

70 Griffith 2002: 217.

71 Hall 2006: 327. For the text of the Peace of Nicias, see Thuc. 5.18 with Hornblower 1996: 469–471.

72 Hall (2006: 328–333) etymologizes the name as 'Son of Trugoidos,' i.e., 'Son of the Comedian'.

73 Robert 1914: 37. Followed by Sutton 1975: 354; Dobrov 2001: 101–103; Hall 2006: 340–341. Bakola 2010: 108–110; cf. Lämmle (2013: 40 n. 52), who does not appear to endorse it; Shaw 2014: 91 n. 42.

74 Robert (1914: 37) proposed Sophocles' lost satyr play *Pandora* or *Sphyrokopoi* ('Hammerers'), for which there are two fragments, as Aristophanes' model. Hall (2006: 340–341) and Bakola (2010: 108–109) have tentatively suggested Aeschylus's *Diktyoulkoi*, or *Netfishers*.

75 Metropolitan Museum inv. 28.57.23 (450–440 BCE; Bérard 1974: § 50; Olson 1998: xxxvi); Rhodes inv. 12.454 (Bérard 1974: § 63; Olson 1998: xxxvii); Ashmolean inv. 525 (Bérard 1974: § 71) is occasionally connected to Sophocles' *Sphyrokopoi*. See Robert 1914: 17–38 with Soph. fr. 482; cf. Olson 1998: xxxvii; Ferrara inv. T. 579 (Bérard 1974: § 30a–c; *KPS*: 376). The ἄνοδος has been detected in Euripides' *IT* and *Hel.*

76 For the trope in satyr play, see Steffen 1965; Hall 2006: 340. For a sceptical view of its connection to *Peace*, see Olson 2002: *ad loc.*

77 For the myth, see Apollod. 2.4.1; Pherec. *FGrHist.* 3F 10.22–26.

78 See Lissarrague 1993: 212. The trochaic tetrameter communicates the rapid movement of the Aristophanic chorus entering in haste (e.g., *Ach.* 204–207, 219–222 with Olson 2002: *ad loc.*; *Eq.* 247–254).

79 Museo Archeologico Nazionale di Spina, inv. 3031.

80 *KPS*: 26.

81 Hall 2006.

82 For similar entreaties, see Soph. fr. 314.229–230 (*Trackers*) and Eur. *Cyc.* 476.

83 Lawler 1964: 117; alternatively called the ποδῶν ῥιπή by Seidensticker 2003: 112. See Griffith's (2005: 170–171) distinction between the movements of satyr and comic choruses.

84 Lawler 1964: 117–118; Seidensticker 2003: 112; Griffith 2005: 170–171. See Seidensticker 2010 on satyr dance, generally.

85 See Griffith (2010: 59) on this particular satyr.

86 Sutton 1980; Bakola 2010: 93.

87 E.g., Aesch. fr. 46a.18–20 (*Dict.*); fr.78c.72–74 (*Theor.*); Soph. fr. 314.39–49 (*Ichn.*); (?) fr. 1130. On the theme generally, see Seaford 1984: 35; Bakola 2005: 54.

88 Griffith (2005: 168) counts twelve astrophic and three strophic passages of lyric. Moreover, as in satyr play, the hauling scene itself originates in choral action (Seidensticker 2003: 109).

89 The nature of the statue's representation is irrecoverable, although we know Aristophanes' contemporaries Eupolis and Plato Comicus mocked it (Σ Pl. *Ap.* 19c). Olson (1998: xliv) suspects it may have been as basic as a hunk of wood with a mask and rich robes. See also Revermann 2006a: 153.

90 Seidensticker 2003:118.

91 Newiger 1957: 115; MacDowell 1995: 185.

92 Pulling in two or more groups: Dover 1972: 138; pulling in four groups of six: Olson 1998: *ad loc.*; Dover 1972: 135; Sommerstein 1985: xvii; and Olson 1998: xliv–xlviii see the *skênê* door as the entrance to the goddess's cave.

93 Sommerstein (1985: *ad loc.*) and Olson (1998: *ad loc.*) link the nautical provenance of Hermes' commands to the specific task of hauling a ship ashore to be beached.

94 A possibility raised by Griffith 2005: 169; Parker 1997: 274 advises caution.

95 For a useful discussion of the politics to which these criticisms allude, see Olson 1998: *ad loc.*

96 See Eur. *Cyc.* 477; Seidensticker 2003: 118.

97 See, e.g., the chorus's refusal to assist Odysseus at Eur. *Cyc.* 632–653.

98 Parker 1997: 272–275. The tetrameter is 'well adapted to the vigorous movement of a chorus that marches into the orchestra at steady pace but not with undue haste' (White 1901: § 168; cf. Ar. *Vesp.* 230–247).

99 Mastronarde 1999, which follows Gould 1996.

100 Griffith 2002: 208–213.

101 Lissarrague 1990.

102 For a handful of short quotations of satyr play in Aristophanic comedy (e.g., *Ran.* 184, 1287; fr. 623), see Shaw 2014: 84–85.

103 Riu (1999: 237–243) explores the insult within the structure of a play.

104 Sommerstein 1998: 109.

105 See Seaford (1984: 39 n. 111, 105) for a list of possible divine/mortal pairings.

106 For commentary, see O'Sullivan and Collard 2013: 254–257. Aeschylus's *Amymone* (*KPS*: 91–97) also featured a 'courtship' of satyrs; cf. Kunsthistorisches Museum (Vienna), inv. IV 101 (420–410 BCE).

107 The maiden is presumably Deianira, daughter of Oeneus and sister of Meleager; see Conrad 1997: 154–159, 284–286; O'Sullivan and Collard 2013: 378–380.

108 Robson (2015: 324) notes the unusual vocabulary διαμηρίζω and στύομαι τριέμβολον.

109 Sommerstein 1998.

110 Scharffenberger 1995.

111 The fragments of *Iris* by Achaeus of Eretria (b. 480) are of little help (see *KPS*: 524–529). Simon (1982: 125–129) suspects (probably incorrectly) that the same play inspired a cup from Capua (490–480 BCE) depicting the assault of Iris on one side and the harassment of Hera on the other.

112 Scharffenberger 1995. Herington (1963) argues (somewhat unconvincingly, I believe) for a parody of the Aeschylean *PV*. Cf. Rau 1967: 176–177.

113 For this depiction of political power, see Ruffell 2013.

114 Lissarrague 1990: 236.

115 For the biography of Agathon, see Austin and Olson 2004: *ad loc.* For the fragments, see Snell and Kannicht 1986: 155–168.

116 Dover 1989: 144.

117 Pl. *Symp.* 213c.

118 Σ Ar. *Ran.* 85. See also Sommerstein 1994: *ad loc.*; Austin and Olson 2004: *ad loc.*; cf. Pl. *Symp.* 193c, *Prt.* 315e, and Xen. *Symp.* 8.32.

119 The 'Genetyllides' were women's goddesses worshipped in Cape Kolias (just south of Phaleron) and associated with nymphomania in comedy and related genres; cf. Ar. *Nub.* 52; *Lys.* 1–3; *Thesm.* 130–133; Paus. 1.4.5.

120 Feminine dress seems to be implied by both Inlaw's earlier comparison of the poet to the prostitute Cyrene (98; with Austin and Olson 2004: *ad loc.*) and his subsequent disguise in female dress from Agathon's own wardrobe (see Muecke 1982: 50).

121 Bobrick 1997: 180; Duncan 2006: 40.

122 Cf. Lämmle's (2013: 48) interesting suggestion that Inlaw's sexual aggression channels comedy's desire to appropriate tragedy as a demonstration of its equality with the loftier genre.

123 See Lissarrague 1990.

124 Σ *Thesm.* 136. Lycurgus was eventually struck blind and afflicted with a divine madness that drove him to massacre his family. The trilogy (see Sommerstein 1996a: 41) included *Edonians* (Aesch. frr. 57–67), *Bassarai* or *Bassarids* (Aesch. frr. 23–25), *Neaniskoi* and the satyr play *Lykourgos* (Aesch. frr. 146–149; for the evidence, see *KPS*: 164–168). Cf. *Il.* 6.130–140; Soph. *Ant.* 955–965; Apollod. 3.34.

125 For commentary, see Austin and Olson 2004: *ad loc.*

126 The classic study of comedy's appeal to feelings of superiority is Bergson 1911; see also Ruffell 2013.

127 See Dobrov's (2007: 251) use of this term to describe an impermeable boundary between satyr play and Old Comedy.

Chapter 4: Poetic Failure and Comic Success in Aristophanes' *Peace*

1 MacDowell 1995: 181.

2 Hall 2006: 328–333.

3 Olson (1998: *ad* 916) describes τρύξ as 'a term applied loosely to any mixture of grapes or grape-fragments with the wine or juice produced from them'.

4 'Must' is from the Latin *mustum, -i.*

5 Dregs: Ar. *Plut.* 1084–1086; new wine: Ar. *Nub.* 50; *Pax* 576 (with Olson 1998: *ad loc.*).

6 I owe special thanks to Stelios Chronopoulos for talking through this idea with me.

7 MacDowell 1995: 180; Hall 2006: 326. Olson (1998: xxv–xxxvi) provides a detailed account of events leading to the Peace of Nicias in 421 BCE. For the text of the agreement, see Thuc. 5.18 with Hornblower 1996: 469–471.

8 Lukewarm assessments of the play include Dover 1972: 137; MacDowell 1995: 181; and Parker 1997: 262. Cassio (1985) and Olson (1998) began the upward trend in study of the play, which now includes Dobrov 2001; Hall 2006: 321–352; Robson 2006: 132–189; Tordoff 2011; Chronopoulos 2017; Zogg 2014; Taplin 2014.

9 For productions in France, see Hall 2006: 323. Peter Hack's successful 1962 stage-production of the play initiated a rich period of adaptations of classical literature in the GDR (Seidensticker 2007: 194–195).

10 E.g., Revermann 2006a: 172–175.

11 For treatments of these institutions as pillars of Greek civilization, see Hes. *Op.* 42–46 (agriculture); *Theog.* 570–616, *Op.* 59–105 (marriage); *Theog.* 556–557 (sacrifice).

12 Jauss 1982: 14–18.

13 For text and commentary, see Olson 2007: 172–175.

14 See, e.g., Olson 2007: 173.

15 See Lowe (2006: 52) on Aristophanic staging.

16 Rosen 1988: 28–31; cf. Cassio 1985: 91. Beetles feature in the iambic poets Semonides (fr. 13 W) and Hipponax (78, 92 W).

17 For Aristophanes' novelty, see D'Angour 2011: 211–216.

18 Rau 1967: 89–97; Olson 1998: *ad* 76–77.

19 Olson 1998: *ad loc.*; cf. Eur. fr. 286b; Rau (1967: 91) adds the tragic parallel of Sophocles' *Ajax* and its hero's similar cry from offstage (cf. Harvey 1971: 364).

20 As in, e.g., Eur. *Med.* 214–266; *Hipp.* 198–249.

21 Webster 1967: 109–111; Riedweg 1990; Collard 1995a: 98–120; and esp. Dixon 2014.

22 *Il.* 6.152–206. Glaucus recounts Bellerophontes' stay at Proetus's house in Tiryns, where the latter's wife, Anteia, falsely accused him of assault after he rebuffed her advances. By overcoming a series of deadly trials ordered by Iobates, Proetus's

father-in-law, the hero wins Iobates' daughter and a share of his kingdom. Hesiod (*Theog.* 319–325) mentions his defeat of the Chimaera and (fr. 43a.81–84 [*Cat.*]) his acquisition of Pegasus as a gift from Poseidon.

23 Collard (1995b: 79–83) summarizes the evidence. An outstanding representation of Proetus, Stheneboea and Bellerophontes is preserved on an Apulian stamnos (*c.* 390) from Gela and now in Boston (MFA, inv. 1900.349); cf. Taplin 2007: 201–204.

24 His motive varies with the source. Σ^T *Il.* 6.202a: bitterness over the death of his children. Pind. *Isthm.* 7.44–48: arrogance.

25 Riedweg 1990: 46–47; Mastronarde 2010: 173.

26 Dixon (2014: 498–499) draws on a conjecture of Scodel's (1997: 226).

27 Hall (2006: 321–352) has outlined the enormous challenges of this role for an actor: delivering a tragic pastiche of alternating anapaests and iambic trimeters, while gesturing and balancing on the beetle swinging from the *mêchanê*; cf. Hourmouziades 1965: 150. For the view that Trygaeus alights on the roof with the switch to trimeters (102), see Olson 1998: *ad loc.*

28 Cf. Dover 1972: 132 n. 1; Olson 1998: xxxv; Casari 2002: 43.

29 Davies and Kathirithamby 1986: 88; see esp. Beavis 1988.

30 Rau 1967: 92; Riedweg 1990: 49 n. 51; Parker 1997: 262; Olson 1998: *ad loc.* The pastiche consists of multiple tragic sources, shifting meters (dactylic tetrameters [114–117], hexameters [118–123], iambic trimeters [124–154], anapaestic dimeters [154–172]), and diction (δώμασιν, 115; πῶλος, ναυσθλώσομαι, 126).

31 Hourmouziades 1965: 152; Rau 1967: 93; Riedweg 1990: 49 n. 51. For a discussion of the fragment, see Collard 1995b: 96; Collard and Cropp 2008: 139.

32 For comedy's use of the fable, see Rothwell 1995 (in *Vesp.*); Schirru 2009.

33 Olson 1998: xxxv.

34 See also Aesop *Fab.* 84, 107, 112 Perry. Aristophanes' reference to the very same fable in his *Wasps* (1401) of the previous year proves that he felt it was sufficiently popular to be recognizable to an audience.

35 The most thorough discussion of the beetle's literary pedigree is Steiner 2008.

36 Steiner 2008: 86–87; Rosen 1988: 32–33.

37 The translation of this passage is based on Henderson 1998 with minor modifications.

38 Griffith 2006a, 2006b.

39 Griffith 2006a: 198.

40 ἥσυχος ἥσυχος, ἠρέμα, κάνθων. / μή μοι σοβαρῶς χώρει λίαν / εὐθὺς ἀπ' ἀρχῆς ῥώμῃ πίσυνος …, 82–84 ('Whoa, whoa, easy boy! / Don't get too wild and / sure of yourself right from the start …').

41 Griffith 2006a.

42 Griffith 2006a: 202.

43 Arist. *Pol.* 4.1289b34–40, 6.1321a5–14; cf. Ar. *Nub.* 69–80.

44 See Griffith (2006a: 226) on the 'ass' jokes of Ar.'s *Frogs* (1–34).

45 Σ^v *Pax* 82; followed by Davies and Kathirithamby 1986: 84; Olson 1998: *ad loc.*

46 Griffith 2006a: 223.

47 Griffith 2006a: 227.

48 For fables with donkeys aspiring to a higher status than they merit, see Griffith 2006a: 224–226.

49 Griffith 2006a: 187.

50 The date of its introduction in fifth-century theatre and the frequency of its use are unknown. Mastronarde (1990: 266) argues for a degree of frequency that others are not prepared to acknowledge (cf. Hourmouziades 1965; Taplin 1977). For a list of the most compelling passages where it is used, see Mastronarde 1990: 286–287.

51 Hughes 2012: 53 fig. 13 (a miniature of a reconstructed *mêchanê*), 77–78.

52 Pickard-Cambridge 1946: 51, 111, 127; Hourmouziades 1965: 154; cf. Mastronarde 1990: 107 n. 68. More neutral treatments are Barrett 1964: 395–396; Taplin 1977: 443–447; 1978: 12.

53 See also Pl. *Cra.* 425d.

54 Hourmouziades (1965: 147–169) argued that use of the crane is signaled in the text by explicit references to 'flying' and accompanying anapaests.

55 Hourmouziades 1965: 146, 155; Mastronarde 1990: 262.

56 Mastronarde 1990: 272–280. The crane's three other appearances in Aristophanic comedy exploit tragic associations, esp. *Nub.* 218; cf. Pl. *Ap.* 19c2–4.

57 See Eur. *And.*, *Bacc.*, *El.*, *Hel.*, *Supp.*, *Hipp.*, *Ion*, *IT*, *Or.*

58 Dunn 1996: 28–31.

59 'Peace' is mentioned at least three times by Euripides: *Herac.* 371–380, *Or.* 1682–1683, and fr. 453. For the cult, see Philoch. 328 F 151; Smith 2011: 78.

60 A fragment (fr. 305) ascribed to Aristophanes' second *Peace* features a brief exchange between an unknown speaker and 'Agriculture' (Γεωργία), who identifies Peace as her nurse, steward, colleague, guardian, daughter and sister.

61 Commentators have advanced various theories to explain this. Sommerstein (1985: *ad loc.*) suggests that it was the combination of the inanimate statue and live attendants that was strange; for Olson (1998: *ad loc.*), it was the manner of introducing the statue; Taplin (2014) argues that its gigantic size (κολοσσικὸν) was what attracted ridicule.

62 For the divine power of the ἄγαλμα, see Gernet 1981; Scodel 1996: 115.

63 But cf. Chronopoulos (2017), who argues compellingly that the second half of *Peace* also acknowledges the social tensions that inevitably emerge after a major economic and political upheaval, even in generally positive circumstances such as peace.

64 Compton-Engle (2015: 61) has perceptively recognized that *Peace* 'studiously avoids making distinctions among its characters' clothing'.

65 Moulton 1981: 93. See also Tordoff's (2011) osphresiological analysis of the plot, which moves from the bad smells of the city at war to the pleasant smells of agriculture and food in the countryside.

66 Ruffell 2000: 475; Wilkins 2000: 128.

67 For solidarity as the chief value of comedy's agricultural economy, see Wilkins 2000: 104.

68 Vernant 1980: 169–185; Foley 1985: 35.

69 For an accessible summary of this 'functionalist' school of ritual theory, see Bell 2009: 23–29.

70 Burkert 1983: 12, 38, 40.

71 Foley 1985: 39–40.

72 Olson 1998: *ad loc.*

73 Variants of σφαγή are found roughly a half dozen times in both Aeschylus and Sophocles, and more than fifty times in Euripides.

74 Olson 1998: *ad loc.*

75 Wilson (2007a: 279) interprets the averted sacrifice as a pointed metatheatrical allusion to 'comic *Nikê*'.

76 Foley 1985: 40. Tragedy's perverted sacrifices are well documented; see Zeitlin 1965; Burkert 1966: 117–121; Foley 1985; Seaford 1994: 369–371.

77 Foley 1985: 40.

78 For treatment of the sacrilege, see Foley 1985: 43–44.

79 Seaford 1994: 342–360.

80 Seaford 1994: 368–369.

81 Schechner 1977: 74–76.

82 Compton-Engle's (2015: 44) comparison of Trygaeus's position, flanked by the two beautiful personifications, to the trophy ceremony of a motor race, where women signify the sexual rewards available to a successful male, is particularly apt in this respect.

83 *Peace* 174, 287, 292–300, 730–731, 734, 962–965, 1022.

84 'Ritual spectating' (Nightingale 2004); 'right of spectating at public festivals' (Hall 2006); 'pilgrimage' (Rutherford 1995). For general studies of *theôria*, see Dillon 1997: 1–26; Rutherford 1995, 2000; Kowalzig 2007.

85 For *theôria* elsewhere in comedy, see Ar. *Plut.* 619–626; frr. 487–503 (*Women Claiming Tent-Sites*); Epich. frr. 68–69 (*Theôroi*); Henioch. fr. 5; Pl. Com. frr. 27–37 (*Festivals*).

86 Nightingale 2004: 41–42.

87 The traditional formula is some variation of 'I give [her] to you for the cultivation of legitimate children' (ταύτην γνησίων παίδων ἐπ᾽ ἀρότῳ σοι δίδωμι); cf. Men. *Dysk.* 842–843; *Peri.* 1013–1014; *Sam.* 726–728. See Harrison 1968: 3–9; Oakley and Sinos 1993.

88 For the conversion of weapons to instruments of farming, see Micah 4:1–4 (cf. Isaiah 2: 2–5).

89 See Olson 1998: *ad loc.* and Totaro 1999: 103–112.

90 For this metaphor becoming reality, see Calame 2004: 175.

91 Other features include the ritual refrain to Hymen, the *makarismos* ('blessing') of the bridal couple (1334–1335), and the lyrical reiziana. On the hymeneal generally, see Page 1955: 71–74 and Swift 2010: 242–245 (esp. 242 on the complexities of generic terminology and specific context). No complete hymeneal from the Archaic and Classical periods survives apart from the fragments of Sappho and a few others. Fifth-century drama presents only variations or parodies, as Eur. *Hipp.* 1131–1152; *Tro.* 308–340. For the song in comedy, see Ar. *Av.* 1731–1743.

92 E.g., brides are flowers, apples and saplings; grooms are, by contrast, horses, Achilles and Hector.

93 For the markedly panhellenic identity of the chorus during Peace's rescue, see *Pax* 508. The folkish, communal emphasis of the wedding song would have lent it a certain panhellenic tone (Parker 1997: 293).

94 For the flight from Athens as a starting point for comedy's utopian experiments, see Ruffell 2000.

95 A point trenchantly argued by Cassio (1985: 139–141). For the osphresiological organization of *Peace*, see Tordoff 2011. On the golden-age imagery of the wedding song, see Calame 2004: 174. Cf. Auger 1979.

96 See e.g., Auger 1979: 80–81; Cassio 1985: 139–147; Calame 2004: 174–176.

97 Carey 2013: 164–165. See also Swift (2010: 255–262) on the mixed gender of the hymeneal chorus.

98 As noted by Cassio (1985: 143), Σ *Pax* 1357 indicates that the chorus addressed these final lines of the play (1357–1359) – ὦ χαίρετε χαίρετ' ἄν- / δρες, κἂν ξυνέπησθέ μοι, / πλακοῦντες ἔδεσθε to the audience.

99 Exceptions include the wedding of *Birds* (1720–1765), Cratinus's marriage to 'Comedy' in the fragmentary *Pytinê*, and possibly a few others.

100 The most important study of tragic marriage is Seaford 1987. See also Craik 1990. Kaimio (2002) shows that tragedy does not uniformly portray marriage negatively. Notable exceptions include Aeschylus's *Egyptians* and *Danaids*, which followed his *Suppliants* (cf. fr. 44); see Sommerstein 1996a: 100–120.

101 Seaford 1987: 106.

102 Seaford 1987: 120–121. Moreover, Haimon's spray of blood across the maiden's white cheek has been seen by some to evoke the defloration of a bride (1238–1241).

103 For the dangers of textiles in tragedy, see esp. Lee 2004.

104 Seaford 1987: 108–110.

105 Seaford 1994: 375.

106 Seaford 1987: 111–112, 120.

107 Seaford 1994: 342–360 and *passim*.
108 Foley 1985: 85.
109 Raaflaub 2009: 238–241.
110 Dover 1972: 137.

Chapter 5: Old Comedy and Lyric Poetry

1 The expression 'song culture' was coined by Herington 1985. Choruses: Calame 2001. Music: Csapo 1999–2000, 2004; Power 2010; LeVen 2014. Dithyramb: Kowalzig 2007. *Khorêgia*: Wilson 2000, 2007b.
2 Garner 1990; Rutherford 1995; Bagordo 2003; Swift 2010.
3 For subjects of melic and iambic poetry, see West 1974: 18; Bowie 1986. For tragedy's trope-oriented appropriation of lyric, see Swift 2010.
4 By 'classic' lyric I mean poetry composed by canonical authors of the Archaic and early Classical period as opposed to late fifth-century, contemporary lyric.
5 On the formal qualities of the parabasis, see Sifakis 1971; Totaro 1999; for biographical content, Hubbard 1991. Silk's (1980) study of 'serious' Aristophanic lyric challenges long-held assumptions about its quality. A useful introduction is Robson 2009.
6 Rosen 1988; Arist. *Poet.* 1448b24–1449a5.
7 Hubbard 1991.
8 Kugelmeier 1996: esp. 1–9.
9 Swift 2010: 42.
10 Timotheus's claim (*PMG* 796.5) to break from the past exemplifies this kind of self-conscious departure.
11 LeVen 2014: 72–83.
12 LeVen (2014: 53–59) raises cogent objections to traditional interpretations of this transitional period.
13 Simonides' death is usually dated to the 460s, Pindar's to 440 (Lefkowitz 2012: 61), and Bacchylides' as late as the 420s.
14 For 'heroic vagueness,' see Easterling 1997; Grethlein 2010: 75.
15 On the misleading nature of the term 'New Music,' see Csapo and Wilson 2009: 278.
16 LeVen (2014: 63) excellently summarizes these changes.
17 Plato describes this in a passage (*Leg.* 700a–701a) discussed in Chapter 6.
18 D'Angour 2011: 29.
19 Barker 1984; D'Angour 2006: 90–91, esp. 95: 'familiarity and repeatability are ways of demonstrating the excellence of "classic"'.
20 For explicit claims to novelty as a strategy for 'classicizing,' see D'Angour 2006: 93.
21 On the fragment, see Olson 2016: 16–19. As KA note, the meter of the passage is not fully understood.

22 For the *iambykê* and *trigônon*, see West 1992: 76–77. For similar sentiments about old and new lyric, see Eup. fr. 395 (Stesichorus); fr. 398 (Pindar).

23 Davidson (2000) identified Gnesippos as an early artist of mime, but cf. Hordern 2003; Prauscello 2006. See esp. Olson 2016: 16–17.

24 This dichotomy underlies the opposition of Aeschylus and Euripides in Aristophanes' *Frogs*, for example.

25 See Karanika 2014: *passim*, esp. 2.

26 See Σ E Ar. *Nub.* 1356aα + b; cf. Rawles 2013: 184.

27 As noted by Rawles 2013: 177.

28 Σ *Ach.* 637. See also Isoc. 15.166; Lavecchia (2000) discusses testimonia of the song's reception.

29 For the Persian Wars in Athenian identity, see Steinbock 2013: 53–54; cf. Andoc. 1.107.

30 Rawles 2013: 177. Kugelmeier (1996: 160) finds two other allusions to Pindaric poetry at Ar. *Av.* 1121 (*Nem.* 1.1) and 1321 (*Pyth.* 8.1); cf. Rawles 2013: 178 n. 11.

31 Parker (1997: 328–333) notes that most of the poet's rhythmic phrases have individual Pindaric parallels; cf. Dunbar 1995: 522–528.

32 Repeated κλῄζω (906, 921, 950), typical of hymns and prayers; μελιγλώσσων (908) (cf. Bacchylid. 3.97, fr. 4.63); φάτις (924); ἀμαρυγά (925); χρυσόθρονε (950); κρυεράν (950).

33 For echoes of Homer and Simonides, see Kugelmeier 1996: 110.

34 See Dunbar 1995: *ad loc.*

35 Dover (1968: *ad Nub.* 338) traces this stock joke to the early fifth century when tyrants and aristocrats still hosted lyric poets; cf. Dunbar 1995: 521.

36 The Pindaric original is fr. 105 b.

37 Hartog 1988; Arist. *Pol.* 1256a32–36.

38 Cf. Kugelmeier (1996: 115), who sees the poet as the modern descendent of the poet as greedy, business operative (cf. Ar. *Pax* 698–699); cf. Martin's (2009: 87) slightly farfetched 'planetary' bard, who 'names himself … in coded bardic fashion' with a verbal gloss on Hesiod's name.

39 E.g., the Simonidean epinician πῖνε πῖν' ἐπὶ συμφοραῖς ('Drink, drink for the results!') in paeonic and trochaic rhythm at Ar. *Eq.* 406 (Σ 405a=512 *PMG*). The Greater Argument of *Clouds* describes learning songs such as 'Pallas, savage City-sacker' and 'the Shout from Afar' (ἢ 'Παλλάδα περσέπολιν δεινάν' ἢ 'τηλέπορόν τι βόαμα') at *Nub.* 967.

40 *IG*³ ii 3028 partly preserves a victorious *khorêgos*'s dedication for a chorus trained by Cinesias.

41 Physical appearance: Ar. fr. 156. He was subject to play-length satire in Strattis's *Cinesias* (c. 408–405 BCE; cf. Orth 2009). For his appearance in comedy, see Kugelmeier 1996: 208–248; Kidd 2014: 89–117. He apparently suffered from a public

attack of diarrhoea some time before 405 (*Ran.* 152–153, 366; *Eccl.* 328–330) and was accused of impiety (Lys. frr. 85–86).

42 Wright 2012: 110–112; cf. Taillardat 1965: § 28; Ar. *Nub.* 331–338.

43 A common trope of lyric (cf. Pind. *Ol.* 2.86–88, *Nem.* 3.80, 5.21; Bacchyl. 5.16–33; Dunbar 1995; Barker 2004; Wright 2012: 112). For the eagle as an image of pre-eminence, see Hubbard 1985: 149–152.

44 D'Angour 2011: 195; see also LeVen 2014: 153–157.

45 Csapo 2004: esp. 225–226.

46 From [Plut.] *De mus.* 30.1141c. For commentary, see Düring 1945; Borthwick 1968; Olson 2007: 182–186.

47 The anonymous author of *On Comedy* describes Pherecrates as an actor for Krates, who later went on to compose domestic comedies with female characters (Koster III.29–31 [=Test. 2a KA]). He won his first victory in 437 (Olson 2007: 413–414).

48 [Plut.] *De mus.* 1141c: Φερεκράτη τὸν κωμικὸν εἰσαγαγεῖν τὴν Μουσικὴν ἐν γυναικείῳ σχήματι, ὅλην κατηκισμένην τὸ σῶμα.

49 For Melanippides' avoidance of astrophic composition, see West 1992: 357–358. The term χορδαῖς ('strings'), from 'χορδή,' is the sheep gut from which lyre strings were fashioned, and plays on the colloquial term for penis.

50 Such καμπαί ('modulations') and cognates are found in unfavourable descriptions of poetic composition (e.g., Ar. *Thesm.* 53) and can denote aggressive (often sexual) bending and twisting.

51 West 1992: 360–361; Olson 2007: 184. A fourth-century BCE vase painting (Museo Provinciale Salerno, inv. 1812) features Phrynis being physically assaulted by 'Pyronides,' hero of Eupolis's *Demes* (see Storey 2003: 116–117, 332).

52 Since one of Phrynis's innovations was increasing the number of cithara strings from seven to nine, it is unclear why he is assigned only five strings here (see Olson 2007: 184).

53 On this mixing, see Csapo and Wilson 2009: 284.

54 Their popular appeal is discussed by West 1992: 370–372; Csapo 2004: 229–245; Roselli 2005.

55 *Mousikē*'s sexual objectification resembles the Muse of Euripides ridiculed by Aeschylus in Aristophanes' *Frogs*: low-class, generically promiscuous, indecent and demotic, she derives from 'whore-songs, Miletus's drinking-songs, Carian pipe-tunes, dirges [and] choruses' (*Ran.* 1301–1303). She is also compared to the prostitute Cyrene and her 'twelve tricks' (*Ran.* 1325–1328).

56 To such critics, the sole remaining – and completely fictional – antidemocratic oases of an earlier prelapsarian socio-cultural order untouched by the New Musical innovations were the idealized Sparta and Crete (Csapo 2004: 241–244, citing Ath. 628b, 632f–633a; Pl. *Leg.* 657b, 660b). See Csapo and Wilson (2009: 286) for the story of Timotheus's punishment for additional cithara strings at a Spartan festival.

57 The most comprehensive study is Horn 1970; see also Willi 2003: 16–41; Carey 2013: 168.

58 See the remarks of Swift 2010: 20–21; cf. Pulleyn's (1997: 43) concise overview of the primary meanings of ὕμνος in ancient Greek sources.

59 Bremer 1981 presents a clear, helpful definition; cf. Pulleyn 1997: 132–155. For formality in the Homeric Hymns, see Janko 1981.

60 In tragedy: Swift 2010: 70–103; in comedy: Kleinknecht 1937; Horn 1970.

61 On the relevance of the Agathon scene to the play's broader thematic concerns of gender, genre and intertextuality, see Whitman 1964: 222; Dover 1972: 162–163; Hansen 1976: 166 n. 7 (with bibliography).

62 Verbs: ὄλβιζε (107), ἀείσατ(ε) (115), κλῄζουσα (116), ἀγάλλετε (128). Willi (2003: 25–26) speculates that multiple references to hymnic singing may have been a feature of Agathon's style. For the devotional tone of the chorus's expression of thanksgiving, see Mantziou 1981: 227–228; cf. *Hym. Hom. Cer.* 9, Anacreon 348 (on Artemis of Magnesia), and further hymns listed in Mantziou 1981.

63 For fuller explication of these features, see Csapo 1999–2000: 417–425; also West 1992: 356–372. 'Dionysiac' includes not only Leto and Artemis, whose cult was widespread in Asia Minor, but technically even the initially named Eleusinian goddesses (99), whose presence is usually explained by the Thesmophoria festival framing the play: Bierl 2009: 142; Austin and Olson 2004: *ad loc.*

64 First recognized by Bothe 1829: *ad Thesm.* 111.

65 For a full treatment, see Parker 1997: 398–405; Furley and Bremer 2001: 350–353; Austin and Olson 2004: *ad loc.*

66 There is disagreement about whether Agathon is wearing all women's clothes (Muecke 1982: 50) or a combination of men and women's (MacDowell 1995: 255). Snyder 1974 examines illustrations of fifth-century vase painting that depict Anacreon's effeminate Ionic dress.

67 ἱμάτιον and στρόφιον (250–251), saffron gown (253), περίθετος (258), and ἔγκυκλος (261).

68 Stone 1981: 22–24; for the comic body, see Foley 2000; Revermann 2006a: 145–159.

69 A Greek formulating a prayer through a hymn searched for the names and titles appropriate to the occasion and perhaps most effective (Bremer 1981: 195).

70 Muecke 1982: 48–49.

71 E.g., Austin and Olson (2004: 87): 'this is not a happy omen for Euripides' great plan'. Cf. Bierl (2009: 149), who claims that Agathonian drama lacks a 'connection to the real world'.

72 Swift 2010: 71–72. Hippolytus's hymn to Artemis (Eur. *Hipp.* 58–71) shares certain formal and dramaturgical features with Agathon's hymn, including Hippolytus acting as an *exarchos* exhorting in dactyls a chorus of male followers.

73 E.g., Soph. *OT* 1086–1109, where the chorus anticipates that Oedipus's discovery of his parentage will be a joyous occasion (Swift 2010: 81–83).

74 On the play, see Webster 1967: 136–143; Harder 1985; Cropp 1995a: 121–147. Aristotle famously singles out the play's recognition at *Poet.* 1454a5; *Eth. Nic.* 1111a11.

75 The following commentary draws from Harder 1985; Cropp 1995a.

76 Polybius (12.26.5), citing Timaeus, reports that the Sicilian statesman Hermocrates quoted lines 1–7 at a peace conference at Gela in 424 BCE (Cropp 1995a: 144).

77 Parker 1997: 84, 150. See also Wilamowitz 1962: 326.

78 Euripides' sequence of choriambs (primarily glyconic and Hipponactean) is given alternating dicolon choriamb + bacchiac.

79 *GMT* §723; cf. Willi's (2003: 33) discussion of the optative as an alternative to the standard imperative.

80 Cf. Kleinknecht 1937: 91–92. The hymn is excluded from both Horn (1970) and Rau (1967: 148 n. 28).

81 For analysis, see esp. Griffith 2013: 134–137.

82 Griffith 2013: 135.

83 Hunter 2009: 25.

84 The scholia cite Eur. *IA* (read *IT*), *Meleager*, *El.*, and *Hypsipyle*. For the meter, see Parker 1997: 506; cf. Stanford 1958: *ad loc.*

85 See Σ *Ach.* 443; cf. Barlow 2008: 20. Mastronarde (2010: 126–145) estimates that roughly sixty per cent of Euripidean stasima have a non-immediate connection to their context.

86 The *melisma*, i.e., the repetition of a syllable over several notes in the melody ('εἰειειειειειλίσσετε,' *Ran.* 1314), parodies a stylistic tendency of the New Music. The term ἐλίσσω itself is a self-conscious reference to the revolving movement of circular dance. Dolphins' 'circling, whirling movements' and the 'tendril' (ἕλιξ) are frequently mentioned in the New Music (Griffith 2013: 147).

87 Csapo 2003: 72

88 Cropp 2000: 239. The halcyon is called πολυπενθής at Hom. *Il.* 9.561–564; Ap. Rhod. 4.362–363; cf. Arist. *Hist. an.* 593b8–12, 616a14–34; Pliny *HN* X.32. For modern studies, see Thompson 1895: 28–32; Arnott 2007: 20–21.

89 Euripidean characters: Ar. *Ran.* 92, 841, 943, 1069, 1071; *Pax* 995. Chattering admittedly describes birds generally in Aristophanes (Taillardat 1965: § 520–523).

90 See Plut. *Mor.* 963c5–d5.

91 Beavis (1988) takes φάλαγγες here as a non-venomous house spider, an 'ἀράχνης.'

92 Aristotle's description (*Hist. an.* 623a8) of the spider's skilled (σοφώτατον) and smooth (γλαφυρώτατον) webs (ὑφαίνει) draws on conventional terms for women's weaving. For the identification of Ar. *Ran.* 1316–1317 with Euripides' *Hypsipyle* (fr. 752f.10), see Borthwick 1994.

93 The spider's web is also evidence of disuse in epic and lyric; see Hom. *Od.* 16.35; Bacchyl. 4. 69–72; Cratin. fr. 202; Eur. fr. 369.1; Pirrotta (2009: 94) surveys the metaphor of web-spinning in Greek thought.

94 E.g., Hom. *Od.* 8.280 (Hephaestus catching Aphrodite and Ares in 'delicate webs,' ἀράχνια λεπτά).

95 Borthwick (1994: 30) counts at least forty instances of *melisma* in Euripides, compared to three each in Aeschylus and Sophocles. For this and other attributes of the *genus tenue*, see O'Sullivan 1992; Wright 2013: 114.

96 λαλία: Ar. *Ach.* 705; cf. *Ran.* 943, 1071.

97 Dover (1993: *ad loc.*) takes ἔπαλλε as transitive; cf. Stanford 1958: *ad loc.*

98 For such zeugmas, see Breitenbach 1934: 209.

99 Euripides shows a marked preference for κανών in expressions of measurement (Stieber 2011: 388–397). For uses of στάδιος, see *Heracl.* 863; *Ion* 497.

100 O'Sullivan 1992: 136; cf. Ar. fr. 656, in which Aristophanes describes Euripides as ἐπιθυμεῖ τὴν γλῶσσαν αὐτοῦ μετρῆσθαι, 'eager to measure out his own tongue'.

101 For Euripides' use of the ἑλικ- root (as well as δινεῖν/δινεύειν) to describe winding things, whirling water, curling ivy at a rate far greater than his peers, see Borthwick 1994: 30.

102 Cf. the sudden embrace of the Euripidean Jocasta (ἀμφίβαλλε μαστὸν ὠλέναισι ματέρος, Eur. *Phoen.* 306) to *Ran.* 1322.

103 See Kaimio (1988: 37) for Euripides' emphasis on the physical contact of embrace and the joy of reunion; cf. Eur. *IT* 793–797, *Ion* 569–584, 1395–1449; *Hel.* 557–567.

104 For Strattis's biography, see esp. Olson 2007: 416–417.

105 Preserved at Ath. 2.69a (cf. Eur. *El.* 432–434). For commentary, see Orth 2009: 267–272.

106 The caterpillar was a garden pest to Greeks (Theophr. *Hist. pl.* 7.5.4.4–5; see Beavis 1988: 243–244). For σατυριδίων μακροκέρκων, see Marchiori (in Canfora 2001: vol. 1 198 n. 7); cf. Edmunds 1957: vol. 1 835.

107 Hall 2006: 295.

108 The best study remains Barner 1971; see also Barlow 1986: 17; Beverly 1997; Hall 2006: 288–320.

109 Σ Eur. *Andr.* 103; Suda μ 1242; Hesychias μ 1465. Hall 2006: 310.

110 For Melanthius's fragments, see Snell and Kannicht 1986: 136–138.

111 On the opening sequence, see Gibert 2004: 141–142; Taplin 2007: 174–176.

112 Andromeda's precise position onstage is unknown. Webster (1967: 193) saw her facing the audience directly with the *skênê* behind her. Gibert (2004) suspects she was at one side, perpendicular to the audience who represented the direction of the sea with the *skênê* as the cave of the shore; cf. Taplin 2007: 176. The 'full lament' of tragedy is distinguished by its placement near the play's end (Wright 1986: 110), e.g., Eur. *Hipp.* 1347–1388; *IA* 1276–1318; see also Barner 1971: 287–290.

113 Webster (1967: 193) surmised this on the evidence of four mid-fifth-century vase paintings, which he believed have been inspired by Sophocles' production; cf. Green 1994: 20–22; Taplin 2007: 33, 174–182.

114 For such 'undercoding' in Greek drama, see Revermann 2006a: 42–43; cf. Elam 2002: 49.

115 On *apotympanismos*, see Austin and Olson 2004: 294–295.

116 Rau 1967: 70; Austin and Olson 2004: *ad loc.* Tropes include addresses to age-mates and lamenting loss of youth (1015, 1030); polypteton (μέλεα…μέλεος, 1037–1038); repetition (1038); cries (1042); anaphora (1043–1044).

117 πῶς ἄν + optative is a standard tragic expression (Rau 1967: 71).

118 Other choral lines folded into the monody include *Thesm.* 1019, 1022–1023.

119 Webster 1967: 194. Echo first appears in poetry as a messenger of fame tasked with relaying news of Olympic victory to the winner's dead father (Pind. *Ol.* 14.20).

120 Specifically, the hero lacks any neighbour to whom he 'might weep (ἀποκλαύσειεν) a groaning lament, evoking one in response (ἀντίτυπον)' (Soph. *Phil.* 691–695; cf. 1458–1460).

121 See Rau 1967: 82–85.

122 For the connotations of συναγωνίζομαι ('sharing the struggle'), see Arist. *Poet.* 1456a25–29; Mastronarde 2010: 147.

123 The text gives no explicit indication that 'Echo' ever appears within the audience's view, and many commentators believe Euripides remains out of sight until he reappears as Perseus (1098). Cf. Hourmouziades' (1965) ingenious conjecture that she ran back-and-forth across roof of the *skênê*.

124 Henderson 1987.

125 Barlow 1986: 10. Parker (1997: 442): 'an "un-Euripidean" excess of metrical diversity.' For the New Music's use of compounds, see Arist. *Poet.* 1457a34; 1459a9; *Rhet.* 1406b1.

126 The words μέλας (28 times) and φόνιος (54 times) are among the commonest epithets found in Euripides (Barlow 1986: 11).

127 The sole appearance of κάλπις in tragedy is Eur. *Hipp.* 123. See Dover (1993: *ad loc.*) on ἀποκλύσω (1340).

128 φωράω is an Attic legal term to describe an approved search of a residence for stolen property (Harrison 1968).

129 For detailed treatments, see Dover (1993: 358–362), Sommerstein (1996b: 277) and Parker (1997: 508–518).

130 For the New Music's influence in this passage, see Csapo 1999–2000: 418.

131 *POxy.* II.219 = *Lyr. Adesp.* 4 Powell [Παῖς ἀλέκτορα ἀπολέσας]. Hunter (2002: 199) dates the content to the early first century CE.

132 As suggested by Hunter 2002: 200.

133 See Ar. *Av.* 489 with Dunbar 1995; Cratin. fr. 279.

134 Csapo 1993a and 1993b are the classic studies.

135 Csapo 1993a: 15. Furthermore, chickens are ἀφροδισιαστικά and fertile: Arist. *Hist. An.* 488b4; *Gen. an.* 769b30. Henderson (1991: 128) notes that πτέρυξ is definitely phallic at Ar. *Lys.* 774, and that while πτερόν is not explicitly so, a handful of texts and images are suggestive.

136 See Revermann 2006a: 152–153. Fluttering expresses erotic excitement at Ar. *Eq.* 1344; Hdt. 2.115.4.

137 Csapo 1993a: 16–17.

138 Stanford (1958) and Sommerstein (1996b: *ad loc.*) recognize the link between monody and Cretan royal women.

139 See Callim, *Hymn* 3.183–224 for a catalogue.

140 Hubbard 2015.

141 Robson 2009: 153–154.

142 Ar. *Eq.* 529–530. See also the old-fashioned love of Phrynichus by the chorus of decrepit old jurors at Ar. *Vesp.* 219–220 (Biles and Olson 2015: *ad loc.*; cf. *Vesp.* 268–269, 1490).

143 Prauscello 2012; see esp. LeVen (2014: 81 n. 31) for additional studies.

Chapter 6: The Feminine Mistake: Household Economy in Aristophanes' *Thesmophoriazusae*

1 See Zeitlin's (1996: 376) summary. Despite its reputation as feminist, *Lysistrata* is much less feminist and pacifist than first-time readers often assume (see Revermann 2010b: 72–77).

2 Gamel (2002) gives a sense of the difficulty of staging this play in the present day. Scharffenberger (2002) discusses a controversial production at the University of Arizona.

3 Dover 1972; Hansen 1976; Zeitlin 1996; Gamel 2002; Scharffenberger 2002; Tzanetou 2002; Austin and Olson 2004. A watershed moment in the study of the play was the identification of Inlaw's sacrifice of the 'wine-baby' (Ar. *Thesm.* 752–753) on the Würzburg Telephus (cf. Chapter 2).

4 E.g., Taplin 1993: 86–87; Walsh 2009: 221–222.

5 Aristophanes' running joke that Euripides introduced 'women in love' (*Ran.* 1043–1044), or 'evil' women – a distortion of his rather nuanced depiction of troubled women as victims of much greater powers (Vellacott 1975; March 1990) – has gone without much scrutiny (Rosen 2008: 145).

6 For each parody, see Rau 1967: 51–53, 53–65, 65–89.

7 Zeitlin 1996.

8 See Pl. *Prt.* 318e. On Protagoras's political theory, see Denyer 2013.

9   Pomeroy 1994: 18–19.

10 Bowie 1993: 220; Cowan 2008: 319.

11 For discussion of this passage and its implications for Aristophanes' view of Euripides and tragedy, see Hall 1997: 125–126; Roselli 2005: 30; Rosen 2008; Hunter 2009: 10–52; Griffith 2012: 125.

12 See also Hdt. 6.70; 9.116; see Austin and Olson 2004: *ad* 496. Stanford (1958: *ad loc.*) cites the use of this word at Thuc. 3.43.3. Dover (1993: *ad loc.*) sees a similar description of roguery in Pl. *Resp.* 409c.

13 The standard study is Ehrenberg 1947: esp. 56.

14 The original idea is sometimes credited to Protagoras. See, e.g., Pl. *Meno* 91a–b; *Resp.* 600; Xen. *Mem.* 3.4.6; Isoc. 15.285.

15 For such plain language as representative of the 'badness' that allowed audiences to draw bad conclusions from his plays, see Rosen 2008: 162–163. Euripides' frequent choices of metaphor to describe his art ('subtle rulers … squared-off words', 956) is seemingly calibrated to appeal to this banausic class (Roselli 2005: 30).

16 Hunter 2009; see also Folch 2015: 124–126.

17 Despite its historical inaccuracies, Plato's account of judgment in the democratic audience nonetheless correctly affirms its link with the fundamental principles of democratic politics (Folch 2015: 126).

18 Rosen (2008: 159) identifies this collaboration as the basis of the 'poetic badness' imputed to Euripides, whose dialogic style encouraged observers to equate its immoral content with the poet's own intentions.

19 Stanford 1958: *ad Ran.* 980–991; see also Csapo 2010: 122.

20 For the alleged misogyny of Euripidean tragedy, see March 1990; Mastronarde 2010: 271–279.

21 For a general treatment of the festival, see Deubner 1966: 50–60. Aristophanes' depiction of the festival is analyzed by Tzanetou 2002 and Faraone 2011.

22 E.g., with prayers (295–311), curses (331–351) and oaths. See McClure 1999: 228–231; Bierl 2009: 174–198.

23 On narrative inevitability, see Burian 1997.

24 On props and their narrative value, see Poe 2000: 284–285.

25 Austin and Olson 2004: *ad loc.* For the fragments of the tragedy, see Collard 1995b. Discussions include Webster 1967: 80–84; Papamichael 1983; Taplin 2007: 201–204.

26 See Eur. fr. 664; cf. Cratin. fr. 299.

27 This may allude to Euripides' lost *Aeolus* and its incestuous relationship of brother and sister (cf. Ar. *Nub.* 1371–1376).

28 Melanippe, described as a 'γυνὴ πονηρὰ' later in the comedy (*Thesm.* 546–547), was depicted sympathetically in *Melanippe the Wise* and *Captive Melanippe*. Aristophanes' disingenuous association of her with the more culpable Phaedra and Stheneboea may have exploited audiences' discomfort with her intelligence

and assertiveness as well as her rape by Poseidon in the former play (Cropp
1995b: 246).

29 Both Theseus and Proetus incur some blame for being manipulated by their wives'
lies (Eur. *Hipp.* 1282–1296; *Sthen.* Hyp. 20–22 [=Test iia]).

30 Austin and Olson 2004: *ad loc.*; cf. Ar. *Vesp.* 112–113, 154–155 (with Biles and Olson
2015: *ad loc.*); *Lys.* 245–246, 264–265.

31 Xen. *Cyn.* 10.1; Arist. *Hist. an.* 608a 26–33; Ael. *NA* 3.2; Poll. 5.17–86; cf. Lilja 1976:
79. House dogs were small and of the Maltese ('Melitaean') family.

32 For a sense of the disruption this kind of animal causes indoors, see Trimalchio's
display of Scylax ('Puppy') to his terrified diners at Petron. *Sat.* 64.7 and the profile
of the uncultured bumpkin answering the door with his aggressive dog (Theophr
4.9–10).

33 Although this is the earliest textual mention of the Laconian key, they would have
been in use at Athens by the early fifth century according to Diels 1914: 46–48. On
the key generally, see Austin and Olson 2004: *ad loc.*; Barton 1972; Whitehead
(1990), who compares the house in *Thesm.* to the city placed under martial law in
Aen. Tact. 10.9–10.

34 As noted by Austin and Olson 2004: *ad* 414–417.

35 Seaford 1987; 1990a; 1990b.

36 All enumerated by Seaford 1990a: 81.

37 For supposititious children in Euripides, see Satyros fr. 39 col. vii (*POxy.* ix 1176)
with Schorn 2002: 299.

38 Inlaw's impersonation is physical and linguistic (Willi 2003: 185).

39 This anxiety is implied, if not explicit, in our sources.

40 A well-known novella theme (Trenkner 1958: 80–84; cf. Ar. *Nub.* 41–52, on
Strepsiades' wife).

41 Sexual intercourse in temples and sanctuaries was strictly forbidden and purification
from recent sexual activity before entering such spaces was mandatory (Dover 1974:
206; Parker 1986: 76; Sommerstein 1994: *ad loc.*).

42 Parker 1986: 76.

43 E.g., the myth of Auge (Apollod. 3.9) and the mother of the Spartan Demaratus (Hdt.
6.68–69).

44 As noted by Porter (1997) and Austin and Olson (2004: *ad loc.*).

45 Though seemingly identified in this passage, mule-grooms were not necessarily
slaves; see Walin 2012b: 23.

46 As Austin and Olson (2004: *ad loc.*) note, the garlic either gives the impression of
being sexually unapproachable or conceals the scent of perfume (see Trenkner
1958: 84). Alternatively, given garlic's use as a stimulant of physical and sexual
aggression in fighting cocks (Csapo 1993b: 117–120; Ar. *Ach.* 156–166, 524–527;
Lys. 458), it might be an aphrodisiac here.

47 I print the text of R (Ravenna 429).

48 See Austin and Olson (2004: *ad loc.*) for the sources. Hughes (2012: 91, 186) describes an ἔγκυκλον.

49 See also Aristotle's (*Poet.* 1454b36) illustration of one type of recognition through the 'voice of the shuttle' (ἡ τῆς κερκίδος φωνή), which exemplifies the dramatic potential of this activity. The phrase originally alludes to Sophocles' *Tereus*; see fr. 595 with the comments of Fitzpatrick and Sommerstein 2006: 183–184.

50 Austin (1975: 187), followed by Austin and Olson (2004) and N. Wilson (2007), emends the text to εὖ κεκαλυμμένον ('well-concealed').

51 Seager (1981: 248) is followed by Sommerstein (1994) and Cowan (2008).

52 On veiling to express shame, see Cairns 1993: 292.

53 Sommerstein (1994: *ad loc.*) suggests the courtyard. Austin and Olson (2004: *ad loc.*) do not specify.

54 Because front entrances were deliberately arranged to make the house's interior court invisible from the street, a wife could reach the courtyard from one of the rooms without being seen by someone entering (Nevett 1999: 69–70).

55 Demosthenes' similar allegation that Medias was purchased from his biological mother by another woman who passed him off (ὑποβαλομένη) as her own (21.149–150) demonstrates the use of this narrative in other public discourses.

56 Walin (2012a) demonstrated the uterine and vaginal qualities of the χύτρα across the Aristophanic corpus (*Eq.* 1030–1034, 1174–1176; *Vesp.* 904; fr. 833; *Plut.* 672–695), an association predated by Hippocratic gynaecology (King 1998: 26; cf. Σ Ar. *Thesm.* 509).

57 Both Sommerstein (1994) and Austin and Olson (2004) are unsure about the joke's meaning: does the crone recognize the husband's penis because she was his nurse or his concubine? For the comic phallus, see Taplin 1993.

58 On comparing a baby to a lion, see Sommerstein (1994: *ad loc.*) and Hdt. 5.92.3

59 Cowan (2008) conjectures that this absurdly delayed 'birth' parodies Hera's cruel extension of Alcmene's labour for nine days before Eileithuia was allowed to release the mother from her pains.

60 Thus Zeitlin 1996: 380: '… out of the typical male discourse of comic theater'.

61 Since nameless wives are merely mentioned at Ar. *Ach.* 262 and *Nub.* 41–55, 59–74, it is commonly (though not universally) believed that Aristophanes' 411 plays are the first to portray such women in comedy (Henderson 2002; Stroup 2004). Aristophanes' older contemporary, Pherecrates, may have portrayed women and domestic life in greater detail, but his fragments do not confirm this.

62 Trenkner (1958: 6) identifies the adultery plot as the classic type of novella. For tropes like the wife meeting her lover, the husband's unexpected return and women sleeping with slaves, see Trenkner 1958: 80–88. A partially preserved script (*c.* first/second century CE) entitled 'The Adulteress' on the verso of *POxy.* 413 preserves a

mistress's savage reaction to rejection by her male slave and plot to poison her husband (161–162).

63 See Johnstone 1994: 233.

64 Silk 2000: 327; see also Tzanetou 2002: 357; Cowan 2008.

65 Note esp. Ruffell (2011: 340): 'What is at stake in the dialogue of tragedy and comedy [in these three plays] is the nature of realism, the effect of different sorts of realism, and the relationship between realism and referentiality.'

66 Ruffell 2011: 346.

67 For an account of discrepant decoding, see Revermann's (2013) analysis of Sophocles' *Electra*. Discrepant 'awareness' is examined in Pfister 1988: 50.

68 On the forensic quality of the speech, see Austin and Olson 2004: 175. On focalization, see De Jong 2014: 67.

69 Rosen 2006. An earlier passage that reflects the subculture of poetic fandom is Strepsiades' claim to be ignorant of the poetry that is currently trendy. He dismissively urges Pheidippides to recite 'whatever it is' (ἅττ᾽ ἐστὶ τὰ σοφὰ ταῦτα), now popularly regarded as σοφά if not Simonides or Aeschylus (Rosen 2006: 32–34).

70 Rosen 2006: 29. See also Farmer (2017: 16, 42–43, and *passim*) for the phenomenon in fifth- and fourth-century fragmentary comic poets.

71 Although Aristophanes exaggerates Euripides' deployment of properties and the extent of their symbolism, Euripides does show a fondness for 'putting ordinary objects to ordinary use' in his tragedy (Revermann 2013: 84).

72 Revermann 2013: 82.

73 Taplin (1986: 172) is a standard treatment of this minimalism.

74 As a source of visual meaning, the mask (here the index of female complexion) can function like a prop (see Tordoff 2013).

75 Poe 2000: 285. Vertruský (1964) explains that the 'action force' of a prop attracts a certain action to it. The absence of plausible intentionality in comic props distinguishes them from tragic ones (Poe 2000: 285–286).

76 Poe 2000.

77 On plausible intentionality, see Poe 2000: 285–286. This is not to say that accumulated props cannot express a larger point in their plots: in *Acharnians* (1097–1133) and *Peace* (255–282), they distinguish life in war and life in peace; in *Thesmophoriazusae*, they underscore women's exploitation of the many responsibilities of οἰκονομία.

78 Taplin 1977; 1978: 31.

79 For this perception of the generic contest, see Silk 2000: 327; Cowan 2008.

80 Cowan 2008: 316.

81 See esp. Bowie 1993: 224; Cowan 2008; cf. Foley 2008.

82 Parker 1986: 82–83.

Conclusion

1   Perhaps a more nuanced attempt to define the influence of Euripides on
    Aristophanes is Ar. fr. 488, in which an unidentified speaker (perhaps Aristophanes)
    acknowledges adopting a version of a second poet's style – seemingly Euripides – but
    with less demotic (ἀγοραίους) content.

Bibliography

Allan, W. (2000), *The Andromache and Euripidean Tragedy*, Oxford: Oxford University Press.

Allan, W. (2008), *Euripides: Helen*, Cambridge: Cambridge University Press.

Aloni, A. and A. Iannucci (2007), *L'elegia greca e l'epigramma dalle origini al V secolo. Con un' appendice sulla 'nuova' elegia di Archiloco*, Florence: Le Monnier Università.

Anderson, M.J. (1997), *The Fall of Troy in Early Greek Poetry and Art*, Oxford: Oxford University Press.

Arnott, W.G. (2007), *Birds in the Ancient World from A To Z*, London: Routledge.

Auger, D. (1979), 'Le Théâtre d'Aristophane: Le Mythe, L' Utopie et Les Femmes', in J. Bonnamour (ed.), *Aristophane, Les Femmes et La Cité*, 71–97, Fontenay aux Roses: E.N.S.

Austin, C. (1975), 'Aristophane, *Thesmophories*, vers 500', in J. Bingen, G. Cambier and G. Nachtergael (eds), *Le Monde Grec. Pensée, Littérature, Histoire, Documents. Hommages à Claire Préaux*, 186–187, Brussels: University of Brussels Press.

Austin, C. and S.D. Olson (2004), *Aristophanes: Thesmophoriazusae*, Oxford: Oxford University Press.

Bagordo, A. (2003), *Reminiszenzen früher Lyrik bei den attischen Tragikern: Beiträge zur Anspielungstechnik und poetischer Tradition*, Munich: C.H. Beck.

Bakola, E. (2005), 'Old Comedy Disguised as Satyr Play: A New Reading of Cratinus' *Dionysalexandros* (*POxy* 663)', *ZPE*, 154: 46–58.

Bakola, E. (2010), *Cratinus and the Art of Comedy*, Oxford: Oxford University Press.

Barker, A. (1984), *Greek Musical Writings. Volume I: The Musician and His Art*, Cambridge: Cambridge University Press.

Barker, A. (2004), 'Transforming the Nightingale: Aspects of Athenian Musical Discourse in the Late-Fifth Century', in P. Murray and P. Wilson (eds), *Music and the Muses. The Culture of Mousike in the Classical Athenian City*, 185–204, Oxford: Oxford University Press.

Barlow, S. (1986), 'The Language of Euripides' Monodies', in J.H. Betts, J.H. Hooker and J.R. Green (eds), *Studies in Honour of T.B.L. Webster, vol. I*, 10–22, London: Bristol Classical Press.

Barlow, S. (2008), *The Imagery of Euripides*, 3rd edn, London: Bristol Classical Press.

Barner, W. (1971), 'Die Monodie', in W. Jens (ed.), *Die Bauformen der Tragödie*, 277–320, Munich: Fink.

Barrett, W.S. (1964), *Euripides. Hippolytus*, Oxford: Oxford University Press.

Barton, I.M. (1972), 'Tranio's Laconian Key', *G&R*, 19 (1): 25–31.

Beavis, I.C. (1988), *Insects and Other Invertebrates in Classical Antiquity*, Exeter: University of Exeter Press.

Beazley, J.D. (1952), 'The New York "Phlyax Vase"', *AJA*, 56 (4): 193–195.

Bedbury, S. (2002), *A New Brand World: Eight Principles for Achieving Brand Leadership in the 21st Century*, New York: Viking.

Bell, C. (2009), *Ritual: Perspectives and Dimensions*, New York: Oxford University Press.

Bennett, S. (1997), *Theatre Audiences: A Theory of Production and Reception*, New York: Routledge.

Bérard, C. (1974), *Anodoi: Essai sur l'Imagerie des Passages Chthoniens*, Rome: Imprimerie Paul Attinger SA.

Bergson, H. (1911), *Laughter: An Essay on the Meaning of the Comic*, London: Macmillan.

Beverly, J. (1997), *The Dramatic Function of Actors' Monody in Later Euripides*, DPhil thesis, Oxford University.

Bevis, M. (2013), *Comedy: A Very Short Introduction*, Oxford: Oxford University Press.

Bieber, M. (1961), *The History of the Greek and Roman Theater*, Princeton, NJ: Princeton University Press.

Bierl, A. (2009), *Ritual and Performativity: The Chorus of Old Comedy*, Washington, DC: Center for Hellenic Studies.

Biles, Z.P. (2002), 'Intertextual Biography in the Rivalry of Cratinus and Aristophanes', *AJP*, 123 (2): 169–204.

Biles, Z.P. (2011), *Aristophanes and the Poetics of Competition*, Cambridge: Cambridge University Press.

Biles, Z.P. and S.D. Olson (2015), *Aristophanes. Wasps*, Oxford: Oxford University Press.

Biles, Z.P. and J. Thorn (2014), 'Rethinking Choregic Iconography in Apulia', in E. Csapo, H.R. Goette, J.R. Green and P. Wilson (eds), *Greek Theatre in the Fourth Century B.C.*, 295–318, Berlin: De Gruyter.

Bobrick, E. (1997), 'The Tyranny of Roles', in G.W. Dobrov (ed.), *The City as Comedy*, 177–197, Chapel Hill, NC: University of North Carolina Press.

Borthwick, E.K. (1968), 'Notes on the Plutarch *De Musica* and the *Cheiron* of Pherecrates', *Hermes* 96 (1): 60–73.

Borthwick, E.K. (1994), 'New Interpretations of Aristophanes' *Frogs* 1249–1328', *Phoenix* 48 (1): 21–41

Bosher, K., ed. (2012), *Theatre Outside Athens*, Cambridge: Cambridge University Press.

Bothe, F.H. (1829), *Aristophanis Thesmophoriazusae*, Leipzig: Hahn.

Bowie, A.M. (1993), *Aristophanes: Myth, Ritual, and Comedy*, Cambridge: Cambridge University Press.

Bowie, A.M. (2000), 'Myth and Ritual in the Rivals of Aristophanes', in D. Harvey and J. Wilkins (eds), *The Rivals of Aristophanes: Studies in Athenian Old Comedy*, 317–339, London: Duckworth and the Classical Press of Wales.

Bowie, E.L. (1986), 'Early Greek Elegy, Symposium, and Public Festival', *JHS*, 106: 13–35.

Bowie, E.L. (2002), 'Ionian Iambos and Attic *Komoidia*: Father and Daughter, or Just Cousins', in A. Willi (ed.), *The Language of Greek Comedy*, 33–50, Oxford: Oxford University Press.

Breitenbach, W. (1934), *Untersuchungen zur Sprache der euripideischen Lyrik*, Stuttgart: Kohlhammer.

Bremer, J. (1981), 'Greek Hymns', in H. Versnel (ed.), *Faith, Hope and Worship: Aspects of Religious Mentality in the Ancient World*, 193–215, Leiden: Brill.

Burgess, J.S. (2001), *The Tradition of the Trojan War in Homer and the Epic Cycle*, Baltimore, MD: Johns Hopkins University Press.

Burian, P. (1997), 'Myth into Muthos: The Shaping of Tragic Plot', in P.E. Easterling (ed.), *The Cambridge Companion to Greek Tragedy*, 178–210, Cambridge: Cambridge University Press.

Burkert, W. (1965), 'Demaratos, Astrabakos und Herakles: Königsmythos und Politik zur Zeit der Perserkriege (Herodot 6, 67–69)', *RhM*, 22 (3): 168–177.

Burkert, W. (1966), 'Greek Tragedy and Sacrificial Ritual', *GRBS*, 7 (2): 87–121.

Burkert, W. (1983), *Homo Necans: The Anthropology of Greek Sacrificial Ritual and Myth*, trans. P. Bing, Berkeley, CA: University of California Press.

Cairns, D.L. (1993), *Aidôs: The Psychology and Ethics of Honour and Shame in Ancient Greek Literature*, Oxford: Oxford University Press.

Calame, C. (2001), *Choruses of Young Women in Ancient Greece: Their Morphology, Religious Role, and Social Functions*, 2nd edn, Lanham, MD: Rowman and Littlefield.

Calame, C. (2004), 'Choral Forms in Aristophanic Comedy', in P. Murray and P. Wilson (eds), *Music and the Muses: The Culture of Mousike in the Classical Athenian City*, 157–184, Oxford: Oxford University Press.

Canfora, L. (2001), *I Deipnosofisti. I Dotti a Banchetto*, Roma: Salerno.

Carey, C. (2013), 'Comedy and the Civic Chorus', in E. Bakola, L. Prauscello and M. Telò (eds), *Greek Comedy and the Discourse of Genres*, 155–174, Cambridge: Cambridge University Press.

Casari, J. (2002), 'La Lutte pour La Paix dans Le Théâtre d' Aristophane', in S. Rochefort-Guillouet (ed.), *Analyses et Réflexions sur Aristophane, La Paix*, 36–45, Paris: Ellipses.

Casolari, F. (2003), *Die Mythentravestie in der griechischen Komödie*, Münster: Aschendorff.

Cassio, A.C. (1985), *Commedia e partecipazione: La Pace di Aristofane*, Napoli: Liguori.

Chronopoulos, S. (2017), *Spott im Drama: Dramatische Funktionen der persönlichen Verspottung in Aristophanes' 'Wespen' und 'Frieden'*, Heidelberg: Verlag Antike.

Collard, C. (1995a), 'Bellerophon', in C. Collard, M. Cropp and K.H. Lee (eds), *Euripides: Selected Fragmentary Plays*, Vol. 1, 98–120, Warminster: Aris and Phillips.

Collard, C. (1995b), 'Stheneboea', in C. Collard, M. Cropp and K.H. Lee (eds), *Euripides: Selected Fragmentary Plays*, Vol. 1, 79–97, Warminster: Aris and Phillips.

Collard, C. and M. Cropp (2008), *Euripides: Fragments: Oedipus-Chrysippus*, Cambridge, MA: Harvard University Press.

Collins, D.B. (1998), *Immortal Armor: The Concept of Alkê in Archaic Greek Poetry*, Lanham, MD: Rowman and Littlefield.

Compton-Engle, G. (2003), 'Control of Costume in Three Plays of Aristophanes', *AJP*, 124 (4): 507–535.

Compton-Engle, G. (2015), *Costume in Aristophanes*, Cambridge: Cambridge University Press.

Connelly, J.B. (1993), 'Narrative and Image in Attic Vase Painting: Ajax and Kassandra at the Trojan Palladion', in P.J. Holliday (ed.), *Narrative and Event in Ancient Art*, 88–129, Cambridge: Cambridge University Press.

Connor, W.R. (1985), 'The Razing of the House in Greek Society', *TAPA* 115: 79–102.

Conrad, G. (1997), *Der Silen: Wandlungen einer Gestalt des griechischen Satyrspiels*, Trier: WVT.

Conte, G.-B. (1992), 'Empirical and Theoretical Approaches to Literary Genre', in K. Galinsky (ed.), *The Interpretation of Roman Poetry: Empiricism or Hermeneutics?*, 104–123, Frankfurt am Main: Lang.

Cowan, R. (2008), 'Nothing to Do with Phaedra? Aristophanes, "Thesmophoriazusae", 497–501', *CQ*, 58 (1): 315–320.

Craik, E.M. (1990), 'Sexual Imagery and Innuendo in *Troades*', in A. Powell (ed.), *Euripides, Women, and Sexuality*, 1–15, London: Routledge.

Croiset, M. (1904), 'Le Dionysalexandros de Cratinos', *Revue des Études Grecques*, 17 (76/77): 297–310.

Cropp, M. (1995a), 'Crespontes', in C. Collard, M. Cropp and K.H. Lee (eds), *Euripides: Selected Fragmentary Plays*, Vol. 1, 121–147, Warminster: Aris and Phillips.

Cropp, M. (1995b), '*Melannipê Desmôtis*', in C. Collard, M. Cropp and K.H. Lee (eds), *Euripides: Selected Fragmentary Plays*, Vol. 1, 240–280, Warminster: Aris and Phillips.

Cropp, M. (1995c), 'Telephus', in C. Collard, M. Cropp and K.H. Lee (eds), *Euripides: Selected Fragmentary Plays*, Vol. 1, 17–52, Warminster: Aris and Phillips.

Cropp, M. (2000), *Euripides: Iphigenia in Tauris*, Warminster: Aris and Phillips.

Csapo, E. (1986), 'A Note on the Würzburg Bell-Crater H5697 ("Telephus Travestitus")', *Phoenix*, 40 (4): 379–392.

Csapo, E. (1993a), 'Deep Ambivalence: Notes on a Greek Cockfight (Parts I)', *Phoenix*, 47 (1): 1–28.

Csapo, E. (1993b), 'Deep Ambivalence: Notes on a Greek Cockfight (Parts II–IV)', *Phoenix*, 47 (2): 115–124.

Csapo, E. (1999–2000), 'Later Euripidean Music', *ICS*, 24/25: 399–426.

Csapo, E. (2003), 'The Dolphins of Dionysus', in E. Csapo and M.C. Miller (eds), *Poetry, Theory and Praxis: The Social Life of Myth, Word and Image*, 69–98, Oxford: Oxbow.

Csapo, E. (2004), 'The Politics of the New Music', in P. Murray and P. Wilson (eds), *Music and the Muses: The Culture of Mousike in the Classical Athenian City*, 207–248, Oxford: Oxford University Press.

Csapo, E. (2010), *Actors and Icons of the Ancient Theater*, Oxford: Wiley-Blackwell.

Csapo, E. and M.C. Miller, eds (2007), *The Origins of Theater in Ancient Greece and Beyond: From Ritual to Drama*, Cambridge: Cambridge University Press.

Csapo, E. and W.J. Slater (1995), *The Context of Ancient Drama*, Ann Arbor, MI: University of Michigan Press.

Csapo, E. and P. Wilson (2009), 'Timotheus the New Musician', in F. Budelmann (ed.), *The Cambridge Companion to Greek Lyric*, 277–293, Cambridge: Cambridge University Press.

Csapo, E., H.R. Goette, J.R. Green and P. Wilson (eds) (2014), *Greek Theatre in the Fourth Century B.C.*, Berlin: De Gruyter.

Currie, B. (2015), 'Cypria', in M. Fantuzzi, D. Konstan and C. Tsagalis (eds), *The Greek Epic Cycle and Its Reception: A Companion*, 281–305, Cambridge: Cambridge University Press.

D'Angour, A. (2006), 'Intimations of the Classical in Early Greek *Mousikê*', in J.I. Porter (ed.), *Classical Pasts: The Classical Traditions of Greece and Rome*, 89–105, Princeton, NJ: Princeton University Press.

D'Angour, A. (2011), *The Greeks and the New: Novelty in Greek Imagination and Experience*, Cambridge: Cambridge University Press.

Davidson, J. (2000), '*Gnesippus Paigniagraphos*: The Comic Poets and the Erotic Mime', in D. Harvey and J. Wilkins (eds), *The Rivals of Aristophanes: Studies in Athenian Old Comedy*, 41–64, London: Duckworth and the Classical Press of Wales.

Davies, M. and J. Kathirithamby (1986), *Greek Insects*, London: Duckworth.

Dawkins, R. (2006), *The Selfish Gene*, 3rd edn, Oxford: Oxford University Press.

De Jong, I.J.F. (2014), *Narratology and Classics. A Practical Guide*, Oxford: Oxford University Press.

Dearden, C.W. (1976), *The Stage of Aristophanes*, London: Atholone Press.

Denoyelle, M. and F. Silvestrelli (2013), 'From Tarporley to Dolon: The Reattribution of the Early South Italian "New York Goose Vase"', *Metropolitan Museum Journal*, 48 (1): 59–71.

Denyer, N. (2013), 'The Political Skill of Protagoras', in V. Harte and M. Lane (eds), *Politeia in Greek and Roman Philosophy*, 155–167, Cambridge: Cambridge University Press.

de Ste Croix, G.E.M. (1972), *The Origins of the Peloponnesian War*, Ithaca, NY: Cornell University Press.

Deubner, L. (1966), *Attische Feste*, Berlin: Akademie-Verlag.

Diels, H. (1914), *Antike Technik*, Leipzig: Teubner.

Dillon, M (1997), *Pilgrims and Pilgrimage in Ancient Greece*, London: Routledge.

Dixon, D.W. (2014), 'Reconsidering Euripides' *Bellerophon*', *CQ*, 64 (2): 493–506.

Dobrov, G.W. (2001), *Figures of Play: Greek Drama and Metafictional Poetics*, Oxford: Oxford University Press.

Dobrov, G.W. (2007), 'Comedy and the Satyr Chorus', *CW*, 100 (3): 251–265.

Dover, K.J. (1963), 'Notes on Aristophanes' *Acharnians*', *Métis*, 15: 6–25.

Dover, K.J. (1968), *Aristophanes: Clouds*, Oxford: Oxford University Press.

Dover, K.J. (1972), *Aristophanic Comedy*, London: Batsford.

Dover, K.J. (1974), *Greek Popular Morality in the Time of Plato and Aristotle*, Oxford: Blackwell.

Dover, K.J. (1989), *Greek Homosexuality*, 2nd edn, Cambridge, MA: Harvard University Press.

Dover, K.J. (1993), *Aristophanes: Frogs*, Oxford: Oxford University Press.

Dunbar, N. (1995), *Aristophanes: Birds*, Oxford: Oxford University Press.

Duncan, A. (2006), *Performance and Identity in the Classical World*, Cambridge: Cambridge University Press.

Dunn, F.M. (1996), *Tragedy's End: Closure and Innovation in Euripidean Drama*, Oxford: Oxford University Press.

Düring, I. (1945), 'Studies in Musical Terminology in Fifth-Century Literature', *Eranos*, 43: 176–197.

Easterling, P.E. (1997), 'Constructing the Heroic', in C. Pelling (ed.), *Greek Tragedy and the Historian*, 21–37, Oxford: Oxford University Press.

Easterling, P.E. and Hall, E. (eds.) (2002), *Greek and Roman Actors: Aspects of an Ancient Profession*, Cambridge: Cambridge University Press.

Edmunds, J.M. (1957), *The Fragments of Attic Comedy*, Vol. 1, Leiden: Brill.

Ehrenberg, V. (1947), 'Polypragmosyne: A Study in Greek Politics', *JHS*, 67: 46–67.

Elam, K. (2002), *The Semiotics of Theatre and Drama*, 2nd edn, London: Routledge.

Fantuzzi, M. and D. Konstan (2013), 'From Achilles' Horses to the Cheese-Seller's Shop: On the History of the Guessing Game in Greek Drama', in E. Bakola, L. Prauscello and M. Telò (eds), *Greek Comedy and the Discourse of Genres*, 256–274, Cambridge: Cambridge University Press.

Faraone, C.A. (2011), 'Curses, Crime Detection, and Conflict Resolution at the Festival of Demeter Thesmophoros', *JHS*, 131: 35–44.

Farmer, M.C. (2017) *Tragedy on the Comic Stage*, New York: Oxford University Press.

Ferguson, N., ed. (1999), *Virtual History: Alternatives and Counterfactuals*, New York: Basic Books.

Fish, S. (1980), *Is There a Text in This Class? The Authority of Interpretive Communities*, Cambridge, MA: Harvard University Press.

Fitzpatrick, D.G. and A.H. Sommerstein (2006), 'Tereus', in A.H. Sommerstein, D. Fitzpatrick and T. Talboy (eds), *Sophocles. Selected Fragmentary Plays*, vol. 1, 141–195, Oxford: Aris and Phillips.

Flory, S.F. (1988), 'Thucydides' Hypotheses about the Peloponnesian War', *TAPA*, 118: 43–56.

Folch, M. (2015), *The City and the Stage. Performance, Genre, and Gender in Plato's Laws*, New York: Oxford University Press.

Foley, H.P. (1985), *Ritual Irony: Poetry and Sacrifice in Euripides*, Ithaca, NY: Cornell University Press.

Foley, H.P. (1988), 'Tragedy and Politics in Aristophanes' *Acharnians*', *JHS*, 108: 33–47.

Foley, H.P. (2000), 'The Comic Body in Greek Art and Drama', in B. Cohen (ed.), *Not the Classical Ideal: Athens and the Construction of the Other in Greek Art*, 275–312, Leiden: Brill.

Foley, H.P. (2008), 'Generic Boundaries in Late Fifth-Century Athens', in M. Revermann and P. Wilson (eds), *Performance, Iconography, Reception: Studies in Honour of Oliver Taplin*, 15–36, Oxford: Oxford University Press.

Forrest, W.G. (1963), 'Aristophanes' *Acharnians*', *Phoenix*, 17 (1): 1–12.

Forsdyke, S. (2005), *Exile, Ostracism, and Democracy: The Politics of Expulsion in Ancient Greece*, Princeton, NJ: Princeton University Press.

Fowler, A. (1982), *Kinds of Literature: An Introduction to the Theory of Genres and Modes*, Cambridge, MA: Harvard University Press.

Friedländer, P. (1907), *Herakles: Sagengeschichtliche Untersuchungen*, Berlin: Weidmannsche Buchhandlung.

Frow, J. (2006), *Genre*, London: Routledge.

Furley, D. and J. Bremer (2001), *Greek Hymns: Band I: A Selection of Greek Religious Poetry from the Archaic to the Hellenistic Period*, Tübingen: Mohr Siebeck.

Gadamer, H.-G. (2013), *Truth and Method*, revised 2nd edn, London: Bloomsbury Academic.

Gamel, M.K. (2002), 'From Thesmophoriazusae to the Julie Thesmo Show: Adaptation, Performance, Reception', *AJP*, 123 (3): 465–499.

Gantz, T. (1993), *Early Greek Myth*, Baltimore, MD: John Hopkins University Press.

Garner, R. (1990), *From Homer to Tragedy: The Art of Allusion in Greek Poetry*, London: Routledge.

Gennette, G. (1997), *Palimpsests: Literature in the Second Degree*, trans. C. Newman and C. Doubinsky, Lincoln/London: University of Nebraska Press.

Gernet, L. (1981), *The Anthropology of Ancient Greece*, Baltimore, MD: Johns Hopkins University Press.

Gibert, J. (1999–2000), 'Falling in Love with Euripides (Andromeda)', *ICS*, 24/25: 75–91.

Gibert, J. (2004), 'Andromeda', in C. Collard, M. Cropp and J. Gilbert (eds), *Euripides: Selected Fragmentary Plays*, vol. 2, 133–155, Oxford: Aris and Phillips.

Gigante, M. (1971), *Rintone e il teatro in Magna Grecia*, Napoli: Guida.

Gilula, D. (1995), 'The Choregoi Vase: Comic Yes, but Angels?', *ZPE*, 109: 5–10.

Giuliani, L. (1996), 'Rhesus between Dream and Death: On the Relation of Image to Literature in Apulian Vase-Painting', *BICS*, 41: 71–86.

Goldhill, S. (1991), *The Poet's Voice: Essays on Poetics and Greek Literature*, Cambridge: Cambridge University Press.

Gomme, A.W. (1938), 'Aristophanes and Politics', *CR* 52 (3): 97–109.

Gould, J. (1996), 'Tragedy and Collective Experience', in M. Silk (ed.), *Tragedy and the Tragic*, 217–256, Oxford: Oxford University Press.

Graham, A.J. (1964), *Colony and Mother City in Ancient Greece*, Manchester: Manchester University Press.

Graham, A.J. (1978), 'The Foundation of Thasos', *BSA*, 73: 61–98.

Green, J.R. (1991), 'On Seeing and Depicting the Theatre in Classical Athens', *GRBS*, 32 (1): 15–50.

Green, J.R. (1994), *Theatre in Ancient Greek Society*, London: Routledge.

Green, J.R. (2000), 'Tragedy and the Spectacle of the Mind: Messenger Speeches, Actors, Narrative, and Audience Imagination in Fourth-Century BCE Vase-Painting', in B. Bergmann and C. Kondoleon (eds), *The Art of Ancient Spectacle*, 36–63, New Haven, CT: Yale University Press.

Green, J.R. (2014), 'Two Phaedras: Euripides and Aristophanes?', in S.D. Olson (ed.), *Ancient Comedy and Reception: Essays in Honor of Jeffrey Henderson*, 94–131, Berlin: De Gruyter.

Green, J.R. (2015), 'Pictures of Pictures of Comedy: Campanian Santia, Athenian Amphitryon, and Plautine *Amphitruo*', in J.R. Green and M. Edwards (eds), *Images and Texts: Papers in Honour of Professor Eric Handley*, 45–80, London: Institute of Classical Studies.

Grenfell, B.P. and Hunt, A.S. (1904), 'Argument of Cratinus' ΔΙΟΝΥΣΑΛΕΞΑΝΔΡΟΣ, no. 663', *The Oxyrhynchus Papyri*, 4: 69–72.

Grethlein, J. (2010), *The Greeks and Their Past: Poetry, Oratory, and History in the Fifth Century BCE*, Cambridge: Cambridge University Press.

Griffith, M. (2002), 'Slaves of Dionysus: Satyrs, Audience, and the Ends of the *Oresteia*', *Clas. Ant.*, 21 (2): 195–258.

Griffith, M. (2005), 'Satyrs, Citizens, and Self-Presentation', in G. Harrison (ed.), *Satyr Drama: Tragedy at Play*, 161–199, Swansea: Classical Press of Wales.

Griffith, M. (2006a), 'Horsepower and Donkeywork: Equids and the Ancient Greek Imagination Part 1', *CPhil*, 101 (3): 185–246.

Griffith, M. (2006b), 'Horsepower and Donkeywork: Equids and the Ancient Greek Imagination Part 2', *CPhil*, 101 (4): 307–358.

Griffith, M. (2008), 'Greek Middlebrow Drama (Something to Do with Aphrodite?)', in M. Revermann and P. Wilson (eds), *Performance, Iconography, Reception: Studies in Honour of Oliver Taplin*, 59–87, Oxford: Oxford University Press.

Griffith, M. (2010), 'Satyr Play and Tragedy, Face to Face', in O. Taplin and R. Wyles (eds), *The Pronomos Vase and its Context*, 47–63, Oxford: Oxford University Press.

Griffith, M. (2011), 'Extended Families, Marriage, and Inter-City Relations in (later) Athenian Tragedy: Dynasts II', in D.M. Carter (ed.), *Why Athens? A Reappraisal of Tragic Politics*, 175–208, Oxford: Oxford University Press.

Griffith, M. (2013), *Aristophanes' Frogs*, Oxford: Oxford University Press.

Guggisberg, P. (1947), *Das Satyrspiel*, Zurich: Leemann.

Hall, E. (1989), *Inventing the Barbarian: Greek Self-Definition through Tragedy*, Oxford: Oxford University Press.

Hall, E. (1997), 'The Sociology of Athenian Tragedy', in P.E. Easterling (ed.), *The Cambridge Companion to Greek Tragedy*, 93–126, Cambridge: Cambridge University Press.

Hall, E. (2006), *The Theatrical Cast of Athens*, Oxford: Oxford University Press.

Hall, J.M. (2002), *Hellenicity: Between Ethnicity and Culture*, Chicago, IL: University of Chicago Press.

Halliwell, S. (1984), 'Aristophanic Satire', *YES*, 14: 6–20.

Halliwell, S. (1993), 'Comedy and Publicity in the Society of the Polis', in A.H. Sommerstein, S. Halliwell, J. Henderson and B. Zimmermann (eds), *Tragedy, Comedy, and the Polis: Papers from the Greek Drama Conference, Nottingham, 18–20 July 1990*, 321–340, Bari: Levante Editori.

Halliwell, S. (1995), *Aristotle: Poetics*, Cambridge, MA: Harvard University Press.

Halliwell, S. (1998), *Aristotle's Poetics*, 2nd edn, Chicago, IL: Chicago University Press.

Handley, E.W. and J. Rea (1957), *The Telephus of Euripides*, London: University of London, Institute of Classical Studies.

Hansen, H. (1976), 'Aristophanes' *Thesmophoriazusae*: Theme, Structure, and Production', *Philol.*, 120 (1): 165–186.

Harder, A. (1985), *Euripides' Kresphontes and Archelaos: Introduction, Text and Commentary*, Leiden: Brill.

Hardwick, L. (2013), 'The Problem of the Spectators: Ancient and Modern', in A. Bakogianni (ed.), *Dialogues with the Past: Classical Reception Theory and Practice*, 11–26, London: University of London.

Harrison, A.R.W. (1968), *The Law of Athens*, vol. 1, 2nd edn, London: Bristol Classical Press.

Hartog, F. (1988), *The Mirror of Herodotus: The Representation of the Other in the Writing of History*, trans. J. Lloyd, Berkeley, CA: University of California Press.

Harvey, F.D. (1971), 'Sick Humour: Aristophanic Parody of a Euripidean Motif?', *Mnemosyne*, 24 (1): 62–65.

Heath, M. (1987), *Political Comedy in Aristophanes*, Göttingen: Vandenhoeck & Ruprecht.

Heath, M. (1990), 'Aristophanes and His Rivals', *G&R*, 37 (2): 143–158.

Hedreen, G. (2001), *Capturing Troy: Narrative Functions of Landscape in Archaic and Early Classical Greek Art*, Ann Arbor, MI: University of Michigan Press.

Henderson, J. (1987), 'Older Women in Attic Old Comedy', *TAPA*, 117: 105–129.

Henderson, J. (1990), 'The Demos and Comic Competition', in J. Winkler and F. Zeitlin (eds), *Nothing to Do with Dionysos? Athenian Drama in its Social Context*, 271–313, Princeton, NJ: Princeton University Press.

Henderson, J. (1991), *The Maculate Muse: Obscene Language in Attic Comedy*, 2nd edn, New York: Oxford University Press.

Henderson, J. (1998), *Aristophanes: Clouds, Wasps, Peace*, Cambridge, MA: Harvard University Press.

Henderson, J. (2002), *Aristophanes: Frogs, Assemblywomen, Wealth*, Cambridge, MA: Harvard University Press.

Henderson, J. (2007), *Aristophanes: Fragments*, Cambridge, MA: Harvard University Press.

Henderson, J. (2007), 'Drama and Democracy', in L.J. Samons (ed.), *The Cambridge Companion to the Age of Pericles*, 179–195, Cambridge: Cambridge University Press.

Herington, J. (1963), 'A Study in the "Prometheia", Part II: "Birds" and "Prometheia"', *Phoenix*, 17 (4): 236–243.

Herington, J. (1985), *Poetry into Drama: Early Tragedy and the Greek Poetic Tradition*, Berkeley, CA: University of California Press.

Hinds, S. (1998), *Allusion and Intertext: Dynamics of Appropriation in Roman Poetry*, Cambridge: Cambridge University Press.

Holley, N.M. (1949), 'The Floating Chest', *JHS*, 69: 39–47.

Hordern, J.H. (2003), 'Gnesippos and the Rivals of Aristophanes', *CQ*, 53 (2): 608–613.

Hordern, J.H. (2004), *Sophron's Mimes: Text, Translation, and Commentary*, Oxford: Oxford University Press.

Horn, W. (1970), *Gebet und Gebetsparodie in den Komödien des Aristophanes*, Nürnberg: Hans Karl.

Hornblower, S. (1996), *A Commentary on Thucydides. Volume I: Books I–III*, Oxford: Oxford University Press.

Hornblower, S. (2011), *Thucydidean Themes*, Oxford: Oxford University Press.

Hose, M. (1990), *Studien zum Chor bei Euripides*, vol. 1, Stuttgart: Teubner.

Hourmouziades, N. (1965), *Production and Imagination in Euripides*, Athens: Greek Society for Humanistic Studies.

Hubbard, T.K. (1991), *The Mask of Comedy: Aristophanes and the Intertextual Parabasis*, Ithaca, NY: Cornell University Press.

Hubbard, T.K., ed. (2000a), *Greek Love Reconsidered*, New York: W. Hamilton Press.

Hubbard, T.K. (2000b), 'Pederasty and Democracy: The Marginalization of a Social Practice', in T.K. Hubbard (ed.), *Greek Love Reconsidered*, 1–11, New York: W. Hamilton Press.

Hubbard, T.K. (2003), *Homosexuality in Greece and Rome: A Sourcebook of Basic Documents*, Berkeley, CA: University of California Press.

Hubbard, T.K. (2006), 'History's First Child Molester: Euripides' *Chrysippus* and the Marginalization of Pederasty in Athenian Democratic Discourse', in J. Davidson, F. Muecke, P. Wilson and K.H. Lee (eds), *Greek Drama III: Essays in Honor of Kevin Lee*, 141–162, London: University of London, Institute of Classical Studies.

Hubbard, T.K. (2015), 'Diachronic Parameters of Athenian Pederasty', in J. González (ed.), *Diachrony: Diachronic Studies of Ancient Greek Literature and Culture*, 363–389, Berlin: De Gruyter.

Hughes, A. (2012), *Performing Greek Comedy*, Cambridge: Cambridge University Press.

Hunter, R.L. (2002), 'Acting Down: The Ideology of Hellenistic Performance', in P.E. Easterling and E. Hall (eds), *Greek and Roman Actors: Aspects of an Ancient Profession*, 189–206, Cambridge: Cambridge University Press.

Hunter, R.L. (2009), *Critical Moments in Classical Literature: Studies in the Ancient View of Literature and Its Uses*, Cambridge: Cambridge University Press.

Hutcheon, L. (1985), *A Theory of Parody: The Teachings of Twentieth-Century Art Forms*, New York: Methuen.

Hutcheon, L. (2006), *A Theory of Adaptation*, New York: Routledge.

Iser, W. (1978), *The Act of Reading: A Theory of Aesthetic Response*, Baltimore, MD: John Hopkins University Press. Translation of *Der Akt des Lesens: Theorie Ästhetischer Wirkung* (1976).

Janko, R. (1981), 'The Structure of the Homeric Hymns: A Study in Genre', *Hermes*, 109: 9–24.

Jauss, H.J. (1982), *Toward an Aesthetic of Reception*, Minneapolis, MN: University of Minnesota Press.

Johnstone, S. (1994), 'Virtuous Toil, Vicious Work: Xenophon on Aristocratic Style', *CPhil*, 89 (3): 219–240.

Kaimio, M. (1988), *Physical Contact in Greek Tragedy*, Helsinki: Academia Scientiarum Fennica.

Kaimio, M. (2002), 'Erotic Experience in the Conjugal Bed: Good Wives in Greek Tragedy', in M.C. Nussbaum and J. Sihvola (eds), *The Sleep of Reason: Erotic Experience and Sexual Ethics in Ancient Greece and Rome*, 95–119, Chicago, IL: University of Chicago Press.

Kannicht, R. (2004), *Tragicorum Graecorum Fragmenta, Vol. 5: Euripides*, Göttingen: Vandenhoeck & Ruprecht.

Karanika, A. (2014), *Voices at Work: Women, Performance, and Labor in Ancient Athens*, Baltimore, MD: Johns Hopkins University Press.

Kidd, S. (2014), *Nonsense and Meaning in Ancient Greek Comedy*, Cambridge: Cambridge University Press.

King, H. (1998), *Hippocrates' Women*, London: Routledge.

Kleinknecht, H. (1937), *Die Gebetsparodie in der Antike*, Stuttgart: Kohlhammer.

Konstantakos, I.M. (2014), 'Comedy in the Fourth Century I: Mythological Burlesque', in M. Fontaine and A.C. Scafuro (eds), *The Oxford Handbook of Greek and Roman Comedy*, 160–180, Oxford: Oxford University Press.

Körte, A. (1893), 'Archäologische Studien zur alten Komödie', *Jahrbuch des Deutschen Archäologischen Instituts*, 8: 61–93.

Körte, A. (1904), 'Die Hypothesis zu Kratinos' Dionysalexandros', *Hermes*, 39 (4): 481–498.

Kossatz-Deissmann, A. (1980), 'Telephus Travestitus', in H.A. Cahn and E. Simon (eds), *Tainia: Festschrift Roland Hampe*, 281–290, Mainz am Rhein: Von Zabern.

Kowalzig, B. (2007), *Singing for the Gods: Performances of Myth and Ritual in Archaic and Classical Greece*, Oxford: Oxford University Press.

Krumeich, R. (1999), 'Einleitung', in R. Krumeich, N. Pechstein and B. Seidensticker (eds), *Das griechische Satyrspiel*, 1–73, Darmstadt: WBG.

Kugelmeier, C. (1996), *Reflexe Früher und Zeitgenössischer Lyrik in der Alten Attischen Komödie*, Stuttgart and Leipzig: Teubner.

Lämmle, R. (2013), *Poetik des Satyrspiels*, Heidelberg: Universitätsverlag Winter.

Lavecchia, S. (2000), *Pindari Dithyramborum Fragmenta*, Roma: Edizioni dell' Ateneo.

Lawler, L.B. (1964), *The Dance of the Ancient Greek Theatre*, Iowa City, IA: University of Iowa Press.

Lear, A. and E. Cantarella (2009), *Images of Ancient Greek Pederasty: Boys Were Their Gods*, London and New York: Routledge.

Lee, M.M. (2004), 'Evil Wealth of Raiment: Deadly πέπλοι in Greek Tragedy', *CJ*, 99 (3): 253–279

Lee, M.M. (2015), *Body, Dress, and Identity in Ancient Greece*, Cambridge: Cambridge University Press.

Lefkowitz (2012), *The Lives of the Greek Poets*, 2nd edn, Baltimore, MD: Johns Hopkins University Press.

LeVen, P. (2014), *The Many-Headed Muse: Tradition and Innovation in Late Classical Lyric Poetry*, Cambridge: Cambridge University Press.

Lilja, S. (1976), *Dogs in Ancient Greek Poetry*, Helsinki: Societas Scientiarum Fennica.

Lissarrague, F. (1990), 'Why Satyrs Are Good to Represent', in J. Winkler and F. Zeitlin (eds), *Nothing to Do with Dionysos? Athenian Drama in its Social Context*, 228–236, Princeton, NJ: Princeton University Press.

Lissarrague, F. (1993), 'On the Wildness of Satyrs', T.H. Carpenter and C.A. Faraone (eds) *Masks of Dionysus*, 207–220, Ithaca, NY: Cornell University Press.

Lissarrague, F. (2010), 'Visuality and Performance', in M.L. Hart (ed.), *The Art of Ancient Greek Theater*, 53–56, Los Angeles, CA: J. Paul Getty Museum.

Lowe, N. (2006), 'Aristophanic Spacecraft', in L. Kozak and J. Rich (eds), *Playing Around Aristophanes*, 48–64, Oxford: Aris & Phillips.

Luppe, W. (1966), 'Die Hypothesis zu Kratinos' Dionysalexandros', *Philol.*, 110 (1/2): 169–193.

MacDowell, D.M. (1995), *Aristophanes and Athens*, Oxford: Oxford University Press.

Mac Sweeney, N. (2013), *Foundation Myths and Politics in Ancient Ionia*, Cambridge: Cambridge University Press.

Mantziou, M. (1981), *Hymns and Hymnal Prayers in Fifth-Century Greek Tragedy with Special Reference to Euripides*, DPhil, University of London.

March, J.R. (1990), 'Euripides the Misogynist?', in A. Powell (ed.), *Euripides, Women, and Sexuality*, 32–75, London: Routledge.

Marincola, J. (2007), 'Odysseus and the Historians', *Syllecta Classica*, 18: 1–79.

Marshall, C.W. (2000), 'Alcestis and the Problem of Protosatyric Drama', *CJ*, 95 (2): 229–238.

Marshall, C.W. (2001), 'A Gander at the Goose Play', *Theatre Journal*, 53 (1): 53–72.

Martin, R. (2009), 'Read on Arrival', in I. Rutherford and R.L. Hunter (eds), *Wandering Poets in Ancient Greek Culture*, 80–104, Cambridge: Cambridge University Press.

Mastronarde, D.J. (1990), 'Actors on High: The Skene Roof, the Crane, and the Gods in Attic Drama', *Clas. Ant.*, 9 (2): 247–294.

Mastronarde, D.J. (1999–2000), 'Euripidean Tragedy and Genre: The Terminology and its Problems', *ICS*, 24/25: 23–39.

Mastronarde, D.J. (2010), *The Art of Euripides: Dramatic Technique and Social Context*, Cambridge: Cambridge University Press.

Mayer, P. (2006), 'Krieg aus Versehen? Zur Funktion und Aussage der Telephos-Geschichte im neuen Archilochos (P. Oxy. 4708, fr. 1)', *ZPE*, 157: 15–18.

Maynard Smith, J. and G.R. Price (1973), 'The Logic of Animal Conflicts', *Nature*, 246 (2 Nov. 1973): 15–18

McClure, L. (1999), *Spoken Like a Woman: Speech and Gender in Athenian Drama*, Princeton, NJ: Princeton University Press.

McGlew, J.F. (2002), *Citizens on Stage: Comedy and Political Culture in the Athenian Democracy*, Ann Arbor, MI: University of Michigan Press.

Medda, E., M.S. Mirto and M.P. Pattoni, eds (2005), *ΚΩΜΩΙΔΟΤΡΑΓΩΙΔΙΑ. Intersezioni del Tragico e del Comico nel Teatro del V secolo a.C.*, Pisa: Edizioni della Normale.

Meineke, A. (1839), *Fragmenta Comicorum Graecorum*, Berlin: Reimer.

Messerschmidt, F. (1932), 'Bühnenbild und Vasenmalerei', *Mitteilungen des Deutschen Archäologischen Instituts*, 47: 122–151.

Miller, J. and D. Muir (2005), *The Business of Brands*, Oxford: Oxford University Press.

Mitchell, A.G. (2009), *Greek Vase-Painting and the Origins of Visual Humour*, Cambridge: Cambridge University Press.

Moret, J.-M. (1975), *L'Ilioupersis dans La Céramique Italiote: Les Mythes et Leur Expression Figurée au IVe Siècle*, Vol. 1, Rome: Institut suisse de Rome.

Most, G.W., ed. (1997), *Collecting Fragments =Fragmente Sammeln*, Göttingen: Vandenhoeck & Ruprecht.

Moulton, C. (1981), *Aristophanic Poetry*, Göttingen: Vandenhoeck & Ruprecht.

Muecke, F. (1982), 'A Portrait of the Artist as a Young Woman', *CQ*, 32 (1): 41–55.

Muniz, A.M. and T.C. O'Guinn (2001), 'Brand Community', *Journal of Consumer Research* 27 (4): 412–432.

Murray, P. and P. Wilson, eds (2004), *Music and the Muses: The Culture of Mousike in the Classical Athenian City*, Oxford: Oxford University Press.

Nafissi, M. (1997), 'Atene e Metaponto: ancora sulla Melanippe Desmotis e i Neleidi', *Ostraka*, 6: 337–57.

Nesselrath, H.-G. (1995), *Die attische mittlere Komödie: Ihre Stellung in der antiken Literaturkritik und Literaturgeschichte*, Berlin: De Gruyter.

Nevett, L.C. (1999), *House and Society in the Ancient Greek World*, Cambridge: Cambridge University Press.

Newiger, H.-J. (1957), *Metapher und Allegorie: Studien zu Aristophanes*, Munich: Metzler.

Nightingale, A (2004), *Spectacles of Truth in Classical Greek Philosophy: Theoria in its Cultural Context*, Cambridge: Cambridge University Press.

Norwood, G. (1931), *Greek Comedy*, London: Methuen.

Oakley, J.H. and R.H. Sinos (1993), *The Wedding in Ancient Athens*, Madison, WI: University of Wisconsin Press.

Obbink, D. (2005), '4708: Archilochus, Elegies (more of VI 854 and XXX 2507)', *The Oxyrhynchus Papyri*, 69: 19–42.

Obbink, D. (2006), 'A New Archilochus Poem', *ZPE*, 156: 1–9.

Olins, W. (2004), *On Brands*, London: Thames and Hudson.

Olson, S.D. (1998), *Aristophanes: Peace*, Oxford: Oxford University Press.

Olson, S.D. (2002), *Aristophanes: Acharnians*, Oxford: Oxford University Press.

Olson, S.D. (2007), *Broken Laughter: Select Fragments of Greek Comedy*, Oxford: Oxford University Press.

Olson, S.D. (2016), *Eupolis Heilotes—Chrysoun Genos (frr. 147–325): Translation and Commentary*, Berlin: Verlag Antike.

Orth, C. (2009), *Strattis, Die Fragmente: ein Kommentar*, Berlin: Verlag Antike.

Osborne, R. (2008), 'Putting Performance into Focus', in M. Revermann and P. Wilson (eds), *Performance, Iconography, Reception: Studies in Honour of Oliver Taplin*, 395–418, Oxford: Oxford University Press.

O'Sullivan, N. (1992), *Alcidamas, Aristophanes, and the Beginnings of Greek Stylistic Theory*, Stuttgart: Steiner.

O'Sullivan, P. and C. Collard (2013), *Euripides. Cyclops and Major Fragments of Greek Satyric Drama*, Oxford: Aris & Phillips.

Page, D.L. (1955), *Sappho and Alcaeus: An Introduction to the Study of Ancient Lesbian Poetry*, Oxford: Oxford University Press.

Panofka, T. (1849a), 'Parodie D' Antigone', in *Dissertations Archéologiques*, 216–221, Paris.

Panofka, T. (1849b), 'Komödienscenen auf Thongefässen', *Archäologische Zeitung*, 7: 18–44.

Papamichael, E.M. (1983), 'Bellerophon and Stheneboea (or Anteia)', *Dodone*, 12: 45–75.

Parker, L.P.E. (1997), *The Songs of Aristophanes*, Oxford: Oxford University Press.

Parker, R. (1986), *Miasma: Pollution and Purification in Early Greek Religion*, Oxford: Oxford University Press.

Pelling, C. (1999), *Literary Texts and the Greek Historian*, London: Routledge.

Pfister, M. (1988), *The Theory and Analysis of Drama*, Cambridge: Cambridge University Press. Translation of *Das Drama* (1977).

Pickard-Cambridge, A. (1927), *Dithyramb, Tragedy and Comedy*, Oxford: Oxford University Press.

Pickard-Cambridge, A. (1946), *The Theatre of Dionysus in Athens*, Oxford: Oxford University Press.

Pirrotta, S. (2009), *Plato Comicus, Die fragmentarischen Komödien: Ein Kommentar*, Berlin: Verlag Antike.

Platter, C. (2007), *Aristophanes and the Carnival of Genres*, Baltimore, MD: Johns Hopkins University Press.

Poe, J.P. (2000), 'Multiplicity, Discontinuity, and Visual Meaning in Aristophanic Comedy', *RhM*, 143 (3/4): 256–295.

Pomeroy, S.B. (1994), *Xenophon. Oeconomicus: A Social and Historical Commentary*, Oxford: Oxford University Press.

Porter, J.R. (1997), 'Adultery by the Book: Lysias 1 (*On the Murder of Eratosthenes*) and Comic *Diegesis*', *Classical Views* 41: 421–453.

Power, T. (2010), *The Culture of Kitharôidia*, Cambridge, MA: Harvard University Press.

Prauscello, L. (2006), 'Looking for the "Other" Gnesippus: Some Notes on Eupolis Fragment 148 K-A', *CPhil*, 101 (1): 52–66.

Prauscello, L. (2012), 'Epinician Sounds: Pindar and Musical Innovation', in P. Agócs, C. Carey and R. Rawles (eds), *Reading the Victory Ode*, 58–82, Cambridge: Cambridge University Press.

Preiser, C. (2000), *Euripides, Telephos: Einleitung, Text, Kommentar*, Hildesheim: Olms.

Pulleyn, S. (1997), *Prayer in Greek Religion*, Oxford: Oxford University Press.

Raaflaub, K. (2009), 'Conceptualizing and Theorizing Peace in Ancient Greece', *TAPA*, 139: 225–250.

Rau, P. (1967), *Paratragödia: Untersuchung einer komischen Form des Aristophanes*, München: Beck.

Rawles, R. (2013), 'Aristophanes' Simonides: Lyric Models for Praise and Blame', in E. Bakola, L. Prauscello and M. Telò (eds), *Greek Comedy and the Discourse of Genres*, 175–201, Cambridge: Cambridge University Press.

Rehm, R. (1988), 'The Staging of Suppliant Scenes', *GRBS*, 29 (3): 263–307.

Revermann, M. (1997), 'Cratinus' Διονυσαλέξανδρος and the Head of Pericles', *JHS*, 117: 197–200.

Revermann, M. (2005), 'The 'Cleveland Medea' Calyx Crater and the Iconography of Ancient Greek Theatre', *Theatre Research International*, 30 (1): 3–18.

Revermann, M. (2006a), *Comic Business: Theatricality, Dramatic Technique, and Performance Contexts of Aristophanic Comedy*, Oxford: Oxford University Press.

Revermann, M. (2006b), 'The Competence of Theatre Audiences in Fifth- and Fourth-Century Athens', *JHS*, 126: 99–124.

Revermann, M. (2010a), 'Situating the Gaze of the Recipient(s): Theatre-Related Vase Paintings and their Contexts of Reception', in I. Gildenhard and M. Revermann (eds), *Beyond the Fifth Century: Interactions with Greek Tragedy from the Fourth Century BCE to the Middle Ages*, 65–93, Berlin: De Gruyter.

Revermann, M. (2010b), 'On Misunderstanding the *Lysistrata*, Productively', in D. Stuttard (ed), *Looking at Lysistrata*, 70–79, London: Bristol Classical Press.

Revermann, M. (2013), 'Generalizing about Props: Greek Drama, Comparator Traditions, and the Analysis of Stage Objects', in G. Harrison and V. Liapis (eds), *Performance in Greek and Roman Theatre*, 77–88, Leiden: Brill.

Riedweg, C. (1990), 'The Atheistic Fragment from Euripides' *Bellerophontes* (286 N²)', *ICS*, 15 (1): 39–53.

Ries, A. and J. Trout (2001), *Positioning: The Battle for Your Mind*, New York: McGraw-Hill.

Riu, X. (1999), *Dionysism and Comedy*, Lanham, MD: Rowman and Littlefield.

Robert, C. (1914), 'Pandora', *Hermes*, 49 (1): 17–38.

Robson, J. (2006), *Humour, Obscenity and Aristophanes*, Tübingen: Gunter Narr.

Robson, J. (2009), *Aristophanes: An Introduction*, London: Duckworth.

Robson, J. (2015), 'Fantastic Sex: Fantasies of Sexual Assault in Aristophanes', in M. Masterson, N.S. Rabinowitz and J. Robson (eds), *Sex in Antiquity: Exploring Gender and Sexuality in the Ancient World*, 315–331, London: Routledge.

Rose, M.A. (1993), *Parody: Ancient, Modern, and Post-Modern*, Cambridge: Cambridge University Press.

Roselli, D.K. (2005), 'Vegetable-Hawking Mom and Fortunate Son: Euripides, Tragic Style, and Reception', *Phoenix*, 59 (1/2): 1–59.

Roselli, D.K. (2011), *Theater of the People: Spectators and Society in Ancient Athens*, Austin, TX: University of Texas Press.

Roselli, D.K. (forthcoming), 'Kings in Rags and Working-Class Heroes in Greek Tragedy'.

Rosen, R.M. (1988), *Old Comedy and the Iambographic Tradition*, Atlanta, GA: Scholars Press.

Rosen, R.M. (2000), 'Cratinus' *Pytine* and the Construction of the Comic Self', in D. Harvey and J. Wilkins (eds), *The Rivals of Aristophanes: Studies in Athenian Old Comedy*, 23–39, London: Duckworth and the Classical Press of Wales.

Rosen, R.M. (2003), 'Aristophanes' *Frogs* and the Contest of Homer and Hesiod', *TAPA*, 134 (2): 295–322.

Rosen, R.M. (2006), 'Aristophanes, Fandom, and the Classicizing of Greek Tragedy', in L. Kozak and J. Rich (eds), *Playing Around Aristophanes*, 27–47, Oxford: Aris & Phillips.

Rosen, R.M. (2008), 'Badness and Intentionality in Aristophanes' *Frogs*', in I. Sluiter and R. Rosen (eds), *Kakos: Badness and Anti-Value in Classical Antiquity*, 143–168, Leiden: Brill.

Rosen, R.M. (2014), 'The Comic Hero', in M. Revermann (ed.), *The Cambridge Companion to Greek Comedy*, 222–240, Cambridge: Cambridge University Press.

Rosen, R.M. (2015), 'Aristophanic Satire and the Pretense of Synchrony', in J. González (ed.), *Diachrony: Diachronic Studies of Ancient Greek Literature and Culture*, 213–231, Berlin: De Gruyter.

Rosen, R.M. and V. Baines (2002), '"I Am Whatever You Say I am . . .": Satiric Program in Juvenal and Eminem', *Classical and Modern Literature,* 22: 103–127.

Rostagni, A. (1956), *Scritti Minori*, vol. 2.1, Torino: Bottega d'Erasmo.

Rothwell, K.S. (1995), 'Aristophanes' *Wasps* and the Sociopolitics of Aesop's *Fables*', *CJ*, 90 (3): 233–254.

Rothwell, K.S. (2007), *Nature, Culture, and the Origins of Greek Comedy: A Study of Animal Choruses*, Cambridge: Cambridge University Press.

Ruffell, I. (2000), 'The World Turned Upside Down: Utopia and Utopianism in the Fragments of Old Comedy', in D. Harvey and J. Wilkins (eds), *The Rivals of Aristophanes: Studies in Athenian Old Comedy*, 473–506, London: Duckworth and the Classical Press of Wales.

Ruffell, I. (2002), 'A Total Write-off: Aristophanes, Cratinus, and the Rhetoric of Comic Competition', *CQ*, 52 (1): 138–163.

Ruffell, I. (2011), *Politics and Anti-Realism in Athenian Old Comedy: The Art of the Impossible*, Oxford: Oxford University Press.

Ruffell, I. (2013), 'Humiliation?: Voyeurism, Violence, and Humor in Old Comedy', *Helios*, 40 (1–2): 247–277.

Rutherford, I (1995), 'Theoric Crisis: The Dangers of Pilgrimage in Greek Religion and Society', *Studi e Materiali di Storia delle Religioni*, 19 (2): 276–292.

Rutherford, I (2000), '*Theoria* and *Darshan*: Pilgrimage as Gaze in Greece and India', *CQ*, 50 (1): 133–146.

Rutherford, R.B. (2012), *Greek Tragic Style: Form, Language, and Interpretation*, Cambridge: Cambridge University Press.

Scharffenberger, E.W. (1995), 'Peisetairos' "Satyric" Treatment of Iris: Aristophanes' *Birds* 1253–6', *JHS*, 115: 172–173.

Scharffenberger, E.W. (2002), 'Aristophanes' *Thesmophoriazousai* and the Challenges of Comic Translation: The Case of William Arrowsmith's *Euripides Agonistes*', *AJP*, 123 (3): 429– 463.

Schechner, R. (1977), 'From Ritual to Theatre and Back: The Structure/Process of the Efficacy-Entertainment Dyad', in *Essays on Performance Theory, 1970–1976*, 63–98, New York: Drama Book Specialists.

Scheer, T.S. (1993), *Mythische Vorväter: Zur Bedeutung griechischer Heroenmythen im Selbstverständnis kleinasiastischer Städte*, Munich: Maris.

Schirru, S. (2009), *La Favola in Aristofane*, Berlin: Verlag Antike.

Schmid, W. (1946), *Geschichte der griechischen Literatur*, vol. 1.4, Munich: Beck.

Schorn, S. (2002), *Satyros aus Kallatis: Sammlung der Fragmente mit Kommentar*, Basel: Schwabe.

Schwarze, J. (1971), *Die Beurteilung des Perikles durch die attische Komödie und ihre historische und historiographische Bedeutung*, Munich: Beck.

Scodel R. (1996), 'Δόμων ἄγαλμα: Virgin Sacrifice and Aesthetic Object', *TAPA*, 126: 111–128.

Scodel R. (1997), 'Review of *Euripides: Selected Fragmentary Plays 1*, C. Collard, M.J. Cropp, and K.H. Lee 1995', *Phoenix*, 51 (2): 226–227.

Seaford, R. (1984), *Euripides: Cyclops*, Oxford: Oxford University Press.

Seaford, R. (1987), 'The Tragic Wedding', *JHS*, 107: 106–130.

Seaford, R. (1990a), 'The Imprisonment of Women in Greek Tragedy', *JHS*, 110: 76–90.

Seaford, R. (1990b), 'The Structural Problems of Marriage in Euripides', in A. Powell (ed.), *Euripides, Women, and Sexuality*, 151–176, London and New York: Routledge.

Seaford, R. (1994), *Reciprocity and Ritual: Homer and Tragedy in the Developing City-State*, Oxford: Oxford University Press.

Seager, R. (1981), 'Notes on Aristophanes', *CQ*, 31 (2): 244–251.

Seidensticker, B. (2003), 'The Chorus in Greek Satyrplay', in E. Csapo and M.C. Miller (eds), *Poetry, Theory, Praxis: The Social Life of Myth, Word and Image in Ancient Greece*, 100–121, Oxford: Oxbow.

Seidensticker, B. (2007), '"Aristophanes is Back!" Peter Hacks's Adaptation of *Peace*', in E. Hall and A. Wrigley (eds), *Aristophanes in Performance, 421 BC–AD 2007*, 194–208, London: Legenda.

Shaw, C.A. (2014), *Satyric Play: The Evolution of Greek Comedy and Satyr Drama*, New York: Oxford University Press.

Shklovsky, V. (2008), *Literature and Cinematography*, trans. I. Masinovsky, Champaign, IL: Dalkey Archive Press.

Sifakis, G.M. (1971), *Parabasis and Animal Choruses: A Contribution to the History of Attic Comedy*, London: The Athlone Press.

Silk, M.S. (1980), 'Aristophanes as a Lyric Poet', in J. Henderson (ed.), *Aristophanes: Essays in Interpretation*, 99–151, Cambridge: Cambridge University Press.

Silk, M.S. (1993), 'Aristophanic Paratragedy', in A.H. Sommerstein, S. Halliwell, J. Henderson and B. Zimmermann (eds), *Tragedy, Comedy, and the Polis: Papers from the Greek Drama Conference, Nottingham, 18–20 July 1990*, 477–504, Bari: Levante Editori.

Silk, M.S. (2000), *Aristophanes and the Definition of Comedy*, Oxford: Oxford University Press.

Silk, M.S. (2013), 'The Greek Dramatic Genres: Theoretical Perspectives', in E. Bakola, L. Prauscello and M. Telò (eds), *Greek Comedy and the Discourse of Genres*, 15–39, Cambridge: Cambridge University Press.

Simon, E. (1982), 'Satyr-plays on Vases in the Time of Aeschylus', in D. Kurtz and B. Sparkes (eds), *The Eye of Greece: Studies in the Art of Athens*, 123–148, Cambridge: Cambridge University Press.

Small, J.P. (1999), 'Time in Space: Narrative in Classical Art', *ABull*, 81 (4): 562–575.

Small, J.P. (2003), *The Parallel Worlds of Classical Art and Text*, Cambridge: Cambridge University Press.

Smith, A. (2004), 'Migrancy, Hybridity, and Postcolonial Literary Studies', in N. Lazarus (ed.), *The Cambridge Companion to Postcolonial Literary Studies*, 241–261, Cambridge: Cambridge University Press.

Smith, A.C. (2011), *Polis and Personification in Classical Athenian Art*, Leiden: Brill.

Snell, B. and R. Kannicht (1986), *Tragicorum Graecorum Fragmenta*, vol. 1, Göttingen: Göttingen: Vandenhoeck & Ruprecht.

Snodgrass, A. (1998), *Homer and the Artists: Text and Picture in Early Greek Art*, Cambridge: Cambridge University Press.

Snyder, J.M. (1974), 'Aristophanes' Agathon as Anacreon', *Hermes*, 102 (2): 244–246.

Sommerstein, A.H. (1985), *Aristophanes: Peace*, Warminster: Aris and Phillips.

Sommerstein, A.H. (1994), *Aristophanes: Thesmophoriazusae*, Warminster: Aris and Phillips.

Sommerstein, A.H. (1996a), *Aeschylean Tragedy*, Bari: Levante.

Sommerstein, A.H. (1996b), *Aristophanes: Frogs*, Warminster: Aris and Phillips.

Sommerstein, A.H. (1998), 'Rape and Young Manhood in Athenian Comedy', in L. Foxhall and J. Salmon (eds), *Thinking Men: Masculinity and its Self-Representation in the Classical Tradition*, 100–114, London: Routledge.

Sommerstein, A.H. (2004), 'Harassing the Satirist: The Alleged Attempts to Prosecute Aristophanes', in I. Sluiter and R.M. Rosen (eds), *Free Speech in Classical Antiquity*, 145–174, Leiden: Brill.

Sommerstein, A.H. (2005), 'A Lover of His Art: The Art-Form as Wife and Mistress in Greek Poetic Imagery', in J. Herrin and E. Stafford (eds), *Personification in the Ancient Greek World: From Antiquity to Byzantium*, 161–171, Aldershot: Ashgate.

Stanford, W.B. (1958), *Aristophanes. The Frogs*, London: Macmillan.

Steffen, W. (1965), 'Der Hilferuf in den Netzfischern des Aischylos und sein Fortleben im griechischen Drama', *Eos*, 55: 38–43.

Steinbock, B. (2013), *Social Memory in Athenian Public Discourse: Uses and Meanings of the Past*, Ann Arbor, MI: University of Michigan Press.

Steiner, D. (2008), 'Beetle Tracks: Entomology, Scatology, and the Discourse of Abuse', in I. Sluiter and R. Rosen (eds), *Kakos: Badness and Anti-Value in Classical Antiquity*, 83–115, Leiden: Brill.

Stewart, A. (1997), 'Telephos/Telepinu and Dionysos: A Distant Light on an Ancient Myth', in R. Dreyfus and E. Schraudolph (eds), *Pergamon: The Telephos Frieze from the Great Altar*, vol. 2, 109–119, San Francisco, CA: Fine Arts Museums of San Francisco.

Stieber, M. (2011), *Euripides and the Language of Craft*, Leiden: Brill.

Stinton, T.C.W. (1965), *Euripides and the Judgement of Paris*, London: Society for the Promotion of Hellenic Studies.

Stone, L.M. (1981), *Costume in Aristophanic Comedy*, New York: Arno Press.

Storey, I.C. (2003), *Eupolis: Poet of Old Comedy*, Oxford: Oxford University Press.

Storey, I.C. (2005), 'But Comedy Has Satyrs Too', in G. Harrison (ed.), *Satyr Drama: Tragedy at Play*, 201–218, Swansea: Classical Press of Wales.

Storey, I.C. (2006), 'On First Looking into Kratinos' *Dionysalexandros*', in L. Kozak and J. Rich (eds), *Playing Around Aristophanes*, 105–125, Oxford: Aris & Phillips.

Strauss, M. (1990), 'Frühe Bilder des Kindes Telephos', *Istanbuler Mitteilungen*, 40: 79–100.

Stroup, S.C. (2004), 'Designing Women: Aristophanes' *Lysistrata* and the "Hetairization" of the Greek Wife', *Arethusa*, 37 (1): 37–73.

Sutton, D.F. (1975), 'The Staging of Anodos Scenes', *Rivista di Studi Classici*, 23: 347–355.

Sutton, D.F. (1980), *The Greek Satyr Play*, Meisenheim am Glan: Hein.

Sutton, D.F. (1984), *The Lost Sophocles*, Lanham, MD: University of America.

Sutton, D.F. (1987), 'The Theatrical Families of Athens', *AJP*, 108: 9–26.

Swift, L.A. (2010), *The Hidden Chorus: Echoes of Genre in Tragic Lyric*, Oxford: Oxford University Press.

Swift, L.A. (2014), 'Telephos On Paros: Genealogy and Myth in the "New Archilochus" Poem (*P Oxy.* 4708)', *CQ*, 64 (2): 433–447.

Taaffe, L. (1993), *Aristophanes and Women*, London: Routledge.

Taillardat, J. (1965), *Les Images d' Aristophane. Études de Langue et de Style*, Paris: Les Belles Lettres.

Taplin, O. (1977), *The Stagecraft of Aeschylus: The Dramatic Use of Exits and Entrances in Greek Tragedy*, Oxford: Oxford University Press.

Taplin, O. (1978), *Greek Tragedy in Action*, Berkeley, CA: University of California Press.

Taplin, O. (1983), 'Tragedy and Trugedy', *CQ*, 33 (2): 331–333.

Taplin, O. (1986), 'Comedy and Tragedy: A Synkrisis', *JHS*, 106: 163–174.

Taplin, O. (1987), 'Classical Phallology, Iconographic Parody, and Potted Aristophanes',
    PCPS, 33: 92–104.
Taplin, O. (1993), *Comic Angels and Other Approaches to Greek Drama through Vase-
    Paintings*, Oxford: Oxford University Press.
Taplin, O. (1996), 'Comedy and the Tragic', in M.S. Silk (ed.), *Tragedy and the Tragic*,
    188–216, Oxford: Oxford University Press.
Taplin, O. (1997), 'The Pictorial Record', in P.E. Easterling (ed.), *The Cambridge
    Companion to Greek Tragedy*, 69–90, Cambridge: Cambridge University Press.
Taplin, O. (2007), *Pots and Plays: Interactions between Tragedy and Greek Vase-painting
    in the Fourth Century B.C.*, Los Angeles, CA: J. Paul Getty Museum.
Taplin, O. (2014), 'Epiphany of a Serious Dionysus in a Comedy?', in S.D. Olson (ed.),
    Ancient Comedy and Reception: Essays in Honor of Jeffrey Henderson, 62–68, Berlin:
    De Gruyter.
Telò, M. (2015), *Aristophanes and the Cloak of Comedy*, Chicago, IL: University of
    Chicago Press.
Thompson, D. (1895), *A Glossary of Greek Birds*, Oxford: Oxford University Press.
Tordoff, R. (2011), 'Excrement, Sacrifice, Commensality: The Osphresiology of
    Aristophanes' *Peace*', *Arethusa*, 44 (2): 167–198.
Tordoff, R. (2013), 'Actors' Properties in Ancient Greek Drama. An Overview', in
    G. Harrison and V. Liapis (eds), *Performance in Greek and Roman Theatre*, 89–110,
    Leiden: Brill.
Tordoff, R. (2014), 'Counterfactual History and Thucydides', in V. Wohl (ed.),
    Probabilities, Hypotheticals, and Counterfactuals in Ancient Greek Thought, 101–121,
    Cambridge: Cambridge University Press.
Totaro, P. (1999), *Le Seconde Parabasi di Aristofane*, Stuttgart: Metzler.
Trendall, A.D. (1936), *Paestan Pottery: A Study in the Red-figured Vases of Paestum*,
    Rome: British School at Rome.
Trendall, A.D. and T.B.L. Webster (1971), *Illustrations of Greek Drama*, London:
    Phaidon.
Trenkner, S. (1958), *The Greek Novella in the Classical Period*, Cambridge: Cambridge
    University Press.
Tzanetou, A. (2002), 'Something to Do with Demeter: Ritual and Performance in
    Aristophanes' *Women at the Thesmophoria*', *AJP*, 123 (3): 329–367.
Vellacott, P. (1975), *Ironic Drama: A Study of Euripides' Method and Meaning*,
    Cambridge: Cambridge University Press.
Veltruský, J. (1964), 'Man and Object in the Theater', in P. Garvin (ed. and trans.), *Prague
    School Reader in Esthetics, Literary Structure, and Style*, 83–91, Washington, DC:
    Georgetown University Press.
Vernant, J-P. (1980), *Myth and Society in Ancient Greece*, trans. J. Lloyd, Brighton:
    Harvester Press.
Walin, D. (2012a), 'The *Chytra* as Vaginal and Uterine Metaphor in Aristophanic
    Comedy', *Annual Meeting of the American Philological Association* (143), Philadelphia.

Walin, D. (2012b), *Slaves, Sex, and Transgression in Greek Old Comedy*, PhD Diss., University of California, Berkeley.

Walsh, D. (2009), *Distorted Ideals in Greek Vase-Painting: The World of Mythological Burlesque*, Cambridge: Cambridge University Press.

Webster, T.B.L. (1948), 'South Italian Vases and Attic Drama', *CQ*, 42 (1/2): 15–27.

Webster, T.B.L. (1967), *The Tragedies of Euripides*, London: Methuen.

Webster, T.B.L. (1970), *Greek Theatre Production*, 2nd edn, London: Methuen.

West, M.L. (1974), *Studies in Greek Elegy and Iambus*, Berlin: De Gruyter.

West, M.L. (1992), *Ancient Greek Music*, Oxford: Oxford University Press.

West, M.L. (2003), *Greek Epic Fragments from the Seventh to the Fifth Centuries BC*, Cambridge, MA: Harvard University Press.

West, M.L. (2013), *The Epic Cycle: A Commentary on the Lost Epics*, Oxford: Oxford University Press.

White, J.W. (1901), *The Verse of Greek Comedy*, London: Macmillan.

Whitehead, D. (1990), 'The Lakonian Key', *CQ*, 40 (1): 267–268.

Whitman, C.H. (1964), *Aristophanes and the Comic Hero*, Cambridge, MA: Harvard University Press.

Wiencke, M. (1954), 'An Epic Theme in Greek Art', *AJA*, 58 (4): 285–306.

Wilamowitz, U. (1962), *Griechische Verskunst*, Berlin: Hermann Gentner.

Wilkins, J. (2000), *The Boastful Chef: The Discourse of Food in Ancient Greek Comedy*, Oxford: Oxford University Press.

Willi, A. (2003), *The Languages of Aristophanes: Aspects of Linguistic Variation in Classical Attic Greek*, Oxford: Oxford University Press.

Wilson, N.G. (2007), *Aristophanis Fabulae*, Oxford: Oxford University Press.

Wilson, P. (2000), *The Athenian Institution of the Khoregia: The Chorus, the City, and the Stage*, Cambridge: Cambridge University Press.

Wilson, P. (2007a), 'Nike's Cosmetics: Dramatic Victory, the End of Comedy, and Beyond', in C. Kraus, S. Goldhill, H.P. Foley and J. Elsner (eds), *Visualizing the Tragic: Drama, Myth, and Ritual in Greek Art and Literature*, 257–287, Oxford: Oxford University Press.

Wilson, P. (2007b), 'Sicilian Choruses', in P. Wilson (ed.), *Greek Theatre and Festivals: Documentary Studies*, 351–377, Oxford: Oxford University Press.

Wilson, P. (2009), 'Thamyris the Thracian: The Archetypal Wandering Poet?', in R. Hunter and I. Rutherford (eds), *Wandering Poets in Ancient Greek Culture*, 46–79, Cambridge: Cambridge University Press.

Wohl, V., (ed.) (2014), *Probabilities, Hypotheticals, and Counterfactuals in Ancient Greek Thought*, Cambridge: Cambridge University Press.

Wohl, V. (2015), *Euripides and the Politics of Form*, Princeton, NJ: Princeton University Press.

Wright, E.S. (1986), *The Form of Laments in Greek Tragedy*, PhD Diss., University of Pennsylvania.

Wright, M. (2007), 'Comedy and the Trojan War', *CQ*, 57 (2): 412–431.

Wright, M. (2012), *The Comedian as Critic: Greek Old Comedy and Poetics*, London: Bloomsbury.

Wyles, R. (2011), *Costume in Greek Tragedy*, London: Bristol Classical Press.

Zeitlin, F.I. (1965), 'The Motif of the Corrupted Sacrifice in Aeschylus' *Oresteia*', *TAPA*, 96: 463–508.

Zeitlin, F.I. (1996), 'Travesties of Gender and Genre in Aristophanes' *Thesmophoriazusae*', in *Playing the Other. Gender and Society in Classical Greek Literature*, Chicago, IL: University of Chicago Press.

Zogg, F. (2014), *Lust am Lesen: Literarische Anspielungen im Frieden des Aristophanes*, Munich: C.H. Beck.

Index Locorum

All references below are cited but not necessarily quoted in the text and notes and also include references of special significance to the core themes of the study. Excluded are references cited purely as *comparanda*.

Cretans
  – fr. 472: 177

Cyclops
  – 175–187: 110

Electra
  – 839–843: 138

Helen
  – 1–67: 5
  – 68–166: 5
  – 528–596: 5
  – 541–659: 6

Medea
  – 1156–1202: 142

Stheneboea
  – fr. 661.5: 191

Telephus
  – fr. 696: 38–39
  – fr. 697: 33–34
  – fr. 705a: 27 n.7
  – frr. 710–711: 40
  – fr. 715: 41 n.77
  – fr. 720: 27 n.7
  – fr. 727c.25–34: 40–41

Trojan Women
  – 309–340: 67

HERMIPPUS
  – fr. 47: 101

HERODOTUS
  Histories
  – 4.1–142: 155

HESIOD
  Theogony
  – 201–202: 139

  Works and Days
  – 42–105: 135
  – 117–118: 135

  Fragments
  – fr. 165.8–17 MW: 34 n.39

HOMER
  Iliad
  – 17.210–212: 31 n.22

  Odyssey
  – 4.499–511: 69 n.71
  – 5.121–124: 177
  – 8.266–366: 98
  – 11.305–310: 177
  – 11.321–325: 177
  – 11.519–521: 34 n.39

HYGINUS
  Fabulae
  – §28: 177

MENANDER
  Dyskolos
  – 842–843: 140 n.87

PAUSANIAS
  – 10.25.5–27.2: 56 n.15

PHERECRATES
  – fr. 155: 156–157

PINDAR
  Odes
  – *Isth.* 5.41: 34 n.40
  – *Ol.* 9.70–73: 34 n.40
  – *Pyth.* 3: 177

  Fragments
  – fr. 76: 152
  – fr. 77: 152–153
  – fr. 105a: 154
  – fr. 105b: 155 n.36

PLATO
  Apology

  Scholium
  – 19c: 105 n.89, 134

  Laws
  – 659b–d: 187
  – 699c: 158
  – 699e: 158
  – 700a–701d: 158
  – 700c–d: 187–188
  – 700e–701a: 188

Index